Advance praise for *Neoliberalism, I*

"Mark Goodale and Nancy Postero's collection offers us a vivid panorama of neoliberalism and its interruption, keeping in mind broader patterns of political economic transformation and civil society struggle. The chapters forcefully demonstrate neoliberalism's investment in violence and regulation, while opening our eyes to civil society's spaces to challenge them. From Buenos Aires to Venezuela, from race to gender, this collection represents an important theoretical and critical engagement with Latin America's current realities."

—Sarah A. Radcliffe, University of Cambridge, author of *Indigenous Development in the Andes: Culture, Power, and Transnationalism*

"*Neoliberalism, Interrupted* makes an important contribution to studying Latin America's rapidly changing socio-political landscape. The volume's authors remind us that the region presents a rich laboratory for experiments that defy existing categories of social and political theory in contradictory, but potentially exciting new ways."

—Philip Oxhorn, McGill University, author of *Sustaining Civil Society: Economic Change, Democracy, and the Social Construction of Citizenship in Latin America*

"This book will resonate with all those interested in one of the most important political questions for Latin America today. The authors resist the temptation to provide easy answers—the essays are subtle and effective, their sophistication buttressed by empirical and theoretical rigor."

—Sian Lazar, University of Cambridge, author of *El Alto, Rebel City: Self and Citizenship in Andean Bolivia*

"This timely collection brings together diverse disciplinary perspectives to explore the limits of neoliberal governmentality in contemporary Latin America. The contributors provide fine-grained, ethnographic analysis of alternatives to the 'Washington Consensus,' both grandiose and grassroots, revealing in the process the promises and contradictions of 'post-neoliberal' political programs and social projects."

—Patrick C. Wilson, University of Lethbridge, coeditor of *Editing Eden: A Reconsideration of Identity, Politics, and Place in Amazonia*

NEOLIBERALISM, INTERRUPTED

NEOLIBERALISM, INTERRUPTED

Social Change and Contested Governance in Contemporary Latin America

Edited by
Mark Goodale and Nancy Postero

Stanford University Press
Stanford, California

Stanford University Press
Stanford, California

This book has been published with the assistance of the Wenner-Gren Foundation.

Printed in the United States of America on acid-free, archival-quality paper

Library of Congress Cataloging-in-Publication Data

Neoliberalism, interrupted : social change and contested governance in contemporary Latin America / edited by Mark Goodale and Nancy Postero.
pages cm
Includes bibliographical references and index.
ISBN 978-0-8047-8452-8 (cloth : alk. paper)—
ISBN 978-0-8047-8453-5 (pbk. : alk. paper)
1. Latin America—Politics and government—1980– 2. Neoliberalism—Latin America. 3. Social change—Latin America. 4. Latin America—Social conditions—1982– 5. Latin America—Economic policy. I. Goodale, Mark, editor of compilation. II. Postero, Nancy Grey, editor of compilation.
F1414.3.N46 2013
980.03—dc23 2012049541

ISBN 978-0-8047-8644-7 (electronic)

Typeset by Westchester Book Composition in 10.5/15 Adobe Garamond

CONTENTS

ACKNOWLEDGMENTS

The first phase of the project that culminated in *Neoliberalism, Interrupted* was a lively and provocative international workshop held over several days in May 2008 at the University of California, San Diego. This meeting, organized around the theme of "Revolution and New Social Imaginaries in Post-neoliberal Latin America," was made possible by the generous support of the Wenner-Gren Foundation for Anthropological Research, and it is to the foundation, its president, Leslie C. Aiello, and its conference program associate, Laurie Obbink, that we owe our principal debt of gratitude. The continuing support of the foundation was critical to the further refinement of the theoretical framework of the volume, which paved the way for the development of the project into a cohesive book.

At the University of California, San Diego (UCSD), our gathering of scholars was given the chance to engage in productive conservations and social encounters in the delightful setting of the La Jolla campus and its environs. We want to acknowledge, in particular, the participation of the Center for Iberian and Latin America Studies (CILAS) and the Department of Anthropology at UCSD for their close collaboration. During a crucial period in the evolution of the project, the editors were given a chance to meet for a week of intensive discussion at Point of View, the center for advanced studies of the School of Conflict Analysis and Resolution (S-CAR), George Mason University, which is located in a nature conservancy on the shores of Belmont Bay, south of Washington, D.C. For this opportunity we thank the administration of S-CAR and, in particular, its former director, Professor Sara Cobb, for her enthusiastic support of this project and, more generally, the idea of a critical ethnographic study of the life of neoliberalism in contemporary Latin America.

We also must acknowledge the dedication of the authors of the volume themselves. They gave much of their intellectual and professional energy to bring this book together through multiple rounds of writing and revision. As a group, they were deeply engaged and ready and willing to take up and help to deepen a theoretical framework that crystallized over months and indeed years. We are also grateful to two anonymous reviewers and to Roger Rouse for comments on previous versions of these texts.

We were also fortunate to have the assistance of a number of graduate students over the years. At George Mason University, Adriana Salcedo, in particular, assisted in a number of important ways, including providing first-draft translations. At UCSD, Eli Elinoff, Jorge Montesinos, Paula Saravia, Devin Beaulieu, and Patrick Kearney were of great help in thinking through the issues, polishing the translations, and providing audiovisual support. Their enthusiasm helped enormously over the long germination of this project. We thank Amy Kennemore for her excellent editorial assistance in the final stages of manuscript production.

The editorial and production staffs at Stanford University Press have been a joy to work with. Kate Wahl, publishing director and editor in chief of the press, was an early supporter of the project, and to her we offer our deepest appreciation. We also received excellent assistance at the press from Emma S. Harper and Frances Malcolm.

Finally, it is our pleasure to recognize the support of important people in our lives. Mark would like to acknowledge the love and inspiration of Romana, Dara, and Isaiah. Nancy thanks Jeff for his loving support; he is always a peaceful refuge in the academic storm.

ABBREVIATIONS

ALBA	Alianza Bolivariana para los Pueblos de Nuestra América (Bolivarian Alliance for the Peoples of Our Americas), regional integration initiative for Latin America and the Caribbean
ANC	Asamblea Nacional Constituyente (National Constituent Assembly), Colombia
ARENA	Allianza Republicana Nationalista (National Republican Alliance), political party, El Salvador
AVC	Alfaro Vive Carajo (Alfaro Lives, Damn It), guerrilla organization, Ecuador
BSA	Bloque Social Alternativo (Alternative Social Bloc), coalition of progressive and left-wing organizations and social movements, Colombia
CA	Constituent Assembly
CAFTA	Central American Free Trade Agreement
CGT	Confederación General de Trabajadores (General Federation of Workers), Argentina

CIMA	Comité de Integración del Macizo Colombiano (Committee for the Integration of the Colombian Massif), social movement, Colombia
CONAC	Consejo Nacional de la Cultura (National Council of Culture), Venezuela
CPE	Constitución Política del Estado (Political Constitution of the State), Bolivia
CRIC	Consejo Regional Indígena del Cauca (Regional Indigenous Council of Cauca), indigenous rights organization, Colombia
CSC	Consejo de la Sociedad Civil (Council on Civil Society), coalition of nongovernmental organizations, Mexico
DERHGO	Desarrollo Rural de Hidalgo, A.C. (Rural Development of Hidalgo), nongovernmental organization, Mexico
DREAM	Development, Relief, and Education for Alien Minors Act, immigration reform, United States
ECLAC	Economic Commission for Latin America and the Caribbean (United Nations)
ELN	Ejército de Liberación Nacional (National Liberation Army)
FARC	Fuerzas Armadas Revolucionarias de Colombia (Revolutionary Armed Forces of Colombia)
FMDR	Fundación Mexicana para el Desarrollo Rural (Mexican Foundation for Rural Development)
FMLN	Frente Farabundo Martí para la Liberación Nacional (Farabundo Martí National Liberation Front), political party, El Salvador
FOSIS	Fondo de Solidaridad e Inversión Social (Solidarity and Social Investment Fund), Chile
FUNDEF	Fundación de Etnomusicología y Folklore (Foundation of Ethnomusicology and Folklore), Venezuela
IIRAIRA	Illegal Immigration Reform and Immigrant Responsibility Act, immigration reform, United States
ILEA	International Law Enforcement Academy for Latin America, United States

IMF	International Monetary Fund
INDEC	Instituto Nacional de Estadística y Censos (National Institute of Statistics and Census), Argentina
ISI	Import substitution industrialization
LPP	Ley de Participación Popular (Law of Popular Participation), Bolivia
MAQL	Movimiento Armado Quintín Lame (Quintín Lame Armed Movement), indigenous guerrilla movement, Colombia
MAS	Movimiento al Socialismo (Movement Toward Socialism), political party, Bolivia
MERCOSUR	Mercado Común del Sur (Common Market of the South), common market agreement among some South American countries
MIDEPLAN	Ministerio de Planificación (Ministry of Planning), Chile
MTD	Movimiento de Trabajadores Desocupados (Movement of Unemployed Workers), Argentina
NAFTA	North American Free Trade Agreement
NGO	Nongovernmental organization
PDVSA	Petróleos de Venezuela, S.A. (Petroleum of Venezuela), state-owned petroleum company
PIDER	Programa de Inversiones para el Desarrollo Rural (Investment Program for Rural Development), Mexico
PJHD	Plan Jefas y Jefes de Hogar Desocupados (Unemployed Heads of Household Plan), Argentina
PLOC	Proyecto de Ley Orgánica de la Cultura (Project of the Organic Law of Culture), Venezuela
PNC	Policía National Civil (National Civil Police), El Salvador
PND	Plan Nacional de Desarrollo (National Development Plan), Bolivia
PNUD	Programa de las Naciones Unidos para el Desarrollo (United Nations Development Program, UNDP)

PRI	Partido Revolucionario Institucional (Institutional Revolutionary Party), political party, Mexico
PRODEMU	Programa de Promoción y Desarrollo de la Mujer (Program for Women's Promotion and Education), Chile
SAP	Structural adjustment program
SENEC	Secretariat for New Experiences in Community Education, Mexico
SERNAM	Servicio Nacional de la Mujer (National Women's Bureau), Chile
TAG	Transnational Anti-Gang unit, collaborative anti-gang effort between the United States and El Salvador
TIPNIS	Territorio Indígena Parque Nacional Isiboro Sécure (Isiboro-Sécure Indigenous Territory and National Park), Bolivia
WTO	World Trade Organization

EDITORS AND CONTRIBUTORS

Mark Goodale is associate professor of conflict analysis and anthropology at George Mason University and series editor of Stanford Studies in Human Rights. He is the author, editor, or coeditor of eight other books, including, most recently, *The Bolivia Reader: Culture, History, Politics* (Duke University Press, 2013), *Human Rights at the Crossroads* (Oxford University Press, 2012), *Mirrors of Justice: Law and Power in the Post–Cold War Era* (Cambridge University Press, 2010), *Surrendering to Utopia: An Anthropology of Human Rights* (Stanford University Press, 2009), *Human Rights: An Anthropological Reader* (Blackwell, 2009), and *Dilemmas of Modernity: Bolivian Encounters with Law and Liberalism* (Stanford University Press, 2008). He is currently writing a new book based on research in Bolivia since 2005 on constitutional revolution and the problem of radical social change.

Nancy Postero is associate professor of anthropology at the University of California, San Diego. She is the author of *Now We Are Citizens: Indigenous Politics in Post-Multicultural Bolivia* (Stanford University Press, 2007) and, with Leon Zamosc, *The Struggle for Indigenous Rights in Latin America* (Sussex, 2003). She recently coedited a special issue of *Latin American Research*

Review titled "Actually Existing Democracies" (2010). She serves as an editor for the *Journal of Latin American and Caribbean Ethnic Studies* (LACES). She is currently completing a new book, *Decolonizing Bolivia*, focusing on political conflicts and spectacular performances in plurinational Bolivia, including analyses of the Constituent Assembly, opposition hunger strikes, and government-sponsored collective marriages.

Marcela Cerrutti received her PhD in sociology at the University of Texas, Austin. She is now a research member of the National Council for Scientific and Technological Research of Argentina (CENEP-Argentina) and professor at the National University of General San Martín. Her areas of specialization are international migration and gender and labor markets in Latin America, and she has numerous publications on these topics. Recently she has published *Health and International Migration: Bolivian Women in Argentina* and *Divided Families and Global Chains of Care: South-American Migration in Spain* (with Alicia Maguid). She serves as editor of the *Revista Latinoamericana de Población.*

Miguel Ángel Contreras Natera is a sociologist and professor of social theory in the School of Sociology at the Central University of Venezuela (UCV). He was the editor of the 2006 volume *Desarrollo, eurocentrismo y economía popular: Más allá del paradigma neoliberal* (Development, Eurocentrism, and popular economy: Beyond the neoliberal paradigm). His most recent work, *Una geopolítica del espíritu* (A geopolitics of the spirit), published in 2011 by the Fundación Centro de Estudios Latinoamericanos Rómulo Gallegos, examines the contemporary relation between social movements and participatory democracy in the context of the enormous political and spiritual transformations in Latin America and the Caribbean.

Sujatha Fernandes is associate professor of sociology at Queens College and the Graduate Center of the City University of New York. She is the author of *Cuba Represent! Cuban Arts, State Power, and the Making of New Revolutionary Cultures* (Duke University Press, 2006), *Who Can Stop the Drums? Urban Social Movements in Chávez's Venezuela* (Duke University Press, 2010), and *Close to the Edge: In Search of the Global Hip Hop Generation* (Verso, 2011). She is currently working on a new research project about social movements and legislative advocacy in New York City.

David Gow is the Edgar R. Baker Professor Emeritus of Anthropology and International Affairs at the Elliott School of International Affairs at the George Washington University. His principal publications include *Countering Development: Indigenous Modernity and the Moral Imagination* (Duke University Press, 2008) and *Implementing Rural Development Projects: Lessons from AID and World Bank Experience* (with Elliott R. Morss) (Westview, 1985). Since 2005 he has been conducting research on politics at the provincial level in Colombia, focusing on the role of social organizations, social movements, and coalitions in the creation and sustainability of alternative public spaces and alternative governments. In collaboration with a Colombian colleague, he has completed a book-length manuscript on the experience of alternative government in the context of political violence, poverty, and struggling democracy.

Alejandro Grimson is professor of anthropology at the National University of General San Martín. Since his early studies of comunication at the University of Buenos Aires and in his PhD in anthropology at the University of Brasilia, he has been invesigating migration processes, border zones, social movements, political cultures, identities, and interculturality. His first book, *Relatos de la diferencia y la igualdad* (Tales of difference and equality) (Eudeba, 1999) won the FELAFACS prize for the best thesis in comunication in Latin America. After publishing edited volumes like *La cultura en las crisis latinoamericanas* (The role of culture in Latin American crises) (CLACSO, 2004), he was awarded the Bernardo Houssay Prize by the Argentine state. His book *La nación en sus límites: Interculturalidad y comunicación* (The limits of the nation: Interculturality and communication) won the prestigious Iberamericano Prize from LASA in 2012. He is now an investigator at CONICET and dean of the Institute de Social Studies at the National University of General San Martín.

Christopher Krupa is assistant professor of anthropology at the University of Toronto. His writings have appeared in *American Ethnologist, Comparative Studies in Society and History*, the edited volume *Subalternity and Difference:*

Reflections from the North and the South (Routledge, 2011), and other publications. He is currently completing an ethnography of labor and desire in Ecuador's cut-flower industry and editing (with David Nugent) a volume on state and parastate complexes in the Andes.

Analiese M. Richard is associate professor of anthropology in the School of International Studies at the University of the Pacific. Her work has appeared in the *Journal of the Royal Anthropological Institute*, the *Political and Legal Anthropology Review*, and the *Journal of Latin American and Caribbean Anthropology*. Her latest research project examines cultures of citizenship, security, and expertise in Mexico's food sovereignty movement.

Veronica Schild is associate professor of political science and director of the Centre for the Study of Theory and Criticism at the University of Western Ontario. She has published extensively on feminism and the women's movement in Chile, on feminism and new market citizenship, and, more recently, on feminism and the neoliberalizing state. Her current research focuses on the relation between institutional feminism and processes of neoliberal governmentality, and she is currently completing a book titled *Contradictions of Emancipation: The Women's Movement, Culture, and the State in Contemporary Chile.*

Elana Zilberg is associate professor in the Department of Communication at the University of California, San Diego. Her book, *Space of Detention: The Making of a Transnational Gang Crisis Between Los Angeles and San Salvador* (Duke University Press, 2011), is an ethnographic account and spatial analysis of how transnational gangs became an issue of central concern for national and regional security. In her newest project, Zilberg examines the historical and contemporary role of rivers in the racialization of space in San Antonio, Texas; Los Angeles, California; and the U.S.-Mexico border region.

CHAPTER I

REVOLUTION AND RETRENCHMENT

Illuminating the Present in Latin America

Mark Goodale and Nancy Postero

THIS VOLUME EXAMINES THE WAYS IN which Latin America, during the last decade, has become a global laboratory. There, new forms of governance, economic structuring, and social mobilization are responding to and at times challenging the continuing hegemony of what the anthropologist James Ferguson (2006) describes as the "neoliberal world order." Yet despite the fact that political leaders in countries like Bolivia, Ecuador, Nicaragua, and Venezuela articulate these responses in the language of revolution, these most radical of regional experiments remain outliers, the exceptions that prove the general rule that the global consolidation of late capitalism through neoliberalism has been merely, if revealingly, interrupted in Latin America. Nevertheless, we argue that these interruptions have important consequences and reveal new horizons of possibility—social, political, economic, theoretical—within a broader, post–Cold War world in which many of the traditional alternatives to late capitalism and neoliberal forms of governance have lost ideological legitimacy and in which even the idea of revolution itself—with its mythological invocations of radical change, righteous violence, and social and moral renewal—is often seen as an anachronism.

At the same time, we also examine the problem of widespread retrenchment of neoliberalism in Latin America, a set of processes that both brings into starker contrast the significance of the exceptional challenges to neoliberalism and underscores the ways in which neoliberal forms of governance and social life have become ideologically detached from their historical contingencies. Without the ever-present specter of the Cold War looming over ongoing struggles over land, racism, and political marginalization, it has become more difficult for social and political radicals in Latin America to bring home the point that the assumptions and structures that perpetuate different forms of inequality are not inevitable. Indeed, as we will see, neoliberal governmentality in Latin America is as naturalizing as elsewhere. Even the most robust and earnest provocations of the conditions that produce vulnerability come up against the lingering effects of the Washington Consensus in Latin America, through which regional political economies came into a forced alignment around market democratization, the withdrawal of the state from service sectors, trade liberalization, and the codification of a high-liberal property-rights regime that extended legal inequalities into new areas like intellectual property and biogenetics (see, e.g., Dezalay and Garth 2002; Oxhorn and Ducatenzeiler 1998).

If in its broadest reach our volume is a critical study of one slice of the contemporary life of neoliberalism in Latin America, it is perhaps not surprising that we have chosen to bring together a diverse group of scholars and intellectuals, both Latin American and Latin Americanist, who present a range of disciplinary, regional, and theoretical perspectives. *Neoliberalism, Interrupted* revolves around case studies of the everyday lives of people and their institutions, caught up in moments of social change and processes of contested governance. The volume's perspectives move between the grounded experiences of neoliberalism in Latin America and more synthetic reflections on meaning, consequence, and the possibility of regional responses to neoliberal hegemony and the articulation of formal alternatives to it. These perspectives are enriched by the critical voices of several prominent Latin American researchers and writers, one of whom (the Venezuelan sociologist Miguel Ángel Contreras Natera), in a provocative postscript to the volume, productively obscures the line between politics and scholarship, manifesto and intellectual inspiration, in a full-throated and deeply theorized plea for a new kind of politics in Latin America.

Taken together, the different critical studies in the volume demonstrate the ways in which the history and politics of contemporary Latin America carry important lessons for scholars, activists, and political leaders in other parts of world with similar histories and structural conditions, including legacies of extractive colonialism and neocolonialism, the influence of Cold War proxyism, interethnic conflict, strong regional identity, and traditions of institutional instability. In this way, the volume adds its collective voice to a growing debate on the meaning and significance of responses to neoliberalism in Latin America and beyond (see, e.g., Arditti 2008; Escobar 2010; Gudynas, Guevara, and Roque 2008; Hershberg and Rosen 2006; Macdonald and Ruckert 2009; Panizza 2009). This body of work reveals a spectrum of responses to what can be described as "maturing neoliberalism," from a Bolivian revolution that is framed as a formal rejection of neoliberalism, to Colombia's deepening recommitment to the full suite of neoliberal social, political, and economic practices.

Where our volume diverges most starkly from this ongoing critical conversation is in the way our case studies lead to a thoroughgoing skepticism about the conventional dichotomies that are used to make sense of social change and contested governance in Latin America: neoliberalism vs. socialism; the Right vs. the Left; indigenous vs. mestizo; national vs. transnational. Instead, we focus on the ways in which a range of unresolved contradictions interconnects various projects for change and resistance to change in Latin America. There is no question that "neoliberalism" remains a powerful discursive framework within which these different moments of crisis and even rupture play out. But our volume suggests that a new ideological landscape is coming into view in Latin America and that it has the potential to dramatically reorient the ways in which social and political change itself is understood, conceptualized, and practiced in the region and beyond.

ILLUMINATING THE PRESENT IN LATIN AMERICA

The present in Latin America is marked by both extraordinary moments of social, political, and economic experimentation and moments of violent resistance and retrenchment. And yet the case studies in this volume resist most of the easy dialectics that have provided analytical cover for those who seek to encompass Latin America within the grand and all-too-often reductive sweep. If it is true, as Walter Mignolo (2005b) argues, that the space of "Latin America" must be apprehended first and foremost as a contested idea, then it is also true that there are multiple strategies for illuminating this ever-shifting and highly fraught idea. We agree with Mignolo that the integrative geospacial concept of "Latin America" remains relevant and indeed, over the last decade, has been even more so. However, we also believe that the kind of coherence Mignolo urges can be understood only through close engagement with actual points of crisis, from the grand (the "refounding" of Bolivia through constitutional reform) to the less visible (the creation of local development alternatives in rural Colombia), from the urban and deeply national (the emergence of a new class of working poor in Chile's cities) to the transnational (the construction of transborder policing strategies between El Salvador and the United States). As Perreault and Martin suggest, neoliberalism produces locally specific and scalar expressions (2005).

For the remainder of this chapter, we draw together the collective lessons from the book's chapters. Taken together, they demonstrate that Latin America has emerged over the last twenty years as a leading edge of social, political, and economic possibility at the same time that specific regions and countries of Latin America reflect the intractability of a range of historical legacies of structural vulnerability. Indeed, the case studies in the volume illuminate the ways in which the currents of neoliberalism create new forms of contestation while simultaneously choking off other possible ideologies and programs for radical social change. This means that in contemporary Latin America, real challenges to the "neoliberal world order" coexist with and even reinforce enduring patterns of exploitation and violence.

Fractured tectonics

In the postscript to the volume, Contreras Natera argues that the disjunctures of the present in Latin America are the result of a prevailing condition he characterizes as "fractured tectonics." What he means is that the contemporary examples of experimentation and contestation in contemporary Latin America are closely entwined with both previously and actually existing ideologies and exploitative practices they seek to overcome. This is not a simple dialectics, however, since the relationship between what he calls "insurgent imaginaries" and their hegemonic antitheses is both variable within different regions and histories of Latin America and much less predictably unstable. Even in the most self-consciously revolutionary nations of Latin America, namely Venezuela and Bolivia, the discursive frame is in fact quite ambiguous since the clarion call for radical social change is at least in part dependent on the language and logics of existing frameworks of governance, economic relations, and social and cultural practices.

In order to understand these multiple fractured tectonics empirically, we must adopt an archaeological methodology that seeks to reveal the ways in which these insurgent frames interpenetrate the national neoliberalisms whose legacies suggest their own contradictions and possibilities. Indeed, as the contributors to this volume demonstrate, the essential task of the critical observer of contemporary Latin America is to clear a path among the rubble that is created when these discursive layers shift, often violently, in order to answer more fundamental questions: What really *are* the meaningful challenges to neoliberalism now? Are they in the melding of human rights discourse with revolutionary socialism, as in Bolivia? Are they in the more gradualist and compromising constitutional reforms of Ecuador? Or are they in the hybrid socialist anti-imperialist nationalism of Chávez's Bolivarian Venezuela? Conversely, does the conservative neoliberal deepening in Peru, Chile, Colombia, and much of Central America, including Mexico, stand apart from the processes of insurgence elsewhere, or does it, in a sense, bracket them?

Moreover, as David Gow (Chapter 4) illustrates, examples of challenges to the hegemony of maturing neoliberalism in Latin America can be found on very small scales indeed, even within a state like Colombia, whose majority politics have, for the time being, definitively rejected the possibility of something like a Bolivian refoundation. Moreover, although the constitutionalist reform moment of the early 1990s seems like a distant memory now, Gow's study points to the development of modest alternatives in the interstices between the summarizing discursive frame of the nation-state and the equally expansive—though now perhaps fatally compromised—ideology of the Fuerzas Armadas Revolucionarias de Colombia (FARC). Interstitial challenges like these are usually ignored or obscured, yet their meanings and importance can, as here, be illuminated by the ethnographic spotlight.

Neoliberal contradictions

Within colonial societies, domination was framed by discourses of race in which indigenous peoples were considered either dangerous savages or children in need of stewardship (Hall 1996). Moreover, throughout the colonial period, tensions in extractive and plantation forms of accumulation produced conflict, as indigenous and slave communities periodically resisted their structural oppression (James 1989; Serulnikov 2003; Stern 1993; Thomson 2002).

These contradictions were not resolved by the formal end of colonialism in Latin America in the first part of the nineteenth century. As they pushed for independence from Spain and Portugal, Creole elites adopted the liberal ideas of the European Enlightenment. Anxious to break with coercive forms of governance and social control, the new Republican states sought liberal solutions to the tensions underlying colonialism, especially the constant threat of ethnic mobilization. As Brooke Larson argues in the case of Andean elites, the effort to recreate colonial societies in terms of liberalism faced a fundamental paradox: mestizo elites looked to "impose universal definitions of free labor and citizenship, as well as to mold national cultures into homogenous wholes (along Eurocentric ideals), while creating the symbols and categories of innate difference in order to set the limits on those 'universalistic' ideals" (Larson 2004, 13). The goal, she suggests, was to "build an apparatus of power that simultaneously incorporated and marginalized peasant political cultures in the forced march to modernity" (ibid., 15).

Liberalism promised universal belonging, yet it was accompanied by a new form of race thinking that merely reorganized "colonial hierarchies subordinating Indianness . . . to the Creole domain of power, civilization, and citizenship" (Larson 2004, 14; see also Mehta 1997). Thus, the promises of liberalism were never completely fulfilled, as indigenous groups and peoples of African descent were denied full participation in the political, economic, and cultural life of the new Republican nation-states. In the process, what we might describe as a Latin American liberalism emerged from regimes of exclusion that cut along racial, ethnic, and intraregional lines and then took root. In his postscript, Contreras Natera describes this contradiction as the result of "the colonial-modern logos," the dominant epistemological and discursive framework for ordering social relations in the wider colonial world.

Throughout the nineteenth and twentieth centuries, various responses to the paradoxical exclusions of liberalism have marked Latin American history and politics (see Goodale 2009; Postero 2007). At the turn of the twentieth century, the Zárate Willka rebellion in Bolivia reprised the insurgencies of the previous century, demonstrating that indigenous demands for land and autonomy had still not been met (Egan 2007; Rivera Cusicanqui 1987). Populist revolutions, such as those in Mexico (1910), Bolivia (1952), Cuba (1959), and Nicaragua (1979), brought to the surface the still-simmering tensions over unequal land tenure and deepening class divisions (Hale 1994; Klein 1992; Knight 1990). By the 1960s and 1970s, decades of development efforts had failed to increase the standards of living for the majority of Latin Americans, and the need to address structural inequalities through agrarian reform and the redistribution of national resources took on new urgency.

In some countries, popularly elected governments—like Allende's in Chile—undertook these reforms. In others—like Peru, El Salvador, and Guatemala—communist social movements in the vernacular resisted liberal reforms and instead pursued revolutionary guerrilla war and the politics of structural transformation in terms of a theory of history marked by cycles of conflict (Degregori 1990; Stern 1998; Stoll 1993; Wood 2003). Many of these movements were in turn violently disrupted by a wave of military dictatorships that swept across the region in the 1970s and 1980s. The end of the Cold War brought this phase of violent revolution and reprisal to a close, and most Latin American countries made the transition to formal democracy. Nevertheless, as the chapters in this volume reveal in different ways, the twinned legacies of revolutionary struggle and the violence of state repression continue to shape arguments for and against alternative models of social change and forms of governance in contemporary Latin America.

The 1980s and 1990s saw the crystallization of neoliberalism as the dominant economic and political paradigm. As David Harvey argues:

> Neoliberalism is in the first instance a theory of political economic practices that proposes that human well-being can best be advanced by liberating individual entrepreneurial freedoms and skills within an institutional framework characterized by strong private property rights, free markets, and free trade. The role of the state is to

create and preserve an institutional framework appropriate to such practices. (Harvey 2005, 2)

In other words, neoliberal governance assumes that the state has a key role to play in capitalist accumulation by diffusing market logics throughout society. This process has taken different forms across Latin America. Elana Zilberg's contribution to this volume (Chapter 9) underscores the violence that often accompanies the diffusion of market logics. She describes the contexts of these struggles as "neoliberal securityscapes" and examines the ways in which unruly outliers are both constructed and disciplined in these ambiguous social and political spaces.

Neoliberalism in Latin America is also constituted through "market democracy," a "purposeful construction and consolidation of neoliberalized state forms, modes of governance, and regulatory relations" (Peck and Tickell 2002, 384). This form of governance emphasizes technocratic administration and the passing of the responsibility for governing from the state to local actors and nongovernmental organizations (NGOs). Scholars have argued that a central element of neoliberal governance is the encouragement of a civic identity in which individuals are urged to take responsibility for their own behavior and welfare (Foucault 1991a; Rose 1996; Postero 2007; Rudnyckyj 2009). Veronica Schild (Chapter 8) argues that, in Chile, these forms of governmentality are visible through two expressions of what she calls an "enabling state." First, the "caring state" targets subjects—especially poor women—and teaches them to be responsible citizens who are able to stand up and make their rights count, exercise their choices as consumers and workers, and make demands upon the state for support in health, pensions, and education. Second, the "punitive state" disciplines those workers who do not comply or who are deemed dangerous.

Legacies of difference and exclusion

Historical legacies of difference and exclusion continue to shape the experiences and consequences of neoliberalism in Latin America. As Patrick Wilson argues, neoliberalism in Latin America continues to be intertwined with racist social and state practices and stubborn ideologies of modernizations and progress (2008, 139). There are several implications of this specific history in the present. First, where a legacy of ethnic or racial exclusion exists, this exacerbates the social costs of neoliberal policies and can come to ground movements of resistance. Second, groups with strong cultural identities can use them as resources for formulating alternatives to neoliberalism. Finally, where subversive discourses of ethnicity or race explicitly frame projects for social change, this heightens existing economic or political conflicts and increases the chances that these conflicts will spiral into cycles of deep social crisis or violence.

In Chapter 2, Postero examines the ways in which neoliberal reforms were extended in Bolivia in the mid-1980s under President Gonzalo Sánchez de Lozada, whose government privatized state-owned enterprises, slashed social services, and lowered barriers to foreign capital and commodities. The result was increased unemployment, especially of miners; a massive migration from rural areas to the cities, as farming became unsustainable; and greater poverty. This period also saw growing organization and activism by indigenous and peasant groups, who linked their ethnically articulated demands for territory and recognition to the social consequences of neoliberal policies.

The Bolivian economic reforms were also paired with a set of neoliberal multicultural reforms that encouraged participation at the municipal level. Even though racism frustrated indigenous efforts to force the redistribution of significant resources, indigenous activists were able to take advantage of the political reforms to form their own political parties and to begin articulating alternative proposals based on their own cultures and *cosmovisiones*, or worldviews. In 2005, after five years of protests by a population exhausted by the effects of neoliberalism, Bolivians elected their first self-identifying indigenous president, Evo Morales. Postero argues that the powerful discursive link between antineoliberalism and decolonialization has served to legitimate the MAS (Movement Toward Socialism) government's agenda to its indigenous constituents despite ongoing resource extraction on indigenous lands and neoliberal engagement with the global market.

David Gow's study of an indigenous local government in Colombia likewise reveals the importance of ethnicity in framing responses to neoliberalism. Gow explains how struggles during the Constituent Assembly of 1991, increasingly militant indigenous and campesino organizing in the following decade, and the political participation of recently demobilized guerrillas all combined to enable an indigenous governor to take power in the Colombian department of Cauca and push for a participatory development project that provided a hopeful alternative to the neoliberal (and corrupt) status quo. This case study reinforces the perhaps obvious but nevertheless important point that responses to neoliberalism take root within particular social and political landscapes. In this particular region of Colombia, a long and successful history of indigenous and peasant organizing within a broad coalition of actors created the preconditions for the formation of a new model of local and regional governance.

Neoliberal violence

In Chapter 9, Elana Zilberg argues that the specter of the Cold War enemy of the state, the Farabundo Martí para la Liberación Nacional (FMLN) guerrilla, continues to haunt neoliberal El Salvador in a new form: the transnational gangster-as-terrorist. The social fear of this transfigured enemy of the neoliberal state has allowed the Salvadoran government to adopt draconian security and policing regulations inspired by the United States. Even more, this transnational state of exception has allowed Salvadoran elites to continue to benefit from their support of the United States and its military and economic interests in the region. In Chapter 4, David Gow likewise demonstrates that even when Colombian activists are able to formulate clear—if local—alternatives to the state's neoliberal agenda, their ability to sustain such structural alternatives is much diminished in a context of institutional state violence.

Violence also shapes the ways in which memory and history are subject to reinterpretation within neoliberalism. As Chris Krupa explains in Chapter 7, the president of Ecuador, Rafael Correa, has used a newly uncovered history of neoliberal violence to support his transition to a "postneoliberal" epoch. Formed by Correa just three months after taking office, Ecuador's truth commission was given the curious charge of investigating human rights abuses committed twenty-five years earlier. The commission's extensive research exposed a public secret lurking in Ecuador's past: that during the early years of the administration of Ecuador's neoliberal "founding father," President León Esteban Febres-Cordero, the government unleashed a wave of terror, first against a small and largely symbolic guerrilla organization and then against all perceived opponents of the regime. Krupa argues that the revelation of this violent past was a necessary complication of Ecuador's reputation as an "island of peace" in the region, but he also draws attention to the effects this historical reconstruction is having in the present moment of social change. The commission's investigations construct a richly analytic narrative that folds Ecuador's broader experience of neoliberalism into the violence used to institutionalize it—marking the period with indisputable evidence of its consequences right when support for an oppositional agenda was most needed by the Correa government.

Similarly, Veronica Schild (Chapter 8) argues that, in Chile, neoliberal actors beyond the state deploy a kind of symbolic violence in the way their work redefines acceptable categories of subjects by targeting certain behaviors and punishing others. She examines how feminist NGOs single out poor women for intervention and urge them to become responsible consumers and service workers in Chile's globalized capitalist economy. Those who succeed receive aid; those who do not are punished and left to be swept into the growing private prison system. At a broader level, Zilberg shows how neoliberal categories of inclusion and exclusion, which depend on particular understandings of legal and illegal subjectivity, circulate transnationally between El Salvador and the United States. "Illegal aliens," deportees, and gang youth are, in a sense, essential to the purposes of a transnational zero-tolerance policing regime that punishes those who defy neoliberal logics of individual responsibility.

Patterns of accumulation and exploitation within and beyond neoliberalism

The chapters in the volume also reveal to different degrees the ways in which particular regimes of accumulation affect the production of responses to neoliberalism in Latin America and are reworking class relations in the process.

In Colombia, Gow argues, indigenous activists who have struggled for decades to obtain land rights now have sufficient class legitimacy to capture governing positions and push for indigenous notions of development. In Ecuador, the *hacendado* class has been transformed into a new political and economic elite through ownership of nontraditional export processes, while their former indigenous *peones* have become the new working class. The old contradictions of race and land are now being debated through the idiom of citizenship, often in harsh and sometimes violent ways.

The Chilean and Salvadoran cases also uncover new class struggles. Schild describes the transformation of the Chilean economy under neoliberalism, where industrialization based on cheap labor and increased consumption destroyed rural production and produced a new class of urban poor. Moreover, as Zilberg explains, in the transnational circuit between the United States and El Salvador, a postwar economy dependent on transnational global market relations produced new categories of neoliberal subjects: poor migrants, service workers, and "gang youth." At the U.S. border, those migrants become "illegal aliens" and "disposable people" subject to state violence (Green 2011). Yet, those same forces have also produced a new transnational class of migrant entrepreneurs who return to their countries of origin to wield much more political and economic power than they could have prior to immigrating (see also Pedersen 2012).

Shifting categories of class also reorient the relationships of other actors working for social change. In her chapter on NGOs in Mexico, Analiese Richard (Chapter 6) argues that NGOs are often either criticized for being "Trojan horses" for market-oriented forms of subjectivity and social action or celebrated as incubators of democratic values and practices. However, this dichotomy ignores the complexity of the specific political and social terrains these civil-society actors inhabit. Richard traces the historical development of the NGO sector in Tulancingo, Mexico, and reveals important contradictions between the class orientation of the organizations' founders and their populist aims, as well as strong connections between NGOs and political elites. She argues that, as a result, Mexican NGOs have been forced to negotiate with a variety of actors within and beyond the state in their own quest to be "taken into account" in policy decisions that affect them and their constituents; this, she maintains, in turn profoundly limits the capacity of local NGOs to openly challenge the neoliberal model. Schild makes a related argument about feminist NGO workers in Chile. She suggests that the neoliberal reforms of the past twenty years have resulted in the restoration of capitalist class power and control. One troubling effect of this has been the morphing of many on the Left into what we might call "the managerial Left"—those concerned more with pragmatic politics than with earlier agendas of sweeping social change.

These cases all demonstrate that Latin America is symptomatic of a dynamic that scholars have been describing more generally: that global late capitalism has produced new and rapidly changing class relations (Comaroff and Comaroff 2000, 2006; Robinson 2006). Although these often come to supersede previous class formations, many of the contradictions of the past are retained and recontextualized into new power struggles and divisions. Moreover, it is becoming increasingly clear that there is no longer one unquestioned model of neoliberal capitalism at work in Latin America. The Venezuelan and Bolivian experiments were a response to a truly popular disillusionment with the neoliberal model in Latin America. Might they be the harbingers of a new epoch in which a radical postneoliberal politics is embedded within and even dependent on the strictures of late capitalism? Both states continue to rely on a development model based on aggressive exploitation and global trade in natural resources even as they legitimize market participation by redistributing some resources to the population and developing nonstate sectors of political action around social movements and regional autonomy (Goodale n.d.; Gudynas 2010).

Something old, something new

The chapters in the volume also uncover something surprising about the possibilities more generally for profound social change in the contemporary world. To the extent to which meaningful challenges to neoliberalism are being developed in certain countries and in particular regions of countries in Latin America, these challenges generate at least two kinds of categories of contradiction and contestation. The first category, which we might call "a transnational entitlement regime," arises out of international discourses on citizenship, human rights, and democratization. It is associated with new conflicts that are the product of the essential hybridity of social change in post–Cold War Latin America, in which decades and centuries-old frameworks for articulating grievances are no longer available and have been replaced by what has now become a global language of social change. This new rhetoric linking human rights to social change and political evolution was first adopted during the postapartheid transition in South Africa. It brings together variants of democratization within a robust human rights framework that emphasizes economic equality, political participation, state responsibility, and the moral dimensions of public life. As Richard A. Wilson argues, this hybrid rhetoric, which is heavily inflected by legacies of liberalism, has become "the archetypal language of democratic transition" in many parts of the world (2001, 1; see also Goodale 2009). Benjamin Arditti similarly describes a common pattern among Latin America's Left, which he calls a "post-liberal politics" (Arditti 2008). And if this discursive framework for radical social change likewise shapes and brackets the current moment in Latin America, then it also necessarily excludes as much as it engenders.

Moreover, this new global model for social change generates alternative forms of contestation, some of which are central and indeed compelled by imperatives internal to the model itself and some of which are caused by the ways in which the model is imposed or implemented within a transnational sphere of activism and social reformism. In Latin America, the case of Bolivia is paradigmatic. With the reelection of Evo Morales in 2009, the MAS government has now turned its attention to the daunting task of implementing the nation's dizzyingly far-reaching new constitution. Even the most sympathetic observers of Bolivia's constitutional revolution have expressed skepticism about the possibilities for its full realization, and Bolivia's citizens continue to be deeply engaged in acrimonious debates about its meaning and implementation. As Postero (Chapter 2) demonstrates, the Morales government has been opposed both by the elites on the Right and by indigenous communities who have been supporters of the Morales regime.

Furthermore, as Sujatha Fernandes (Chapter 3) shows us, the beneficiaries of state-directed challenges to neoliberalism can be unpredictable. In the case of Venezuela, state rhetoric of resistance to U.S. imperialism is reinterpreted by urban community activists as resistance to power itself, including the power of the anti-imperialist Bolivarian state. Although their invocation of the surging multitudes has been justly criticized for its ambiguity and paradoxical lack of political form, Hardt and Negri's 2000 manifesto against empire did get something right, which the chapters in the present volume reinforce in different ways: that populations empowered by the hybrid rhetorics of the post–Cold War era can be creatively subversive in ways that both support and undermine the idea of the postneoliberal state.

Nonetheless, in the second category of contradictions and contestation generated by the range of responses to neoliberalism in contemporary Latin America, a category we might call a "regime of exclusion," we find something quite different: the resurgence of conflicts over structural tensions that have their roots in colonial legacies of inequality and exploitation. Even in countries like Bolivia, Venezuela, and Ecuador, enduring patterns of inequality in land tenure and access to political power remain. Although the traditional political class may have been displaced, "revolutionaries" have become a new class of elites who have to be concerned with consolidating power even as they exercise it in the service of revolutionary goals. What is more, the logics of global commodity markets mean that countries like Venezuela and Bolivia must still play ball through the mechanisms of the public-private partnerships that provoked so much social anger during the late 1990s and early 2000s.

Neoliberal and postneoliberal subject making

Apart from the ways in which the chapters in the volume reveal new patterns of social change and old legacies of exploitation and vulnerability in Latin America, they also bring us up close to the people whose lives are affected by the fractured tectonics of the present. The ongoing legacy of neoliberalism in Latin America is one in which particular moral and cultural projects have been shaped by the logics of neoliberal governmentality. Indeed, the moral, political, and economic dimensions of the current conjuncture unfolding in Latin American are intertwined in ways that both resonate more broadly and appear highly specific when viewed through an ethnographic lens. And yet the question of subjectivity is critical because in the end both the forces compelling the retrenchment of neoliberalism and those offering alternatives must be expressed in terms of *categories* of everyday lives that can be understood and appreciated only through the ethnography of the helter-skelter of social practice (Berlant 2007; Stewart 2007). What is so fascinating, in particular, about what these chapters reveal on this question is the way in which subjectivity itself, the process by which identity is performed, justified, and resisted within or against state projects, is mirrored on both sides of the neoliberal moment.

Thus, in the countries that have entered a period of conservative neoliberal resistance to broader political and economic realignment (e.g., Chile,

Colombia, Mexico, Peru), neoliberal subjectivity has become coextensive with citizenship itself, something that for the time being makes the emergence of alternative imaginaries unthinkable. However, in countries (e.g., Bolivia, Venezuela, Ecuador) whose revolutionary governments self-consciously locate themselves on the other side of neoliberalism, a historical and discursive conjuncture that might be rightly called "postneoliberal" (Grimson 2007), subjectivity is no longer simply derived from the logics of neoliberal governmentality. Instead, as new models of subject making that are based in an ethics of social responsibility are promoted, they come into conflict with subjectivities associated with broader—and earlier—regimes of exclusion.

Nevertheless, as Contreras Natera argues in the postscript, this link between subjectivity and governance—or subjectivity *as* governance—can become unstable during times of social and economic contradiction. He insists, for example, that contemporary South America is riven by a continent-wide fracturing that makes possible the emergence of a Hardt and Negri-like multitude. And yet, as Fernandes explains in her chapter on public-sector workers in Contreras Natera's same Bolivarian Venezuela, the moral project of revolution reveals its own contradictions and can create unintended social, political, and ethical forms. These new structures, in turn, modulate the scope of revolution itself; they bracket the outer limits of alternatives to neoliberalism.

The role and ideology of the state

The set of implications for understanding the contested present in Latin America relates to both the role and the ideology of the state. The volume's chapters present a rich historical and ethnographic tapestry of the state and suggest important lessons for locating the state in relation to new instruments of social change and new rhetorics of resistance to the structures of global capital.

To begin, it is important to periodize the rise of the neoliberal state. In Latin America the neoliberal state was constituted quite intentionally through a national-international-transnational nexus of actors who were faced with the problem of how to make the notoriously centralized and centralizing Latin American state more efficient and responsive within networks of capital that could not tolerate political obstruction. The result, as Schild discusses in the case of the Chilean state, was the emergence of public-private partnerships, dominated, however, by private transnational capital, which required the Latin American state to radically decentralize its functioning and social responsibilities. Although the official framing of decentralization throughout Latin America was almost always political—so-called market democracy as a further and more advanced stage in a process of civilian rule and democratization that began in the mid-1980s, for example—in fact, the most far-reaching and indeed catalytic consequences of the "Washington Consensus" were often economic and experienced by people at the level of prices, property, resource use, and basic social and human services (see Perreault and Martin 2005).

There is no better example of this than the 1999–2000 "water war" in Bolivia, in which the water concern in the Cochabamba Valley was privatized and contracted to a multinational company, which promised the coming of the holy trinity of cheaper prices, better infrastructure, and better customer service (see Olivera 2004; Shultz 2009). In fact, the result was a total upending of the social life of water provisioning, which had created a system of water allocation based on local norms and networks. Even more dramatic, the cost of water for customers rose by an average of 43 percent, leading to widespread social unrest and the crystallization of antineoliberalism as a framework for broader and later social mobilization (Shultz 2009, 18).

Cerrutti and Grimson (Chapter 5) discuss the responses of social movements to neoliberalism in Argentina, thus demonstrating another way the role of the state has changed but not disappeared. They show how the focus of urban social movements shifted from basic questions of housing and land tenure in the 1970s and 1980s to demands arising from the massive unemployment that accompanied the neoliberal reforms in the 1990s. The creative protests of neighborhood groups and unions of unemployed workers pushed the Argentine state under Menem to create a national works program that employed millions at soup kitchens and community centers. They argue that, rather than signaling the end of the welfare state, under neoliberalism the Argentine state, by heavily subsidizing unemployment and offering food to the indigent population, became more important than ever in the domestic economy of poor households.

In addition, although the policies of the neoliberal state that created the greatest lines of division in Latin America were often economic, the decentralization of the state was experienced as a retreat in other important spheres as well. As Elana Zilberg argues, the El Salvadoran state became unable to control what many would argue is the primary function of the modern state: citizen security (Moodie 2006; Goldstein 2004). Because of El Salvador's legacy of civil war and its destructive aftermath, the country was particularly susceptible to a political ideology of decentralization that required the state to divest itself of many of its obligations. However, what makes El Salvador a kind of worst-case scenario is the fact that a flow of immigration had been created with the United States that allowed veterans of both civil and gang wars to cross national boundaries. This vibrant transnational criminality—whose presence in El Salvador made life after the civil war traumatic in newly violent ways—became the target of the intervention of U.S. and international institutions, which ended up producing even more violence. Indeed, when policing and the control of national borders cease to fall strictly within the competencies and obligations of the state, the very nature of the state is called into question.

Thus, even in the cases of El Salvador and Chile, where neoliberalism has been firmly consolidated, the state nevertheless remains vital. Indeed, a central finding of this volume is that the state is often the key point of reference in relation to which political, cultural, legal, and economic mobilization must be articulated. This is true in countries where the state has become deeply and unshakably neoliberalized (e.g., Chile, Colombia, Argentina); in countries where the state remained stubbornly centralized throughout the period of neoliberal consolidation (e.g., Brazil, Costa Rica, to a lesser extent Paraguay); and, perhaps most bedeviling for our theoretical, if not ethnographic, purposes, in countries where the direct challenge to neoliberalism and its colonial antecedents was made both against and always in relation to the state, which was understood as an enduring symbol of colonialist (if not colonial) structures of exploitation and violence (e.g., Bolivia and Venezuela).

In the first group of countries, the classical neoliberal state reinforces its own stranglehold on processes of political activism and subject making—among others—precisely as it delegates legal and moral responsibilities to actors beyond the boundaries of state agencies and established political parties. This hallmark of neoliberal governmentality makes all citizens responsible state actors even as they become actors of the state. Furthermore, when all citizens, even (or especially) those who view their own projects in opposition to the state, become state actors, the possibilities for real challenges to state power can become severely foreshortened. A powerful and indeed poignant example of this foreshortening can be seen in Winifred Tate's (2007) study of the culture and politics of human rights activism in Colombia. As she argues, the Colombian state created a landscape on which nonstate, human rights institutions could both proliferate and flourish. But as these NGOs became more and more the vehicles for witnessing and then expressing popular discontent with the ongoing culture of violence in Colombia, they became more and more intertwined with a state that had proven incapable of moving from "symbolic" to "instrumental" efficacy, as Mauricio García Villegas has argued (1993). In this way, state power increased by proxy.

In the second group of countries, what the Chilean historian Claudio Véliz (1980) calls "the centralist tradition in Latin America" allowed the state to consolidate its power even during the highpoint of the Washington consensus in the 1990s. The retreat into a kind of democratic authoritarianism provided a model of stability through the late 1990s and into the early 2000s for a region that was descending into greater levels of instability, even if this fracturing was also a sign of popular discontent and resistance. For Latin American states in the throes of democratic authoritarianism, power was concentrated not only in the traditional spheres and ways—landed property, political exclusion, state suppression of dissent—but also in new, less overt, ways since the demands to soften and decentralize state power were so influential at a regional level. Either way, the power and inevitability of the state were reinforced.

In the third group of countries, like Bolivia and Venezuela, the state has been reconstituted as an essential agent of social and political mobilization and change even where "the state" itself had always existed as a "summarizing key symbol" (Ortner 1973) of exploitation, exclusion, violence—that is, everything that was to be eliminated through the processes of *refundación*. The revolutionary government of Chávez's Venezuela has established what Arturo Escobar (2010) calls a "neo-developmentalist" state as the foundation for experiments in postneoliberalism. Yet, as Fernandes (Chapter 3) shows us, even as poor barrio residents contemplate open acts of cultural resistance observable by the state, they at the same time reaffirm the essential role of the Venezuelan state as the source of funding, political inspiration, and social ideology.

If this is true more generally of the arguably postneoliberal states in Latin America (Bolivia, Ecuador, Venezuela), then postneoliberalism does not point necessarily to a withering away of the state, as some in Bolivia's hodge-podge of social movement revolutionaries, in particular, were led to believe (see Goodale n.d.). As Postero (Chapter 2) shows, this is also a source of great consternation for Morales's critics. In the absence of a legitimate post-Westphalian framework at the broader regional or even global level, the logics of the modern or liberal state will continue to provide the architecture within which challenges to neoliberalism in Latin America must be made.

In order to understand both how powerful this model of the state continues to be and also how the new Bolivian constitution or the earlier Zapatista Good Governance Councils (see Speed 2008) provide tantalizing glimmers of the kind of "postliberal" future that scholars like Escobar envision, we believe it is important to draw a distinction between *the state* and *forms of governance*. There is no question, as our volume demonstrates, that the (liberal or modern) state continues to be the dominant form of governance in Latin America. But if a form of governance is a particular mode of social ordering, then we can see the Bolivian constitutional experiment based on the visions and demands of indigenous social movements and the Zapatista governance councils as forms of governance that are grounded in non- or postliberal logics. In the case of Bolivia, the very much still-emergent form of governance that is expressed most clearly in the recent Law of Autonomy (2010), while embedded in the shell of the liberal state, is nevertheless a discursive and political expression of something quite different: a profound challenge to the interrelationship between state power and governance or, perhaps more accurately, state power *as* governance.

Much like the Zapatista *juntas de buen gobierno* that Speed writes about, the Bolivian constitution offers a model of governance in which decision making, rights, and obligations are radically horizontalized and centrifugal; power, in the traditional sense, radiates outward (not downward) through and in relation to communities, ethnic groups, social movements, and local political parties, however incipient. The result is a form of governance that orders but does not control; is structurally plural and pluralizing; and is derived from an ethics of social life—expressed through the popular slogan *vivir bien*, or "to live well"—rather than from the kind of biopolitics associated with the modern state. Yet, as Postero explains in her chapter, the process of implementing this new form of governance has generated its own tensions based on internal divisions within the broader coalition of MAS supporters and the compromises necessary to continue extractive forms of economic development as a precondition for social reform.

CONCLUSION: HORIZONS OF POSSIBILITY

In his clarion call for new mobilizations of power and identity in Latin America, Contreras Natera argues that alternatives to the hegemony of both the neoliberal state and market will not be of lasting consequence unless they are preceded by what he calls a "dislocation in the foundations of the colonial-modern logos." By this he means that the parameters of radical social, political, and economic change in Latin America must be widened through new projections of what is possible. Latin Americans must be willing to envision social logics and forms of governance and economy that do not yet exist. This is a methodology for a new model of insurgency, one that challenges lines of power, racial and ethnic ideology, and rationales of market exclusion and inclusion not through the deployment of violence or a direct attack on the institutions of the state but through a social process that Contreras Natera describes as "critical and deconstructive thinking."

Nonetheless, as the chapters in this volume demonstrate in no uncertain terms, the neoliberalization of Latin America accelerated the deepening of ideologies that, among other things, naturalize and flatten out their own historical contingency. In the absence of clear alternatives to neoliberalism with similar legacies of political legitimacy and historical durability, it has become more difficult for radicals in contemporary Latin America to gain much regional traction. This is another reason that it has become all too easy to analytically marginalize the sociopolitical experiments in countries like Bolivia and Venezuela. In addition, it does not help that the Bolivian revolution, for example, is understood by some of its protagonists as a revolution *toward socialism*, when in fact its constitution and broader ethnopolitical lines of restructuring suggest a radically hybrid form of governance that defies the existing categories of social and political theory.

Taken as a whole, the chapters in the volume point to the challenges that confront the vision and desires of intellectuals like Contreras Natera and political and social leaders throughout Latin America who strive for a post-neoliberal future, one in which the region will once again be at the vanguard of global activism and revolutionary militancy. As the life-threatening illness of Hugo Chávez has underscored, challenges to neoliberalism in Latin America are still largely embodied in the trajectories of charismatic leaders, whose quests for political power can overshadow both the efforts of more obscure activists and the goals of the revolution itself. This has also prevented the emergence of a viable transregional, postneoliberal alignment. Instead, we see what might be described as "national postneoliberalisms," or the development of "post-neoliberalism in one country." These national experiments nevertheless reveal something beyond the constraints of the neoliberal world order. They point the way to new horizons of possibility even if their broader implications are still incipient or deeply contested. And they are, without question, suffused with the kind of insurgent imaginary that Contreras Natera urges, even as neoliberalism becomes more rooted and discursively naturalized throughout much of Latin America.

PART ONE

THE POSTNEOLIBERAL CHALLENGE

CHAPTER 2

BOLIVIA'S CHALLENGE TO "COLONIAL NEOLIBERALISM"

Nancy Postero

SOON AFTER INDIGENOUS LEADER EVO Morales was elected president of Bolivia in 2005, he visited Fidel Castro in Cuba. There, with much fanfare, the two leaders announced a partnership designed to eradicate illiteracy in Bolivia. Shortly afterward, Morales went to Venezuela, where he met with Hugo Chávez. Together, they denounced free-market economics, saying they were uniting in a "fight against neoliberalism and imperialism." Chávez termed the warm new relationship between Bolivia, Cuba, and Venezuela an "axis of good"—a pointed reference to George Bush's "axis of evil"—and promised to supply Bolivia with diesel fuel, money for social programs, and support for Bolivia's stance against U.S. drug eradication programs (St. John 2006). Since then, Morales has moved beyond these dramatic rhetorical displays to the difficult business of governing. In the process, he and his MAS (Movement Toward Socialism) party have offered serious challenges to the neoliberal model that has been dominant for the last few decades, returning to public ownership many resources that were privatized during the neoliberal era, particularly natural gas; expanding social services; and making significant redistributions to Bolivia's neediest people.

In this chapter, I examine the so-called postneoliberal moment in Bolivia, focusing on the contradictions that have emerged in the process (Webber 2011). Clearly, the economic transformations the MAS has enacted are reversing many of the neoliberal policies of the last decades, but just as neoliberalism was never complete, neither is the current administration's reversal of it. As a result, the Bolivian experiment to reformulate the neoliberal state cannot be evaluated simply by its adherence to or rejection of neoliberal economic policies. Instead, I focus on the transformations this challenge to neoliberalism is producing, especially in the relation between the state and Bolivia's diverse indigenous population. All development models link economic policies to political and social goals. In Bolivia, this is explicit, as the MAS economic or development model is part of a political-cultural revolution to "refound the nation" and "decolonize" a society made up of nearly 70 percent indigenous people. The MAS project is based on an understanding that the indigenous peoples, peasants, and popular social movements that make up its constituency suffered from structures of race and class domination that were the legacy of colonialism and that neoliberalism exacerbated these inequalities. Just as neoliberalism combined economic and political reforms to promote "market democracy," so the "radical democracy" project in Bolivia responding to it is addressing both cultural recognition and economic changes. One important way in which these two are linked in Bolivia's new constitution is through the notion of *vivir bien* (to live well), a form of sustainable development that promises to alter Bolivia's long history of development, based on aggressive exploitation and global sales of its natural resources. This ongoing project offers an important and highly visible alternative to neoliberalism as it has been practiced for the last few decades, but it is marked by internal tensions and deep contestations. Thus, rather than postneoliberal, it may be more accurate to characterize the MAS's administration as a hybrid that holds conflicting models of neoliberal extractivism and indigenous sustainability in an unstable tension.

I begin by defining neoliberalism and tracing its enactment and effects in Bolivia. Bolivia's governments have been implementing neoliberal policies since the early 1980s, but the 1990s saw a deepening of this strategy. Yet, by 2000, a decade of economic and social crisis had left Bolivians deeply frustrated with the neoliberal model. The next five years saw a wave of protests and insurrections that culminated in the election of Morales. I then turn to the transformations occurring in Bolivia since Morales's election. I describe the MAS government's interventions in the economy and pay special attention to the National Development Plan, published in 2006. I then turn to the contents of the new constitution passed in 2009, which codifies many rights for Bolivia's indigenous citizens. By linking their opposition to neoliberalism to centuries-old struggles against colonial domination and racism, the MAS forged a powerful discourse that legitimated its new national agenda and gave it enormous political power. Yet, as the Morales administration continues to privilege a natural-resource extraction model that sacrifices some of Bolivia's poorest and most vulnerable indigenous communities, its political hegemony has begun to weaken.

PRACTICES OF NEOLIBERAL ORTHODOXY

The philosophy of neoliberalism focuses on the relation between the state, the market, and individuals. David Harvey suggests that "neoliberalism is in the first instance a theory of political economic practices that proposes that human well-being can best be advanced by liberating individual entrepreneurial freedoms and skills within an institutional framework characterized by strong private property rights, free markets, and free trade" (Harvey 2005, 2). Within this framework, the state should be restricted to those functions necessary, for instance, to guarantee the proper functioning of markets and the integrity of money, courts, private property (ibid.).

This model, derived from classic economic liberalism, emerged as a philosophy in the post–World War II period but was not put into effect until the 1970s, when the failures of import substitution industrialization (ISI) and raging debt left Latin American countries vulnerable to a new philosophy of development. As the development model favored in Latin America since the 1950s, ISI promoted inward-oriented economic growth and industrialization by limiting foreign trade and investment through protectionist policies (Perreault and Martin 2005). By merging Keynesian welfare economics and dependency theory, ISI recognized that (peripheral) Latin American countries that were producing raw materials were structurally dependent upon global markets controlled by (core) industrialized countries. Although ISI produced enormous economic growth in some countries, it had serious negative effects—it exacerbated trade deficits, caused inflation, increased debt, and brought about huge rural-to-urban displacement (ibid.). Beginning in the Reagan and Thatcher eras, in what has been called the "Washington Consensus," the philosophy of neoliberalism took hold in the centers of power, especially in the World Bank (WB) and the International Monetary Fund (IMF). In this first phase of neoliberal practice, these institutions gave loans to debt-ridden countries in exchange for promises to abide by the banks' prescriptions for economic health. These "structural adjustment programs" (SAPs) instituted an orthodox set of reforms: states were to privatize state-owned enterprises, radically reduce social spending, deregulate industry, orient industry toward export, and drop all subsidies and trade barriers. A critical part of the model was the creation of a favorable climate for free trade and the encouragement of foreign investment. This included a renewed emphasis on natural-resource extraction and efforts to develop regional and global trade agreements. In Bolivia, these reforms were begun in the early 1980s, as the country emerged from dictatorship. In his two terms as president (1992–1997, 2002–2003) President Gonzalo Sánchez de Lozada deepened these measures by privatizing public enterprises, eliminating public jobs, cutting social services, and ending subsidies to farmers (see Arze and Kruse 2004; Kohl and Farthing 2006; Postero 2007).

The justification for these radical transformations was that the "deviations" encouraged under ISI—tariffs, quotas, and subsidies for domestic industry—had deformed the correct functioning of the market. Once the market was allowed to function efficiently, with every country acting on the basis of its competitive advantages (like cheap labor and raw materials), economic benefits would supposedly flow to all. However, the overwhelming result of two decades of neoliberal practices has been the opposite: a dramatic redistribution of wealth from the poorest people in the hemisphere to the richest (Duménil and Lévy, cited in Harvey 2005, 16), thereby exacerbating rather than reducing the "uneven geographies of development" (Perreault and Martin 2005, 197). Over the last decade, scholars have carefully documented the ways wealth has been redistributed under this framework. Harvey suggests that the main mechanism is "accumulation by dispossession," whereby property, land, and labor are increasingly privatized and commoditized (Harvey 2005, 19). Others have described the ways neoliberal state policies act to reverse the flow of wealth from the poor—and increasingly the middle class—to the rich by cutting social spending, which then forces the population to shoulder the burdens of education, health care, and so on (ibid., 164). Feminist scholars have described how these processes have gendered effects, as poverty is increasingly feminized (Elson 1995).

In Bolivia, the neoliberal reforms of the 1990s had devastating effects (Postero 2007, 190–193). Economic analysts Carlos Arze and Tom Kruse explain that the state abandoned its role as the country's principal employer. Thousands of miners at the state mining corporation were retired, and mid-level bureaucrats were laid off. In the 1990s, capitalization (privatization) of most publicly owned enterprises further cut public-sector employment (Arze and Kruse 2004, 27). This restructuring of the labor market produced a huge pool of unemployed workers who turned to the informal market for fragile and uncertain subsistence. Second, the state lost money in the process of privatization. Promised dividends from capitalization partners did not appear, and the shares retained by the state went to pension plans also controlled by the capitalist partners. This meant that control over most of the country's economic surplus passed into the hands of foreign investors without producing new income for the state (ibid., 25). Third, market liberalization reforms severely affected Bolivian industry, which had been supported by protective barriers. Fourth, Bolivia's farm economy, which is the principal provider of products for domestic consumption, was devastated by the commercial liberalization. Large numbers of rural farmers and herders were bankrupted because they were unable to compete with cheaper supplies from abroad. This led to a massive increase in agricultural imports, which substitute for national production, and an emptying of the countryside and a massive migration to urban areas (ibid., 26). The U.S.-driven policy of coca eradication caused the loss of substantial resources (a government office estimated $610 million between 1997 and 2000) and the destruction of thousands of jobs directly or indirectly linked to this agricultural production (ibid.).

As the poor shouldered these burdens, incomes rose for the dominant classes, especially the "transnational capitalist class" and local economic and political elites tied to transnational capital (Robinson 2006, 142). The crisis caused a huge migration of Bolivians to other countries, especially Argentina and Spain. The result was an increasing sense among most Bolivians that the elite, in conjunction with the transnational capitalist classes, had commandeered control of what was formerly considered national patrimony, the economy of the country. This was especially clear at the end of the Sánchez de Lozada government, when it was revealed that the president had secretly signed contracts with transnational gas companies in which the royalty percentages were far below that demanded by law.

Given the disastrous results for the majority of Bolivians, one might wonder why they went along with neoliberalism for as long as they did. One important mechanism that cannot be ignored is state violence. Despite the importance in neoliberal philosophy of minimizing the state, the state did not, in fact, disappear. Certain parts of the state apparatus, such as social services, education, and health care, were, of course, dismantled, but the coercive aspect of the state remained in full force. This was all too clear in the 2003 "gas war," when protestors in El Alto and La Paz demonstrated against plans to pipe natural gas from the lowlands to Chilean ports and on to the United States and Mexico. The Sánchez de Lozada government met the protestors with military force, killing more than eighty people and wounding nearly five hundred. This draws our attention to the underlying violence of these economic structures and institutions and to the continued threat of oppression that compels compliance. As chapters 7–9 in this volume (by Krupa, Schild, and Zilberg) also point out, ultimately, neoliberal states, like liberal ones, rely on the fundamental threat of sovereign violence.

THE SECOND STAGE: MARKET DEMOCRACIES

Nonetheless, we cannot explain the hegemony of neoliberalism strictly through coercion, whether that takes place at the national or the transnational level. After the initial years of harsh neoliberal restructuring, a new discursive regime began to emerge and, in effect, fostered certain consent (Kohl and Farthing 2009). Responding to the terrible social costs of the first phase, the WB and the IMF responded by modifying the hard-line neoliberal agenda, at least to some degree. Early programs to ameliorate the effects of the SAPs—the so-called social emergency funds—gave way to what many perceived as a "kinder, gentler" version of neoliberalism, what Peck and Tickell call "roll-back neoliberalism" (2002, 384). A central strategy was to pair economic reforms with a discourse of "market democracy." That is, a linkage between free trade and democracy promotion resulted in policies such as decentralization (the devolution of state power to cities and regions), on the one hand, and the empowerment of civil society, on the other. This discourse was marked by two sets of practices. First, neoliberalism regulated and rationalized conduct through both "public," or state, mechanisms *and* "private" arenas, such as corporations, nongovernmental organizations (NGOs), and individual actions (Foucault 1991a; Rose 1996). Thus, many of the duties of the state—health, education, policing—were passed to private actors by selling state enterprises, by reorganizing service providers along economic-enterprise models, or by outsourcing to NGOs or private actors (Burchell 1996; Schild 2000). The increasing role of international agencies like the World Bank and the IMF and of international NGOs amounts to a kind of transnational governance that acts to transfer sovereignty away from the state (Ferguson and Gupta 2002; Ferguson 2006). The second set of practices promotes and imbues a particular political rationality in individuals (Brown 2003; Burchell 1996; Foucault 1991a; Rose 1996).

The Bolivian Law of Popular Participation (LPP) was a prime example of neoliberal government. A Bolivian version of decentralization, the LPP distributed national-level monies to municipalities and created new political institutions to foster and manage responsible citizens, challenging older and more contentious corporate forms of civil society like miners' unions and peasant organizations. Under the program, adopted as part of the neoliberal reforms of the mid-1990s, indigenous and social movements were encouraged to participate in development and budget decisions at the municipal level. Nongovernmental organizations that were facilitating this new form of citizenship imbued these subjects with a new logic of responsibility and efficiency in their role as citizens (Postero 2007, chap. 5). However, although this plan did recognize indigenous people as legitimate actors, I have argued that, in most cases, it did not function to significantly redistribute resources. The overarching racism in the country and the continuing control of elite political parties made it difficult for indigenous people and their representatives to gain any meaningful access to the political process. Rather, the LPP acted—initially, at least—to justify and soften the harsh effects of economic restructuring by presenting the state as democratic and receptive to the cultural and political demands of long-oppressed indigenous citizens (Postero 2007).

This points to the importance of civil society as a site for both the construction of and the resistance to neoliberalism. Civil society, that supposedly autonomous sphere where citizens exercise their freedom and responsibilities, is an essential element of classic political liberalism, which posited the "rights-bearing citizen-subject," whose freedom was sacrosanct. The Law of Popular Participation legitimated the neoliberal state by creating new categories of citizenship, which were then taken up by indigenous and poor people, who began to expect that they had rights to participate in the society and the economy. Finding little opportunity to exercise those rights through existing institutions, however, indigenous and popular social movements fought back. First, they took to the streets. In the 2000 "water war," factory workers, rural irrigators, and a wide spectrum of urban residents joined in massive protests against a water-privatization plan implemented by the city of Cochabamba. This was followed that same year by mobilizations by campesinos and coca growers, who blocked the highways. This wave of social unrest culminated in the 2003 "gas war," mentioned earlier, in which a broad spectrum of urban indigenous people, labor, and students rejected plans to allow transnational corporations export natural gas, which they considered "patrimony." Condemning a pattern of foreign and elite profit from the resources and labor of poor Bolivians, they demanded the resignation of the president and the nationalization of gas.

The following years saw the rise of new political parties based in popular and indigenous social movements, most notably the MAS, which emerged primarily from the efforts of the *cocaleros*, the coca-growers' union in the Chapare region of the Cochabamba tropics. The MAS's struggles against government- and U.S.-backed drug-eradication policies positioned it as a key player in the oppositional politics of Bolivia. Beginning in 2002, the MAS brought together a number of other movements—labor, peasants, lowland indigenous peoples—and began to gain control of municipal governments. As both Albro and Lazar describe in their ethnographies of urban political contestations, a central reason for the MAS's success was that it employed political models based in populism and Andean communal organizations and combined traditional patron-client relations with new discourses of citizenship and indigenous rights (Albro 2010; Lazar 2008). In 2005, the MAS gained a majority of seats in the national parliament and captured the presidency as well. Evo Morales, the indigenous leader of the coca-growers' union, made antineoliberalism a central part of his presidential campaign. He explained the October uprising as a sign of "the exhaustion of neoliberalism" (Morales 2003). Relying both on what Madrid (2008) calls "ethnopopulism" and on classic antidependency narratives, Morales held himself out as the representative of the "people" (in contrast to the corrupt political elite) and promised to nationalize gas resources, restore Bolivia's sovereignty (long eroded by its dependence on U.S. and foreign aid), and institute national development based on indigenous values and social justice for the poor.

THE 2006 NATIONAL DEVELOPMENT PLAN AND THE DISCOURSE OF COLONIAL NEOLIBERALISM

Once in power, the MAS made significant steps to transform the relation between the state and the market and overturn the neoliberal project of the previous decades. The fundamental change was to make the state a primary actor in economic development. This was an overt contestation of orthodox neoliberal ideology—but not practices—about the separation of the economic and the political. The government issued a roadmap to its plans in June 2006, when it published the Plan Nacional de Desarrollo (National Development Plan) (PND 2006). Although much of the PND was never implemented, it is worth taking a close look at its language to understand both how the MAS discursively linked neoliberalism to colonialism and how it located its alternative project within indigenous customs and potentials.

The plan describes the goal of national development as "remov[ing], from its roots, the profound social inequality and inhuman exclusion which oppress the majority of the Bolivian population, particularly those of indigenous origin" (PND 2006, 1). This inequality, the plan makes clear, is the product of colonialism, capitalism, and neoliberalism. Colonialism, continuing through the Republican period, denied indigenous peoples not only their dignity and their labor but also their right to the means of production, especially land. Then, the capitalist "primary export model" of silver and tin mining deepened these inequalities by benefiting a small nucleus of oligarchs. Throughout the first half of the twentieth century, most of Bolivia's natural riches were exported to other countries, along with the profits from their exploitation. The reforms of the 1952 revolution, including nationalization of the mines, were not enough to overcome the original causes of the structural inequalities and social exclusions. Instead, the state capitalism of the second half of the century gave rise to new regional oligarchs who appropriated state patrimony. This period ended in a crisis of external debt and hyperinflation, ushering in the neoliberal period (ibid.).

The neoliberal model, says the plan, exacerbated the concentration of wealth by giving access to means of production and jobs to one-tenth of the population. This "inequality and social discrimination, called 'poverty' by neoliberal colonialism," led to compensatory measures such as the "poverty-reduction" policies that often accompanied structural-adjustment programs and, more recently, the "millennium development goals." Although this amounted to recognition of the failure of the market and the need for state intervention, neoliberal antipoverty efforts continued to be subject to the logic of the market. Consequently, NGOs and foreign aid stepped into this void with "development" projects, but since they did not address the fundamental causes, they could not resolve the problems; instead, they created projects that catered to foreign objectives, debilitated the government, and wasted enormous amounts of money. Thus, under neoliberalism, the development of the country was subject to the interests of multilateral organizations and transnational corporations (PND 2006, 3).

This model of development failed because "it is the product of a system of ethnic, cultural, and political domination, impregnated with racism" (PND 2006, 12). The plan proposed an alternative model of development, which arose from social demands of the "majority of the population," whose voices were silenced by neoliberalism. Because neoliberalism conceived of development as "exclusively associated with economic growth, delinked from the State or politics," "it expropriated from the people their right to propose and debate their common future" (ibid., 9). Instead, the plan offered a new model, called *vivir bien* (to live well). Derived from the *cosmovisión* (worldview) of indigenous peoples, it refers to communitarian forms of *convivencia*, or living together. It implies intercultural respect and symmetries of power: "One cannot live well if others live badly" (ibid., 10). The plan argues that this collective notion of well-being is very different from Western notions of individual well-being, which can be obtained at the expense of others or the environment. It also differs from Western notions in that it goes beyond the material and economic to include values such as emotions, recognition, difference, social prestige, and dignity (ibid., 10).

The plan insisted that implementation of this alternative form of development would require the state to intervene as "promoter and protagonist of national development" (PND 2006, 4). The state would act to transform society and the economy but would do so "only if all peoples and cultures are present in the economic and political decisions of the State" (ibid., 15). This meant that the people's "capacity to decide" would have to be recuperated within a new notion of the nation that recognized the pluriethnicity and multiculturality of the country, as well as the vitality of the social movements. Finally, the plan suggested that these newly empowered social actors would create a new state during democratic debate in the Constituent Assembly.

Several aspects of this document require comment. First, the document returns time and again to its assertion that the foundation of Bolivian society is its indigenous peoples, tying the well-being of all Bolivians and the nation as a whole to its native peoples and social movements. By characterizing the majority of the population as indigenous, however, it elides the complex relationship between race and class that has led poor Bolivians to identify in some periods as *campesinos* (peasant farmers) and in others as *indígenas* or *pueblos originarios* (indigenous or original peoples) (Albó 2000; Canessa 2006; Postero 2007). It also erases and delegitimizes other nonindigenous sectors, demonizing the *mestizos*, who held power in previous eras. Most important, in proposing an alternative to "colonial neoliberalism" based upon these idealized indigenous values, it blurs the differences between Bolivia's many indigenous groups' histories, cultures, languages, and spiritual beliefs by constructing an authenticity based upon the supposed shared values of harmony, complementarity, and communitarian forms of living. Yet, it combines these values drawn from the indigenous repertoire with the tried and true values of liberalism, linking them to the internationally recognized discourses of multiculturalism, environmental sustainability, democratization, and human rights. The document demonstrates the very rich repertoire of "indigenous culture and values" and how flexibly it can be adapted. Morales has used this discourse to great advantage on the national and international stage, claiming to find answers to global problems, including climate change, in the cosmovisión of Bolivia's indigenous people (see Morales 2006).

Second, the narrative told in the document links neoliberalism and colonialism as stages in a coherent, long-term model of cultural and economic exploitation. The document explains that its authors reject the neoliberal definition of development as strictly economic or material and intentionally redefine development to include cultural and political rights, especially human dignity and human rights. Thus, for these authors, development must be understood in terms of cultural values and forms of social organization (PND 2006, 12). As we have seen, however, neoliberalism was never strictly economic in practice. Neoliberal governance also encouraged particular values and notions of civil-society organization and produced a certain kind of responsible, self-disciplining subject (Li 2007; Postero 2007). Although the MAS rhetoric challenging "colonial neoliberalism" may seem hyperbolic, it does render visible the workings of capitalism, especially those of neoliberalism. It gives voice to the reality that Bolivia's poor and indigenous people know *en carne propia* (in their flesh and bones): the market is not a neutral site but one that reinforces existing power relations of race and class. Thus, as Morales declared at his inauguration, his victory marked not only the end of neoliberalism but also the beginning of a "cultural revolution" (Morales 2006). In this way, this discourse legitimates MAS's national agenda to its constituents and to the world. That is, the MAS does not offer its project merely as a different economic model to be debated among dueling economists. Rather, it holds itself out as creating a new nation based on social justice and multicultural equality. By yoking its discourse of "anticolonial neoliberalism" to liberal discourses of human rights and democratization, the MAS legitimates its policies much more powerfully than it could by merely invoking Keynesian welfare or socialist economic models.

However, this discursive strategy also raised the political stakes as Bolivians engaged in overtly cultural struggles. During the multicultural 1990s, identity politics were central to neoliberal governance, yet there was some sense that racism was gradually diminishing as the state recognized indigenous cultures and leadership and encouraged intercultural understanding. That sense disappeared, however, and was replaced by a stark polarization of the population. Although many indigenous people felt their interests were being taken into account at long last, many other Bolivians feared a focus on race and culture despite all the rhetoric about equality. Such fears motivated much of the resistance to the MAS agenda and made it even harder to enact. In the lowlands, white and mestizo opposition leaders argued for political and economic autonomy from the central state, focusing on self-government and the ability to benefit from the resources exploited in their regions. Underlying these demands, however, was a deeply subjective resistance, much of it expressed in cultural and racialized terms. Lowland leaders describe themselves as representing a different culture, with different customs and history, and argue that the Morales government is a dictatorship that violates human rights (Fabricant and Postero forthcoming). During the tense period around the passing of the constitution in 2008, racist violence shocked the country by exposing deep schisms. Overt racism seems to have lessened slightly in recent years, as the right wing has lost political power, but the divisions remain.

CHANGING THE ROLE OF THE STATE

The most salient aspect of Morales's antineoliberal program had already begun as the plan was being developed. In May 2006 Morales declared he was nationalizing the oil and gas sector and ordered the Bolivian army to take over the foreign-owned natural-gas installations in the eastern section of the country. Gas and mining resources were nationalized by the state after the 1952 revolution and run by state-owned companies until the neoliberal era, when they were privatized. As a result, there is a long collective memory of the state's involvement in the exploitation of what is considered the national patrimony. Perhaps even more important, the mines generated numerous jobs with good salaries, benefits, and high status associated with working for the nation (Nash 1979). The miners' layoffs in the late 1980s as part of the neoliberal restructuring were perceived by many as a blow to the dignity of Bolivia's working people (see Nash 1992). Thus Morales struck a deep emotional populist and nationalist chord when he staged the takeover in May 2007.

Clearly, this reassertion of the state's role in the economy defies the neoliberal model and signals a reversion of the waves of privatizations in the 1990s. Yet, it is not just a return to the past. Morales did not seize the assets of the foreign corporations working the gas concessions. Rather, the nationalization decree gave the companies six months to renegotiate their contracts with the state. It also sharply raised taxes and royalties on gas producers and created the *Impuestos Directos de los Hidrocarburos*, or direct taxes from natural gas profits. Previously, companies received on the order of 82 percent of the profits, which left the Bolivian state with only a small portion. The new taxes, royalties, and renegotiated contracts changed these proportions; now the central government receives about 54 percent of the profits (after operating costs and funding the state-owned gas company) (Andean Information Network 2007a, 2007b). Morales's "nationalization" plan was therefore a savvy political move that masked a highly pragmatic strategy with the rhetoric of populism. Although many of his constituents might have preferred complete state control, Bolivia simply does not have the enormous capital necessary for oil and gas exploration, exploitation, and distribution. This arrangement also demonstrates that the Morales model is not an end to the primary export model so decried in the PND. Like the Venezuelan case described by Fernandes in Chapter 3 of this volume, Morales and his economic advisers see that Bolivia's national development must remain linked to global capitalism.

As a result of this reassertion of control over profits from its natural resources, Bolivia radically altered its financial situation. Government income from oil and gas went from US$173 million in 2002 to an estimated US$1.57 billion in 2007 (Andean Information Network 2008). Much of this was due to the fact that oil prices rose dramatically for the first years of the MAS administration—to nearly five times greater than during the Sánchez de Lozada years (Laserna Rojas, Miranda Pacheco, and Torrico 2009, 31). For the first time Bolivia began to experience a surplus, which reached 5 percent of the gross domestic product in 2008, and it amassed large international reserves—almost $8.5 billion (Weisbrot, Ray, and Johnston 2009, 13, 20). Using this surplus in its fiscal policy, Bolivia was able to manage the financial downturn much better than other countries in the region (ibid.). Moreover, the economy registered an annual growth of 5.2 percent from 2006 to 2009.

This has shrunk during the recession, but Bolivia is still among the top countries for projected growth in the hemisphere (ibid., 2).

The health of Bolivia's economic situation is widely contested from both the Right and the Left. Conservative economist Roberto Laserna Rojas argues that the Morales government falls into the classic *rentier* mentality of previous governments inasmuch as it views hydrocarbon resources as something to be plundered without concern for making the country more productive or creating jobs (Laserna Rojas , Miranda Pachecho, and Torrico 2009). Moreover, he points out that since the renegotiation of the oil contracts, Bolivia's "partners" have invested far less money, exploring and producing at levels far below the neoliberal years (ibid., 23). Marxist analyst Jeffery Webber, on the other hand, characterizes the Morales development model as disappointingly reformist and argues that it reinforces existing class and capitalist structures through a neostructuralist development model that favors transnational corporations, the agricultural elite, and fiscal security over real structural change that benefits the poor (Webber 2011). In a more sympathetic analysis, Kaup argues that the Morales government continues to be constrained in its options by the "path-dependent" effects of the neoliberal years, which set Bolivia on a development trajectory that is very difficult to change. Even though it was able to renegotiate the rents from its natural-gas resources, it was not able to make radical changes to the material constraints of gas extraction, transport, and use, which keep it supplying gas that benefits its neighbors' development projects more than its own (Kaup 2010).

Clearly, the Bolivian economy has faced difficulties. Gas and mineral prices have dropped in the last few years, reducing revenue. In 2007 the United States slapped trade sanctions on Bolivia under the Andean Trade Protection and Drug Eradication Act (ATPDEA), thereby precluding Bolivian exports to the United States. And in December 2010, citing concerns that much of Bolivia's highly subsidized oil and gas was being sold on the black market in neighboring countries, Morales announced he was cutting fuel subsidies and raising domestic prices, a classic neoliberal shock-therapy move. After massive demonstrations and strikes protesting the "*gasolinazo*," Morales backed down (Quiroga 2011). Bolivia's challenge is to invest further in the sector so as to be able both to meet growing domestic demand and to export to its neighbors, particularly Argentina and Brazil (Kaup 2010; UPI 2010).

Meanwhile, some of the oil companies scared away in the "nationalization" have returned. Petrobras, Brazil's national oil company announced in early 2011 that it would explore three new fields in Bolivia (*Wall Street Journal* 2011). Inflation also continues to plague the country. In February 2011 popular sectors led by the workers' union, the Central Obrero Boliviano (COB), and neighborhood groups held massive demonstrations protesting planned hikes in the transportation prices and calling for increases in the minimum salaries. In June 2012 the police held massive strikes, demanding pay raises. Thus, Bolivia's economic picture is not yet settled, but there is no doubt that the massive influx of money from the oil and gas sector and its large reserves has changed the country's ability to maneuver.

The looming question is, of course, how free Bolivia is to implement different models, given the hegemony of global capitalism and the particular neoliberal forms it has taken. Ten years ago, Bolivia's reforms would have met stiff resistance from the IMF and the World Bank, those external enforcers of neoliberal orthodoxy. Now, however, those institutions have much less influence across the continent, as countries have reduced their debt and found alternative sources of funding, especially from petroleum-rich Venezuela. In 2001 most of Bolivia's debt to the World Bank and the IMF was cancelled as part of the loan forgiveness program for highly indebted and poor countries, and in 2006, after twenty years of funding tied to strict neoliberal conditionalities, Bolivia let its last agreement with the IMF expire. It also recently received debt relief from the Inter-American Development Bank (IADB 2008). Economist Mark Weisbrot argues that these developments are much more important than they may appear, as they demonstrate the fading power of multilateral banks like the IMF to dictate policy to the region. The result, he suggests, is that countries like Bolivia have a much freer hand in their attempts to rethink their economies and the role of the state (Weisbrot 2006).

REDISTRIBUTION AND DEMOCRATIZATION

Uruguayan ecologist Eduardo Gudynas argues that in "progressive neo-extractivist" countries, the state gives resource extraction greater legitimacy by redistributing some of the surplus to the population (Gudynas 2010). That is exactly what Bolivia has done. Like Venezuela, the Bolivian government began using state hydrocarbon resources for national development projects to initiate new forms of public spending, state subsidies, and social security programs. Direct taxes from natural-gas profits are distributed to public universities, municipalities, departments (regional governments), and indigenous groups (see Laserna Rojas, Miranda Pachecho, and Torrico 2009). At the national level, the government instituted two cash-transfer programs: a popular retirement account for senior citizens, called the Renta Dignidad, and a subsidy for children attending school, called the Juancito Pinto program. More than 1.7 million students received the payment each school year. Additionally, with Cuba's help, the central government funded a national literacy program; a "zero-malnutrition" program to eliminate childhood malnutrition; and a large campaign for eye health (Weisbrot and Sandoval 2007). Some question whether these are truly forms of redistribution since they do not raise the standard of living in a significant way (Webber 2011). Considering that, overall, there has been very limited social spending by the Bolivian government and very little improvement in the poverty rate since Morales's election, I share this critique (Weisbrot, Ray, and Johnston 2009, 16–19). Some new studies argue, however, that these cash transfers allow the poor to invest money in the projects most likely to increase their production and income (Chaudhry 2011). More study appears necessary, but for now we can say that the programs are enormously popular among Bolivia's poor and indigenous majority, Morales's main constituency.

Another central part of the Morales agenda has been agrarian reform. During the neoliberal years, there were legislative reforms intended to rationalize land titles, including granting collective titles to indigenous groups for the first time. Yet, these efforts met with limited success, as large landholders refused to cooperate and the government showed little will to enforce existing laws that required landholders to demonstrate that their lands fulfilled a "social function." As a result, Bolivia continues to have one of the most unequal land-distribution patterns in the continent, and the great majority of rural indigenous people live in poverty (Weisbrot and Sandoval 2008). Land reform is one of the most pressing demands from Morales's base, as unequal land ownership has maintained the privileges of the white and mestizo elite. The National Development Plan declared, "It is necessary that the State establish procedures and formulas that facilitate a more democratic distribution of income and wealth, of which land is a basic element" (PND 2006, 16). Not surprisingly, such statements are threatening to the elite of the lowland departments, whose livelihood is based on agribusiness and ranching on large landholdings (Valdivia 2010). It is also threatening to the nation's lowland indigenous people, who fought for many years to gain collective control of their territories.

THE CONSTITUENT ASSEMBLY

Agrarian reform was also at the center of the 2006–2007 Constituent Assembly (CA), a yearlong meeting to rewrite the constitution. The CA was a long-held demand of indigenous groups, who claimed that the elite had drafted the previous constitutional frameworks without any input from the great majority of Bolivians. Many Bolivians felt that during the neoliberal years, public decision making, especially on natural resources, had been privatized and made by a small group of elite along with transnational corporations. The CA was supposed to be an effort to reverse this, to return this function to the people, through a process of "direct democracy."

The CA opened in August of 2006 to international fanfare, the source of enormous hope for many Bolivians. As the MAS held a majority of the delegates, it intended to use this liberal democratic instrument to fashion a new national developmentalist state with a clear popular mandate to carry out its agenda, including agrarian reform. Unfortunately, the assembly's process was marred by partisan struggles, opposition boycotts, and dramatic episodes of street violence. (See Postero 2010 for a discussion of the troubling tactics the MAS used to get the draft constitution passed.) Not surprisingly, there was significant contestation over fundamental issues. On one side of the political spectrum, pushing the MAS from the Left, was the Pacto Unidad, a coalition of indigenous and peasant organizations. They urged a refounding of the plurinational state and the establishment of "indigenous autonomy," which would give Andean and Amazonian communities expansive jurisdiction to protect their living areas and livelihoods and especially to restrict the power of timber, mining, and oil multinationals to exploit and destroy their territories (Regalsky 2010, 45; Tapia 2011).

On the other side were the civic committees of the lowland departments, which represent the elite land-owning and business class and are collectively referred to as the Media Luna, or Half Moon (so named because of the shape of this region). This sector mounted an all-out battle for regional or departmental autonomy, meaning a system in which departments have the ability to tax, legislate, and make decisions about development projects, free from the oversight of La Paz. The civic committees acted in constant opposition, boycotting meetings of the Constituent Assembly, and mounting a massive hunger strike. In the middle of the CA, they held a referendum to legitimize their autonomy efforts (even though the electoral court ruled the vote illegal). This struggle was marked by violence and a sharp uptick in racial conflicts. Lowland leaders framed the dispute as a fight between the Indians, who control the central government and want to take land from its legitimate owners, and the lowland peoples, who are struggling for freedom from an authoritarian state. They strongly opposed the land-holding limits in the draft constitution and argued that such reforms should be left up to the departments. In September 2008 events turned even more difficult. In Santa Cruz, opposition groups took over central-government agencies such as the tax office, the state telephone company, customs, and most notably the agrarian-reform offices, claiming they were now under the control of the department. Then, in the northern department of the Pando, opposition groups carried out a massacre of more than thirty MAS supporters, most of whom were indigenous peasants. This event finally turned the tide of public opinion and opened the way to a negotiated settlement between the MAS and opposition groups, in which the MAS made significant concessions to the opposition. Despite Morales's rhetorical commitment to decolonization, the MAS favored the pragmatic politics of governing over immediate implementation of indigenous and peasant demands (Bautista 2011; Regalsky 2010; Tapia 2011).

THE NEW CONSTITUTION

Because of the tense process in which it was written, contested, and finally approved, the new 2009 constitution is both inspiring and contradictory. The preamble of the Constitución Política del Estado (CPE) sets the tone:

> The Bolivian people, composed of a plurality, from the depths of history, inspired by the struggles of the past; by the indigenous anticolonial uprising; by independence;

by the popular struggles of liberation; by the indigenous social movement and union marches; by the water and October (gas) wars; by the struggles for land and territory, and with the memory of our martyrs, construct a new State. . . . We leave in the past the colonial, republican, and neoliberal State . . . and refound Bolivia. (CPE 2008, preamble)

The plurinational Bolivia that emerges from the text of the constitution is a profoundly liberal one based on intercultural respect, human rights, and the rule of law. It provides for new forms of autonomous governments at the departmental, regional, and municipal levels and creates a new (albeit limited) form of self-government called "indigenous autonomy." It allows indigenous peoples to develop their own territories, speak their languages, and assert sovereignty. It calls for group rights but also protects individual rights and private property, and it establishes a strong state responsible for general welfare (Albro 2010). The CPE requires the state to constitute a "just and harmonious society without discrimination or exploitation, consolidating plurinational identities," and charges it with guaranteeing the "well-being, development, security, protection, and equal dignity of all persons, nations, peoples, and communities," as well as equal access to education, health, and work (CPE 2008, art. 9). The constitution provides for a number of different ways in which to exercise democracy, from direct and participatory, such as assemblies, referenda, and citizen initiatives; to classic representation by elections; to communitarian, where communities designate their representatives according to indigenous custom (article 10). Most interestingly, the constitution declares that "the sovereign people, through organized civil society, will participate in the design of public policy" and will exercise "social control in public administration at all levels of the state" (CPE 2008, art. 241). Here we see much of what was described in the National Development Plan: the recuperation of the people's right to decide, which was denied by both colonialism and neoliberalism. The document also includes decidedly unliberal aspects, like article 8, which defines the principles, values, and goals (*fines*) of the state. It declares that the state will assume and promote a number of indigenous ethical-moral principles, including the Aymara code of not being lazy, lying, or stealing; the Guaraní notion of the harmonious life, and the Quechua idea of the noble path (CPE 2008, art. 8).

This interesting mix reflects the fact that the constitution is the product of a wide spectrum of desires and hopes. It represents the demands of indigenous people who have been marginalized for centuries but are now attempting to make liberal institutions speak to their lives and values, thus "vernacularizing" liberalism (see Engle Merry 1997, 2006; Postero 2010). It reflects the aspirations and experiences of social activists, who have used the medium of civil-society organizations to push for change. It bears the mark of indigenous and leftist intellectuals who are taking advantage of this chance to put into action the "decolonial" theories that have been sustaining them for decades (see, e.g., Bautista 2011; Escobar 2010; Patzi Paco 1999, 2002, 2005; Mamani Ramírez 2004, 2006; Tapia 2011; Zibechi 2010). Yet, it also reflects the realpolitik of the MAS, which was forced to moderate many of the articles to reach agreement with the many sectors that opposed their agenda. For instance, the CPE section on agrarian reform limited the amount of land individuals could hold (the electorate got to choose whether the limit would be 5,000 or 10,000 hectares; they voted for the former). This was enormously important to the indigenous people as it broke a pattern of land holding that reached all the way back to colonial times. Yet, in the negotiations with the civic committees in September 2008, the MAS agreed to make the limitation prospective rather than retroactive, thus protecting the holdings of the lowlands elite. This contradicted much of what the Pacto Unidad had pushed for and the elected delegates to the CA had approved (Regalsky 2010, 37). This seeming betrayal has prompted many in indigenous and peasant circles to share Regalsky's critique:

> I argue that the Morales government is not heading a revolutionary, state-transforming process representing the interests of the majority of the citizenry (the indigenous population and the working class) but attempting to balance indigenous demands with those of the dominant and still powerful landowning class (aligned with business interests centered in Santa Cruz) in order to create new conditions for governance. . . . The MAS is attempting to reinvent the Bolivian nation-state. (Regalsky 2010, 35–36)

The most common critique of the new Bolivian state is that it has consolidated enormous power to the central state. While the CPE makes possible different levels of government through the various forms of autonomy, in fact the Law of Autonomy passed in 2010 limits the "competencias," or the areas of jurisdiction of each level of government. Under the law, the departments and indigenous autonomies have the right to self-govern and to make decisions about their development. In practice, however, this freedom is quite limited by the funding structure, which continues to funnel most monies through the central government. The departments and indigenous municipalities have very limited abilities to tax or to raise funds. Most advocates of departmental autonomy consider the autonomy a disappointing fraud. Critics make similar assessments of the indigenous autonomy provisions, which are much diluted from the original idea proposed by the Pacto Unidad at the CA (Garcés 2011; Postero forthcoming; Tapia 2011). The new law makes it very difficult for communities to qualify for the status, so instead of making broad transformations in land ownership hoped for, only eleven indigenous communities have begun the process.

EXTRACTIVISM

But nothing is creating more conflict than Morales's continued commitment to natural-resource extraction. One the one hand, Morales represents himself as a committed environmentalist whose desire to protect the Pachamama (Mother Earth) is the result of indigenous beliefs and practices. Both the 2009 constitution and the New Law of Mother Earth (2010) call on the state and the Bolivian people to protect the environment. On the other hand, the Bolivian economy continues to be what scholars call "extractivist," an economy centered on the export of raw materials, such as minerals, fossil fuels, and agricultural commodities (Gudynas 2010; Ruíz Marrero 2011). This is not new. Bolivia has exported primary materials since the Spaniards began mining gold and silver, through the long years of tin, to the recent years of petroleum and natural gas (Farthing 2009). The neoliberal period saw an expansion of this model, as natural gas began to be discovered and exploited by transnational corporations. Across Latin America, many on the Left criticized their countries' extractivist models for the dependence on exports, the enormous power of foreign businesses, the minimal state presence in the economy, and the weak taxation systems (Gudynas 2010). Others pointed out that extractivism is "ecologically destructive and keeps the global South in misery, dependence, and underdevelopment" (Ruíz Marrero 2011). So, many hoped the new progressive postneoliberal governments would also move to a "postextractivist" stance. This is not necessarily a postcapitalist move. Instead, they advocated ending their dependency on first-world powers, diversifying production, and industrializing products (Gudynas 2010). Indigenous groups in Bolivia also pushed the state for more plural forms of economy that would be centered on social and communitarian forms of production and distribution, focusing more on the well-being of local communities than on foreign corporate profit. Prada and Arkonada describe this model as "passing beyond the extractivist model to a productive model, combining industrialization with food sovereignty and harmony with Mother Earth" (Prada and Arkonada 2011). They also urge the government to move away from exploiting fossil fuels and to pursue renewable and alternative sources of energy instead. Yet the Morales government, facing the urgent needs of the poorest country in South America, has not moved to end this model. Instead, it has supported ongoing projects and promoted several new ones of its own.

As I discuss in detail elsewhere (Postero 2013), Bolivia's main source of income comes from the exploitation of hydrocarbons, mainly in the form of natural gas. Most of the approximately 350 oil and gas wells are located in the Chaco area, in the dry lowlands in the southeast. Eighty-three percent of the reserves lie under the lands of the Guaraní indigenous people, who, despite years of protests, have had limited success against the transnational oil companies, who have polluted the communities' lands in the process of drilling and extraction (Perreault 2008).

Gas is not the only mineral resource of importance, however. Indigenous protests have focused on the San Cristobal mine, a massive open-pit silver, lead, and zinc mine operated by Japanese Sumitomo Corporation in the Nor Lípez province of Potosí department, which, indigenous and peasant leaders say, uses massive amounts of water from the aquifer below the mine without paying for it, drying up streams and polluting rivers with toxic refuse (Carvajal 2010; Weinberg 2010). Morales's government gave a huge concession to the Indian company Jindal to mine iron ore at the Mutún site near Puerto Suarez, in the eastern Amazon area, near the border with Brazil. Activists worry about the toxic by-products that might result if this largest iron-ore mine in South America is built. There is already serious damage from the highway that will support the mine. It is part of the new Bio-Oceanic Highway, planned as part of the Initiative for the Integration of the Regional Infrastructure of South America (IIRSA). The portion of that road already under construction from Santa Cruz to Puerto Suarez traverses the department of Santa Cruz, across the dry forest lands of the Chiquitano people. The Organización Indígena Chiquitana (OICH) has been protesting this road since its inception in 2000, citing serious damage to the fragile ecosystems along the road's trajectory, as well as the lack of consultation with their authorities, bad working conditions, and the increase in social problems, including prostitution (Bailaba Parapaino 2004; ERBOL 2010a).

Morales is aggressively pursuing several new megaprojects that have the potential to create devastating impacts. The most important are the giant new lithium fields in the vast salt flat in southwestern Bolivia, the Salar de Uyuni. The newly discovered fields contain about half the world's known lithium—5.4 million tons (Howard 2009; Romero 2009; Wright 2010). A Bolivian-owned lithium-processing plant broke ground in 2008 and plans to begin making batteries within a year or so. Eventually, with the help of joint ventures, Bolivia wants to produce electric cars. However, as with any other nonrenewable resource, producing lithium will likely take its toll on the fragile ecosystem of the Salar and the Rio Grande delta, where flamingos breed. To exploit the lithium, Bolivia will create large brine beds and evaporation ponds and then reinject the leftover salt, thereby increasing the salinity of the rivers, which local people use to irrigate their farms. Because of the high percentage of magnesium mixed with the lithium, it must be treated with toxic chemicals prior to evaporation. Critics argue that the government has not yet carried out sufficient water or environmental studies, but the Meridian Institute, an independent-energy think tank, concluded that to extract enough lithium to meet even 10 percent of global automotive demand would cause irreversible and widespread damage to these environments (Meridian International Research 2008).

Clearly, Bolivia's historical extractive legacy is ongoing and continues to create terrible environmental damage, much of which is borne by indigenous peoples at the local level. Yet Morales and his government endorse these practices as necessary to defend their cultural revolution and to maintain national sovereignty. Vice President García Linera made clear the government's priorities:

We are going to construct highways, we will drill wells, we will industrialize our country preserving our resources in consultation with the people, but we need resources

> to generate development, for education, transport, and the health of our people. We are not going to turn ourselves into park rangers for the powers of the North, who live happily, while we continue in poverty. (ERBOL 2010b, my translation)

For Morales, there is no contradiction between his *pachamamista* discourse and his continued support for these megaprojects because he sees industrialization and economic progress as a fundamental part of his mandate from his constituents. Most Bolivians believed the neoliberal leaders of the 1990s cared more about putting dollars into their own pockets and those of their international corporate friends than building a just and prosperous Bolivia. So, the majority of Bolivians, and that includes many indigenous people, are proud of the nationalization and delighted that Morales et al. reversed the unfair terms of the gas business. They *want* lithium to be developed, and they want their standards of living to improve. This is part of *pachakuti*, the turning of the timetable, the change of destiny. This is the time for the formerly poor to receive their fair share. Article 8 of the constitution itself reflects this by declaring the state to be sustained by values of social justice, distribution and redistribution of products and social goods, and the indigenous notion of living well. In the very next article, it declares the state has the obligation to carry out industrialization and development (CPE, articles 8–9). Here, again, we see how the discursive link between antineoliberalism and decolonialization works to legitimate the MAS's populist national development project. We also see how the MAS calls upon this development model to support sovereignty. As Maria Josefina Saldaña-Portillo argues:

> It is precisely the marriage of development and decolonization that discursively legitimates the extraction of resources and productive capacity in a way the civilizing mission of colonialism never could. The extraction of resources and productive capacity is ordained as the principal course of action for a decolonized nation to achieve and maintain sovereignty. (2003, 22)

Yet this model also requires some sacrifices. Gudynas points out that such "progressive neoextractivist" models ignore the social and environmental damages that result. "It's the paradox of macroeconomic well-being at the cost of local harm" (cited in Salazar 2010). Over the last few years, Morales's government has rejected protests against the effects of these projects and accused indigenous groups and peasants of impeding development or causing harm to the country (Bebbington 2009; Gudynas 2010, 7). This was clear in 2010, when the Plurinational Assembly debated the law implementing the new constitution's notions of autonomy. When the Confederación de Pueblos Indígenas de Bolivia (CIDOB), the lowland indigenous organization, protested that the MAS version of the law did not take into account their demands, the government suggested that the CIDOB was financed by the U.S. Agency for International Development. But Morales's willingness to sacrifice lowland indigenous people became a source of international concern in 2011, when the government made public its plan to put in a highway from the coca-growing region of Chapare to San Ignacio de Moxos, crossing the country's most important national park and indigenous territory, the Territorio Indígena Parque Nacional Isiboro Sécure (TIPNIS). Ignoring constitutional requirements to consult with indigenous peoples prior to any development that would affect them, Morales declared the road would be put in regardless of whether they agreed. Again, Morales and his ministers accused the indigenous of being manipulated by NGOs and standing in the way of progress for all Bolivians (García Linera 2011). As the whole country watched on television, lowland indigenous groups staged a massive march from the Beni to La Paz in protest. Environmentalists, students, and right-wing opposition leaders rallied to their cause. Finally, on September 25, the national police intercepted the demonstration and violently assaulted the marchers, beating them, firing teargas, and causing many injuries. This shocking event and the public anger it sparked turned the tide, and the government finally relented. When the marchers arrived in La Paz, where a massive and supportive public welcomed them, the government signed an agreement that the TIPNIS would be *intangible*, or untouchable, pending a new community consultation. As of this writing, the situation remains in flux, however, as different indigenous groups struggle to represent the community and the government continues to push for the development of the road. Whatever the solution, the government's response to the demands of both the indigenous peoples and the environmentalists to find an alternative path for the road demonstrated once again the huge gap between the government's Pachamama discourse and its extractivist development model.

CONCLUSION

This chapter has traced political, economic, and cultural transformations in Bolivia since the election of Evo Morales and described the forging of a powerful discursive regime linking antineoliberalism and decolonization. Clearly, the Bolivian national development project is a direct challenge to the neoliberal project of the previous decades. I have described the many ways in which the Morales government has rolled back the structural reforms of the 1980s and 1990s, giving the state a central role in the economy and making efforts to redistribute resources to the Bolivian people. Responding to the demands of Bolivia's poor and indigenous citizens, the Morales government has pressed forward with an ambitious experiment intended to reembed economic policies within social and cultural structures. Employing a creative use of indigenous values, it has put forth a utopian model of radical democracy that makes state-controlled economic justice a centerpiece. This, in itself, challenges neoliberalism, which passed off questions of justice to the responsible individual or the market. But can a government that relies on the same capitalist-based resource-extraction model that all previous governments relied on be termed postneoliberal? To use Arturo Escobar's terms, although Morales's Bolivia may be "antineoliberal," it is clearly neither "postcapitalism" nor "postdevelopment" (Escobar 2010). To this we must add, it certainly is not "postextractivist."

Right-wing critics, especially the lowlands civic committees and their militants, call Morales an authoritarian and liken him to Venezuela's Chávez. Many MAS supporters have left the government because of frustrations with the tight control Morales and his inner circle exert over the workings of the administration. There is fear of a one-party state. People on all sides have expressed their frustration with the Constituent Assembly, the outcome of which was widely seen as controlled by Morales and his MAS party. In addition, almost everyone criticizes the inefficiency of the state, which has not been able to administer much of the new income or really put into effect the radical agenda it promised (Kohl 2010).

Many on the Left criticize Morales for being a reformer rather than a revolutionary (see Petras 2007; Webber 2006, 2011). Sociologist Raúl Prada, the former vice minister of strategic planning and a key MAS intellectual at the Constituent Assembly, criticizes the Morales government for focusing on macroeconomic stability rather than on the high social costs it brings. This strategy proves to him that the MAS has spent more time restoring the liberal nation-state than constructing the communitarian intercultural plurinational state envisioned by social movements and codified in the new constitution. He urges the government to continue the *proceso de cambio* (the process of change) and to complete the work of decolonizing the country (Prada and Arkonada 2011).

These differing critiques make visible the complex tensions with which the MAS must contend as it formulates a new development model. So, going forward, will Bolivia's challenge to colonial neoliberalism amount in the end to "capitalism with an indigenous face," or can the alternative visions that motivated this challenge be put into practice? Are these critiques a sign of serious ruptures in Morales's support or merely expressions of the "creative tensions within the national-popular block," as Vice President García Linera suggests (García Linera 2011: 23)? This remains to be seen. However, economist Javier Gómez suggests that throughout all of these crises, Bolivia is struggling to find a model that is right for the twenty-first century. "Post-Keynesianism is not yet thought out," he says. "We need to think more about what the role of the state should be" (personal communication, June 2008, La Paz). This is precisely what we are seeing today as Bolivia's people engage in both utopian thinking and disagreement to move from a "postneoliberal" rhetoric to new forms of government.

CHAPTER 3

CULTURE AND NEOLIBERAL RATIONALITIES IN POSTNEOLIBERAL VENEZUELA

Sujatha Fernandes

DURING THE MONTH OF JUNE, RESIDENTS of the popular Caracas parish of San Agustín celebrate the San Juan fiesta with a daylong procession through the barrio, singing, dancing, and drumming. When I arrived at this event in San Agustín in 2004, it was already in full swing. Men, women, and children were leading the procession down the main street, waving brightly colored flags that are said to purify the road ahead of them. Two young men, Alexander Arteaga and Raúl Britto, moved through the crowd offering people *aguardiente*, a liquor made from sugarcane, from bottles slung around their necks. In rural areas, the procession traditionally passes by the church so that San Juan can be blessed by the priest. But in the urban context, at times the priests refuse to bless San Juan or participate in the festival.

"Here we have an issue." Raúl told me. "When we go to the church, the priests don't want to bless San Juan. Every year this happens."

Alexander added, "And today we had a mass because for months we've been requesting a mass for the saint, and we wanted to know why the priest didn't want to bless the saint."

"Why doesn't the church see this fiesta as part of the church?" I asked them.

"They say that this isn't part of the church, but I've been to the church at times, and they talk about San Juan," replied Raúl. "They say that this isn't a religious issue, and that's why they can't bless San Juan. But it is a religious issue; it's the religion that we have."

"The priests have refused many times to do the mass for San Juan in the Church of Fátima and of Nazaret," added Alexander.

Raúl continued:

> But San Juan has to be blessed by the priest, by God, because we go purifying the path, and we don't want problems with anyone. Anyway, San Juan was a man of the church; he was a baptist. We had to bring him [the San Juan statue] to the church and say, "Please, give this damned guy some holy water 'cause we're missing out on the party." The priest thought it was a joke, and it's not. This is a religion for us, that we love and respect. Why do they always reject us when we're working so hard? . . . Just because we're in the Central [region], which is Caracas, the heart of Caracas, why do they reject us? The president says, "Nobody gets rid of me" (*A mi no me mueve nadie*), and that's San Juan now. The police also want to dominate us, but they are very mistaken. Who thinks that they can stop the drums of San Agustín here?

Fiesta organizers Raúl and Alexander exemplify the new social subjects emerging as protagonists in contemporary Latin America. Barrio residents involved in the fiestas make frequent reference to the process of social change initiated under President Hugo Chávez, who has carried out a radical antineoliberal program for redistribution and regional integration, invoking the vision of early nineteenth-century Republican leader Simón Bolívar. The residents identify icons such as San Juan with the figure of Chávez as a way of bolstering the legitimacy of their cultural movements. Cultural identity has provided an idiom for the expression of class and racial cleavages in an emerging battleground between multiple competing tendencies in Venezuelan society. However, as fiesta organizers and other cultural producers begin to develop links with state institutions and official sectors of Chavismo, they confront the neoliberal rationalities and logics embedded within state institutions.

In this chapter I argue that "culture" has emerged as a crucial site of struggle in the Chávez era. As I demonstrate, the meaning of "culture" is highly contested. For now, I refer to it as the arts, everyday activities, and popular traditions practiced by people and sponsored by institutions. The field of culture has received greater public funding through oil revenues and local government under Chávez than under his predecessors, but it also remains articulated to private investment and global circuits of capital. These contradictory tendencies are manifested in cultural institutions, which seek to incorporate cultural producers into a state-building agenda but are at the same time guided by neoliberal rationalities that emphasize the utility of culture in ameliorating social conditions and generating revenue. Although cultural bodies like Fundarte and the mayor's office view culture as both a means of political integration and a strategy for building social capital, barrio residents speak to the spiritual value of culture and of culture as a way of being. The conflict between arts administrators and barrio residents is expressive of the contradiction at the heart of what I term the "hybrid postneoliberal state." As the fiestas have adapted from being covert activities subject to policing to cultural festivities promoted by the Chávez government, cultural producers have been confronted with these new rationalities of governance.

The chapter begins with a historical and theoretical description of the postneoliberal state. I describe my methodology of "everyday wars of position," which moves beyond the terrain of official actors and policy to examine the kinds of social change brought about by urban sectors in their daily interactions and struggles. I go on to explore the evolution of cultural policy in Venezuela and focus on shifts that took place during the neoliberal era of the 1990s and the postneoliberal period of the early 2000s. The chapter then looks specifically at the clashes between the instrumental rationalities embedded within certain state-identified programs, groups, and institutions and the everyday, local practices of some barrio-based cultural and community organizations. Transferring our focus from the institutional actors to the everyday state-society interactions helps to illuminate the workings of neoliberalism even within an avowedly antineoliberal order.

THE HYBRID STATE IN A POSTNEOLIBERAL ERA

The specific configuration of social actors under Chávez is shaped by histories of the developmental and neoliberal state. In order for us to comprehend the constraints and obstacles that confront new social subjects as they construct alternative futures, it is important to outline the history and nature of state formation under neoliberalism, as Goodale and Postero suggest in Chapter 1 of this volume. Even though Chávez's administration has been broadly described as antineoliberal, I suggest rather that it is a postneoliberal order, one in which neoliberalism is no longer the dominant guiding policy, although it continues to surface in a range of conflicting rationalities and policies that are brought into an uneasy coexistence. In the spectrum of hybrid states emerging throughout Latin America, the postneoliberal state creates greater spaces for alternative movements than does the full-fledged hegemonic project of the "enabling" state in Chile, as described by Veronica Schild in Chapter 8 of this volume.

As others have pointed out, the historical experiences of state formation in Venezuela must be understood in relation to the exploitation of petroleum. Due to its oil largesse, the Venezuelan state has differed from other peripheral states that were structured around the extraction and distribution of surplus value. For Fernando Coronil (2000), what distinguished the Venezuelan state was its organization around the appropriation and distribution of ground rent. Although Chávez has consistently drawn strong popular support for his return to a policy of capturing and redistributing oil rents, his project is facing a new stage of capitalism, where production and accumulation have been globalized. This has made it harder for individual nations to sustain independent polities and economies (Robinson 2003). As Coronil has noted, the state is torn by its desire to both subsidize gasoline on the local market and obtain international rents, while maintaining the global competitiveness of the oil industry: "While as the sovereign owner of the subsoil the state has sought to obtain ever-larger rents by increasing oil prices and regulating supply, as a capitalist it must seek to obtain profits through productive investments in the global market" (Coronil 2000). The insertion of Venezuela into a global order requires certain policy adjustments and concessions that do not always mesh with Chávez's antineoliberal rhetoric.

The debate over whether the Chávez government is proneoliberal or antineoliberal has also tended to revolve around its economic policy. Neoliberalism is typically understood as an encompassing set of economic policies that attempt to privatize and deregulate the economy in order to promote free trade, foreign direct investment, and export-oriented industrialization. Some argue that the Chávez administration has pursued antineoliberal measures by reversing the reduction of social spending and assigning resources to health and education that envision universal coverage despite the tight constraints of the international context (Parker 2005). Others contend that the Chávez government has pursued macroeconomic stability rather than confronting multinational capital (Vera 2001) and that despite Chávez's rhetoric there have been no ruptures with foreign creditors or oil clients (Petras and Veltmeyer 2005, ix). However, following Wendy Brown (2003), I argue that we must look at neoliberalism not just as a set of economic policies but also as one mode of the modern form of power that Michel Foucault (1991a) labeled "governmentality." Governmentality refers to knowledge and techniques that are concerned with the regulation of everyday conduct. Neoliberal governmentality involves the extension of market rationality, based on an instrumental calculation of cost and benefit, to all state practices, as well as formerly noneconomic domains (Brown 2003, 4). As Aihwa Ong (2006) argues, these rationalities and techniques can predominate even in contexts where neoliberalism as an economic doctrine is not central. I suggest that this is the case in Chávez's Venezuela, a postneoliberal formation that has adopted significant antineoliberal reforms, while its ongoing subjection to the requirements of a global economy has given impetus to neoliberal rationalities and techniques in a range of state and nonstate arenas.

Under Chávez, there has been an attempt to divide up the national territory into what Ong calls "zones of graduated sovereignty," where "developmental decisions favor the fragmentation of the national space into various noncontiguous zones and promote the differential regulation of populations who can be connected to or disconnected from global circuits of capital" (Ong 2006, 77). Post-2002 social policy has focused on creating a protected zone where the welfare apparatus could be cushioned from the demands and rationalities of global markets. Funds are channeled directly from the state-owned oil company, PDVSA, to a series of social-welfare "missions" established by the Chávez government. For example, PDVSA manages a yearly fund of some $US4.85 billion from oil revenue, and this is all channeled into social programs.[1] This considerable reserve fund, even if linked to a volatile and nonrenewable natural resource, has allowed the state to disconnect social-welfare provision from global circuits of capital. Nonetheless, other zones continue to be articulated to foreign and private capital to different degrees, including culture and communications, mining and hydrocarbons, and the manufacturing sector. These zones are subject to market calculations, as they are tied more directly to global circuits of capital. I argue that it is in these zones that the contradictions of the postneoliberal state under Chávez are most apparent.

In contrast to the ideal type formulations of neoliberalism as a set of economic reforms that were adopted uniformly in Third-World debtor nations, there is a growing sense that neoliberalism is a "moving target, subject to hybridizations" (Craig and Porter 2006, 21) and consists of "different rationalities and techniques, often working at odds with each other" (Ong 2006, 95). Neoliberal governmentality is just one modality of power working among others. In Venezuela under Chávez, neoliberal rationality fuses with a rentier liberalism in the contours of a hybrid-state formation. The task of ethnography is to identify the scope of liberal and neoliberal logics as they collide with new forms of collective action. It is often the disjunctures between antineoliberal rhetoric and market-based rationalities that open a space for critique by social movements. This raises the specter of not just a postneoliberal order but also a postneoliberal social imaginary, where alternative visions are being put on the agenda by social movements. According to Alejandro Grimson and Gabriel Kessler (2005, 191), the postneoliberal imaginary refers to the new contestatory narratives and forms of collective action that are dislodging neoliberalism from its quasihegemonic position. As Nancy Postero (2007) argues, the emergence of alternative and collective responses to neoliberalism shows the limitations of theories of neoliberal governmentality, which have tended to focus mainly on the production of consent to regimes of structural adjustment.[2] We need to combine Foucaultian theories of governmentality with a Gramscian notion of hegemony in order to account more fully for the contested nature of power.

Just as in earlier eras of Venezuelan politics, class struggle in the Chávez era has centered on the state and access to the state. In contrast to earlier periods, the unifying nature of the state as a force that claims to stand above and bring together different classes has been disrupted in favor of a polity divided by race and class (Coronil 2000). Sectors of the poor and marginalized majority have aligned themselves with Chávez in order to wrest control of the state—and its considerable oil resources—away from the hands of the multinationals and the privileged, transnational elites. Ongoing struggles for control of the state apparatus include the general elections of 1998, Chávez's running for reelection in 1999 under a new constitution, the general elections of 2006, and responses from the opposition, which orchestrated a coup in April 2002 and attempted to legally remove Chávez from office by means of a recall referendum in August 2004. Urban social movements were central participants in these battles.

However, beyond these larger struggles over the state apparatus, I argue that the structures and discourses of exclusion are being contested in a range of quotidian sites through everyday wars of position. My phrase "everyday wars of position" combines Antonio Gramsci's (1971) term with James Scott's (2000) concept of "everyday forms" of resistance and *lo cotidiano* (the everyday), invoked by the social movements themselves to describe the multiple battles that they participated in daily on numerous fronts. Although Gramsci was concerned with hegemony in a negative sense as domination, he was also interested in it in a positive sense, such as the way in which subordinate populations employ wars of position to remake their material and social worlds. He used the military metaphor "wars of position" to describe political struggle between classes. In contrast to the Leninist notion of a vanguard party that would lead the working classes to victory, Gramsci (1971, 234) saw conflict as occurring in the trenches of society, where incremental changes could help to shift the relation of the forces in conflict and build counterhegemonies. For example, wars of position are being fought in Venezuela in the area of culture and cultural production.

CULTURAL INSTITUTIONS, NEOLIBERAL LOGICS, AND POPULAR CULTURE PRODUCERS

Cultural institutions and private corporations have traditionally sponsored culture as an instrument of ideological cohesion. In a neoliberal era, culture became subject to a new legitimation based on utility. The contradictory impulses of the political use of culture and its subordination to a market-based rationality continue to play themselves out in the laws and programs of the postneoliberal state.

Historically, state sponsorship of culture in Latin America meant that the state controlled and sometimes subsidized the culture industries. In Argentina, Brazil, and Mexico during the 1920s and 1930s, the state mobilized cultural forms such as the samba, carnival, murals, and the tango in an attempt to unify the population during the stage of import substitution industrialization (Yúdice 2003, 70). In Venezuela, state promotion of popular culture as part of a national culture came later, beginning with a brief period of democratic rule from 1945 to 1948 and followed by an era of national-populist democratic rule from the late 1950s to the 1980s. Under the auspices of the Folklore Service, headed by Rómulo Gallegos, Juan Liscano choreographed a five-day folklore performance in Caracas in 1946 with groups from around the country. Through this and subsequent performances, the image of San Juan became the center of a new national identity and was publicized to the country as a whole (Guss 1993, 456). During the 1970s, the oil boom facilitated a distribution of wealth to the cultural sector. As David Guss argues, the government began playing an increasingly important role in cultural renewal as it formulated the first comprehensive cultural plan and created the Consejo Nacional de la Cultura (National Council of Culture, CONAC), which coordinated cultural activities and the arts throughout the nation (Guss 2000, 100). In 1971 the Afro-Venezuela coastal village of Curiepe was proclaimed the "National Folklore Village." State patronage also became tied to a clientelist system, as drummers in Curiepe received nominal payments from the political party in power (ibid., 42). Amid nationalization of the iron and oil industries in 1975, state sponsorship of culture helped to bolster a fervent nationalism and contributed to a system of patronage.

The 1980s witnessed a growing commercialization of culture, but corporations still concentrated on promoting a national identity in order to sell products. As Venezuela was hit by the debt crisis, the significant reduction in state funding for cultural programs was offset by corporations such as Cigarrera Bigott. Cigarrera Bigott was a Venezuelan tobacco company with a national reputation, which was purchased by the transnational cartel British American Tobacco in 1922. In his comprehensive analysis of the company, Guss (2000) relates that British American Tobacco remains one of the world's largest cigarette manufacturers and Britain's third largest industrial enterprise. In 1963, British American Tobacco established the Fundación Bigott (Bigott Foundation) primarily as a philanthropic association designed to help workers finance their homes. During the nationalist years of the 1970s, as foreign-owned companies began undergoing nationalization, Bigott had sought to associate itself with the sphere of national culture by sponsoring cultural initiatives and workshops (ibid., 94).

This plan proved fruitful in 1981, when the government of Luis Herrera Campíns outlawed all tobacco and alcohol advertising on television and radio. As Guss (2000, 96) recounts, the Fundación Bigott began to invest more heavily in the field of popular culture as a way of promoting itself without advertising cigarettes. Two of the main aspects of this campaign were cultural workshops and television programs. The popular culture workshops were part of an ambitious nationwide program established to teach local forms of Venezuelan music and dance. Groups that emerged from these cultural workshops were important forces in new projects of cultural renewal in the barrios. Nonetheless, radical cultural groups found that it was a delicate balancing act for them to accept support from a corporation and for Bigott to work with leftist groups; as Guss says, this balance worked only if each group thought it were using the other (ibid., 111). Ricardo Hernández, a fiesta organizer in the parish of Catia, justified it this way: "In some ways Bigott served our interests. Actually we utilized it because it allowed us to meet people from isolated regions that later we ourselves began to visit. We began to gain their confidence and then to apply their techniques in the urban communities" (personal interview). Bigott also produced a television series on popular culture in the mid- to late 1980s, which included more than 140 programs. Instead of mentioning its brand, the programs displayed the company's logo with the name of the Fundación Bigott (Guss 2000, 116). In addition, Bigott developed the magazine *Revista Bigott* through its publications program, a rural radio series in the tobacco-growing states, and grants for culture-related activities. Through these programs, the tobacco corporation redefined popular culture and the company itself as symbolic of national values and identity (ibid., 102). In some ways, corporations had replaced the role of the state in patronizing national-popular culture and disseminating vernacular forms.

An important shift took place during the 1990s with the election of Carlos Andres Pérez and the neoliberal turn ushered in by his government. In this period, culture was recast as a product or merchandise for consumption. As Yolanda Salas argues, "the *pueblo*, the subject and actor of the popular, is substituted by the product that should be advertised via the mass media" (2003, 162). The "popular" was being transformed into the "consumer." At this time, other corporations were pursuing programs in popular culture, thereby introducing competition for Bigott. These companies included the Fundación para la Cultura Urbana (Foundation for Urban Culture), affiliated with the Grupo de Empresas Econoinvest; the Centro Cultural Corp Banca, funded by the Corp Banca, a private bank; Fundación Pampero, a program of Pampero Rum; and the Fundación Polar, founded by the beer company Polar.[3] In a neoliberal climate of greater openness to foreign investors, private foundations were less interested in promoting national identity as a way to market themselves and more direct about publicizing their products. The new director of Bigott, Antonio López Ortega, told Guss in an interview that, after 1991, "the foundation decided to completely abandon its old course and start coming out in public and begin speaking really clearly about our programs, our achievements, and the various objectives we've accomplished" (Guss 2000, 123). Bigott became more straightforward in its publicity language, integrating its cultural activities into a promotional campaign.

However, the transition was more than the recasting of culture as a commodity. As George Yúdice argues, in a neoliberal era the field of culture itself becomes regulated by an economic rationality based on utility. States and foundations actively employ instrumentalized art and culture to improve social conditions, support civic participation, or spur economic growth (Yúdice 2003, 11). Along these lines, Pérez's Eighth National Plan proposed to deal with poverty and create economic efficiency by deepening cultural development, as promoted by international foundations such as UNESCO and the World Bank. In the section titled "The New Strategy of Cultural Change," the plan lists the nature and contributions of culture in development, including "culture as a factor and means of development," "harmonization of growth with social well-being," "culture as a distinctive end of economic growth," and "culture as a right and public service" (CORDIPLAN 1990, 113). Another policy released a few months later as the Plan of Sociocultural Participation proposed to "develop a culture with strategic value, that is, one that permits a more positive insertion into social life and the field of labor" (Baptista and Marchionda 1992). Instead of seeing culture as an end in itself, it was increasingly considered a means of promoting development and economic growth and of ameliorating social problems. As state expenditures in the arts were reduced, private foundations like Bigott were given an expanded role to play in meeting these goals.

After Chávez was elected in 1998, cultural producers encountered conflicting rationalities that included both the use of culture for political gain and integration—especially as state financing of the arts was revitalized—and a utilitarian approach to culture as a resource in which to invest. Fiesta organizers, cultural producers, and residents countered these logics of the hybrid state with alternative views of culture as a way of being and as linked to their everyday lives and religious beliefs.

Chávez implemented new policies for arts funding. In 2000 the Proyecto de Ley Orgánica de la Cultura (Project of the Organic Law of Culture, PLOC), jointly designed by the Ministry of Education, Culture, and Sport and CONAC, established the approach of the Chávez government as contrary to the dominant neoliberal models by increasing the state's patronage of culture; in addition, it highlighted the importance of the state in protecting and preserving cultural patrimony (Proyecto Ley Orgánica de la Cultura 2000). The Chávez government has channeled oil revenues into the sponsorship of culture and made greater funds available to municipal governments. Local-level councils such as Fundarte, a foundation for culture and the arts established by the mayor of the Libertador municipality, have played an increasingly important role in the funding and stimulation of cultural forms such as urban fiestas.

This increase in state sponsorship of fiestas was evident between the 2004 celebrations, a description of which opens this chapter, and the 2005 celebrations. During the San Juan festivities in San Agustín in July 2005, Raúl and the other members of the fiesta *cofradía* (guild) were outfitted in identical yellow T-shirts that read "San Juan–San Agustín." Although the T-shirts did not advertise the sponsor, they had been provided by the city's Chavista mayor, Juan Barreto. Fundarte had also helped organize the fiesta. The previous year, when opposition mayor Alfredo Peña had been in power, the fiestas had had more of an oppositional and subversive nature. In 2005, despite accepting state support and wearing the T-shirts, barrio residents spoke about wanting to maintain the fiestas as religious events and not as tools for partisan intervention. The following quotation from Raúl illustrates some of the ambivalences occasioned by state support:

> Fundarte is with the *proceso*. It has always existed and has helped us, but at times we don't want to politicize our culture, and Fundarte is another institution of the government. Now we ourselves are the government, the people are the government; it is no longer Fundarte or Freddy Bernal or Chávez; it is the people. . . . We don't receive money from the state. And we don't want the state to suddenly come and tell us they're gonna give us millions of *bolívares*. No, this is culture; it is a religious issue, not political. We want the community to be united.

Raúl strategically places himself both inside and outside the state as he considers the contradictions of state funding. He draws on the official slogan, *El estado somos todos* (We are all the state). After many years of organizing the fiestas with scarce resources, Raúl welcomes the access to state resources made possible under Chávez. Yet he also wants to maintain the autonomy of culture from politicization, meaning intervention by partisan interests that could introduce divisions. Against a notion of culture as a tool for political integration, Raúl affirms its spiritual and religious dimensions.

These ambiguities of state funding for fiestas were also apparent at the national meeting of black saints, directed by Williams Ochoa in June 2005. The mayor's office gave money to bring in groups from around the country for processions and seminars in the barrio Carmen of La Vega, as well as for a large concert in the Plaza O'Leary in Caracas, where various groups gave short presentations to the crowd. The event at Plaza O'Leary was reminiscent of Liscano's staged events, in which fiestas served as spectacles for popular consumption. This staging of fiestas reintroduced the idea of the artist as performer, of having a separate stage, and of paying the artist. As barrio activist Freddy Mendoza has observed, in the local fiestas, "Drummers are not seen as artists. They are the part of the community that produces the music . . . the artist is not distinct from the community" (personal interview). Because the performers and the audience at the O'Leary concert felt uncomfortable with the format, several groups called for the removal of the stage, saying that the event was a religious ritual, not a public concert. Finally, in the last performance by the San Juaneros from Caracas, audience members climbed up onto the stage, and everyone joined in the singing, disrupting the production of the event as spectacle. Then the *tambores* were brought out into the crowd, and the audience broke up into small circles in which people were dancing and drumming.

The staged event reinforced a static and reified notion of cultural practices that contrasted with the more fluid understanding of culture among barrio communities. Another illustration of this was the continued use of the concept of "folklore" by state administrators and foundations. The cultural institution for the promotion of traditional cultures was called the Fundación de Etnomusicología y Folklore (Foundation of Ethnomusicology and Folklore, FUNDEF).[4] Guss (2000, 114) recounts that Bigott also had a notion of folklore as a detachable object, as evidenced by its later policies of "defolklorization," or the repackaging of culture for the middle and upper classes, and by the view of folklore as a commodity, prevalent in the 1990s and beyond. Ochoa, among others, was critical of the notion of folklore:

> For a long time we called our culture folklore, but we eliminated the term because it identified us first with our language and later with our way of being. It seemed to us that folklore was a cold term and the people in the countryside, for instance with respect to the *bailes de tambor* (dances of the drums), they didn't call this folklore, they called it *bailes de tambor*. (personal interview)

Ochoa points out that the categories and framing of traditional cultures in terms of language groups is arbitrary and not reflective of the ways in which people themselves conceive their cultural practices.

Increased state funding under Chávez promoted the idea of culture as a tool for creating national cohesion and achieving political integration. At the same time, however, the field of culture continued to be oriented toward foreign and private investment. According to Title V of the PLOC, "With the goal of incorporating private investment as a substantial source of financing, it [the law] establishes a regime of fiscal incentives in agreement with the principles, criteria, and procedural norms envisioned in Chapter II." Early on in the Chávez administration, relationships between cultural institutions and corporations were established. In October 1999 the Ministry of Education,

Culture, and Sport signed an agreement with the Fundación Bigott, offering technical assistance to specialist instructors working in the areas of traditional dance and music. More than 1,200 instructors were funded to travel around the country holding culture workshops. Each workshop cost 1–1.5 million bolívares, or about US$620–$940 (Salas 2003, 167). In 2000 the director of Bigott, López Ortega, was appointed to the Ministry of Education, Culture, and Sport. Bigott, along with the Central Bank of Venezuela, the Fundación Polar, and the Corporación Andina de Fomento (CAF), lobbied for the formulation and approval of a *ley de mecenazgo* (law of patronage) to provide fiscal incentives for private companies to invest in the arts. López Ortega argued his case in terms of the financial benefits of encouraging private investment: "The Law of Mecenazgo in Brazil, approved in 1993, has converted Brazilian culture industries into the second largest product for export in Mercosur" (Calcaño, n.d.). These corporations pushed for the development of culture as an export industry and for its conversion into a profitable activity in Venezuela.

In the promotion of culture, the Chávez administration defended its alliances with the tobacco company. Salas, an anthropologist who was the director of FUNDEF from 1998 to 2001, relates that during her time in this position she encountered an attitude of complacence among high cultural officials in the Ministry of Education, Culture, and Sport toward both the contradictions represented by the dominant involvement of Bigott in cultural programs and the "strategic alliances" between the state and this transnational corporation. In her dealings with cultural officials, Salas encountered "silence in response to my proposals, defense of the excellent quality of the activities of the Bigott Foundation, and, in addition, arguments that defended the importance of the income received by the state from the collection of taxes on the sale of cigarettes" (2003: 165). In Salas's experience, state officials mimicked the company's promotional discourse with regard to its success in cultural affairs and excellence of production, ignoring the public health implications of addiction and illness caused by smoking (ibid., 164). From early on, private capital was assured a stable environment to continue investing in culture.

The orientation of the arts toward private investment has encouraged the prevalence of market-based calculations within state-sponsored programs.

The utilitarian approach to culture as a service or product with the objective of enhancing growth and development is clearly outlined in the PLOC. Article 133 of the law declares that "The state, by way of the Cultural System of Culture, will promote the creation of Cultural Agencies, with the goal of increasing the offering of cultural goods and services and promoting economic growth." As Yúdice argues, the utilitarian idea of culture as a resource entails its management. There is a subordination of technicians to administrators, and artists are required to manage the social aspects. Arts administrators as "managerial professionals" become intermediaries between funding sources and artists or communities (2003, 12). This technocratic management of culture by arts administrators is evident in the policies and practices of cultural institutions under Chávez.

Under a plan of cultural funding, the Chávez government has created new administrative bodies to determine the allocation of resources for culture, the distribution of the population, the degree of importance of certain cultural traditions, and the areas that should be promoted (Wisotski 2006, 21). Although the idea is to democratize the cultural sphere, it continues to be managed and regulated by technocratic principles. In 2006 Fundarte began implementing a program known as Joint Programming: Operative Plan of Diagnostic Revision. I was present at a meeting at Fundarte on February 9 of that year, where arts administrators drew up a list of their priorities for the organization of cultural activities in the barrios. These priorities included a census of possible facilitators in the barrios, heightening the profile of these select facilitators, and building a local investigation team to study cultural practices, such as the fiestas. As Li argues in the context of World Bank development programs in Indonesia, informal practices and relationships have to be rendered technical to prepare for an intervention. Experts must identify groups and enroll social forces, and then these groups can be funded, counted, legitimated, and replicated (Li 2007, 235). As cultural practices and communities were rendered technical, they were also prioritized according to instrumental ends.

As they discussed how to proceed, several arts administrators at Fundarte argued that the leaders of the local community should draw up and present their own proposals to Fundarte for funding since they know their needs better than anyone else. However, others took a more paternalistic approach. One administrator said that Fundarte should create proposals on behalf of all of the community groups, based on Fundarte's institutional diagnosis and line (*lineamiento*). "The fiestas in the communities are too general and undefined," she said. "They don't address their necessities." This administrator's assessment of fiestas as "general" and "undefined" is another way of saying that they do not serve instrumental purposes, such as resolving the residents' basic necessities. Rather, according to this perspective, there is a need for expert diagnosis from the arts administrators to consider how fiestas could be mobilized to improve living conditions in the community. The discussion reveals the intersection between neoliberal-technocratic discourses and what Li (2007) identifies as the "will to improve," which is present in all development interventions. Arts administrators are self-styled experts who presume to know better than local leaders what is good for the community.

The technocratic management of culture was apparent as well in a workshop presented by an arts administrator at San Agustín's privately owned Alameda Theater, which had been abandoned. In April 2004 fiesta organizers and residents of the parish occupied and restored the structure and renamed it the Casa Cultural Teatro Alameda. Certain cultural institutions became involved in the Casa Cultural after the takeover and sent arts administrators to the barrio to hold workshops for the residents. Although well intentioned and socially committed to their work, these administrators are beholden to instrumental notions of culture as a resource.

Through state-promoted activities and workshops at the Casa Cultural, arts administrators sought to promote the strategic notions of culture as showcased in the PLOC. On July 25, 2004, a facilitator from the Cinemateca Nacional (National Film Library), María Borges, held a workshop at the Casa Cultural. Borges, a white, middle-class, professionally trained woman, was the coordinator of the Program of Associated Cinema Halls. The workshop was attended by about thirty residents active in the Casa Cultural, men and women of all ages. Borges began by displaying the following handwritten statement, titled "Strategic Actions for Cultural Change," on a large sheet of paper:

- new cultural legislation
- regionalization, decentralization

- reordering of public cultural administration
- designing cultural policies around national and regional development plans
- organization of social and cultural networks
- creation of regional cultural advisories
- autonomous institutes and state foundations for regional and municipal cultural development
- qualitative institutional evaluation and programming for assigning resources
- private participation in cultural development

As Borges spoke about the government priorities for culture, she referred to the residents as "beneficiaries" of resources rather than active participants. Borges's statement reflected the technocratic approach to cultural policy that has become standard under neoliberal administrations, which focus on decentralization; as a consequence, cultural promotion devolves from the national government to regional and local governments. Culture is viewed as a resource that can be linked to "national and regional development," primarily through tourism and the development of social capital. The idea of "qualitative evaluation and programming for assigning resources" seeks to apply market-based calculations in order to determine the benefits and costs of a particular program so as to justify investment. Finally, the statement mentions private participation in cultural development in line with Title V of the PLOC.

Cultural institutions such as the Cinemateca Nacional promote forms of neoliberal instrumentality, but they often clash with the residents' goals and perspectives. In the workshop, Borges asked the participants to break up into groups, each of which was to define what it considered "culture." The groups wrote the following notes on large pieces of paper that had been handed to them for this purpose:

> Group 1: Culture is "the everyday" of the people. Culture is to carry out events on the sociopolitical level.
>
> Group 2: [Culture is] values [that are] created by people and passed from generation to generation.

> Group 3: Culture is everything around us. It is what people do collectively in their community and in a specific place.
>
> Group 4: [Culture consists of] actions, teachings, and knowledge of the family, the sector, the city, and oneself; [culture is] a process that transforms.

The workshop participants' definitions indicated their understanding of and relation to culture. These barrio residents saw culture as what they create in their everyday lives. For them, culture is not a universal category but a local process of sociopolitical change linked to the family, the neighborhood, "a specific place." Borges interpreted their responses through an instrumental notion of culture as social capital or resource. For the first group, she said, "What you are talking about here when you say '*realizar eventos*' [carry out events] is diffusion." Borges situated Group 1's response in a framework of cultural promotion. For Group 2, she said that "*valores*" [values] refer to "our cultural patrimony, our local, regional, and national identity." Again, Borges imposed her own framework on the responses: local culture exists for the creation of a greater national culture. In reality, however, the participants had not mentioned national identity. Borges sought to reformulate and reinterpret the participants' responses to fit the framework that she sought to impose.

Borges then initiated a discussion of what she referred to as "strategic lines," which she said were drawn from the National Plan of Culture embodied in the PLOC. The handwritten diagram she showed the group displayed the following: Cultural Public Intervention → Body of Cultural Policy → Organizational Culture. Borges explained that the participants needed to raise their activities to the level of "organizational culture." Ironically, the 278 members of the community had already organized and achieved what no previous group had ever done: the takeover and running of the Casa Cultural. Borges's paternalistic approach was apparent in her pedagogy: she would pose questions to the participants and answer them herself. At one point she asked, "Why do we work in culture?" She responded as follows: "Work in culture should have the objective of offering services to the community and allowing the community to consume its products." In addition to being "beneficiaries" of services, the residents were also repositioned as "consumers." Borges illustrated her argument with another handwritten diagram on a large sheet of paper pinned to the board:

Inputs → Organization → Results: Achievement of Common Objective
Resources
Medium
(human, material)

Borges's diagram and explanation reflect a highly technocratic and instrumental approach to culture. Conceived of as an economically utilitarian model, people become "inputs" and "resources" whose labor must produce certain "results." Institutions like the World Bank employ such discourse of "social capital," which looks on people as "untapped human resources" of development planning (Laurie, Andolina, and Radcliffe 2002, 253). As Borges had explained earlier, the results must be demonstrable in measurable terms in order to qualify for state funding. The workshop participants' reaction to Borges was one of general indifference and boredom. Some participants doodled, while others stared blankly into space. As an outsider and clearly someone from a different class, Borges had little credibility there.

CONCLUSION

As collaboration between cultural producers and arts administrators increases, a struggle is emerging over the nature and uses of culture. Instrumental approaches to culture either as a tool for political integration or as a service or product designed to ameliorate social problems and promote economic growth have been decried by both groups. But under the cultural legislation of the hybrid postneoliberal state these strategies overlap and combine. They are an indication of some of the obstacles faced by culturally based movements that are attempting to bring about social change from "below," through cultural activities, takeovers, and other forms of community action. As the editors of this volume have stated, the parameters of the possible have been uniquely circumscribed for both nation-states and social actors in the context of the ending of the Cold War.

At the same time, like Nancy Postero's (Chapter 2) and David Gow's (Chapter 4) contributions to this volume, this chapter has also discussed various ways that ordinary people take up agency in the construction of new postneoliberal subjectivities. Whereas arts administrators look to the utility of culture, emphasizing reified and technocratic interpretations of cultural practices, fiesta organizers and residents offer alternative versions of culture as a way of being, as a local category linked to place, and as a component of religious rituals. Place- and identity-based politics may enable novel forms of contestation as corporatist bodies such as trade unions and political parties recede in importance. As stated in the introduction to the volume, hybrid governments in Bolivia, Venezuela, and elsewhere have created new horizons of possibility and insurgent imaginaries. Whether this politics can engender alternative kinds of postneoliberal social formations and collectivity remains to be seen.

PART TWO

MICROPOLITICS OF HISTORY AND PRACTICE

CHAPTER 4

"EN MINGA POR EL CAUCA"

Alternative Government in Colombia, 2001–2003

David Gow

THE CHALLENGE OF ALTERNATIVE GOVERNMENT

In the fall of 2000 the voters in the department of Cauca, located in southwestern Colombia, elected Taita Floro Tunubalá as governor for the next three years. During his election campaign, Tunubalá had promised that, if elected, he would establish an alternative government that would be guided by an alternate plan that would address head on the U.S.-supported Plan Colombia, with its emphasis on security and drugs. But the plan was meant to be more than that. According to Diego Jaramillo, one of Tunubalá's advisers:

> At the end of the day it [the Alternate Plan] was to propose an alternative to neoliberalism, to propose an alternative to the capitalist model that was generating inequality, injustice, all this question about the military, all that it was producing and contributing to a very strong impact in terms of the communities . . . the Alternate Plan had to be one that would orient the social organizations in their struggle.[1]

This chapter is a case study of how one departmental government tried to counter the neoliberal orthodoxy that has prevailed in Colombia for the past thirty years. This approach has been both exacerbated by the prevalence of drugs, violence, and corruption and characterized by increased privatization of the state, decreased governmental presence and investment (particularly at departmental and municipal levels), strengthened forces of law and order, and the pursuit of free-market policies that have adversely affected agriculture and other sectors of the economy. The chapter explores the possibilities of social change in light of the overarching strength of neoliberalism and its allies.

Latin America has witnessed the rise of several governments with agendas focused on improving the social and economic situation of those people whom the state has marginalized or even abandoned. These "alternative" regimes have challenged past development models, especially the neoliberal agendas of free-market economics. For instance, "progressive" or "radical" regimes have attempted to include those whom the traditional political parties or elites had previously excluded from political participation, and part of the "Pink Tide" has been connected with socialism or leftist politics. Here I use the term "alternative" government to mean progressive since one of Tunubalá's major objectives was to implement participatory democracy, which would be inclusive, provide a basis for questioning, and thereby slowly change the political and social status quo. Hence, the creation of such a government makes it possible to study how the local population can be integrated into social and political processes that can improve the residents' standard of living, enable them to share political power, and present a different way of thinking about their families' future. In Latin America, few such studies have been conducted at the provincial or departmental level, partly because such governments have historically been weak, fiscally and politically, and the research focus tends to be on the national level and the politics of the capital city (Whitehead and Gray-Molina 2003).[2] In spite of the many processes of decentralization that have been implemented Latin American, academics have concluded that research at the municipal rather than the departmental level may be more productive. Thus it is potentially useful to glean ideas and suggestions from the recent social-science literature since many of the problems and issues encountered at the municipal level may facilitate a better understanding of those encountered at the departmental level.

Recent scholarship from the north has tended to focus on countries such as Bolivia, Brazil, Ecuador, and Mexico, which have all supported potentially radical reforms at the municipal level over the past two decades.[3] The major premise justifying the creation of an alternative government is the hope that conditions, however they are defined, will improve. Although strengthening participation and improving governance may be problematic, the key question is, how can an alternative local government contribute to "the creation of a more human, just, and open state"? (Bebbington, Delamaza, and Villar 2006, 319).[4] The same authors (ibid., 319–320) argue that alternative government should focus on improving the quality of life, specifically alleviating poverty by allocating resources to provide public goods and implementing programs to address inequity. Although neoliberalism may address poverty alleviation, it rarely, if ever, tackles issues of inequity. Although their case studies at the municipal level in Brazil, Colombia, Ecuador, and Chile do not demonstrate such tangible results, they do suggest that the experience of alternative government can contribute to stronger feelings of collective identity, the creation of an "us" among the various participating actors. In other words, alternative government has a moral and a political dimension.

These suggestions are important as they demonstrate one of the major problems of studying this topic: the tension that exists between the goals of alternative development and the realities of what actually happens. In her comparative study of municipal government in Ecuador and Bolivia, Van Cott (2008) considers whether the new institutional arrangements established at the local level, those that survived a change in administration and were open to all, actually resulted in "better local governance," specifically, improvements in the quality of democracy and the empowerment of citizens. "Radical democracy," which focuses on values, culture, and the deepening of democracy by making it more participatory and deliberative, is the form of alternative government that interests Van Cott. Although the various approaches chosen to effect this form of radical democracy overlap somewhat, she identifies three schools of thought: the participatory, the associative, and the deliberative (ibid., 15–19). The factors that she identifies as contributing to institutional innovation at the municipal level, common to all three types of radical democracy, are the legal and political context, local leadership, and "support from a cohesive, organic, political party rooted in civil society" (ibid., 211). Although these findings are hardly surprising, they do underline the political dimension.

Leadership plays an important role in any form of government, and several researchers have looked more closely at it in the context of alternative government. In Ecuador, Van Cott found that the more sustainable alternative governments were led by mayors who built successful relationships with other groups, thus ensuring that deliberations were open and more democratic and avoiding the creation of a "deliberative elite" (Van Cott 2008, 84–85). Sunstein (2003) has argued that such a group, in the absence of other perspectives, runs the risk of becoming an insulated enclave and adopting more extreme views, leading to group polarization, or alternatively of becoming monolithic and set in its own dogma.

In his comparative study of municipal government in Bolivia, Ecuador, and Peru, Cameron (2010, 318–324) deals directly with the issue of power and politics and questions some of the conventional wisdom. First, he emphasizes the key role of community-based organizations as a training ground for developing important political and administrative skills. According to Van Cott (2008) and Grindle (2007), these skills will help to build and sustain local institutions from the bottom up. Second, Cameron (2010) pinpoints the ambiguous and sometimes contentious relationships between local governments and other local organizations, such as social movements or federations. From his perspective, local government cannot function effectively without autonomy, and local organizations are no longer the exclusive brokers or intermediaries with the local population. Third, he maintains that the role of political parties is much less important than the literature indicates since the existing political parties practiced partisan politics and were riven by factional conflicts. In all six of the cases that he studied, relative autonomy from political parties was an important factor in the process of deepening democracy. Finally, linkages between the local and broader social movements and political parties facilitated participation in larger struggles and redistributive reforms at the national level.

This also holds for the departmental level; in fact, what happens there should be understood in terms of its relationship with the national government. Research in Colombia in the past decade has attempted to explain the differences among the country's thirty-two departments and their relationships—political, economic, and cultural—with the national government in terms of "the differential presence of the state," the historical legacy of the central government's inability to completely control the national territory or to monopolize the use of violence (González González and Otero Bahamón 2010, 31). As a result, the presence and depth of state institutions differ considerably depending on a specific department's level of integration. The more a department is integrated into the national economy, the greater the presence of state institutions. The less a department is thus integrated, the weaker the presence of these institutions and the state's need to rely on local elites. Some have called this a selective modernization of the state, and others term it a form of dualism in which "modern, impersonal" institutions are counterposed to "traditional," clientelistic ones. In the most extreme cases, the presence of the state is either almost nonexistent or reduced primarily to a military presence. However, this typology describes rather than explains the nature of the state and its behavior.

Das and Poole (2004, 4) argue that a study of the margins, where the state's institutions are at best clientelistic and at worst almost nonexistent, can offer a unique perspective on the state because "it suggests that such margins are a necessary entailment of the state, much as the exception is a necessary component of the rule." Drawing on the work of Agamben (1998) and Benjamin (1986 [1978]), they propose that the former's concept of the "state of exception" is a theory of state sovereignty that is both inside and outside the law, a dynamic process that can take many forms, of which war is the classic example. War can redraw boundaries and redefine who is a citizen and who is not (Das and Poole 2004, 12–13). In practice, this may mean that the state's monopoly on the use of violence may be shared with or delegated to other groups such as local elites or paramilitaries, reinforcing Foucault's (1997) recognition of the multiple locations of power.[5] In the case of Colombia, Sanford suggests that the nation is a contested space "in which citizenship and state sovereignty are reconstituted at the margins" (2004, 257).

While the pragmatic objective of a viable alternative government may well be to improve people's quality of life through improved delivery of public services and the implementation of programs to address inequity, there are also grander, more transcendental objectives directly related to the pursuit of citizenship. As Dagnino eloquently states, "What is at stake, in fact, in struggles over citizenship in Latin America is more than the right to be included as a full member of society; it is the right to participate in the very definition of that society and its political system" (2003, 215). This claim is worthy of further investigation since the experience on the ground may be very different. People's quest for citizenship may be motivated by a variety of factors, tangible and intangible, and the realities encountered contradictory. Although these elements do not necessarily invalidate the quest, they can temper some of the more normative assumptions about the process. For example, Cameron (2010, 334) maintains that people view the benefits of local democracy in both abstract and practical terms. On one hand, there is increased respect, dignity, and political autonomy, but there is also more interest in the distribution of resources rather than the process of decision making, particularly when these resources were allocated to public works, which "stood as symbols of modernity in rural communities where dignity and community pride were partly connected to self-perceptions of modernization" (ibid., 336).

The experience of alternative government can potentially transform the ways in which people imagine themselves and their social and political interactions. The desire for a good life, health, and happiness is universal, though it may differ depending on one's education, class, and ethnicity (Appadurai 2004). Nevertheless, Ferguson (2006) reminds us of the pervasive presence of inequality and exclusion, issues that can severely temper aspirations and often play a causal role in the emergence of alternative governments. Because these do not evolve in a vacuum, Hetherington (1998) has suggested that the success or failure of new social movements, particularly those directed at changing society and electing alternative governments, cannot be viewed solely in instrumental political terms. Other criteria such as solidarity, community, and alternative visions of how society should be structured need to be considered as well. Such experiences can affect those most directly involved in constructive ways, particularly those with a personal history of political activism. Hirschman (1984) proposes that people who have participated in earlier, sometimes more radical movements that generally failed to achieve their objectives, often because of official oppression, do not necessarily lose their desire for political change or collective action. He refers to this enduring phenomenon as social energy and maintains that it is capable of reappearing under certain conditions, but perhaps in a somewhat different form.

In the case of contemporary Colombia, there are few studies of alternative government at either the departmental or the municipal level, yet interesting examples of both exist, implemented over the past two decades in various parts of the country. One such example is the alternative government of Taita Floro Tunubalá. This case is of particular interest for several reasons. First, it demonstrates clearly that alternatives to neoliberalism take root within particular social and political landscapes. Here, increasingly militant indigenous and campesino organizing, combined with the political participation of recently demobilized guerrillas, enabled an indigenous governor to assume power in Cauca department and push for a participatory development project that provided a hopeful alternative to the neoliberal (and corrupt) status quo.

Second, and perhaps more important, this example addresses a problematic question: What difference did this alternative government make? If the tangible results were few, can one talk of a symbolic legacy? If so, of what does it consist and what does it mean? Is it unrealistic to think that much could be changed in such a hostile environment, one characterized by a national government that under successive presidents stressed neoliberalism and security and in a department shackled by increasing violence, accumulated debt, and perennial poverty? Why do people persist in their claims against the state? This is an attempt to answer the question Heller (1990) has posed: "Good people exist; how is this possible?" (cited in Jelin 2003, 310).

THE STATE OF THE "REAL COUNTRY"

At the turn of the last century and the beginning of the new millennium, rural Colombia epitomized many of the worst elements of inequitable development in spite of its characterization as "high human development" by the United Nations Development Program (UNDP) in its most recent Human Development Index, which ranked the nation ranked 87 out of a total of 187 reporting countries. The state is highly centralized, and the major policy and fiscal decisions are made in the capital, Bogotá, leaving the departmental and municipal governments frustrated, poor, and powerless. Income distribution is highly skewed, the most extreme in Latin America. At the end of the first decade of the twenty-first century, the Gini coefficient was 58.5, the percentage of people living below the poverty line was 46.8, and the quintile income ratio was 24.8 (i.e., the average income of the richest 20 percent was almost 25 times that of the poorest 20 percent).[6]

The ownership of land was highly concentrated, a trend that has become more pronounced since the 1980s. Although accurate data are hard to come by, in 2009, 18 of the country's 32 departments had Gini ratios greater than 0.8, indicating that land distribution was highly skewed. During the period 2000–2009, the Gini ratio increased in 23 departments. The number of small farmers (less than 50 hectares) increased by 16 percent and comprised 88 percent of all landowners, while the numbers of medium-size (50–500 hectares) and large farmers (more than 500 hectares) increased by 14.3 and 32.6 percent, respectively. In 2009, 1.6 percent of landowners classified as large controlled 28.5 percent of the land, while the small farmers controlled about a third (Programa de las Naciones Unidos para el Desarrollo 2011, 198–205). Using a different set of criteria, the land-tenure situation is even more alarming, with 79.3 of farmers classified as small farmers occupying 10.6 percent of the available land and 1.15 percent classified as large farmers occupying 52.2 percent of the land (ibid., 205–206).

But this is only part of the picture. In 1985, total land area was 114 million hectares, of which 14 million hectares (roughly 12.3 percent of the total) were classified as potentially arable. In 1987, 36.8 percent of the arable land was cultivated, but by 1999 this had decreased to 30.6 percent (Guigale, Lafourcade, and Luff 2003, 560–564). The land "shortage," referred to by some commentators as a "land reform in reverse," has been exacerbated by the massive displacement of nearly four million rural people in the past twenty years, driven off their land by armed agents of both the Left and the Right.

The advent of neoliberalism, introduced during the presidency of César Gavíria in the early 1990s, only exacerbated the situation by reducing tariffs on imported food, in the process jeopardizing the livelihoods of many rural families; by encouraging large-scale commercial agriculture and ranching, often at the expense of the domestic market; by refusing to accept the need for land reform in various parts of the country; and by "rationalizing" government expenditures so that the provision of essential social services, such as education and health, was diluted.

Political corruption is now rampant at all levels of society, fueled by a drug economy that has effectively inserted itself into the political process, a situation that has steadily deteriorated over the past decade. There is an ongoing, low-intensity civil war characterized by a diminished but resilient long-term guerrilla presence, countered by the more recent paramilitary presence, closely associated with the military, the drug lords, and the political and economic elites. In certain regions of the country, where the state's presence is minimal, power has been shared with the guerrillas, as well as the paramilitary and criminal groups, sometimes composed of ex-guerrillas, ex-paramilitaries, and common criminals. When the elites have felt unduly threatened by the possibility of political change that threatened the status quo, they have acted decisively and brutally. In an eight-month period in 1989 and 1990, three presidential candidates, all progressive in one way or another, were assassinated.[7]

Partly in response to these tragic events, Gavíria launched the Constituent Assembly (La Asamblea Nacional Constituyente, ANC) and in the process created a political opportunity for those previously marginalized and ignored. The mandate for the assembly was broad, challenging, and contentious and was designed to resolve the growing political crisis and "provide a forum for national reconciliation between what Colombian commentators called 'the political country' and the 'real country'" (Van Cott 2000, 51). The origins of the crisis were twofold. On the one hand, there was the lack of legitimacy on the part of the traditional political elites, both liberal and conservative, who had ruled the country since La Violencia in the 1950s, a decade of bloody violence sparked by the assassination of Jorge Elícier Gaitán on April 9, 1948, a widely popular presidential candidate from the Liberal Party. This had contributed to increasing social exclusion, social unrest, political apathy, and corruption. On the other hand, the widespread social decomposition went hand in hand with increasing levels of violence provoked by the guerrillas, the paramilitaries, the state, and particularly the drug cartels (Dugas 1993a).

Three indigenous delegates participated in the Constitutional Assembly, two of whom came from Cauca: Alfonso Peña, a recently demobilized guerrilla leader, and Lorenzo Muelas, a leader from Guambía and a member of the same ethnic group as Tunubalá (Peña Chepe 1991). All three, together with many other delegates, highlighted the multiethnic and pluricultural character of the Colombian people, supported the rights of ethnic groups, and argued for the protection of civil rights and the provision of social guarantees. Nevertheless, there was some opposition within the ANC to indigenous rights and multiculturalism, and it was only when Lorenzo Muelas threatened to resign that an agreement was reached. As a result, these themes were incorporated into the new constitution, whose principal goals (e.g., making democratic institutions more participatory; creating stronger, independent judicial institutions; decentralizing administrative functions and political powers) favored the indigenous movement and called for a more inclusive definition of the nation (Peñaranda 1999).[8] In addition, the new constitution favored political pluralism and the creation of new political parties, free from the dominance exercised by the traditional parties. According to some, this made possible the election of Taita Floro Tunubalá and his *gobierno alternativo* in Cauca less than a decade later (Navarro 2001).[9] However, it should be made clear that the ANC built on and stimulated a process that had had already been under way for some time.

Important as the ANC was, it did not address certain controversial but highly relevant topics, such as the economy, security, and subsoil rights, which were directly affected by the government's neoliberal policies. When Tunubalá came to power a decade later, the first two, the economy and security, were to have an adverse effect on his government. One cannot govern without resources, and, in an effort to rationalize budgets at the departmental level, in 1999 the national government passed draconian legislation, the infamous Ley 550, which made incoming governments responsible for the repayment of the accumulated debts of their predecessors. In practice, this tied Tunubalá's hands even before he took office and left him nothing for productive or innovative investment of any sort. When he did take office, Plan Colombia, with its focus on drug eradication and the strengthening of the army and police, was well under way, and Cauca was one of its centers of operation. Initiated under the government of Pastrana in the late 1990s, this emphasis on security only increased when Uribe took over as president in 2002, in the middle of Tunubalá's term in office and became Washington's closest ally in Latin America. In a sense, Tunubalá's victory was a response to these neoliberal policies that had adversely affected the department's predominantly agricultural economy, while at the same time encouraging the growth of a drug economy, which was often supported by the increasing presence of paramilitary forces and the active participation of the guerrilla movements.

THE STATE OF CAUCA

The department of Cauca, located in the southwestern part of the country, is famous for its coffee, sugar, agricultural products, and livestock, as well as an alternative economy based on the cultivation and processing of illegal crops such as coca, marijuana, and opium. It is also known for its social, economic, and political inequalities, its political violence, with the active, ongoing presence of armed groups, particularly the Fuerzas Armadas Revolucionarias de Colombia (FARC) and to a lesser extent the Ejército de Liberación Nacional (ELN), as well as the paramilitaries, and, finally, its history of mobilization by marginalized indigenous and peasant groups, active participants in various ongoing social movements. This well-tested capacity to organize at the local level bore fruit on Sunday, October 29, 2000, when Tunubalá, a local leader, teacher, and politician, was elected governor. His election was noteworthy for several reasons. As a member of the Guambiano ethnic group, he was the first elected indigenous governor in the history of Colombia, a country where less than 2 percent of the population regards itself as indigenous. He was elected without the backing of a political party. Instead, his supporters created the Bloque Social Alternativo (BSA), a coalition of progressive and left-wing organizations and social movements that included unions, small farmers, teachers, indigenous-rights organizations, regional organizations, and the Alianza Social Indígena, a political party established in 1991 by the demobilized members of the Movimiento Armado Quintín Lame (MAQL), a home-grown, primarily indigenous guerrilla movement. Voter turnout for the election was the highest on record, and the total number of votes cast was more than twice the usual number.

Although Cauca's indigenous population is relatively sizeable, estimated at around 25 percent of an overall population of about 1.3 million, Tunubalá did not receive their overall support. Many indigenous voters chose instead to back his opponent, a decent but rather conventional doctor supported by the ruling Liberal Party, which has long dominated departmental politics. He received strong support in Popayán, the departmental capital, a heavily mestizo city with a population of around 250,000, which he carried by 15,000 votes, a margin sufficient to win him the election. His success was due partly to the widespread disgust with the ruling Liberal Party incumbent, who was a scion of the local elites, corrupt, unaccountable, a devout practitioner of politiquería and of "business as usual." Concerns were also raised that the incumbent had allowed Cauca to become ungovernable because he was unwilling or unable to deal with the increasing levels of violence.[10]

But there were other, more powerful historical factors at work. In the decade prior to the issuance of the new constitution, there were popular mobilizations in Cauca, usually in the form of demonstrations and marches led by either the indigenous movement or the growing peasant movements in El Macizo, in the southern part of the department. The constitutional reform of 1986 allowed for the direct election of mayors and council members at the municipal level in 1988. In the 1992 elections, for example, twenty-one of the thirty-eight mayors elected were associated with neither of the two traditional parties (Ruíz et al. 2003, 53). The mobilizations had their roots in the rural population's growing dissatisfaction and frustration with the national government in Bogotá and its reluctance, if not outright refusal, to honor its commitments to provide the necessary resources for the social and economic development of the more abandoned and excluded regions of the department. This pattern continued throughout the 1990s, and although neoliberalism certainly played a role, the national government was also perpetuating a long-held practice of breaking its promises. As a result, these social movements became stronger and better organized. More people participated, and the strategies they pursued (e.g., the capacity and willingness to close the Pan-American Highway, the main artery connecting northern and southern Colombia, with its direct link to neighboring Ecuador and Peru) became more radical. Direct action proved to be an effective way of awakening public opinion and forcing the state to respond publicly, neatly summarized as "A kilometer of the Pan-American is worth more than ten seats in congress" (Herrera Rivera 2003, 132). Nonetheless, the feeling of abandonment by the state was widespread throughout Cauca.

The year 1999 was pivotal. In June the Consejo Regional Indígena del Cauca (CRIC), the oldest indigenous-rights organization in Colombia (founded in 1971), successfully closed the highway for eleven days. The protest, supported by 12,000 people, was directed against the national government's continuing failure to fulfill its promises to the indigenous people of Cauca to finance health care and education, part of the neoliberal agenda to limit or privatize, and its failure to address the perennial issues of land reform and the escalating political violence. During the mobilization, the civic guard, composed of young men and women from the participating communities, was responsible for successfully maintaining law and order. The guerrillas were banned, as were drugs and alcohol. Although there had been earlier large-scale mobilizations protesting essentially the same issues, little had been accomplished (Espinosa 2005). However, the closing of the highway in 1999 was different since it involved more people and lasted longer, although the resulting negotiations with the government achieved little at first. One more immediate result, however, was the establishment of La María-Piendamó as an alternative political space.

This was a precursor to a more widespread and more prolonged closing of the highway later that same year. On November 1, 1999, the Comité de Integración del Macizo Colombiano (CIMA) closed the highway for twenty-five days, blocking it both north and south of Popayán, effectively cutting the city off from the rest of the country and bringing all north-south transportation to a complete standstill. As a result, trade with neighboring Ecuador, Colombia's third major trading partner after the United States and Venezuela, was put on hold. Upwards of 60,000 people, both rural and urban, were involved. Participants included schoolteachers, peasants, Afro-Colombians, indigenous people, and, increasingly, the people of Popayán. The strike, the Paro del Macizo as it came to be called, was in support of the same demands that the people of El Macizo had been making since the 1980s and that the national government, in spite of its commitments regarding the provision of services and the building of a basic infrastructure, had refused to honor. Although the police were present in force and the army was rumored to be arriving at any moment, the strike was nonviolent, and the participating groups took turns maintaining law and order.[11]

Direct negotiations between the leaders of CIMA and representatives of the national government were long and drawn out, but the government finally capitulated and agreed, once again, to most of CIMA's demands. This time, however, the government actually delivered on some of its promises, specifically with regard to the provision of services and improvements in infrastructure. As with the mobilization of the indigenous movement earlier that year, the national government's response was partly justified by its neoliberal policies, which also, ironically, helped end the strike. The closing of the Pan-American Highway and its damaging effect on Colombia's trade with neighboring countries, as well as the immediate impact on Cauca's economy, were other important factors. These actions shook the economic elites of Cauca, and Tunubalá's successors vowed to keep the highway open at all costs, a promise they have been able to keep only by resorting to military force.

As a result of their collective experience and relative success, participants and supporters felt inspired to take on greater challenges, specifically in the political arena (Jaramillo 2005). In comparison with earlier efforts to organize, mobilize, and negotiate directly with the state, the Paro del Macizo had lasted longer, received more recognition, and gained wider support. Thanks to the demonstrators' staying powers and the leadership's negotiating skills, CIMA had obliged the departmental and national governments to take it seriously and negotiate in good faith. The increasing drain on the regional economy was another key factor: it frightened those in power and brought them to the negotiating table. By successfully closing the Pan-American Highway for a substantial length of time, dissident groups had successfully demonstrated that they could essentially bring the regional economy to a standstill.[12]

Nonetheless, the political Left in Cauca, as in other parts of the country, was highly skeptical of electoral politics and preferred to take to the streets rather than participate in elections since its members were convinced that most elections were rigged and that most politicians were not to be trusted. Wilson Bonilla, then president of La Central Unitaria de Trabajadores de Colombia in Cauca, the trade-union federation, explained that, until the mobilization, the only way to get anything done in the department, such as building a road, providing running water, or making sure the local hospital functioned, was through direct action, usually in the form of a strike, sometimes successful but often not. The success of CIMA helped to change this mentality:

> We who had not participated in it [the electoral process] saw the great possibility of doing so. There were some doubts, some opposition because many of us who were opposed, including me, I was always opposed to participating in the elections because, here in Colombia, he who counts the votes is the one who elects [the winner].[13]

It was this change of attitude that contributed to the formation of the BSA, which, as mentioned earlier, was a coalition of various local organizations and social movements, some of whose members had been active participants in the CIMA blockade. They selected Taita Floro Tunubalá as their candidate and got him elected as the first indigenous governor of Cauca, an achievement that would have been impossible earlier.

THE ALTERNATIVE GOVERNMENT OF TAITA FLORO TUNUBALÁ

When asked what motivated him to run for governor, Tunubalá identified several key factors. First, he knew Cauca well and had experienced at first hand the widespread poverty and nonpresence of the state throughout the department. In addition, he had been an active participant for the preceding twenty-five years in the struggle to recover indigenous lands expropriated by mestizos. He was actively involved in the Constitutional Assembly and, later, was one of the first indigenous senators in the country. He had also been governor of the Guambianos, one of the more politically experienced indigenous groups in the department. Finally, since there had never really been a development plan for Cauca, he and his cabinet would have an opportunity to offer an alternative form of government and a different plan for developing the department.[14]

In his acceptance speech after winning the October election, Tunubalá appealed to all of the inhabitants of Cauca—mestizo, indigenous, and Afro-Colombian—to work together to address the major issues confronting the province: poverty, corruption, violence, freedom from liability, narcotrafficking, and unemployment (Tunubalá 2000). This appeal was captured in the phrase *en minga por el Cauca*, which became one of the guiding principles of his government, the idea that people should work together for the common good, building on the Andean tradition of *minga*, which is still practiced on a regular basis in many indigenous communities of Cauca. The objective was to create political space for all social, political, and economic sectors to participate in the construction of a Cauca that would include all of its citizens. The basis for this transformation would be a social and economic development plan that would respect human rights, practice sustainable development, and promote regional democracy. From the very beginning of his administration, Tunubalá and his cabinet were determined that theirs would be "an alternative government." To this end they identified themselves as participatory democrats, people who, according to Van Cott, seek to increase opportunities for citizens to participate in government decision-making processes at the local level, innovations that may eventually lead to structural changes in government institutions at a higher level.

In his inaugural speech to the departmental assembly two months later, in January 2001, Tunubalá stressed the gravity of the departmental government's financial situation; the outgoing governor had left his successor with huge debts to repay, effectively tying his hands and leaving him with few resources to invest in the department. The agricultural sector, the backbone of Cauca's legal economy, had been ignored, a consequence partly of the state's policies, which had liberalized the sector and allowed the importation of cheaper foodstuffs from neighboring countries. Peasants continued to cultivate illegal crops, such as coca, opium, and marijuana. The state, under the umbrella of the U.S.-supported Plan Colombia, contributed to the militarization of development in the department by battling the armed groups on the one hand and eradicating the illegal crops by aerial spraying on the other without offering much in the way of viable economic alternatives. Tunubalá called for an integrated policy to fight the poverty, inequality, corruption, and injustice in the state while respecting the local population and making possible "a life with dignity." This call was directed particularly at the armed groups of the Left, the Right, and the state.[15]

In selecting the members of his cabinet, Tunubalá intentionally did not appoint any indigenous individuals but instead, to the extent possible, chose people who represented the interests of the various constituencies in the BSA, which had elected him. Over time, a small inner group emerged, many of whose members had spent their adult lives working for social, political, and economic change. There was Henry Caballero, a Quintín, who had occupied a key position in the MAQL and had demonstrated considerable skill in negotiating with the state. He was named secretary, second in command, and acting governor when Tunubalá was out of town. Caballero later moved on to a newly created position within the administration responsible for human rights. There was Milton Guzmán, a medical doctor closely identified with CRIC, who was appointed secretary of health. Hermes Idrobo, from El Macizo, closely identified with CIMA, was named secretary of education. In spite of the general budget constraints, he and Guzmán were able to plan and implement programs in their respective sectors as a result of the system of direct transfers (*transferencias*) from the state, introduced through legislation enacted in the 1990s and stemming from the new constitution. There was Darío Delgado, manager of *la licorera*, the government-owned distillery, with a background in the trade-union movement. Diego Jaramillo, the governor's adviser, was a political philosopher at the University of Cauca and manager of the Plan Alterno. The final member of this inner group, María Eugenia Castro, was responsible for administration and finance and had overall responsibility for managing the repayment of the inherited departmental debt. She had a very different background in business and banking, and her selection was a shrewd political move that calmed the concerns of creditors and the private sector in general.[16] It was this inner group that was to provide the leadership and backbone of his administration.

Even before Tunubalá took office, his life was threatened, as was Jaramillo's. In fact, this threat of political violence was a constant throughout Tunubalá's three years in office. The FARC worked unceasingly to undermine his authority and credibility. In Tunubalá's first year of office, the FARC kidnapped three employees of the Deutsche Gesellschaft für Technische Zusammenarbeit GmbH, the German development-assistance agency, which had worked in Cauca during the previous decade and was well respected for its ability to work effectively in areas of conflict. One of the kidnapped men managed to escape, and the two others were released some months later, presumably after payment of a ransom. What was particularly galling for Tunubalá was the fact that they were held in a region of Cauca that is predominantly indigenous. In his second year, the FARC threatened the lives of the mayors of all of Cauca's municipalities in an attempt to force them to resign or face the consequences. The FARC has a long history of assassinating elected local officials, mestizo, indigenous, and Afro-Colombian. Some mayors resigned, some stood firm and were assassinated, and others moved their offices to the larger towns, where they felt more secure. This tense situation lasted for approximately six months. At that time the FARC accepted the fact that neither Tunubalá nor the mayors could be easily or permanently cowed.

There were also the expectations of those who had elected him, partly in the hope of obtaining personal favors but more in terms of radical change since Tunubalá had promised that his would be an alternative government. The fact that he was indigenous did not necessarily help him when indigenous issues came to the fore, however. As governor, he represented the state, in this case as president of the republic and not just of indigenous citizens: "He was *from* the community but no longer *of* it" (Rappaport 2005, 272). Although he did have responsibilities to the members of the coalition that elected him, these were tempered by the stark reality that he had to work within the existing political and administrative system:

> I told them [the social organizations] that Cauca was part of Colombia, of a nation, of a state and that I had to submit to the existing norms in this country and that I could not do what the communities were thinking, and immediately many sectors did not understand, did not want to understand.[17]

Perhaps coincidentally, the coalition never really functioned as a coalition but rather as individuals and the specific organizations they represented, who advised and supported Tunubalá and his cabinet in their role as concerned and engaged citizens. A similar situation developed with Tunubalá's elected supporters in the departmental assembly, who tended to function as individuals with specific interests, hardly a novel situation in a highly centralized country such as Colombia, where departmental governors and assemblies have historically been weak.[18] At the end of Tunubalá's three years, the coalition that had originally elected him selected a candidate to replace him. This individual, who was a native of Cauca and an ex-member of the M-19, had had a distinguished political and professional career in Bogotá. However, he was defeated by a member of one of Popayán's ruling families, a one-time member of congress and an ex-cabinet minister. The governor-elect personified everything that Tunubalá and his government had fought against. Voter turnout dropped precipitously—by approximately half.

THE EFFECTS OF THE VIOLENCE

When Tunubalá took office, one of the major concerns was the governability of Cauca, the extent to which it was even possible to govern the department, given its recent history of corruption, mass mobilization, political violence, and drug cultivation and trafficking. The situation was exacerbated when Álvaro Uribe assumed the presidency halfway through Tunubalá's term of office, replacing the more moderate Andres Pastrana. Uribe pushed a strong neoliberal agenda for the country, with a focus on security, direct confrontation with the guerrillas, a continuation of the war against drugs, and increasingly close relationships with the United States. As a result, he was viewed as a major, conservative U.S. ally in Latin America, one of the few. Even before he was elected, Uribe made it clear that he strongly disapproved of Tunubalá's alternative government and all that it stood for. From the very beginning of his presidency, he made every effort to thwart Tunubalá's initiatives and did little to support either him or his government. Hence the state itself became another major hindrance to a more responsible government since it provided only minimal support to improve the well-being of the population as a whole, a clear demonstration of what González González and Otero Bahamón somewhat euphemistically refer to as "the differential presence of the state" (2010, 31).

When Tunubalá took office in 2001, the level and incidence of violence throughout Cauca had reached crisis proportions, and he strongly criticized "the armed actors," an inclusive term that refers to all those who bear arms, including those who do so in the name of the state, specifically the police and the army, arguing that "peace is an obligation to fight poverty, inequality, corruption, and injustice."[19] But peace never came, and, in fact, over the years the violence steadily intensified. Tunubalá wanted to push for a reduction in the level of violence, arguing strongly, together with the governors of the neighboring departments, that they should have the right to negotiate directly with the guerrillas since they understood local needs, conditions, and constraints much better than any potential negotiators from Bogotá appointed by the president. Nonetheless, violence in various forms was to plague his years in office and leave him saddened by its permanent presence. In his final report, which summarized what his government had achieved, he talked about the moments of pain he experienced when he was informed of the murders and kidnappings, the takeovers of towns, and the destruction of infrastructure, perpetrated by the guerrillas and the paramilitaries, "situations that made me feel most helpless."[20]

The seminal 2003 Programa de las Naciones Unidos para el Desarrollo (PNUD) study *El conflicto: Callejón con salida* (The conflict: A way out) identified the most vulnerable municipalities in Colombia in the early 2000s, where vulnerability was measured as a combination of level of violence and level of governability. Of Cauca's forty-one municipalities, eighteen were so classified (45 percent of the department) (PNUD 2003, 486–491). Many of these municipalities still figure prominently in the news almost a decade later. Among the ten that were classified as the most vulnerable in the country, four were in Cauca. Tunubalá just happened to become governor at a time when the twin problems of violence and governability were particularly acute.

The government's neoliberal policies, particularly under Uribe, contributed little to reducing the level of violence in Cauca, and this holds for all of the armed groups. Their presence in a locality made the delivery of social services, such as health and education, a hazardous undertaking and the provision of security, in the form of a permanent police station, a constant challenge. In the early 2000s, the FARC had a presence throughout the department, with six fronts, a mobile column, and a mobile block (Ruíz et al. 2003, 38). The greatest challenge FARC posed to the governability of Cauca was its attempt to force the mayors to either resign or run the risk of being assassinated. This was part of a national strategy that was implemented in February 2002 after the collapse of the peace talks in San Vicente de Caguán; its purpose was to weaken local institutions of governance, particularly the municipalities. Some of the mayors in Cauca chose to stand their ground in defense of their autonomy, territory, and culture, generally those where the population was predominantly indigenous. The townspeople would not let their mayors resign, and the FARC responded by occupying the respective town centers. Many mayors submitted their resignations to Tunubalá, who refused to accept them. As mentioned earlier, some stayed in their municipalities but kept a low profile and scaled back their work, while others relocated to the larger urban centers, such as Popayán or Cali, where they and their families felt more secure. Overall, 25 percent had to run their municipalities from elsewhere by means of faxes, telephone calls, and personal messengers.[21] As a result of these threats, the provision of public services such as water, bill collection, street cleaning, payment of schoolteachers, and health subsidies quickly deteriorated.[22]

In January 2003, twelve of the threatened mayors agreed to return to their hometowns in spite of the fact that the national government had not provided them with the requested security: bodyguards and armored vehicles. Nevertheless, they were determined to fulfill their responsibilities. In September 2003, the month before the local elections, the FARC started assassinating local leaders in El Macizo, where two mayors and five municipal council members were killed in a continuation of the FARC's long-term campaign to subdue and control strategic parts of the department. El Macizo was particularly appealing because of its almost complete abandonment by the state, which facilitated the production of illegal crops, communication with and access to the neighboring departments of Caquetá, Huila, and Putumayo, and the existence of a corridor to the Pacific Coast for the trafficking of drugs (Ruíz et al. 2003, 39).

The paramilitaries started working in Cauca in 1998, expanding on the base they had already established in the neighboring department of Valle. They announced the "official" arrival of their first contingent in a letter directed to César Negret, then governor of Cauca (Ruíz et al. 2003, 40). From 2001 to 2003, an additional three detachments operated in the department. Starting in the north, they steadily spread throughout the department, though their major focus continued to be the north, the center, and the Pacific Coast.

The paramilitaries would enter a given region for a variety of reasons: to fight the guerrillas; to exclude or eliminate any opposition to local elites; to control strategic corridors, usually for the benefit of the *narcotraficantes*; or to strengthen the already powerful, local economic interests (Zuñiga 2010, 69). From early on there was close collusion between the police and the army on one hand and the paramilitaries on the other. In contrast to the FARC, the paramilitaries were active primarily in urban areas, where they carried out numerous acts of violence or made threats to do so.

Their most egregious act was the massacre in Alta Naya in April 2001. The region, located in the northwestern part of the department, had been settled by indigenous, mestizo, and Afro-Colombian families who, for the past fifteen years, had cultivated coca under the control of the FARC and the ELN.[23] The massacre, which occurred during Easter week, left forty people dead, displaced nearly 400, and was prompted by the quest for territory, control over an important corridor for the shipment of arms and drugs between the Pacific coast and the northern part of the department.[24] The paramilitaries were also motivated by a desire for revenge since they suspected that families in the region had cared for some of the people kidnapped by the guerrillas two years earlier, a form of collaboration punishable, in their eyes, by death. Several hundred paramilitaries were involved, and eyewitness estimates ranged from two to five hundred. This was to be the most outrageous massacre during Tunubalá's tenure in office because of the number of people affected and the extreme violence demonstrated. According to one eyewitness:

> A neighbor threw himself on a paramilitary who was going to shoot him and wrested his gun from him, with such bad luck that the rifle turned and he did not know how to fire it. They took him, dragged him, opened him up with a chainsaw, and chopped him up.[25]

The governor strongly criticized Bogotá for dragging its feet in providing the necessary security for those from the attorney general's office who were trying to investigate what had happened and condemned the perpetrators for committing a form of genocide.[26]

The military were also viewed with distrust. An abortive attempt by some of the mayors in El Macizo, whose lives were threatened by the FARC, to negotiate directly with the local *comandante*, elicited strong censure from Bogotá. The mayors, accompanied by Humberto Urrego, the peace adviser in Cauca, had met with the local FARC commander in Santa Rosa to answer charges that they were supposedly promoting the paramilitary presence in the region. The FARC had threatened the lives of all four mayors and held them responsible for the return of the police and the stationing of a military battalion in the region. The meeting lasted only half an hour. During that time the mayors explained their situation, but the FARC was adamant: all four had to resign; otherwise, they would be killed. On the return trip to Popayán, the group was stopped by the FARC, who shot and killed one of the mayors.

President Uribe denounced such direct dealings between a departmental government and the FARC. Urrego defended his action by pointing out that the mayors had requested his presence as an independent observer and that he had complied because this was humanitarian action, which was covered by international humanitarian law.[27] The surviving mayors likewise demonstrated their independence from and disdain for the dictates of Bogotá. One mayor responded forcefully to the government's insistence that only Bogotá had the authority to talk with the guerrillas: "It doesn't matter if I'm punished because I have a clear conscience. It's one thing to issue orders from Bogotá and something quite distinct to govern in the other Colombia, where the police withdrew 19 years ago and where the army hasn't gone for 11 years."[28] As a mayor temporarily in exile, he felt strongly about the mayors' obligations to their constituencies and their responsibility to improve conditions in their communities even though they risked losing their lives at the hands of "those who are intolerant."[29]

Shortly after reports reached Popayán that the town of Santa Rosa was under siege by the FARC, who had cut off all transportation in and out of the town and also forbidden residents, including the mayor, his cabinet, and the town's doctors, to leave their homes. Santa Rosa had no police station, and there had been little government presence for the past twenty years. The government responded by sending in the army, whose arrival was delayed by the weather, the topography, and the numerous landmines planted by the FARC. The commanding general accused the FARC of using the local population as a human shield for protection. A month earlier, the people had protested the government's burned-earth policy and indiscriminate bombing, which had displaced many residents.[30]

The siege lasted six days. At that time the army had successfully managed to occupy the town, drive out the FARC, and liberate the population. In a cabinet meeting, however, the governor, relying on information provided by a local commission from Santa Rosa, stated that it was the army and not the FARC that had restricted movement in and out of town and had prohibited access to certain organizations: "The colonel said that as long as they [the military] are there, human-rights organizations will not be allowed to enter while they kick out the guerrillas."[31] This does not appear to have been an isolated case. In a communal assembly held in another town earlier that year, the participants accused the army of committing abuses against the municipalities of El Macizo on the grounds that the residents were all collaborators with the guerrillas.[32] At the cabinet meeting, members stated that the national government had politicized the assault on Santa Rosa for two reasons: first, it wished to show its strength at the expense of the departmental government; second, it wanted to wash its hands of the whole business and blame the departmental government for whatever happened to the civilian population.[33]

EMPTY COFFERS: DEBT AND FINANCIAL ACCOUNTABILITY

If violence and the threat of violence were the major external factors that limited the effectiveness of Tunubalá's government, then payment of the financial debt, inherited from the previous administration, was the major internal constraint. Repayment of the debt, debilitating as it was, demonstrated the seriousness and commitment of Tunubalá's government. In contrast to the violence, which continued to worsen, debts could be dealt with but at a considerable political cost since repayment left less money for the business of government in terms of investments, programs, salaries, and the provision of essential services. The legal responsibility to pay off the debt provided Tunubalá's critics with an opportunity to challenge his progressive credentials; the more radical ones argued that he should have refused to pay, mobilized his followers, and marched on the presidential palace in Bogotá at the head of the group. The more political critics, whether members of the BSA or deputies in the Departmental Assembly, used the obligation to pay off the debt as a weapon for undermining Tunubalá's efforts to reform politics in Cauca.

When the new cabinet took office in January 2001, the members were shocked to find that their offices had few furnishings and that many had even been stripped bare. Although Tunubalá knew about the debt, he was taken aback by what he found: "Negret [the previous governor] was so extreme when they handed over the government building to me, the departmental office was simply a room with not even any chairs. They handed it over to us completely empty. That was appalling—without tables, without chairs, without anything."[34]

While this shocked many of the new cabinet officers, the threadbare environment was symptomatic of a much deeper malaise: empty coffers. The new cabinet discovered that the outgoing government had been so short of funds that it had put up for sale some of the government's assets, specifically land and buildings. Four days earlier, the outgoing governor had signed an agreement with the Ministry of Finance, which committed the incoming government and succeeding governments to repay Cauca's accumulated debts, as stipulated in Ley 550. Approved in 1999, the law, as it applied to departmental governments, was designed to strengthen their capacity to fulfill their financial obligations; improve their administrative, financial, and accounting procedures; and guarantee their contributions to departmental pension funds.[35] In other words, this law was an attempt to hold departmental governments financially accountable, a key component of the neoliberal agenda to rationalize government spending.

In the agreement signed by Negret, the government committed to repaying the debt over a period of ten years. Although the initial debt preceded the government of Negret, it had almost doubled during his years in office.[36] The agreement was approved by the outgoing Departmental Assembly.[37] After taking office, the new government discovered another unacknowledged debt to cover outstanding payments to state employees fired by the previous incumbent.[38] Negret had started negotiating the restructuring of the accumulated debt in March 2000, at which time it looked like his hand-picked successor, the Liberal Party candidate, would win the election. Had he won, the indications are that the repayment schedule would have been less onerous and more manageable, a point made by a columnist at *El Informativo*, an independent weekly published in Popayán.[39] However, it appears that, with Tunubalá's victory, the conditions were rewritten and made much stricter, according to several members of Tunubalá's cabinet. At no time during the two-month period following his election did the government consult him or any of his designated cabinet members. The agreement was a done deal, completed with no participation whatsoever on the part of the incoming government.

The onerous nature of these debt obligations can be better understood by placing them in the context of the department's financial statements from 2001 to 2004. For the period in question, total annual revenue remained relatively constant, and the gradual increase was primarily the result of improved tax collection.[40] What is particularly striking about these numbers, however, is the heavy dependency on the central government in the form of financial transfers through the Sistema General de Participaciones, which was restricted for use almost exclusively in the education sector: 84 percent in 2001, 80 percent in 2002, and 72 percent in 2003.[41] A much smaller percentage was utilized for the provision of general public services: 19 percent in 2001, 12 percent in 2002, and 19 percent in 2003.

The magnitude of the challenge facing Tunubalá's government of cannot be overstated since the debt had to be repaid out of savings made on the revenue generated by the department, which was never very much in the first place but was designated primarily for running the government, which included everything from the payment of salaries to the upkeep of vehicles. Law 617 of 2000 mandated that in such situations the estimated "regular" budget had to be reduced by 30 percent. In this case, the savings were to be achieved primarily through a reduction in personnel: 99 people out of a total workforce of 240 were to be dismissed. Revenue at the departmental level came primarily from taxes of various sorts. In 2003 the department generated 19 percent of its total revenue, 49 percent of which came from the consumption of liquor produced by La Licorera, the government-owned distillery, as well as additional taxes on beer consumption and gasoline. In addition, personal taxes in the form of income taxes and property taxes had increased by 17 percent over the previous year. Furthermore, the government had paid off the outstanding debts in three of the four categories (labor and pensions, public entities, social security, and other creditors). Only one category, the largest, remained, which included financial entities and credits from the national government.[42] But the government of Tunubalá accepted the conditions imposed by the agreement as written. The departmental Chamber of Commerce congratulated it for its rigorous fulfillment of the agreement, which provided the necessary conditions of stability and viability, such that by 2004, the year after Tunubalá stepped down, the department was able to generate funds for social investment.[43]

What the Tunubalá government found particularly galling was the fact that each year the department generated a surplus, which, under the terms of the agreement, was automatically applied to repaying the debt. As a result, Tunubalá had very few resources and little leeway to finance any additional activities at the local level. This had immediate implications for the new government. In his capacity as governmental secretary, Henry Caballero, who was often the first cabinet member to arrive on the scene after an outbreak of violence, often felt frustrated and powerless because the government had little material support to offer. This inability to assist also had political implications, and local perceptions of the government changed accordingly:

> We would arrive at some tragedy, and let's say not even in terms of providing a coffin or something because there was nothing. . . . So the very presence was very wearing. So if you did not arrive as a representative of the government, it was a problem since in some way it showed that we were not showing solidarity with those communities or that we were not denouncing the events that were happening.[44]

However, it was not just the lack of funds to deal with emergencies that was frustrating. Equally galling was the lack of funds to "do development." With the exception of health and education, which were directly financed by the central government, there was little or no government support for productive investment in programs and projects. As a result, Tunubalá was obliged to look elsewhere—to North America and especially to Europe, where his Alternate Plan, with its focus on social development, was viewed as an appealing alternative to the more aggressive security and drug-eradication strategy pursued by the U.S. government under its Plan Colombia. Often dressed in Guambiano attire, Tunubalá became, in fact, an ambassador for Cauca and Colombia. These trips were effective inasmuch as they provided support for various types of development programs, some of which were implemented only after Tunubalá had stepped down from office.

THE ALTERNATE PLAN

On these trips Tunubalá presented his Alternate Plan (El Plan Alterno) as an antidote to the U.S.-supported Plan Colombia, a national program designed to fight the guerrillas. Plan Colombia proposed to accomplish this in two ways: first, by strengthening the army and the police, and second, by reducing, if not eliminating, the production of illegal crops through aerial fumigation and replacing them with more socially acceptable but less profitable agricultural crops and commodities (Departamento del Cauca 2001). Better known outside Colombia, where international donors viewed it much more favorably than did the national government, the Alternate Plan proposed a number of radical ways of reorganizing the political and developmental culture of Cauca. The agenda included a focus on popular participation, viable alternatives to illegal crops, direct negotiations with the guerrillas, and a form of regional autonomy from neighboring departments. It was even well received by the U.S. Department of State, which Tunubalá visited on three occasions. Tunubalá recalled these visits as follows:

They [the U.S. State Department] said, "No, at the end of the day you are right in [opposing] aerial spraying. For the first time we are seeing six governors [from southwestern Colombia] of territorial entities defending what is yours. That's the policy and it's good. But we are part of the government, and here it is the president who calls the shots." At that time it was Clinton, on the first visit. "We are part of Clinton's team, and he has ordered aerial spraying of illicit crops. That's why we are going to spray."[45]

In an interview given after his first year in office, Tunubalá stressed the process followed in preparing the plan, which was strongly participatory and attempted to capture the diversity of Cauca and include as many different perspectives as possible—indigenous, peasant, intellectual, academic, worker, and so on (Jaramillo Salgado 2001). The document itself is short, only thirty-seven pages long, divided into five sections, and although it focuses primarily on alternative ways to deal with illegal crops, the first section provides the context and justification (Departamento del Cauca 2001). The plan emphasizes the untapped development potential of Cauca with regard to its natural environment and its cultural diversity. It also highlights the importance of the people of Cauca and their potential role in changing the situation, based on their local development plans, but with much broader objectives than the usual productive and economic goals, specifically the reconstruction of the social fabric (*el tejido social*), which holds society together.

The plan proposes a general strategy for resolving the major issues confronting Cauca, ranging from the manual eradication of illegal crops and their replacement with legal, economically viable alternatives, the creation of chains of production with the direct involvement of the private sector, to a more equitable distribution of health services. What distinguishes this development plan from more conventional ones is the attention that it places on human rights, the rule of law, and the strengthening of civil society, specifically the indigenous movement and the social organizations that helped elect Tunubalá in the first place. The objective was to empower these groups to participate in solving the ongoing armed conflict. At the same time the plan pressured the government to deliver on its earlier promises to social organizations (a recurring complaint) to recognize and assist the victims of the war, those directly affected and those displaced; to initiate land reform in the province, a very sensitive political issue; and to protect the environment since the headwaters of four of Colombia's major rivers are in El Macizo. Furthermore, this plan proposed a regional approach involving several of the neighboring departments, where alternative governments were also in power, developing an idea for territorial redistribution that was proposed in the 1991 constitution but never implemented (Departamento de Nariño 2001).

The plan was a direct challenge to the neoliberal policies pursued by the national government. First, in shaping society, the emphasis was on social organizations rather than the private sector or the government. Although both the private sector and the government still had important roles to play, social organizations, regarded with suspicion by those in power, would play an increasingly important role. Second, the plan proposed a regional approach to solving economic and political issues. In the case of drugs, for example, it argued for a more humane procedure, combined with sustainable economic alternatives. In the case of security, it argued for the right of departmental governors to negotiate directly with the guerrillas, a tactic roundly rejected by the national government. Up to this point, the national government had regarded regional movements with a certain trepidation. Moreover, security was the prerogative of the president and his cabinet. Third, the plan proposed a more equitable approach to development: it would include not just the marginalized but also the displaced, a growing issue in Cauca when the plan was written and one that continues today. Fourth, it emphasized the importance of protecting natural resources and the environment, an issue that has only grown in importance in the past decade. In essence, the plan argued for a more socially responsible form of government, while at the same time encouraging more active participation by all sectors of society.

The plan was produced by the social organizations that participated in the successful blockade of the Pan-American Highway in November 1999. A few months later, in February 2000, the organizations got together to discuss the unfulfilled promises of the national government and began a process of uniting their efforts to make the government comply with its obligations. This meeting marked the birth of the process that would culminate in the Plan Alterno. Meetings continued over the ensuing months and, once the BSA was formed at the end of July, it took over. The BSA was aware that, if Tunubalá elected, he would have credibility as the leader of an alternative government only if they produced something quite distinct from Plan Colombia, which was then in the process of being implemented. The body of the plan, more a call to arms than a blueprint for action, was produced before Tunubalá took office, and, although there are various drafts, the one generally used to negotiate dates from his first month in office. Much of the substance was produced during a two-day workshop held a month after Tunubalá was elected and a mere five weeks before he took office, on January 1, 2001. Titled *Encuentro de organizaciones sociales: Construcción de alternativas al Plan Colombia*, the workshop brought together 1,500 participants, many of whom belonged to organizations that were part of the BSA and had supported Tunubalá's campaign. The workshop was held in La María, thirty kilometers north of Popayán on a bluff overlooking the Pan-American Highway, mentioned earlier in this chapter, and site of a large mobilization of 12,000 people by the indigenous movement the previous year (1999), which had closed the highway for eleven days. La María was established later that year to mark the five-hundredth anniversary of the Spanish invasion of the Americas. The objective was to create an alternative political space where civil society could resolve conflicts and negotiate peace (Consejo Regional Indígena del Cauca n.d.). In the intervening years, La María has continued to play this role by hosting a variety of activities and events (often critical of the state) where subaltern counterpublics can "formulate oppositional interpretations of their identities, interests, and needs" (Fraser 1997, 81).

Although anthropology has made important contributions to the analysis of development plans as forms of discourse (Escobar 1995; Grillo 1997), more recent work has been critical of their "discursive determinism" (Moore 2000) and has argued, at least in the case of documents produced by international donors, that they cannot be read at face value without reference to the arguments, interests, and different perspectives they include, explicitly or implicitly. Such texts have to be reinterpreted to reveal the social relations that produced them: "In short, a sociology of the document is needed . . . [where] policy ideas (especially ambiguous ones like good governance, ownership, or civil society) take social form, being important less for *what* they say than *who* they bring together; how they enrol, unite, or divide" (Mosse 2005, 15).

Given the importance attached to this document, one can argue that the process by means of which the plan was created was just as important as the actual substance, for it demonstrated the potential to form an alternative government that would be participatory, democratic, and willing to oppose the state's neoliberal policies, including Plan Colombia. While the Plan Alterno is usually thought of as a product of Tunubalá's government, it was in fact a product of the social organizations that helped elect him. This is an extremely important point, one that was forcefully driven home by Milton Guzmán, a cabinet member: "We did not produce the Alternate Plan. The Alternate Plan was produced by the social organizations before the time of Floro's government. That is not a legacy of ours."[46]

The workshop followed the standard format used on such occasions: guest speakers, key questions, group work, reports, and plenary session. One of the guest speakers, a long-time activist in charge of communications in CRIC, raised two key questions in his presentation: First, will it be possible for the social organizations to propose an Alternate Plan and a moral condemnation of the consequences of Plan Colombia? And second, with whom are we going to negotiate an Alternate Plan if the national government depends on the United States and the International Monetary Fund? (La María 2000, 14–15). These questions informed the work of the groups that were dealing with production; the environment; civil and political rights; economic, social, and cultural rights; and the rights of the people. These groups raised most of the issues dealt with in the actual Alternate Plan but went out of their way to reiterate the importance of building on the plans already produced at the municipal and community levels; the experience gained earlier in the year when negotiating with the state during the two blockades of the Pan-American Highway; the rights guaranteed in the 1991 constitution; and the organizational capacity to make their own decisions.[47]

A SYMBOL OF THE POSSIBLE

The fact that Tunubalá and several members of his deliberative elite should regard the Plan Alterno as their most important legacy should be viewed in the larger context in which it was produced. Although the document itself and the process that made it possible occurred at a specific moment, its appeal and importance are historical, political, economic, and symbolic. The document is historical because it built on the recent efforts and experiences of others, particularly the M-19 and the MAQL, the Constitutional Assembly, the Paro del Macizo, and the creation of La María. It is political because it challenges the status quo and the prevailing power relations within the department and proposes a regional basis for dealing with the central government. It is also economic since it argues for land reform and a more equitable system of economic production. What is most striking about the plan is that it proposes little that is radically new or different; much of it is based on ideas and proposals already prevalent at that time in left-wing and progressive organizations in Cauca and neighboring provinces. What is new and different is the integration of these various strands of thinking into a single document through a process of participatory democracy and elite deliberation, a document that at one time was better known and more highly regarded outside Colombia than within it. There is, however, one radical aspect. In the plan, Tunubalá and his government were questioning the authority and credibility of the president, first Pastrana and then Uribe, since foreign policy and domestic security are the president's constitutional prerogatives, a crucial aspect of the challenge to neoliberalism discussed earlier.

In terms of everyday politics and the conditions and constraints under which Tunubalá and his cabinet took office, one can argue that they achieved a great deal during their three years in office, whether it was fiscal responsibility (paying off the department's inherited debts), confronting the FARC head on and effectively demonstrating that it was not an acceptable alternative, achieving advances in education and health, although both fields were affected by privatization policies, and proving that it was possible to have honest government at the departmental level. Their alternative government did contribute to stronger feelings of collective identity (Bebbington, Delamaza, and Villar 2006) by pursuing the interests of the department as a whole rather than catering to the special interests of the individual members of the BSA. However, this also proved to be their Achilles' heel: the coalition that elected Tunubalá did not endure for long after the election, a circumstance that severely limited the possibility of institutional innovation. This supports Van Cott's (2008) argument about sustainability, mentioned earlier, and the importance of determining whether such innovations can survive a change of administration and contribute to better governance. If there is no institutional base (e.g., a political party or a social movement) to support the innovations, then they will not survive. If they do, it will be in symbolic form, such as the Alternate Plan.

As a result of her work in Ecuador, Paley (2009) emphasizes the important role that social movements can play in supporting alternative governments in the areas of accountability, transparency, program proposals, and leadership development. More crucial is their support in transcending departmental and national boundaries and linking up with transnational networks, as well as sustaining the struggle for civil, human, and cultural rights. During Tunubalá's alternative government, this rights-based struggle was an important component of his agenda, but it did not become institutionalized. Without institutionalization, his successor could comfortably revert to the status quo ante, that is, the situation prevailing when Tunubalá entered office three years earlier. The social movement that had coalesced to support his candidacy and election did not endure. If it had, his government might have been more effective, and the movement might have consolidated its support behind a more appealing candidate who would have continued the work started by Tunabalá's alternative government. But that did not happen.

One can argue that the Alternate Plan operationalizes what Dagnino (2003, 215), in her discussion of citizenship mentioned earlier, called citizens' right for full inclusion and the right to participate in the definition of society and its political system. This was the rationale for the focus on social organizations, themselves the products of a violent and conflict-ridden context, one that perhaps made possible the emergence of a government such as Tunubalá's. If this is the case, it would substantiate Sanford's (2004, 257) argument that citizenship and sovereignty can be reconstituted at the margins of the state, in places such as Cauca. But such reconstitution comes at a price. Tunubalá had to deal not only with violence, drugs, poverty, and repayment of the department's accumulated debts but also with a hostile national government that justified many of its actions in the name of neoliberalism. The Alternate Plan remains as a symbol of the possible, indeed, proof that good people do exist and that hope has not been extinguished.

CHAPTER 5

NEOLIBERAL REFORMS AND PROTEST IN BUENOS AIRES

Marcela Cerrutti and Alejandro Grimson

Translated by Nancy Postero and Adriana Salcedo

IN THE CONTEXT OF LATIN AMERICA, THE case of Buenos Aires and Argentina stands out as extreme in various ways. Argentina was one of the countries where neoliberal reforms were implemented in the most radical way, and because of this, both the social structure and the structure of labor opportunities were transformed. Similarly, the landscape of popular organizations, their forms of action, and their agendas and claims have changed as protests have intensified over time.

For most of the twentieth century, Argentine society distinguished itself from its neighbors by its large middle class and relatively egalitarian social structure. However, since the last coup d'état, in 1976, Argentina has experienced a significant transformation linked to the abandonment of the import substitution industrialization (ISI) model and the adoption of a new neoliberal model based on economic opening and deregulation. Radical changes in the economy were accompanied by a set of institutional transformations, the most salient of which was the transformation of the role of the state. Liberalization of markets, including the labor market, has been a central pillar of the policies implemented since the early 1990s. Although many Latin American countries have adopted neoliberal policies in the last two decades, Argentina is perhaps a paradigmatic case because of the radical application of these policies and the celerity of the process. In the late 1990s Argentina occupied a special place both for the dimension of its economic downturn and the significant deterioration in the standards of living of its population, as well as for the diverse responses that emerged from civil society.

This chapter describes the drastic transformations experienced by Argentine society and the diverse civil society responses during this process, focusing on the metropolitan area of Buenos Aires. We examine the effects of neoliberal policies on the capacity of the productive structure to generate jobs and, consequently, income for its inhabitants; on the spatial expression of the changes in the structure of opportunities; and on the different forms of popular reaction. We begin by briefly examining the changes in the economic and institutional model and its social effects. In this sense, we analyze the main tendencies in labor markets, particularly those related to unemployment, the precariousness of employment, and the evolution of the informal sector. Elsewhere, we have addressed the impacts of these transformations on income distribution, the growth of poverty, and spatial segmentation of the population in greater detail (Cerrutti and Grimson 2004). Here we focus on the different responses by civil society to these major transformations. Specifically, we analyze the changes in the agendas of popular sectors, as well as the different types of organizations, forms of identification, and action.

FROM THE CRISIS OF THE SUBSTITUTIVE MODEL TO THE NEOLIBERAL MODEL

Since the early 1970s, the institutions and policies that dominated the period of import substitution were transformed or openly dismantled. The crisis of the substitution model and the adoption of structural adjustment policies and economic deregulation constitute a complex process carried out over two decades. As in many Latin American countries, the tools used during the substitution period were tariff protection, subsidies to industrial activities, and the state's broad intervention in the economy (Thorp 1994). Until the 1950s, the process of industrialization was mainly labor intensive, based on import substitution of nondurable goods for local production. During this period, the development of industry was linked to satisfying growing domestic consumption by an expanding working class (Dorfman 1983). During those years, the economic, social, and political centrality of Buenos Aires was reinforced. Economies of scale and an expanding consumer market stimulated the establishment and concentration of manufacturing and a broad set of services in the metropolitan area of Buenos Aires.[1]

Despite its relative success, especially since World War II, the import-substitution strategy began to show its weaknesses in Argentina, mainly as a result of the endemic lack of dynamism in exports (Mallon and Sourrouille 1975). The critical problem of the trade balance, when added to the sharp conflicts over distribution, recurring political crises, and changes in international conditions, led to a long period (1975–1990) of crisis and economic stagnation (which included a disastrous attempt to liberalize the economy between 1976 and 1982) and was exacerbated by the need to administer a huge external debt. With the arrival of democracy in 1984, the economy was strangled by external debt payments. The government tried repeatedly and without much success to stabilize the economy and meet its external obligations.

Although the Economic Commission for Latin America and the Caribbean has characterized the 1980s as the "lost decade" for Latin America as a whole, Argentina was one of the countries that suffered most of all. As an example, between 1981 and 1989 its gross domestic product fell by 23.5 percent (Comisión Económica para America Latina y el Caribe 1997). In the early 1990s and with a new government led by the Justicialista Party, an aggressive combination of stabilization policies, deregulation, and structural reforms began being implemented (Bustos 1995; Centro de Estudios Bonaerenses 1995). The principal policies adopted were a currency convertibility system,[2] the privatization of enterprises and public services, the deregulation of capital and labor markets, fiscal reform, and regional integration (MERCOSUR, or the Common Market of the South). These policies had a series of negative impacts on both the economic structure and the labor market.

Using special powers,[3] the government privatized the main public companies (e.g., gas and oil production, telephone, electricity, water, trains), reduced or eliminated certain mining and industrial production, and deregulated the financial system. In this way, it first reduced employer contributions to the social security system, then privatized it and also introduced a reform to the labor law, aimed at lowering the costs of hiring and firing. These policies significantly increased Argentina's foreign trade.[4] However, the combination of economic liberalization measures and increasingly overvalued currency resulted in a significant imbalance between imports and exports. The most obvious impact was the crisis of local industry and the growing problems in the trade balance.

For a few years after 1991, the economy not only suffered terrible inflation but also showed high growth,[5] sustained largely by an influx of foreign capital into the newly privatized enterprises and other short-term investments. Despite economic growth, unemployment began to rise (from 5.2 percent in 1991 to 12.2 percent in 1994). In 1995, the new model suffered a massive flight of foreign capital as a result of the rise of interest rates in the United States and the 1994 crisis in Mexico. The inflexibility of the convertibility system, which was unable to mitigate the impacts of shock, and the lack of active social policies led to a historic leap in the already high unemployment rate (from 12 percent in 1994 to more than 18 percent in 1995) and poverty levels.

It was not until late 1996 that the economy began to show signs of recovery. However, this recovery did not last long: in 1998 the economy again went into recession and continued to deteriorate. In late 2001, the acute social and economic situation, coupled with apparent government inaction, triggered a dramatic institutional crisis that culminated in the overthrow of the new government, which had emerged in opposition to former president Carlos Menem (1989–1999). The transitional government that emerged from that crisis ended the convertibility plan. The consequence was a sharp devaluation, which, in economic terms, quickly began to have positive effects on the trade balance and the production of local goods. In 2003, a new elected government took power. This new government, while also Justicialista, also proclaimed a paradigm shift.

Much has changed in Argentina since this crisis, as we discuss later. Yet the late 1990s and early 2000s were a defining moment with regard to the ways in which popular organizations resisted and adapted to neoliberal policies.

CIVIL RESPONSES TO NEOLIBERAL TRANSFORMATIONS

Civil society responded in various ways to the social panorama described earlier. Different historical phases give rise to diverse types of organizations that have a range of claims, identities, and modes of action. Argentina has a strong union tradition and a dense organizational network in neighborhoods. State terrorism during the military dictatorship resulted in the murder and disappearance of almost an entire generation of popular and student leaders. Despite this, during the 1980s, when the country was once again under constitutional rule, intense protests calling attention to human rights, unions, housing, and education took place.

The contrast between the ideological and cultural environment of the 1970s and 1990s is obviously significant. Labor unions were central actors in Argentina's political life in the 1970s. During the five and a half years of Raúl Alfonsín's government (1983–1989) alone, the General Labor Confederation called thirteen general strikes. In contrast, the 1990s were characterized by the loss of labor's leadership role and the emergence of new phenomena. When Perón came to power in 1989 and with the extreme application of neoliberal prescriptions by President Carlos Menem, the big labor unions became *officialistas*, or government supporters. Integrated into the administration, labor negotiations focused on issues such as management of the unions' welfare funds and limits on immigration, while the unemployment rate grew by 300–400 percent.

During the rise of neoliberalism in Argentina, a broad social consensus was necessary to establish a system of convertibility of the peso and the dollar, which continued until January 2002. After an initial wave of strikes and protests to avert the wave of privatization, the big unions (which were already losing members) were co-opted by the Judicialista government. Meanwhile, for their part, many members of the middle class were seduced by access to consumer goods through credit and wages, which were paid in dollars, and thereby endorsed the new policies, which promised quick access to First-World status.[6]

During the early 1990s, certain features of the social protests of the previous decade were consolidated. There was

> an abundant mobilization of collective resources, . . . a high degree of fragmentation and low durability in the protests . . . , a concentration of union-related claims in service and state unions . . . , a growing array of civic protest with a markedly diversified nature and with clear features of location and singularity. Therefore, they were highly fragmented and unlikely to build subjects unified through action with any permanence in time or extension in space. (Schuster and Pereyra 2001, 59–60)

Nevertheless, by the end of the decade, this situation had changed. Subjects with new identities had appeared, such as the *piqueteros*,[7] organizations of unemployed people who organized roadblocks, or workers who reclaimed factories. It is therefore necessary to distinguish at least two moments in the 1990s: the first phase of the neoliberal boom (expressed by the reelection of President Menem in 1995) and a phase of crisis. Growing economic stagnation and outright recession since the second half of 1998 combined with a political legitimacy that was slowly undermined by an increase in poverty, unemployment, and corruption. Meanwhile, new organizations and modes of popular protest began emerging with varying intensity. After intense strikes in 1989 and 1990, the protests declined dramatically until they began to escalate slightly with the increase in roadblocks in 1997.

The model's crisis of legitimacy and the dramatic economic predicament grew until the situation reached a critical point in December 2001. In a context of recession, high unemployment, and the banking crisis, the government was paralyzed except for a decision to drastically restrict access to money deposited in banks (*el corralito*). This resulted in a *cacerolazo*[8] on December 19 and mobilizations on December 20, which culminated in the resignation of the president. In December 2001, 859 cacerolazos took place; in January 2002, 706; in February, 310; and in March, only 139. In fact, it is likely that in 2002 there were more street demonstrations than in the prior fifteen years.

At least five popular organizational processes that are worth highlighting developed between the late 1990s and 2003. First, barter networks were formed, through which people tried to resolve or at least alleviate money shortages by informally exchanging goods or knowledge with others. At its peak, these networks involved two million people (Hintze 2003). Second, popular or community kitchens expanded, receiving funding from local governments and eventually private donors. These guaranteed a meal or a glass of milk to children and adults who were on the brink of poverty. Third, groups of unemployed workers emerged and expanded, organizing to demand work and "employment plans" from the state to ensure their subsistence. Fourth, neighborhood assemblies appeared, mostly in middle-class neighborhoods. Their mobilization and commitment responded not only to the economic necessity of assembly members (who did not necessarily have bank accounts or were homeless or unemployed) but also to the larger political and institutional crisis of representation. Finally, we draw attention to the many factories and other businesses that were reclaimed by their workers after bankruptcies, closures, or abandonment by their previous owners.

These measures arose at different times to respond to different conflicts. The neighborhood assemblies were formed as a consequence of the currency crisis of December 2001. The organizations of unemployed workers date back to the second half of the 1990s (in Greater Buenos Aires, they began to appear in 1997). The popular kitchens emerged in the late 1980s, during the hyperinflation crisis, after which the meal plans run by the state were restricted. The barter-exchange nodes appeared in the mid-1990s. The majority of the factories were taken over and recovered by their workers in late 2001 as a collective response to the loss of jobs in a grim situation.

Each of these processes had a different dynamic. Barter underwent an explosion from late 2001 until mid-2002, and then a major crisis and subsequent disruption led to its disappearance as a social phenomenon. Popular assemblies boomed in the first half of 2002 but began to decline rapidly. Although a few assemblies continue in specific neighborhoods, compared to the ways in which the middle classes were involved socially and politically during that time, they have lost their importance today. This is precisely because these sectors gradually withdrew from such participation. In contrast, the phenomena associated with the poor had a different dynamic. The popular kitchens, organizations of unemployed workers, and reclaimed factories continued to operate. This does not mean that they did not change. In fact, a certain institutionalization was evident, as well as fragmentation and a crisis within the piquetero phenomenon and the political dynamic still operating in the recovered enterprises.

Now, how can one study these responses? Immediately after the 2001 crisis, there were many simplistic analyses of the "radical change" in the political culture of popular sectors, as well as of the traditional political parties' ability to rebuild legitimacy and hegemony. On the other hand, with the subsequent stabilization, GDP growth, and strong evidence of fragmentation of the popular sector, most argued that this was just a crisis like so many others and that everything has remained the same. In our discussion of the transformations, we position ourselves between those who warned of a total breakdown and those who guaranteed complete continuity.

THE AGENDA OF THE POPULAR SECTORS IN FOUR BUENOS AIRES NEIGHBORHOODS: FROM HOUSING TO WORK

We carried out ethnographic research in four Buenos Aires neighborhoods between November 2002 and July 2003.[9] These studies were complemented with a close monitoring of political processes in the media and four other contemporary case studies. To understand the processes of organization and collective action in Buenos Aires we developed a territorial approach, analyzing a diverse set of individuals within a particular locale (Portes and Walton 1976, 73). We studied the organizational and political life of popular neighborhoods. We chose the four areas for the diversity of their histories, traditions, and problems, seeking to express the various structural processes of four different metropolitan areas: a *villa miseria* (shantytown) in the center of the city of Buenos Aires; an *asentamiento* (informal settlement) in a southern suburb of Greater Buenos Aires; an area with settlements and workers' neighborhoods in the west; and a popular working-class district in the northwest.[10]

During the import substitution model (and its demise), the urbanization process was unable to deal adequately with the central issues of housing and living conditions (e.g., public lighting, sanitation, water) in these neighborhoods. This problem was generalized throughout the metropolitan areas of the region. Portes and Walton have argued that "rather than occupational or income needs, it is the demand for housing that has most effectively politicized the poor" (1976, 74). As mentioned earlier, compared with other Latin American countries, in Argentina, unions have played an exceptionally important role in previous decades. However, if we look at the popular neighborhoods, the stories of shantytowns and informal settlements show a gradual and extensive improvement in housing. Although this is an ongoing issue in urban areas, the rise in unemployment and underemployment during the 1990s displaced housing as the principal concern in these neighborhoods. Thus, even though housing was a key element of popular organizing during the import substitution model, work became the primary rallying point in Buenos Aires after the rise of neoliberalism.

The neighborhoods in which the study was conducted clearly illustrated these transformations. The urbanization process in Buenos Aires was accompanied by a shortage of legally habitable land. New neighborhood organizations were born as a response to the problems of urban space and access to services. These groups, along with the unions, were of prime importance for these areas in the late 1980s. Neighborhood organizations originated for various purposes: to occupy new lands, to distribute lots collectively, to defend spontaneous land occupations against "eradication" by the government (this was very common during the military dictatorship of the late 1970s), to look for a better way to integrate the neighborhood into the city, and to work for a better quality of life. There were also sports and cultural groups and eventually several that addressed municipal taxes (González Bombal 1989).

In many neighborhoods in the midnineties, the housing problem seems to have found possible solutions (asphalt, services, and, in a few cases, land tenure), although the unemployment rate increasingly affected the households and the social networks to which they belonged. This resulted in a transformation of the political agenda of the urban poor. In Greater Buenos Aires, some organizations that had emerged in the 1980s to claim land and housing were transformed in the second half of the 1990s into organizations of unemployed workers, who demanded employment and employment policies from the state. A key organization emerged, the Movimiento de Trabajadores Desocupados (Movement of Unemployed Workers, or MTD). In other cases, there was not such a direct continuity, but neighborhoods with a history of collective struggle for land coincided with those with strong organizations of unemployed workers. This shift from an agenda of land/housing to work is part of a broader movement. An analysis of popular neighborhoods indicates a combination of a strong Peronist clientelist network, a scarcity of other political organizations, and development of new religious groups before 1997 or 1998 (Semán 2000). When we compare this situation to that of the first half of the 1970s or the 1980s, we see a historic change that is a product of the transition from a place with "high organizational density and levels of political mobilization . . . to a space characterized by organizational desertification and low levels of political mobilization" (Auyero 2001a, 62).

Therefore, the sociopolitical diagnosis of "organizational desertification" was placed in a context of transition where (besides the dictatorship's disruptive impact) the impulses of urbanization in the neighborhoods had diminished, given some limited improvements. Meanwhile, the unemployment issue had already become the central problem but was still without any organizational response. At this stage, in contrast to European countries, which have strong state policies on unemployment, for the unemployed in Argentina, "instead of the centrality of rights and public policies, the market [appeared] as the only possible scenario with which to try to overcome the situation" (Kessler 1996, 112).

THE EMERGENCE OF UNEMPLOYED ORGANIZATIONS

During the early 1990s, organizational processes in Greater Buenos Aires were marked by crisis and disorientation. As grassroots organizations disappeared or lost members, the importance of clientelistic relations grew. Neighborhoods that had been "bedroom communities" for factory workers with very low unemployment rates became neighborhoods of unemployed workers. Various forms of activism emerged, sometimes through patronage networks and sometimes through independent organizations such as collective community kitchens and open-air meal centers. Basically, these groups demanded more food from the state, free bus fares for the unemployed, medicine, and similar types of assistance.

One of these organizations in Florencio Varela decided to imitate the roadblocks that had been organized in the interior of the country. Its members blocked a route for several days and, in response, received from the government several hundred "social plans" for the unemployed. Social plans were a form of unemployment compensation in which the beneficiary received a fixed monthly payment.[11] That achievement of the Varela organization of unemployed workers transformed the agenda of many small grassroots groups. Demands for social plans began to spread. Those plans—designed during the

Menem administration to appease the voters in the interior of the country before the election—were extended after the elections in 1997, but more organizations began calling for them.

The groups were generally unable to obtain enough plans to assist everyone in need. However, their limited success brought new unemployed people to the organizations, thus expanding demand. As a result of the additional requests, the government tried to cancel or reduce the plans, sometimes by raising questions about legal requirements. To counteract these tactics, the people pressured the bureaucrats in the state ministries and agencies and at the same time pushed for additional new plans.

The beneficiaries were required to work as a "counterpart" in exchange for the benefit, which usually meant they would perform tasks supervised by the municipality. Thus, every time an organization of unemployed individuals successfully obtained these plans, it lost members: those who received the benefits found themselves carrying out activities controlled by the local governments and even by the *punteros* (local leaders) of the parties that they had fought against. They began demanding that the labor they contributed be carried out within their own organizations. This allowed them to develop different productive and communitarian enterprises (e.g., bakeries, brick making factories, sewing and tailoring ventures, construction) while keeping their membership. Thus, these individuals worked for their organizations and mobilized to demand more social programs for their unemployed neighbors. By the time this had become an established system, the grassroots organizations of unemployed workers had become a sort of union.

This process combined two key elements of urban space—the neighborhood and transportation—in a particular way. In the neoliberal period, a new layer of segregation was added to the classic segregation of neighborhoods already typical of Buenos Aires, converting the neighborhood into a sort of overall institution of misery. Without work, people could not even pay for transportation out of their neighborhoods. The confinement was not legal but economic. This was one neighborhood parameter around which the unemployed organized. How did these people, who were increasingly immobile and locked up in their neighborhoods, protest? First, they blocked streets, traffic, and the general movement of the city to prevent—as much as possible—urban life from continuing as if they did not exist. As the organizations joined forces, gathered more neighbors, and coordinated with other districts, they did not block the traffic on just any street or road. They realized they could protest on the urban border par excellence: the bridges linking the capital with Greater Buenos Aires. In the southern part of the city, those bridges cross the river known as El Riachuelo. This area was the first industrial zone and, therefore, the oldest working-class neighborhood. Currently full of abandoned factories, it has a high proportion of poor and unemployed residents, in contrast to the northern part of the city. In a city with a number of borders, these areas can become scenarios of social protest. The bridges that cross those borders became shared scenarios of political dispute. Within this framework, the piqueteros came to imagine the possibility of protesting by blocking access to the federal capital at these sites. El Puente Pueyrredón, the main southern viaduct, became a key site for their actions. A violent police crackdown took place on that bridge on June 26, 2002, which culminated in the murder of two piqueteros. In fact, the widespread condemnation of these killings led interim President Dualde to advance by six months the handing over of his administration to his successor.

THE "UNEMPLOYED HEAD OF HOUSEHOLD PLAN" AND POPULAR ORGANIZATIONS

In Buenos Aires, any attempt to characterize a popular organization must address at least three inevitable questions. First, how many plans does it have? That is, how many people in a particular organization give their counterpart labor to the Plan Jefas y Jefes de Hogar Desocupados (Unemployed Heads of Household Plan, or PJHD)? Second, how does the organization get those plans? And third, how does it distribute them? In other words, all people's organizations either have been transformed by the PJHD or, because of it, have managed to become intermediaries between the state and the people. The few that have decided not to manage these plans now represent very few people.[12]

The government advertised the PJHD as a right that beneficiaries could process without intermediaries, in contrast to previous unemployment plans. To receive benefits, one had to go directly to the municipal distribution centers, comply with the requirements, and then would receive the benefit. The plans are distributed by the National Ministry of Work through the advisory councils, where the municipality has a strong presence and acts as the implementation agency for the plans. There is coordination by locality to reach specific organizations where the counterpart labor is to be done. The creation of the councils with the proposal that the unemployment organizations be integrated with them sparked a debate about the co-opting of these (until then independent) organizations through the plans. Thus, although the massive activist groups in one of the communities we studied, La Matanza, were integrated, the autonomous organizations of the south and those linked to leftist political parties refused to follow suit. At the same time, the media began distinguishing between "hard piqueteros" and "soft piqueteros."

In Greater Buenos Aires, approximately 5 percent of the inhabitants had a plan of this kind by 2003. At the national level, there were approximately two million plans, of which only 5 percent (approximately 100,000 plans) were administered by organizations of unemployed workers; the rest were managed by local governments. This number implies that the jobs the municipality assigned—such as sweeping and digging up streets and even administrative projects—were insufficient for all those who needed work. To find additional projects, the local governments signed up organizations and institutions where counterpart labor could be done. For example, with sometimes more and sometimes less political favoritism, the municipality would send around ten beneficiaries to a neighborhood kitchen that used to rely on volunteers. As a result, any social organization could be turned into a potential site of counterpart labor. Thus, although in theory there was no need for intermediaries to apply for benefits from the plan, the need for counterpart labor implied in practice that either the organizations where the work could be done could apply for the plans or the municipality could offer them. So, in a popular neighborhood in Buenos Aires, almost any neighborhood organization now administers a certain number of plans. Community kitchens, microentrepreneurial businesses, daycare centers, nongovernmental organizations (NGOs), and housing cooperatives all administer plans, as do workers' organizations at reclaimed factories and associations of unemployed workers. Obviously, many organizations have created an enormous number of work groups to absorb the counterpart labor positions. This means that these people depend on these associations to carry out the counterpart service demanded by the state.

Thus, the plans represent a common element between organizations that are very heterogeneous in origin, performance, and types of projects. Nevertheless, significant differences between the organizations began appearing in the number of plans they offered, the way they obtained the plans, and the way they managed them. Since the number of plans that a group supervises is a sign of its power in the neighborhood, those that have one or two hundred plans are usually either aligned or allied with the municipal agency or are allowed to exercise social and political pressure relatively autonomously. In the latter case, this autonomy could not be linked to the municipality, as is demonstrated by organizations of the unemployed.

All of the organizations of unemployed workers obtained the first group of plans (known as *planes trabajar*) as a result of their demonstrations (blocking streets and bridges). In the years following, they also obtained plans through negotiations. The proportion of such plans among the piquetero organizations varies. Some of the groups (e.g., FTV) tended to negotiate without roadblocks, whereas others combined both elements. However, in every case, difficult deliberations were held with the state. The leader of a radicalized organization of the unemployed told us that "until the revolution is done, everything is negotiation; when negotiation is not needed, it is because you are stronger than they are." This formula, although expressed as a general organizational strategy, was the consequence of the government policy of extending plans in order to gauge the strength of a group. In other words, to enhance its position, the radicalized organization played a game of "push and pull" according to the dynamic of street strikes, loss of plans, threats of more blockades, negotiations, and so on. If the government policy became less flexible, it was very difficult for the radicalized sectors to consider negotiation while bolstering its forces.

As the plans were obtained through actual or potential direct action, the piquetero organizations made active participation in their demonstrations a requirement for membership. Such coercion, however, was highly debated in moral terms. It has been denounced as a mode of political clientelism by different state sectors. The organizations' point of view is that only those who are willing to fight may become members and that this obligation is a component of consciousness raising. All of this implies significant differences between the piquetero organizations, which obtain plans by themselves, and the NGOs and popular kitchens, which receive plans because of their direct links with the municipality.

The novelty of the piquetes' actions and the diverse types of social plans they administer made these organizations fascinating laboratories in which to test various questions from the social sciences. It became clear, however, that it was inappropriate to speak about the withdrawal of the state. After more than a decade of extreme neoliberalism, a state that was capable of distributing two million plans could not be described as "absent." One must be precise with regard to the aspects of the state that have been retracted and those that have been transformed; one must also analyze the relational and associative consequences of this process. In addition, the plans have presented different political questions to the social agents. Certain small groups from the piquetero movement criticized the acceptance of social plans inasmuch as they considered this a form of surrender to or co-optation by the state. From the state's perspective, the plans sometimes seemed to be a big mistake since the unemployed groups consolidated and grew politically as a result of these plans. From our point of view, both the state and the piqueteros assigned more power to the various actors than they really had, especially in specific political contexts. Such belief in the actors' agency obscures the fact that the relative stability of both the plans and the piqueteros at the end of 2002 was the result of a complex historical process, in which one side demanded many more things in addition to plans and the other side intended to give much less.

PLANS, WORK, AND POLITICS

For many of the plan beneficiaries, the meaning of the counterpart labor evolved from stopgap work to job. On the one hand, for a young person who has never worked, a project that lasts for four hours a day and brings in 150 pesos is easily understood as a part-time job. A number of youths who belonged to the piquetero organizations affirmed that "this is the job I have for now." On the other hand, many of those with an extensive working career do not consider these jobs an obligation to avoid but an opportunity to continue undertaking useful tasks in exchange for money. A particular segment of workers with twenty or more years of work experience and several years of unemployment see the plan as the recovery of lost dignity, dignity associated with work and a culture of work. Other beneficiaries, however, consider such work a fundamental resource that has resulted from the diversification of subsistence strategies.

The meaning given to the plan as "work" converged with the logic of governmentality. Evidently, the government reinforced the idea that the beneficiaries were no longer unemployed. That was how the Instituto Nacional de Estadística y Censos (National Institute of Statistics and Census, or INDEC) characterized it, saying this criterion reduces the unemployment rate in the country. This complex combination of the beneficiaries' own perception and the needs of the government in many cases transforms a program that was conceived of as a social policy to contain unemployment into a policy of employment.

With regard to the relationship between the organizations and the unemployed workers, it was inevitable that the plans would become an end in themselves for the vast majority of unemployed, who were members of the various organizations. This led them to belong to an organization in ways that went beyond a political commitment and/or identification with the specific objectives or principles of the organization. In many cases, membership in an organization made it possible for a worker to obtain a plan, which otherwise would have meant standing in long lines at distribution centers, mistreatment by municipal agents, travel costs, and a complete lack of protection on top of the stresses already felt due to unemployment and exclusion.

The question is whether the piquetero movements sought to transform not only the identity of the popular community association (previously Peronist) but also the relational model. In other words, did the piqueteros successfully transform the identification of certain popular sectors, or are they the result of a broader cultural transformation? The answer is nuanced. There may be organizations whose identity is not Peronist but that operate according to the cultural and relational model of Peronism. That is, they have identified themselves with other political traditions (in this case, the Left) but are forced to make the political linkages required by the Peronist political cultures and traditions that they say they reject.

When social demands increase (because people's own resources are reduced) or when the supply of public resources diminishes (because of budget or supply emergencies), a crisis arises in the social and political links, which, as happened in certain areas in 2001 and early 2002, can threaten subsistence. This generally implies a predicament for the clientelist network to the extent that the ties of reciprocity are broken and people need food and medicine, not explanations. When resources become scarce, protests increase. Nonetheless, it is rare for neighbors to organize autonomously and democratically in such situations. When this does happen, it is typically because of encounters between these neighbors and a group of social militants who are acting without particular interests. However, in general what happens is that, whether by contacting other clientelist organizations or by generating new intermediaries to replace the previous ones, a clientelist network reorganizes and replaces the earlier one. Even though in some cases this network remains in the Peronist orbit, a break with Peronism often occurs in terms of institutions and identification. It would be wrong to see such a rupture as absolute and general. It is not general because it involves only a few of the popular sectors. It is not absolute because it looks for new models of identity more than new relational models.

A number of organizations of the unemployed assume the disarming of clientelist linkages in particular and hierarchical linkages in general as a political objective. They try to distinguish themselves by avoiding "registering people in plans" as a means of expanding the movement. Instead, they offer a "place of struggle," an "organization to fight," or a "tool to fight for genuine work" and accept "plans that are won in the struggle" as a way of subsisting while the process evolves. New notions of autonomy and collective action are considered pedagogical objectives for a political project, and, with certain limitations, they have achieved some changes in the direction they proposed. However, the social relationships instituted by Peronist clientelism are present even in these organizations. In other words, the relational culture of Peronism works as a pole of attraction for organizational processes that oppose it. In piquetero organizations that openly reject any form of clientelism, we have witnessed didactic expositions by members who express frustration because a person who has participated for years in an organization continues asking for food as if the organization were a Peronist (assistentialist and clientelist) municipality. Moreover, other members adopt and greatly value the distinction between one type of link and another. Ultimately, one must distinguish between finding strong obstacles to proposal for change and basing a project on the reproduction of this relational culture.

We have explained this analysis to members of an MTD, an organization of unemployed workers. They argued that those who sign up as members do so not only for the plans since it would be simpler to obtain them from the *punteros*, whose counterpart labor positions are more flexible and do not require the beneficiaries to frequently participate in protests. They suggest that the neighbors choose an organization that also does not give them orders and allows them to express themselves and make decisions. In other words, they emphasize that a change of a different order occurred, namely one of culture and identity. A macroanalysis would express this as a "crisis of representation" such as the one in 2001, the results of which are evident in the different responses mentioned at the outset. Continuing in this vein, it is worth indicating that the social processes tend to either institutionalize themselves or dissolve. If the crisis and the new phenomena are understood in this way, one must characterize the movements that proposed to effect such a change during this period as a minority within the "piquetero movement." They were very visible—but a minority nevertheless.

ANALYZING THE TRANSFORMATIONS

In the course of this chapter, we have proposed to respond to the question of how Buenos Aires changed from the crisis of the import substitution model during the early neoliberal years. There are at least five transformations that we consider significant. They are as follows: the changes in the role of the state; the transformations in the structure of work opportunities; the growing social exclusion and the emergence of the new urban poor; the emphasis on processes of spatial segregation; and the modes of popular protest.

First, let us clarify the meaning of "the end of the welfare state." Although the state substantially changed its presence, it did not disappear, and we postulate that, after a decade of neoliberal reforms, it took on an enormous importance in the daily life and the subsistence of an important share of the population. It was no longer the state that developed and controlled public enterprises (with varying degrees of efficiency), many of which were strategic for development (e.g., petroleum, energy, communications, air transport, roads). These enterprises were privatized, and their workforce was reduced. It was also no longer the state that maintained a legal framework of social and labor protection. The labor laws were modified fundamentally due to pressure from the employers, and the social security system, which was also privatized, was going through a crisis at least as serious as the one it experienced when it depended on the state.

The effects of the macroeconomic policies that supplanted those that were dominant during the import substitution era only increased vulnerability in the labor market. The process of economic opening and deregulation affected the role of different economic sectors and their ability to generate sufficient employment for the population. The clearest proof of this lay in the labor market's increasing vulnerability, which translated into very high levels of open unemployment and a significant vulnerability even among those with jobs. With this structural transformation, unemployment and misery increased dramatically. However, although it might seem paradoxical, a consequence of this was that the public sector itself began to assume responsibility in part for the numerous victims of the process, starting with the serious crisis suffered in the country. By heavily subsidizing unemployment and providing food to the indigent population, the state became more important than ever before in the domestic economy. On the other hand, the state remained very present in its repressive activity, both potential and actual.

Work in factories continued to decline dramatically, and second jobs, or "moonlighting"—increasingly scarce and subject to economic fluctuations—were not sufficient to provide a minimum income to thousands of Argentines. So how did resources enter the popular neighborhoods? Historically, the main source of incomes was wages, whether formal or informal. With a greatly deteriorated labor market, on the one hand the relative and in some cases absolute importance of crime increases, and on the other hand the relative importance of public assistance increases, although its absolute importance decreases. Therefore, on the whole there were fewer resources to distribute; paradoxically, however, the state played a more important role.

The deterioration of living conditions was not the same for everyone. Minority sectors of the population benefited from the fruits of economic opening and deregulation. The direct consequence of this was an increase in social inequality. Throughout the twentieth century, Argentina offered a certain hope for upward social mobility. This changed in the 1990s because an important share of the popular sectors that had aspired to improve their living conditions (whether their own or those of their children) remained excluded. The dichotomy, as in other neoliberal models, stopped being "above/below" and came to be "inside/outside." The poorest sectors, deprived of work, remained more spatially marginalized than ever. This, together with the proliferation of luxurious housing complexes, country clubs, and gated communities, meant that movement between social sectors was greatly reduced. Workers' bedroom communities were converted into spaces for the unemployed, for those expelled from the social system. In our view, neoliberalism qualitatively deepened the ancient urban boundaries of Buenos Aires by transforming many popular neighborhoods into social ghettos, into totalizing institutions of misery.

A difference can therefore be established between Buenos Aires and other metropolitan areas of the region. All of the neighborhoods that we analyzed were part of the city, and their residents had worked to insert themselves into it to an increasing extent. If they were not excluded entirely, it was because their organizations were able to obtain admittedly scarce resources that enabled a partial inclusion. The plans and public assistance were not exclusively resources for survival; they also constituted a precarious link with the state, an (insufficient) recognition of the right to assistance.

In this context, the ways in which the popular urban sectors organized and protested also suffered major transformations. If one compares this period with the decades of the 1960s and 1970s, which were characterized by broad political mobilization in Argentina's main cities and by a strong presence of political parties, the changes were enormous. Although our fieldwork does not allow us to make comparisons, it does allow us to reflect on how the space of the factory and of production, as well as their respective organizations, tended to lose influence relative to the space of the neighborhood and of reproduction. It is therefore not an accident that the only common factor for all neighborhoods was the wide presence of popular community kitchens and that the common feature among the new organizations was their territorial nature. These shared characteristics were linked to the main problems of the urban poor. Considering the demands of the popular organizations, public opinion polls, and social studies conducted in the area, these problems were unemployment, insufficient food, insecurity, access to land and housing, health, education, and low incomes. The relative weight of these problems has varied in the last few decades. In fact, unemployment, food, and insecurity were not crucial problems in the 1980s.

If we ask ourselves how the marginalized survived, it is hard not to agree with the answer given by Lomnitz (1998 [1975]): using and strengthening their networks. The characteristics of the social networks are deservedly a relevant dimension of comparative analysis in recent decades. Although one could diagnose a "shrinking of social networks" (Auyero 2001b), the question then arises as to whether as a result of this, new forms of association or organization would not have emerged. Historically, a person inserted in a broad social network was assisted by the members of the network, who, having work or other types of resources, could offer them help if the need arose. In the context of the crisis that resulted from the neoliberal era, such assumptions become unreliable since the overall resources of the network were reduced significantly. An important share of the popular sector no longer had a stable job, which, in the context of reductions in social plans, drained the potential resources for the network. Thus, the relationship between networks, associations, and the state transformed over time.

Svampa and Pereyra (2003) put forward the sociological question of why it was that in Argentina new social movements of the unemployed emerged since unemployment is a common problem in many other countries. To answer this question, they identified a set of relevant factors. Whereas in other countries the state had strong political networks that were able to contain issues, these did not exist in Argentina. Whereas in other countries, demands for work were channeled through traditional labor unions, in Argentina these institutions supported the policy of currency convertibility. Whereas in other countries people drew on the fabric of the community, networks of survival, and—we would add—an extended informal sector, in Argentina these proved insufficient to soften such a heavy fall. This combined with the impact of unemployment in a relatively integrated and largely salaried society, in contrast to others in Latin America (ibid., 11–13).

These three shortcomings (of the state, of the unions, and of the community networks) can be considered together as notable features of Argentine history that explain the piquetero phenomenon. The relevance of the state in Argentine history is closely linked to the fact that the lack of employment was transformed into a political demand. Something similar occurred with the long tradition of unions and associations, which was reformulated into the new organizations as a result of the desertion of union leaders and the inadequacy of existing networks. That is to say, the very political culture of the popular sectors, the particular presence of the state, the union tradition, and the crisis of resources among social networks are the factors that explain the phenomenon.

Given that the social plans were obtained following the piquetes, we see again the presence of the state, "unions," and networks: that is, there was a decree that establishes a right, a set of organizations that claimed it and administered plans, and a social script that became relevant in the search for the plan, in the growth of organizations, and in the groups in which the counterpart labor is carried out. In other words, with the neoliberal policies, the state withdrew from social protection for vast popular sectors. This generated a vacuum, a "desert," because the old unions, parties, and institutions, which in other contexts have been channels for resistance, no longer fulfilled this role. In this framework a new demand arose, which, at some indeterminate point in the process, institutionalized itself as a "neighborhood union of the unemployed." This only consolidated itself with the reappearance of the state (it, in fact, made the state reappear through its actions) both in its repressive dimension and in its social dimension. "The demonstrators in the streets direct themselves to the national state, demanding their reinsertion in it" (Delamata 2002, 130).

In 1976, Portes and Walton highlighted some social tendencies in the "politics of urban poverty" in Latin America, which might be worth contrasting with the situation encountered in Buenos Aires at the start of the new millennium. The first one indicated that the political conduct of the poor is defined by rationality when confronted with structural circumstances. The current research questions deal more with the specific characteristics that this rationality acquires in different contexts than with demonstrating the existence of this rationality in and of itself. Although in certain situations it may be channeled through neighborhood or electoral participation, at other times it can lead to street protests against the state.

The second tendency referred to the fact that the axis of political organizing of marginalized groups was linked to their most urgent problem, which could not be solved through individual means: access to land and housing. The Argentine case demonstrates a significant change in defining the most pressing problem as it has passed from land and housing to employment. The third tendency was linked to the relatively greater weight of communal organizations centered around local questions as the preferred vehicles for political action. This tendency could not be sustained so clearly in the current Argentine context, although this is not because political parties gained greater relevance—in fact, they suffered a massive process of disaffiliation. What happened is that since the main demand, the struggle for employment, is basically not local, new types of interrelations emerged between the local and the national. These interrelations are more similar to union traditions than to strictly political traditions. The dynamic of high political fragmentation of piquetero organizations and reclaimed factories (the same in 2002 and 2003 in the case of the popular assemblies) could not be explained by the relevance of the local. On the contrary, a study should attempt to reconstruct the interlocking dimensions of political culture that together contribute to a constant fragmentation.

The fourth tendency emphasized the historicity of the organizations and the transformations in relation to their instrumental value. In our opinion, this tendency is particularly relevant for understanding the recent evolution of popular organizations as well as to account for the phase that began in Argentina once the most critical moment of the economic and political crisis had passed. We have mentioned how organizations, networks, and practices such as barter and the assemblies that emerged during the crisis lost their relevance and vitality for various reasons. On the other hand, we have analyzed how this pressing social problem of unemployment at some point came to be approached collectively, and as a result of the relative success of these collective actions and their leaders, hundreds of grassroots organizations that fought for, obtained, and administered social plans emerged and consolidated. It is clear that in order to understand the evolution of the organizations one should not lose sight of the critical role of government, which developed strategies to weaken the most oppositional organizations.

The fifth tendency referred to the fact that the relative absence of political radicalization was not due to a lack of deep frustration but rather to the perception that it was not feasible to challenge the existing order. To confirm this tendency in the Argentine case would require a broader empirical study. In any case we can point out that toward the end of 2001 and the beginning of 2002, broad-based social sectors declared their perception that the existing order was no longer viable. This led to generalized rejection of hegemony much more than it affirmed the viability of a change in any specific direction. From our point of view, political radicalism had reached its limits in the mobilization of piqueteros and the Left in the Plaza de Mayo on December 20, 2002 (Grimson 2003b). One year later a similar action showed the existence of consolidated piquetero organizations, but they were without the capacity to appeal to middle-class sectors, who were completely absent.

The sixth tendency referred to the key role of external intervention in political action and the dependency this action generates in such circumstances. When can we be certain that an intervention is "external"? This is a complex issue. Thus, for example, various takeovers of factories occurred at the workers' initiative, but to subsist and advance, the workers had to establish links with different types of (union, political, legal) "brokers." Something similar happened with community kitchens, which emerged from the neighbors' initiative. Ultimately, the existence of a group of social and political militants with a certain trajectory or experience was a necessary condition for the emergence of a piquetero group. External intervention may not be essential for the emergence of certain organizational processes, but its mediation with the general conditions is a sine qua non for their institutionalization.

Finally, if we compare the situation of current popular organizations at the turn of the century with that prevailing in the 1970s, we must necessarily contrast the characteristics of militancy. Although there were large organizations in the earlier period that promoted the "proletarization" and channeled links with the popular middle-class neighborhoods, in the later period political organizations of this type had become less relevant. What stands out is that since the second half of the 1990s, an entire group of middle-class sectors decided to undertake social and political activities in popular neighborhoods without any institutional mediation at all. The crisis of the political parties did not imply the end of militancy in Buenos Aires but rather the emergence of a new type of militancy, which is often "external" in terms of its social origin, although not always in terms of the formation of a political organization.

CONCLUSION AND POSTSCRIPT

The analyses and arguments of this chapter are based on statistical data and ethnographic evidence from social organizations from 2003 to 2004. In 2003 Argentina closed the transitional moment that began with the renunciation of President De La Rúa on December 20, 2001, and the megadevaluation of currency that multiplied the poverty, misery, and responses of society. Between 2003 and 2011 it was quite difficult to ensure that the official social indicators were collected in a rigorous and exhaustive manner. Starting in 2007, after an ill-considered official policy with respect to the National Institute of Statistics and Census, the official statistics have become objects of great debate, and now some of the indicators are highly questionable. As a result, we cannot make a point-to-point comparison. Nevertheless, we can say that Argentina has changed greatly between 2003 and 2011. It is widely accepted that during this period the economy grew at around 8 percent annually (with the exception of 2009 because of the international crisis). During the first years of this remarkable growth, detractors argued that the increase was due exclusively to the recuperation of losses suffered during the 1998–2002 recession. Later, when these markers easily overcame those of previous years, critics claimed that this was due only to the "tailwind" effect of the rise in prices of soy and other commodities. What is certain is that Argentina abandoned the idea that the state should only promote the free market and increasingly began to intervene in diverse processes while overturning crucial political policies of neoliberalism.

Since there no longer exists a relation of merely receiving and applying the measures of international organizations, as during the neoliberal years, the political economy has tended in the direction of more regulation, but without trying to obtain homogeneous results. The privatizations of the telephone, electricity, gas, and petroleum companies have basically not been affected. In contrast, the privatization of the retirement funds was annulled, and, with the approval of Congress, it returned to being a national delivery system. One measure with perhaps less structural depth but much symbolic significance was the renationalization of Aerolíneas Argentinas, the country's airline. In this general context, one can say with sufficient certainty that unemployment was reduced to one-third of the level it reached during the currency-convertibility period, now around 8 percent. Without a doubt, this is the most forceful indicator that the growth of the recent period has created employment. The critics often point out that this growth was based, besides the "tailwind," on an expansive political economy that generated high inflation. The inflation rate is the subject of the greatest disagreements because the statistics of both the INDEC (less than 10 percent annually for 2010) and the opposition (which refers to rates up to 30 percent annually) are very improbable.

In terms of social policies, the government implemented diverse measures to try to reduce poverty and misery. The principal means has been the implementation of the Asignación Universal por Hijo (Universal Child Allocation) program, whereby families receive both health services and fixed sums for each child that attends school. Other measures have been work subsidies and the creation of cooperatives, as well as the expansion of retirement benefits for those workers who, because of their work in the informal or "black" market, did not make contributions to the retirement funds. Evidently these and other policies reduced the misery and poverty, but we cannot provide numbers, as there is no consensus about them. There are vast sectors where government workers cannot make ends meet without receiving subsidies, called the *salario social*, or social salary, the most notable of which are public health and public transport. Nevertheless, there has been some recuperation of workers' real salaries as a result of joint annual negotiations, and some branches have received increases that keep up with or sometimes surpass the inflation rates. A new debate has to do with whether a moderate reduction in inequality has occurred. The statistics demonstrate that inequality was considerably reduced between 2003 and 2007. The government maintains that this tendency continued after this period, whereas the opposition asserts that inflation neutralized the positive effects of the salary increases. Nevertheless, it is impossible to corroborate their visions because the data for this period are so unreliable. No tax reforms have been designed to reduce inequality.

This scenario is very different from the one the neighborhoods and social organizations of the unemployed faced in the late 1990s and the beginning of 2000. The growth of employment, especially the growth of formal and even industrial jobs, bestowed some authority on the unions in Argentina that they had not had for many years. Thus, not only were the claims of "the end of the state" silenced by various active policies of the government, but declarations about "the end of work" and the political implications thereof were also exposed as unfounded speculations. In 2003 and 2004 we saw a slow integration of movements of the unemployed, some of which were brought about by the government. In other cases, for example in the autonomous or Marxist movements, groups integrated into the "space-time" of traditional protest. That is, if the earlier roadblocks were intended to disrupt what was happening, these later mobilizations tended to routinize their demands and integrate them into the urban landscape. In effect, in spatial terms, the protests were displaced from the urban borders to their traditional places in the central zones. In this transformation, the movements' main ultimatum changed from a political demand based on employment as a condition of integration, to a growing number of small marches to claim a specific number of social plans. Slowly, an important part of the bases of these protests began to provide certain work opportunities. The various movements of the unemployed utilized different strategies to deal with this fact, and here we cannot analyze them all. However, in social terms, it is evident that the movements of unemployed workers are no longer particularly relevant, although many of them continue to press socially and politically for this and other issues.

The Confederación General de Trabajadores (General Federation of Workers, or CGT) now occupies a central place in Argentine politics, supporting the government but trying to press for new social demands and hoping to create a new agenda (like the participation of workers in corporate profits), while demanding greater participation in the distribution of government jobs for party members. It has even gone so far as to state that the official formula for elections should incorporate someone from the CGT as a candidate for vice president. The unions are not completely unified, however. The minority Central de Trabajadores Argentinos (Argentine Workers Union), born in the 1990s to confront neoliberalism and to democratize the unions, has split into two factions: an oppositional sector and a sector that strongly supports the government. One important part of the largest unions continues to be led by the same leaders who supported the principal measures implemented by Menem in the 1990s. Nevertheless, the most prominent union figure is a leader with a Peronist background but who confronted neoliberalism from the traditional union perspective.

The displacement "from the factory to the neighborhood" that we describe in this chapter, and that many read as an inevitable and definitive path in the 1990s, was a social response to a specific state of affairs. Now we are seeing the culmination of another displacement, one that has placed the unions in a crucial position that, in its own way, does not diminish the diversification of the means of organization and the protests of civil society. Now new themes (e.g., the environment, ethnic diversity, sexual orientation) are being incorporated into these protests. The successes of the past are now being strengthened in terms of human rights. This amounts to a new state of affairs, with new politics and both new and old social actors. New questions and new challenges will emerge from this situation.

CHAPTER 6

"TAKEN INTO ACCOUNT"

Democratic Change and Contradiction in Mexico's Third Sector

Analiese M. Richard

ON DECEMBER 16, 2010, PRESIDENT Felipe Calderón bestowed the third annual Premio Nacional de Acción Voluntaria y Solidaria (National Prize for Volunteerism and Solidarity) on two exemplary Mexican citizens and one organization during a gala luncheon held at Los Pinos (the presidential residence). The three winners were all associated with children's charities, including group homes for at-risk and homeless youth. That same day, human rights activist Marisela Escobedo Ortiz was gunned down in front of city hall in the northern capital of Chihuahua. She had been leading a protest against the lack of official attention to the victims of Mexico's epidemic of cartel-related violence. Escobedo Ortiz had begun organizing in response to the murder of her daughter in Ciudad Juárez by the daughter's boyfriend, reputedly an associate of one of the most violent mafias, the ex-paramilitary group known as the Zetas. Despite the suspect's confession, three judges failed to convict him. The murder of Escobedo Ortiz served as a lightning rod for popular criticism of Calderón's war on the cartels, a war many Mexicans seemed to think he was losing badly. In the speech delivered at Los Pinos, Calderón lauded the assembled nongovernmental organizations (NGOs), foundations, and volunteers as "the good guys," who "thankfully outnumber the bad guys," whose exploits earned them greater publicity. Their efforts, he insisted, served as the "engine" of democratic reform in Mexico, leading the nation toward reconstruction of the common good by reclaiming a sense of social solidarity. He admonished the assembled functionaries and cabinet members to "take into account" the proposals and priorities of the "third sector" (Calderón 2010). Calderón's expansion of the state's security apparatus as a means of confronting the unresolved contradictions provoked by Mexico's ongoing experiment with neoliberal democracy has been roundly criticized, especially his administration's failure to protect victims and community organizers such as Escobedo Ortiz. However, there has been comparatively little concrete analysis of either the ways in which the growth of the NGO sector, Calderón's "good guys," has been channeled toward similar aims or the complex relationships between these new organizational forms and earlier historical forms of civic action.

Delivered in a moment of heightened political, economic, and social insecurity, Calderón's speech laid out a vision of active citizenship in neoliberal Mexico. According to Calderón, NGO volunteers foment solidarity, one of the greatest virtues of Mexican civic life: "To be in solidarity," he said, "means to be responsible not only for one's own destiny but also for the destiny of others. The moment human beings forget this essential part of their own nature . . . is precisely when we end up with problems like the ones we now face" (2010). Although acknowledging that the state has a legal responsibility to provide its citizens with basic services and protections, Calderón declared that the work of NGOs is "more significant" than that of the state because to act on behalf of another outside the realm of one's legal or social obligations, to take others into consideration in an act of charity, is to contribute to "the construction of the common good." He characterized the work of "organized civil society" as central to Mexico's democratic transition, praising the work of NGOs in "pluralizing the public agenda" and reducing barriers to participation in democratic governance. However, his remarks also revealed a slippage between citizenship and charity as categories of social action, which has become increasingly common in official discourse. In the grassroots struggle for democratic reform, Mexican NGOs functioned as an alternative to corrupt political parties by helping to organize the civil-society coalitions that pushed for free elections and institutional change. The efforts of many such NGOs were aimed at developing the capacity of marginalized groups to claim their rights as citizens and to participate in formal political processes. Economic development projects formed an integral part of this enterprise as a means of countering the deep social inequality that rendered many Mexicans citizens in name only. However, even as political figures from the Right and the center have adopted the language of democratic citizenship over the course of the last decade and a half, the identification of democratic principles with social equality, which was fundamental to the pro-democracy movement, seems to be been left aside. This discursive shift is related to contradictions produced by the interaction of what Goodale and Postero (Chapter 1 in this volume) identify as the primary categories of contradiction and contestation in contemporary Latin America—the "transitional entitlement regime," which has provided activists and authorities with a common idiom for articulating democratic transitions, and "regimes of exclusion" rooted in enduring structural tensions. As a result, inequality becomes naturalized. Instead of posing problems for democracy, marginalization and exclusion are invoked as opportunities for the entrepreneurial enactment of civic virtue.

Even calls to attend to citizens' most basic political and social rights must confront the legacy of the Washington Consensus. As elsewhere in Latin America, the once-radical notion of civil-society "participation" in governance as a means of deepening democratic citizenship has been reappropriated to further the neoliberal aims of reducing the social role of the state (Dagnino 2003; Paley 2001). In Mexico, the growth of the nonprofit sector, which has come to be known as "organized civil society," produced deep tensions between an "assistential" mode of civic action and more radical transformative projects. This tension is marked by contrasting the frames of citizenship (concerned with common rights and obligations as well as civic deliberation among equals) and philanthropy (emphasizing voluntary gifts contributed to a particular social cause outside the realm of social obligation) through which NGO personnel interpret and articulate their experiences. Although acknowledging the role played by the "third sector" in creating the conditions of possibility for opposition electoral victories, the past two Partido Acción Nacional administrations have also sought to channel the organizational efforts of NGOs into projects more compatible with neoliberal visions of the "common good." This chapter analyzes the often-contradictory modes of civic engagement facilitated by NGOs during the last decade of Mexico's "democratic transition," highlighting the categories of social action through which NGO workers make sense of their own interventions.

As Bornstein notes for India and as Calderón's own words reveal, the global growth of the "third sector" in the neoliberal era has been accompanied by a shift away from teleological narratives of national progress associated with the development era toward "metaphors of repair" (Bornstein 2012, 16). During the last thirty years the neoliberal project has "polarized" Mexico (Dussel 2000), producing contradictions that have led to massive social inequality, increased poverty and dispossession, violence and insecurity, and widespread political abstentionism periodically punctuated by localized uprisings. The present situation bears little resemblance to the outcomes predicted by the hegemonic democratization theories of the 1990s, which assumed that economic liberalization accompanying the creation of free markets would propel deeper political change in the form of liberal democracy. The upwelling of NGOs was interpreted as an indication of social stability and civic health, an impression now contradicted by growing violence. More than a century after the Mexican Revolution, the country possesses many of the trappings of liberal democratic institutions, but the meaning of democracy is still widely debated in society. Institutional reform over the last decade has been largely directed at securing individual liberties, while issues of redistributive justice raised during the pro-democracy movements of the 1980s and 1990s have remained unresolved and in many places become more acute. Modes of democratic participation have also come under scrutiny as human rights activism and traditional forms of public social protest are increasingly criminalized, leaving activists vulnerable to intimidation and reprisals (Correas 2007; Fundación para el Debido Proceso Legal 2010).

Where does this leave the actors Calderón names as "organized civil society"? Using a case study of NGOs located in the Tulancingo Valley of the state of Hidalgo, I argue that the modes of engagement facilitated by these organizations cannot be properly understood without considering their transnational dimensions or the relationship of NGOs to earlier historical forms of collective social and civic action. The historical development of Tulancingo's NGO sector reveals important contradictions between the class orientation of the organizations' founders and their populist aims, as well as strong connections between the aims and methods of NGOs and those of the political class with whom they are intimately, if sometimes uncomfortably, engaged. Moreover, this case demonstrates the ways in which Mexican NGOs have been forced to negotiate with a variety of actors within and beyond the state in their own quest to be "taken into account" in policy decisions that affect them and their constituents. Academic debates over whether NGOs are best understood as Trojan horses for introducing market-oriented forms of subjectivity and social action or as incubators of democratic values and practices have tended to ignore the transformations to which these universalizing forms are subjected as they become embedded in specific political and social terrains. This case demonstrates that the negotiations involved in being "taken into account" in Mexico have profoundly shaped the capacity of local NGOs to openly challenge the neoliberal model, leaving them to confront a political landscape in which activism is dismissed as uncivil while charity stands in for democratic citizenship.

NEOLIBERAL RESTRUCTURING AND THE RISE OF THE THIRD SECTOR

For many outside observers, the 2000 presidential election certified Mexico's transformation into a Western-style market democracy. Although opposition candidate Vicente Fox's victory seemed to confirm the hopes of transition theorists and investors alike, the ensuing decade of neoliberal entrenchment has led many to question the direction of democratic reforms in Mexico. Mexico's experiments with neoliberal restructuring began as a project of elite technocrats and politicians within the ruling party. In the wake of the "lost decade" of the 1980s, groups within the economics ministry, many of them trained in U.S. universities, sought to "modernize" Mexico's political economy by reducing state ownership and regulation while promoting trade and foreign investment. They sought primarily to leverage Mexico's connections to the United States and during the last twenty years have increasingly emphasized this relationship over their ties with the rest of Latin America (Rus and Tinker Salas 2006, 7). President Carlos Salinas (1988–1994) promoted NAFTA (the North American Free Trade Agreement) as the key to Mexico's entry into the First World, and even after the opposition victory of 2000 many of the tenets of his approach have been recycled by successive administrations. Political reforms were part of that package, both as a response to pressure from movements for both human rights and indigenous rights and protest movements that resisted earlier rounds of structural adjustment, as well as the need to assure investors of the rule of law and political stability. However, Mexico's one-party state was able to push through painful economic reforms due to a near monopoly on political power. The institutional reforms advocated by even the most progressive branches of the PRI (the Partido Revolutionario Institucional, or Institutional Revolutionary Party) were limited to what Centeno (1994) has called "democracy within reason," amounting in practice to cleaner elections accompanied by the cordoning off of economic policy from political contestation. However, the relative autonomy of those elites in instituting their reform program was attenuated after 1994. The eruption of the Zapatista rebellion and the popularity it enjoyed both at home and abroad made it impossible for the government to ignore resistance to neoliberalism or to contain it via the conventional combination of repression and patronage. In addition, the devaluation of the peso and the concomitant U.S. bailout meant that much of Mexico's economic policy would continue to be determined from without, according to Washington Consensus orthodoxy. Structural adjustment trimmed the legal responsibilities of the state for social services, and political reforms opened up new arenas for citizen participation in government. The period of the 1990s was marked by an NGO "boom" in Mexico as organized groups sought to take advantage of these domestic openings and enhanced international funding opportunities. Various NGOs played a vital role in producing the democratic transition, but their modes of engagement with the state and international and domestic funders during this period and in the years directly following the 2000 elections would profoundly shape the future course of Mexican democracy.

Mexico is considered part of a larger "third wave" of democratic transitions that began in the late twentieth century. The "transition paradigm" launched during the Reagan administration aspired to provide a universal academic model for understanding political upheaval and change in authoritarian regimes. Democratic transition was portrayed as an orderly progression of key stages: "opening" (a period of political liberalization and struggle resulting in the weakening of the regime), "breakthrough" (the fall of the regime and the rise of a new system, marked by free elections), and finally "consolidation" (a slow process of institutional reforms and the strengthening of civil society and democratic culture) (Carothers 2002). Although this model was largely ahistorical, it was congruent with the neoliberal paradigm of mainstream economics, which focused on the primacy of economic freedom and implied that political freedom would naturally follow. The transition model deeply influenced the agendas of major international foundations and funding agencies working in Mexico in the 1990s and early 2000s, especially with regard to projects aimed at supporting the "consolidation" stage. However, philosophical traditions dating back to the early days of the republic warned that entrenched relationships of social dependency posed a serious obstacle to the free participation of the marginalized classes in the public sphere, giving rise to a class of entrepreneurial political intermediaries (Hale 1989). The growth of a "third sector" was promoted by both Mexican intellectuals and international observers as an antidote to this problem of representation, a laboratory for producing active democratic citizens (Deakin 2001; Putnam 2000). Both philanthropic and governmental efforts to foment "civic engagement" focused on developing an "independent civil society" as a step toward democratic consolidation (Carothers 2002). These efforts were often coterminous with economic development projects that encouraged various forms of "participation" by target populations as a means of organizing consent around and making recipients more responsible for project outcomes (Cook and Kothari 2001). In this context, the proliferation of NGOs was regarded as an indication of the strength of civil society in overcoming corporatism and forging new forms of civic engagement (Olvera Rivera 1999; Verduzco, List, and Salamon 2002).

In practice, however, the political, economic, and social changes mediated by NGOs were much more complex and contradictory (Richard 2009). To begin with, the "third sector" is not an internally coherent institutional category. It names a grab bag of entities that in practice might see themselves as diametrically opposed (gay-rights activists and Catholic educational institutions, for example). It also encapsulates organizations with a variety of missions and methods, as well as complex relationships to local and international funders and constituents. Nonetheless, within official political discourse, it has come to serve as shorthand for "organized" civil society, an imagined "space of participation" for citizens beyond both political parties and "popular sectors." This means that the promotion of NGOs may also lend itself to the domestication of other forms of citizen participation, such as protest movements. In Mexico as in other parts of Latin America, the neoliberal ethic of private interest is moderated by the recognition of the need for mechanisms to promote social integration and cohesion in the face of extreme socioeconomic polarization. Though the model of solidarity Calderón espouses is rooted in the recognition of a common humanity, it focuses on the development of philanthropic subjects rather than the resolution of structural inequality. In the absence of a discernable national project or new social contract, Calderón's 2010 speech reflects the increasingly common official promotion of voluntaristic social solidarity, a new mode of privatizing the common good.

In order to understand the role of NGOs in producing these changes, one must examine the political and social contexts in which they emerged in the late twentieth century. The problem of the production of liberal subjects that animated Mexican political philosophy in the late nineteenth century has been reframed in struggles over forms of political participation, demonstrating how evolving notions of social cooperation may work to reinsert hierarchies and power inequalities into the "liberal" space of the "third sector." Burawoy and Verdery (1999) argue that forms of political power and models of rule that precede democratic transitions are not simply "wiped clean" in the ensuing cultural transformation but instead deeply inform both the changes and responses to them. Mexico has a long history of "cultural revolutions" in which contested projects of rule have been negotiated following extended periods of social upheaval (Corrigan 1994). At each of these historical junctures, different approaches have been proposed for balancing individual freedoms with collective entitlements and reconciling Western political ideologies with indigenous forms of government (Hale 1989; Lomnitz 2001). Contrary to the assumptions of many transition theorists, civic associations have a long history in Mexico, predating both populism and revolutionary nationalism (Forment 2003). Carlos Forment argues that "third-wave" transition models tend to overemphasize electoral politics and institutional change, obscuring some interesting continuities and long-term trends. Among them is the interaction between daily practices and institutional structures in the creation of a unique democratic tradition rooted in the idiom of "Civic Catholicism," which Forment describes as an ethic of reasoned self-rule enacted via a rich associational life, derived from the Jesuit doctrine of probabilism. He argues that civic democracy "understood in Toquevillian terms as a daily practice and form of life rooted in social equality, mutual recognition, and political liberty" (Forment 2003, xi) was already in existence in Mexico by the mid-nineteenth century, although it has sometimes coexisted and sometimes conflicted with authoritarianism. According to Forment, these civic democratic practices have at times enabled people to live "with their backs to the state" (ibid.). Although Forment's central purpose is to argue for a new historical understanding of "democratization" in Latin America, his insights can also be extended to interrogate the ways in which NGOs are related to earlier associational forms. In twentieth-century Mexican history, as we shall see later, NGOs emerged precisely as a means for people to "live with their backs to the state" and later became a means of organizing to hold the state accountable to citizens. However, the articulation between NGOs and "antipolitics" also aided their incorporation as "partners" in projects of neoliberal rule in ways that ultimately limit their social and political autonomy.

The constitutive exclusions of liberal political institutions have been roundly critiqued (Brown 1998, 2003; Mehta 1999), but Forment's conceptualization of "Civic Catholicism" also fails to adequately address the entrenched social inequality and tolerance of hierarchy characteristic of this form of associational life. Shefner warns that the current fascination with "civil society" in Latin America tends to obfuscate both the class roots of the neoliberal project and the role of some social-assistance NGOs in preserving social peace during a period of retrenchment in which class divisions have deepened sharply (2007, 184). During the 1980s, Mexico's largely urban middle class was "organized by non-governmental organizations focused on democratization and human rights" (Shefner 2007, 191). During the democratization movement, they formed coalitions with urban popular movements and peasant organizations to push a common political agenda, but their efforts focused mostly on electoral accountability and voter rights. After the 2000 elections, the coalitions that had formed around reforming political governance found it difficult to achieve consensus on strategies for confronting the social contradictions produced by neoliberalism (ibid., 194). Entrenched inequality remains as great a problem in the posttransition era as it was for neo-Tocquevillian analyses of transition that emphasized the impact of traditions of dependency and deference on the development of a democratic public sphere.

Finally, the academic literature on the rise of the "third sector" in Mexico has concentrated primarily on problematic interactions with state agencies and political parties, paying comparatively little attention to its transnational character. The NGO boom was not just part of an upwelling of civic participation in Mexico itself, against a historically authoritarian state, but rather took place within a context of U.S. expansion and a series of concomitant trends in the way NGOs were managed and funding agendas were set. Moreover, NGOs are simultaneously local and transnational, and their forms of intervention into the lives of local populations allow other transnational actors to circumvent states to enact their own programs of change. To challenge state strategies of rule, NGOs themselves may appeal to transnational ideals and networks (Fischer 1997). In addition, NGOs have become the preferred conduits for foreign development and humanitarian aid. They allow international agencies to bypass regimes they view as corrupt or inefficient and "fit" their proprietary aid models into local settings in a more direct way (Carroll 1992; Fischer 1997). Ferguson and Gupta (2002) argue that nonstate actors like NGOs are inherently implicated in neoliberal modalities of government. In their view, transnational NGO networks may in fact constitute a new mode of "transnational governmentality," which introduces techniques of self-government to devolve both the risks and responsibilities of development interventions onto the local organizations (ibid., 989). In turn, NGOs must use these same logics in evaluating, creating, and manage projects. This affects how they relate to project participants as well as to other NGOs (Elyachar 2002; Fisher, 1997; Leve and Karim 2001). A brief scan of the history of NGOs in Mexico reveals how the earliest independent organizations arose in connection with larger transnational networks that focused on human rights and democratization and how such transnational trends remain important in both ideological and material terms.

Although few scholars agree on the precise moment at which Mexico's "transition to democracy" began, most acknowledge the influence of the 1968 Tlatelolco massacre on the development of the NGOs, which would eventually lead the democratization movement of the late 1990s. Independent unions and student movements had been active for some time prior to this event, but the 1968 massacre marked a very public loss of legitimacy on the part of the Mexican state. This was soon followed by a series of external blows to the PRI's monopoly on power, including the 1980s debt crisis, which reduced the capacity of the corporatist apparatus to contain discontent through patronage, population growth leading to land invasions throughout the countryside, and a growing liberation theology movement that encouraged Catholics to question authoritarian hierarchies. De la Peña (2007) describes the NGOs that emerged during this period as primarily "voluntary associations made up of mostly young, university-educated men and women who dedicate anywhere from a few years to their whole lives to service work for reasons ranging from religious convictions, to humanitarian visions, to beliefs in nonparty politics" (323).

These nascent NGOs played a crucial role in supporting grassroots organizing efforts and helping to consolidate their gains. In response, the populist Echeverría administration (1970–1976) attempted to monopolize social organizing by co-opting and persecuting independent NGOs as well as by bolstering social programs channeled through the PRI's corporatist sectors. However, the government's failure to respond adequately in the aftermath of the devastating 1985 Mexico City earthquake enabled independent organizations to exploit the growing cracks in PRI hegemony. The earthquake became a historical watershed of the same proportions as Tlatelolco in the life of the Mexican NGO sector (Aguilar Valenzuela 1997). In addition to the "neighborly" response of the city's residents in the face of government indecision, indifference, and ineptitude, an outpouring of international aid was mobilized in record time. Although a good deal of this assistance came in the form of state-to-state aid packages and recovery loans from international agencies such as the World Bank, many private international donors, concerned with the Mexican government's reputation for corruption and inefficiency, sought out NGOs to channel their contributions to the victims. These international partnerships bolstered the bargaining power of the new organizations. The loss of state legitimacy further provided an opening for social movements and NGOs to assert rights to associational autonomy, beginning an iterative cycle of negotiations with political officials and reformist or technocratic state managers (Fox and Hernández 1992, 156).

At the same time, a series of civil wars in Central America unleashed a flood of refugees whose flight northward would also impact the development of Mexico's "third sector." Researcher and activist Sergio Aguayo asserts that Mexico opened to human rights from the south rather than from the north, as NGOs on the ground in southern Mexico teamed up with international aid workers to address the refugee crisis.[1] The Diocese of San Cristóbal, headed by Bishop Samuel Ruiz, campaigned for asylum for Central American refugees as a defense of universal human rights, a concept disseminated through the combined efforts of Mexican and international activists. As a consequence of these dynamics, the language of individual human rights gained legitimacy within Mexico and helped to foster communication and collaboration among new social movements, NGOs, and international agencies. Strong national-level coalitions among Mexican NGOs, like Alianza Cívica, Movimiento Ciudadano para la Democracia, and Red "Todos los Derechos para Todos," helped to build popular grassroots support for the pro-democracy movement. However, the banner of individual freedom and community self-sufficiency was later taken up by state authorities in their own restructuring efforts. They called upon citizens to convert the failures of structural adjustment into entrepreneurial opportunities by cultivating networks of social solidarity independent of the shrinking state-welfare apparatus, such as hometown associations that funneled capital from Mexican workers abroad into local infrastructural improvements. Neoliberal reforms, which moved Mexico away from state-led development and a corporatist system of political representation, entailed the dismantling of the social-welfare apparatus, privatization of state-owned enterprises, labor-market flexibilization, and the opening of national markets to trade and investment. The accompanying spate of social problems—including poverty, malnutrition, disease, and violent crime—has not been effectively addressed under the market model. Thus, NGOs emerged as a response both to opportunities created by the loss of PRI legitimacy and to new sources of international aid and have struggled to respond to the social contradictions created by neoliberalism.

"WHAT WILL WE DO FOR OUR *PATRIA*?" DERHGO'S HISTORY AS CASE STUDY

Founded in 1978, Rural Development of Hidalgo (DERHGO) is one of the oldest surviving independent NGOs in Mexico. Its history is representative of the far-reaching social changes that the country has experienced during the last three decades of neoliberal reforms. The state of Hidalgo has earned a reputation as stronghold of *caciquismo*, where a small number of powerful families have managed to maintain political control for extended periods. The PRI has long dominated the political landscape both by patronage and by force. Initially, DERHGO was allowed to carry out select development projects that officials in the national and state governments considered to be in their own interests, as those projects were aimed at ameliorating the rural poverty that had led to violent land invasions in other regions of Hidalgo. Hence the political and social role NGOs like DERHGO have constructed for themselves during the last three decades has been profoundly shaped by their ongoing negotiations with political elites and state agencies over the extent of their organizational autonomy.

Like many other Mexican development projects, DERHGO was born of a spirit of nationalistic solidarity. A chance meeting between two childhood friends in 1974 spawned a project of civic improvement that would eventually help to reshape the social, political, and economic landscape of the region. Both young men were descended from distinguished local families. One, whose family was important to the local cattle industry, had spent his adolescence and early twenties in a seminary on the northern border, studying for the priesthood. A conflict with his superiors over his espousal of liberation theology ended his clerical ambitions, and, after spending a few years as a bank clerk in the capital, he returned home to Tulancingo to manage the family dairy business following the death of his father. In his spare time he led a popular Boy Scout troop. He was also the informal leader of a local salon composed of young businesspeople and others drawn from the cream of Tulancingo society.

The other, whose father was an expatriate merchant and whose mother's family owned a large hacienda, had known the first young man since they were both schoolboys. He completed advanced degrees in geology and engineering abroad and held a brief professorship at the Universidad Nacional Autónoma de México before becoming a private consultant. Out for a Sunday stroll around the plaza, the old friends ran into one another on the steps of the cathedral. They caught up on one another's lives—one's academic success, the other's unanticipated exit from the priesthood and his struggles with his new family responsibilities. They exchanged news about mutual friends and chatted about the changing times in Mexico and Latin America. Recounting the incident some thirty years later, the first claimed he would never forget the intensity with which his friend had looked him in the eye and asked, "*y ahora, que vamos a hacer por nuestra patria*? (and now, what are we going to do for our country?)." The desire to shape the future of their nation and to bring the exciting changes they had witnessed elsewhere to their provincial hometown inspired them to launch a series of projects together over the course of the next decade. How that brand of civic improvement came to be linked with the people and problems of the countryside has much to with a set of broader political dynamics that brought renewed attention both to unresolved agrarian questions and changing modes of civic participation.

At that point, most Mexican NGOs were influenced by the values of Civic Catholicism if not directly affiliated with the church. In the 1960s the aftermath of the Cuban Revolution also inspired the United States to launch the Alliance for Progress, an aid program to Latin American countries that sought to prevent the spread of communism by combating poverty through development and counterinsurgency assistance. The "era of developmentalism" that ensued was complemented by the Vatican's own anticommunism efforts, summed up in the Populorum Progressio. In the late 1960s and early 1970s central Mexico served as the backdrop for a growing movement among progressive bishops committed to the tenets of liberation theology. Bishop Sergio Méndez Arceo of Cuernavaca encouraged the development of Christian base communities among the rural and urban poor. Although the idea of enacting a "preferential option for the poor" proved quite influential in many quarters, as the 1970s wore on, various forces sought to tame the radical tendencies of the liberation theology movement. Pope Paul's death and the appointment of the more conservative Pope John Paul II (along with a cadre of new, Right-leaning bishops) meant an end to official support for liberation theology. In Mexico itself, President Echeverría's populist authoritarian administration sought to relegitimize the government following the public outcry over Tlatololco and to foreclose spaces of rebellion through a campaign of co-optation and persecution of independent NGOs (Aguilar Valenzuela 1997). The NGOs that managed to survive under Echeverría were mostly church-related charities and service organizations or local branches of international organizations like the Soroptomists, Lions' Club, Boy Scouts, and Rotary Club, which had been imported from the United States under the "Good Neighbor" policy.

In the 1970s a series of intertwined economic, political, and social tensions put the agrarian question back on the national agenda in a dramatic way. The two young men from Tulancingo began contemplating a joint project that would combine youth service, poverty alleviation, and rural development throughout the Tulancingo River Valley. In 1977 the pair began meeting in Mexico City with representatives of the Fundación Mexicana para el Desarrollo Rural (Mexican Foundation for Rural Development, or FMDR). The FMDR, funded in large part by Don Lorenzo Servitje (owner of Grupo Bimbo), had evolved from the Union of Catholic Businessmen (UDEC) in the mid-1960s. A reformist group inspired by both the Alliance for Progress and the Populorum Progressio, the FMDR was dedicated to combating poverty in the countryside in order to prevent popular insurgent movements. They were worried about the possible consequences of *ejido* collectivization and land redistribution for large commercial farms in the north. As an alternative to the government's efforts at rural development, which they considered to be "antibusiness," the FMDR organized a national network of regional development centers dedicated to reducing poverty in the countryside by increasing the productivity of *campesinos*, or peasant farmers (Gordon 1998). According to DERHGO's cofounder, the early FMDR espoused a philosophy of "entrepreneurial solidarity" whereby Christian businessmen would use their social position and economic and political contacts to give a "hand up" to poor campesinos and set them on the path toward entrepreneurship. The FMDR saw lack of access to credit as the primary obstacle to entrepreneurship; given that ejidal lands could not serve as collateral for commercial bank loans and since government development loans were inefficiently managed and often politically motivated, most campesinos had little hope of obtaining credit. The key to their strategy was the *aval*, a countersigning practice whereby wealthy and respected members of the FMDR would vouch for the creditworthiness of campesino cooperatives, thereby enabling them to secure commercial loans. After a series of meetings with officials in the head office, DERHGO was founded as a regional center in the FMDR network. They began by naming a board of directors composed of prominent businessmen from Tulancingo and Mexico City.[2]

The local context into which DERHGO was born was a product both of the way the agrarian question was framed in the national agenda of the late 1970s and how those policy debates and programs were articulated to the particular conditions of rural Hidalgo. Given a population that was more than 80 percent rural, mostly engaged in subsistence agriculture, and its proximity to the capital, Hidalgo appeared on the national political radar as a potential hotspot of insurgency. Hidalgo had long been regarded as Mexico City's provincial preserve, providing both food and migrant labor for the industrialization of the capital, as well as serving as a training ground for PRI politicians. Agrarian violence had already erupted in the Huasteca, a region to the northeast of Tulancingo with a ranching economy and a large indigenous population. The expansion and intensification of cattle ranching by large landowners, often in disputed territory claimed by indigenous ejidos, provoked a series of bloody skirmishes between independent campesino organizations and the ranchers' private militias (*guardias blancas*). The conflict in the Huasteca brought to the surface a whole series of class tensions that had intensified as growing population density had resulted in elevated levels of rural unemployment, leading both to out-migration and to new demands for land redistribution. Though ranching occupied a large amount of arable land, it provided relatively few local jobs. As the ranches expanded, the region became a fertile ground for insurgency (Gutierrez 1990; Schryer 1990; Vargas Gonzalez 1998).

If the danger of rural rebellion caught the attention of PRI politicians and planners in the capital, then the close social ties connecting major Hidalgan officials to key national political figures and institutions facilitated the flow of federal resources to the formerly neglected province. In the late 1970s and early 1980s two key figures, Jorge Rojo Lugo and Guillermo Rossell de la Lama, were able to convince the national government to invest in the development of rural Hidalgo. Rojo Lugo, who hailed from a powerful Huastecan political family, was elected governor in 1975. He was later appointed secretary of agrarian reform by his old school friend José López Portillo, then president of the country, which enabled him to direct substantial federal funds toward the resolution of the Huastecan conflict. He undertook a massive program of "economic modernization," called the Plan Huasteca. Rojo Lugo's successor was Guillermo Rossell de la Lama, a member of the earliest generation of PRI technocrats who had occupied important planning posts in the national government and the PRI before attaining the governorship (Valdespino Castillo 1992, 87–90). In the 1980s, he reorganized Plan Huasteca according to a dual strategy of land-tenancy regularization and regional pacification, employing funds from federal development and antipoverty programs like Programa de Inversiones Para para el Desarrollo Rural (Investment Program for Rural Development, PIDER) and Sistema Alimentario Mexicano (Mexican Food System). Both Rojo Lugo and Rossell sought to stem the spread of agrarian revolt to other parts of the state, but the post-1968 political climate forced them to consider strategies other than brute repression.

The conflict in the Huasteca would enable DERHGO's founders to launch their project in the infamously conservative Valley of Tulancingo with a modicum of official support, a factor crucial to their success. During a brief stint in the state government under Rojo Lugo, one managed to enlist the former governor's endorsement of DERHGO's development vision. The PRI establishment viewed the growth of independent campesino organizations as a threat to the social and political order, but Rojo Lugo saw a clear advantage in allowing DERHGO to attempt the development of rural communities in the valley. The governor hoped to harness the "helping hand" of this new branch of the FMDR to weed out unrest before it reached the southern part of the state. In fact, Rojo Lugo took a personal role in drumming up political and financial support for the project among the local elites. He helped DERHGO's founders to plan a benefit banquet at a local hacienda, to which he personally invited the region's most prominent businesspeople and ranchers. By the end of the evening, they had succeeded in soliciting enough pledges to provide a comfortable endowment for their new organization.

Their initial efforts were directed at subsistence producers (both *ejiditarios* and small-property owners) spread out over the entire Valley of Tulancingo. In addition, DERHGO's early strategy, copied directly from the FMDR, was to increase the productivity of these small farmers through credit injections and technology transfer. The NGO quickly identified access to water as the key to boosting productivity in this semiarid region. Most smallholder parcels were rain fed rather than irrigated and were prone to wind erosion in the dry season and flash flooding in the rainy season. Both of these processes depleted the precious topsoil of the plain and limited the types of crops that could be grown and the number of potential growing cycles per year. Moreover, campesinos were forced to travel for miles to procure water for drinking, cooking, washing, and watering their livestock at rivers controlled by powerful ranchers. As DERHGO staff members discovered through their recruiting chats with campesinos, many dreamed of owning a cow whose milk could be sold for cash. Access to water sources and irrigation technology would enable them not only to increase their production of basic crops such as corn and beans but also to sow pasturage with which to support livestock, in addition to redirecting female labor power from water procurement to other productive tasks. With this in mind, DERHGO soon settled on a development strategy that hinged on the perforation of cooperatively managed wells in rural communities.

Through their affiliation with the FMDR, DERHGO formed working relationships with government agencies, international aid organizations, and private banks to finance its projects. PIDER was typical of the semiclientelism that characterized the relationships between state agencies and rural development organizations. Funded in part by the World Bank, PIDER aimed to preserve the social peace in regions of growing tension by funding infrastructure and farm-credit projects involving community participation (Fox 1994, 162–163). The promoters of DERHGO would identify and organize development groups in rural communities, provide technical and planning assistance for their projects, and guide them through the official paperwork necessary to secure funding. Environmental studies and drilling/access permits were arranged through PIDER, while commercial credit was procured through the SOMEX Bank, with *avales* and backing from FMDR. Once a well had been perforated, irrigation systems built, and pasturage cultivation demonstrated, DERHGO would inaugurate a local project with Heifer International (Cadena de la Vida). This U.S.-based international aid organization, founded by Christian relief workers, provides livestock to families in impoverished communities who agree to "pass on the gift" by donating future female offspring to others. The Ford Foundation sponsored educational projects in six of DERHGO's project sites, and the Inter-American Foundation awarded grants for heavy equipment. Through DERHGO's efforts, twenty-two wells were perforated in rural communities, converting seventeen hundred hectares of land to irrigation and transforming the valley into a small-scale dairy region. By the mid-1980s, a dairy cooperative organized by DERHGO was producing an average of 90,746 liters of milk per month and running three distribution centers within the city of Tulancingo. In addition, DERHGO arranged retreats for and exchanges between its campesino cooperatives and groups from other regions to compare experiences and techniques, as well as to build a sense of solidarity and shared purpose.

As a result of its search for new approaches to popular education, in 1986 DERHGO joined a network of local liberation theology and development groups organized by the Secretariat for New Experiences in Community Education (SENEC). Based in a working-class neighborhood of Mexico City, SENEC was the brainchild of Francesc Botey, a Piarist missionary priest from Barcelona. Twice yearly the members of SENEC communities sent delegates to participate in popular *encuentros* (meetings). Each community took turns hosting a weeklong retreat in which participants conducted workshops on current events and social issues, performed popular theater, sang songs, prayed, and worked on development projects together. The SENEC encuentros were organized thematically and were designed not only to provide a group-building experience but also to disseminate information and analysis. One of the encuentros dealt with the issue of Third-World indebtedness and featured workshops on the role of the International Monetary Fund in dictating domestic policy to debtor nations. Another focused on democracy and human rights, with performance pieces on the different Mexican political parties and a mock election, designed to prepare delegates to participate actively in the ill-fated 1988 presidential election.

Although the FMDR was pleased with the results of DERHGO's development projects, the leadership of the foundation became increasingly uncomfortable with the organization's popular education program. To promote economic self-reliance and democratic political participation, DERHGO's personnel had begun promoting "integrated" development projects in poor farming villages, combining infrastructural projects with popular education. Members of DERHGO were encouraged to participate in regional assemblies of popular organizations, and some DERHGO staff promoted the founding of a sister organization dedicated to protecting human rights. The distinction the PRI made between "political" and "social" organizing placed limits on the strategy of NGOs like DERHGO:

> The classical political bargain required official incorporation of social groups under state tutelage in exchange for access to social programs. Mass protest that was strictly "social" was sometimes tolerated, but if it was perceived as "political" (that is, challenging the hegemony of the ruling party), the usual mix of partial concessions with repression shifted toward the latter. (Fox 1994, 159–160)

Hence, DERHGO's shift from a primarily philanthropic orientation to an approach aimed at fostering rural civic engagement, particularly one framed in terms of claiming political and social rights, brought about tension both with the FMDR and with key figures in the PRI, whose tacit support had enabled the organization's early inroads. A rift emerged between FMDR's national directorate and DERHGO during this era as FMDR began to accuse DERHGO of drifting toward "political" rather than "social" aims. In 1985 FMDR funding of the Tulancingo center was cut off. At the same time problems erupted in the relationship between DERHGO and SOMEX. Refusing to confine its role to the recruitment and organization of credit applicants for the bank, DERHGO directed its efforts instead toward developing "integral" projects in the communities. The bank responded by withdrawing its partnership, claiming that DERHGO's failure to recruit new groups at its previous pace meant that their joint venture was no longer financially worthwhile. Soon afterward, Mexico suffered a series of major currency devaluations, which effectively decapitalized DERHGO by drastically shrinking the real value of its endowment. By the 1990s FMDR had founded a new regional affiliate in Tulancingo, the Hidalgan Foundation for Rural Service (FHAR). The FHAR continued the FMDR's long-standing focus on rural development projects aimed at increasing agricultural productivity and commercialization and, as its name suggests, frames its intervention in the idiom of charitable "service." In contrast, DERHGO redirected its program toward rural popular education, human rights, and fair-trade initiatives.

Although social and economic demands formed the primary agendas of Mexican social movements in the 1970s, by the 1980s the focus had begun to shift toward calls for human rights and democratization. This shift, which accompanied crises of state legitimacy and accountability, was characterized in part by demands from NGOs for official recognition and the beginning of long struggle to institutionalize their role in policymaking. Thus NGOs came to serve as institutional links between grassroots movements and intellectuals and "in the process, a new sense of citizenship . . . emerged, combining community-based self-organization for socioeconomic development with a political push for accountable government" (Fox and Hernández 1992, 168). This new framework encouraged many more NGOs and movements to become involved in electoral politics but often from the side of voter education and poll monitoring rather than direct engagement with political parties or candidates. Horizontal alliances among civil-society groups later enabled the successful growth of the prodemocracy movement of the 1990s. Umbrella groups like Alianza Cívica (Civic Alliance) skillfully leveraged international media attention and human rights discourse in order to pressure their government into a series of important reforms. Tulancingo NGO workers warmly recalled this period of activism as a time when local civil-society groups shared a sense of purpose and hope for the future, worked together closely, and interacted regularly with colleagues from around the country. They envisioned a future where these tightly networked NGOs would continue to act as independent monitors of the state and advocates for citizen rights. Given the important role NGOs had played in the pro-democracy movement, they expected to wield greater influence in policy discussions at the local and national levels and to receive public support.

Ironically, in the years immediately following Fox's victory, the Mexican NGO sector slid into a period of disenchantment. After championing free elections as the instrument of democratic change, many found themselves shut out of decision-making processes dominated by appointed technocrats. When the outcomes of those decisions led to further economic hardship, the NGOs were called upon to fill in for shrinking social services. In the 1970s and 1980s DERHGO had been accused of spreading communism, and in the 1990s it was celebrated locally as a champion of democracy, but by the date of its twenty-fifth anniversary in 2003 it was largely ignored by the state. One of the cofounders of DERHGO found this disappointing. "It is better to be thought dangerous," he said, "than not to be thought of at all."[3]

THE STRUGGLE TO BE TAKEN INTO ACCOUNT: HIDALGAN NGOS AFTER THE *ALTERNANCIA*

In period immediately following the 2000 election, many of the NGO coalitions that had helped to organize the pro-democracy and human rights movements began to fall apart, leaving their former members isolated from one another. In their place a series of major NGOs like Marta Sahagún de Fox's foundation, called Vamos Mexico (Let's Go, Mexico!), organized on the North American nonprofit model, have risen to national prominence. The number of grant-maker and pass-through foundations in Mexico has grown rapidly, opening Mexican NGOs up to corporate and international sponsorship (Natal, Greaves, Lainé, and García 2002; Verduzco, List, and Salamon 2002). Whereas many older organizations founded during the 1970s and 1980s pursued deprofessionalization and popular education as models for social solidarity, the newcomers promote professionalism and technical assessment, relating to their constituents more as consultants than as companions on the road to national progress.

These changes have prompted reflection on the shifting composition of the "third sector" and its relationships to the state. In social-science and activist circles during the late 1990s, this tension manifested itself in a series of debates on public-private partnerships. A heavily cited article by development scholar Faranak Miraftab, republished in *Sociedad Civil: Análisis y Debates* (the journal of Mexico City's Fundación DEMOS), asked whether it was possible for NGOs to use state funds or partner with state agencies without compromising their organizational autonomy. To what extent must NGOs engage in "flirting with the enemy" (Miraftab 1997)? What were the available means by which NGOs might participate in policy-making processes without becoming co-opted? Although the normative tone of these debates often obscured the complex political and social compromises that had enabled the emergence of Mexican NGOs in the first place, they indexed a growing anxiety over the increasingly difficult institutional position of NGOs.

In Mexico, NGOs established for public benefit are officially designated as *asociaciones civiles*, or civic associations. In order to operate legally, they must apply both to the Public Registry of Property and to the Federal Taxpayers Registry. The formal paperwork entailed by this process is infamously burdensome. According to the NGO Law Monitor, published by the International Center for Not-for-Profit Law:

> A number of reports have to be filed such as government funding reports, fiscal reports to the federal government, as well as the local government: monthly, annual, transparency, social security reports, audits, information for the Transparency web page . . . reports to the government where an organization receives public funds, reports to the ministry of the field of activities, like the Education Ministry, reports to the Labor Ministry, reports to the Ministry of Social Development where an organization is registered with the Registry of Social Development, and reports to federal and state tax authorities. (International Center for Not-for-Profit Law 2011)

At DERHGO, for example, this official documentation customarily required the labor of one full-time employee and periodic assistance from a local accounting firm. Hence, although no legal barriers prevented any Mexican citizen from founding an NGO, the resources and level of education required for official inclusion within this "space of participation" effectively barred all but the small middle and upper classes.

Beginning in the 1980s the federal Finance Ministry also began to treat NGOs and cooperatives as if they were large businesses or tax shelters by taxing them at high rates. In fact, it was not until 2007 that the Mexican legislature approved a bill that exempted private donations to nonprofits from federal taxes. The NGOs interpreted this treatment as an attempt to broaden the federal tax base and impose greater control on their operations (Fox and Hernández 1992, 185–186). It has served as a rallying point during the last two decades as they have sought to institutionalize their social and political role vis-à-vis both state and society. In 1994 a coalition of NGOs called the Council on Civil Society (Consejo de la Sociedad Civil, or CSC), led by the Mexican Center for Philanthropy (Centro Mexicano para la Filantropía, or CEMEFI) began to lobby the Mexican Congress in favor of the creation of a

Law of Promotion for Civil Society Organizations. The purpose of the legislation was to publicly recognize their role in Mexican society, provide an official legal framework for partnerships with state agencies, and enable NGOs to participate in official policy-making processes. The number of NGOs had exploded in the late 1990s, and many began to look for new sources of support and ways of participating in public decision-making processes. The quest for public legal recognition became especially urgent after the 2000 elections, as the large pro-democracy coalitions lost their common focus and, consequently, their political clout.

While the leaders of some Tulancingo NGOs began to support candidates from particular political parties, others quietly cultivated relationships with multiple groups of political elites simultaneously. Still other organizations, particularly newcomers affiliated with prominent international NGOs, or INGOs, had not yet developed strong political reputations. Yet to publicly ally with one particular political position was to endanger the organization's legitimacy as a "social" rather than "political" actor, authorized to represent the interests of "civil society" in general rather than those of a particular class or faction. These implicit "rules of the game" linked contemporary NGO practices to both the ethic of "Civic Catholicism" as well as the earlier organizing categories deployed by the PRI. They were also related to an emergent phenomenon in Tulancingo politics; a growing number of politicians, seeking to secure the nomination of their parties to candidacy for high office but prevented by new electoral rules from engaging in some of the more blatant methods of vote buying, had taken to founding charities or assistential development NGOs whose sole purpose was to purchase goodwill and name recognition through "good works." The most well-known example is that of the Fundación Hidalguense, which was used to promote the political career of the infamous Hidalgan PRI politician Gerardo Sosa Castelán (Rivera Flores 2004). In fact, the growth of alternative parties after the 2000 elections, far from signaling a fundamental shift in power, merely enabled lesser members of these powerful families to seize new opportunities for political advancement. Likewise, it is possible to interpret the growth of NGOs during this period as a response in part to new political opportunities rather than a transparent upwelling of civic engagement.

In December 2003 the CSC sponsored the Hidalgo State NGO Forum in the capital city of Pachuca as part of a national organizing drive in support of its legislative efforts. In the library of the Arturo Herrera Cabañas Foundation, representatives of more than a dozen NGOs from the region gathered to discuss the common problems they faced following the 2000 elections. The organizations ranged from indigenous media groups to development organizations, education and health-care service groups, and artists' collectives. What emerged from their discussions was a clear understanding of NGOs as legitimate representatives of civil society with a moral imperative to respond to social needs. They demanded to be "taken into account" by the politicians and technocrats who had shifted so much responsibility onto their shoulders.

While most of the participants in the forum agreed on the importance of presenting a united front, there was little consensus on what sorts of organizations should be included under the law and how a unified agenda might be articulated. Much of the disagreement took place over whether merely "assistential" organizations (viewed by the forum participants as paternalistic charities) should be included in the definition of an NGO. Magazine (2003) describes the circulation of a similar discourse among NGOs working with street children in Mexico City during that same period, noting that there the critique of *asistencialismo* rested upon the potential of charitable giving to foster dependency on the part of recipients. Likewise, conversations at the Hidalgo State NGO Forum centered on the perceived tendency of this mode of philanthropy to reinforce patron-client relationships rather than fostering rights-based democratic citizenship. Some participants also questioned whether NGOs, who represented diverse sets of issues and constituents, could reasonably be expected to support a single social or political agenda; this also seemed to them reminiscent of patronage politics rather than pluralistic democracy. They feared the "third sector" might be transformed into yet another interest group grafted onto old pyramidal political models.

Despite these disagreements, however, the participants were consistent in their characterizations of NGOs as both representatives of and mentors for "civil society." Participants agreed that the services they provided were by all rights owed by the state to its citizens, but NGOs had taken on the responsibility for their delivery, as the state was either ineffective or unresponsive. As one participant put it, "all civic organizations are for the public benefit. Therefore, they ought to be supported with legal and financial guarantees, and with funds." Thus NGOs were posed as voluntary public advocates for the fulfillment of the social rights of citizens. As advocates of the "common good" of the nation, they were deserving of government recognition and support regardless of whether their organizational objective was social transformation or temporary assistance to the needy (Richard 2009).

The new Law for the Promotion of Activities Undertaken by Civil Society Organizations, for which the CSC was lobbying, seemed to offer a juridical basis for such a relationship but also presented the forum participants with a threat to their organizational autonomy. Although NGOs had long used personal connections to power brokers and participation in popular demonstrations as means of influencing the public agenda, the proposed law did not concretely specify additional channels for them to participate in policymaking. Given the high degree of "connectivity" between the NGO leaders and the political class, participants in the forum also quickly pointed out the possibility that the proposed law might merely provide a new source of official funds for patronage. One representative of the CSC suggested that self-regulation and transparency in the use of state funds (specifically, setting up a system of reporting that would feed into a public-information clearinghouse) might be a partial solution. On the whole, however, participants seemed nervous about the implied shift in their organizations' identities from democratic activists to social-service intermediaries. One later complained that she was particularly troubled by the notion that the new law, although recognizing the importance of NGOs' work for Mexican society, would ultimately make them more accountable to the state than to the rest of society.

After a decade of negotiation, the final version of the Law for the Promotion of Activities Undertaken by Civil Society Organizations was signed by President Vicente Fox in 2004. In 2005 an official federal registry of NGOs was created. Registration is required of any NGO that wishes to access federal funds or participate in public-private partnerships created by the Ministry of Social Development or other federal entities. Applicants are required to rewrite their bylaws to conform to a single federal standard and are limited to applying for funds from already existing programs (rather than proposing new ones). The final version of the law not only prohibits NGOs that receive state funding from supporting particular candidates (as expected) but also contains a provision prohibiting them from engaging in any political activity intended to influence legislation. Hence the law encourages the activities of NGOs that are complementary to the state's social-development goals, but it does not provide a direct or legitimate means of influencing the formulation of those goals. Moreover, although NGOs are no longer subject to the sort of government harassment many experienced in the 1970s and 1980s, the International Center for Not-for-Profit Law (2011) found that they "are often not provided adequate protection by the government in the face of threats and violence from others."

During the period of democratic disenchantment that followed Fox's election, the staff of DERHGO, like the members of other Hidalgan NGOs, saw clear advantages to the unified pursuit of official federal recognition and support. By the end of the decade, however, few of their initial concerns about the possible modes by which their work might be "taken into account" by the state had been resolved. Some of the older NGOs in Tulancingo declined to petition for inclusion in the National Registry of Civil Society Organizations on the grounds that the costs in labor and resources outweighed any potential benefits. Others like DERHGO and its sister organization, the Sergio Méndez Arceo Human Rights Committee, took part in a campaign of "nonconformist" NGOs, which have rejected the registration process outright as antidemocratic and continue to operate "informally." By 2010 most of the Tulancingo NGOs listed in the *Registro Nacional* were relative newcomers, not in existence during the period leading up to the 2000 elections. By controlling the way "organized civil society" is managed and by excluding groups that are not defined in this way from deep "participation" and dialogue on policy, the Mexican state is able to define the category of its legitimate interlocutors as well as the scope of any dialogue. From a historical perspective these developments seem not so much to break with earlier state tactics but rather to modify them for a new era.

CONCLUSION: NGOS AND NEOLIBERAL DEMOCRACY IN MEXICO

The neoliberal project is currently in crisis in Mexico on both economic and political grounds. The contradictions that have emerged since 2000 demonstrate that transition theories that assumed that political liberalization would naturally follow from economic liberalization were either naïve or shortsighted. Moreover, the neo-Tocquevillian fascination with NGOs as laboratories for democratic citizenship tended to oversimplify both their (often undemocratic) internal dynamics as well as the complex ways in which they are embedded in particular political, social, and economic contexts. More than a decade after the fact, it appears that the overwhelming academic focus on the 2000 elections as the defining moment in Mexico's democratic transition was a red herring. The "government of change" created via that election proved not to be as important (or as indicative of change) as the upwelling of associational life that preceded it or the ways in which the democratic "wave" was alternately channeled and fragmented afterward. One part of that hegemonic transition narrative portrayed the surge in the number of NGOs as indicative of the growth of civil society in the form of a "third sector," through which the Mexican people might govern themselves. We can see this at work in Calderón's reworking of the meaning of the grassroots struggle for democracy and his recasting of the role of "organized civil society" in Mexico's future. However, the model of active citizenship embodied in modern Mexican NGOs is related to earlier historical practices, both democratic and hierarchical. The growth of the "third sector" and the forms of social action it has enabled, which are now posed as a remedy for the social rifts created by neoliberal retrenchment, are both a response to and a product of the ways the neoliberal project has been negotiated in Mexico in the last thirty years. Bornstein (2012) underlines the importance of investigating how these emergent "forms of giving and helping," which take place both within and outside formal institutional frameworks, are related to older, culturally grounded models of gift exchange and social solidarity. I further argue that if we wish to evaluate the influence of NGOs as emergent forms, we must attend to the complex ways in which the shifting political landscapes in which they take root help to shape the forms of intervention it is possible for them to undertake and the compromising relationships they must negotiate.

As Fox and Hernández (1992) point out, the first wave of modern Mexican NGOs to emerge in the 1970s and 1980s were oriented around a dual mission—organizing communities for socioeconomic development and self-reliance and organizing broad-based coalitions in favor of accountable government. Groups like DERHGO undertook these projects with a view to transforming Mexican society into a more egalitarian system where the ritualized social and economic dependency of the poor upon the powerful would no longer prevent them from claiming their rights as citizens. Nonetheless, the tacit political rules of the era dictated that NGOs limit themselves to modes of civic action that could be read primarily as social assistance rather than political critique in order to avoid scrutiny and possible repression. By operating in gray areas, as DERHGO did in rebellion-prone rural Hidalgo, and by creating broad-based coalitions, NGOs helped to organize and structure the pro-democracy movement of the 1980s and 1990s. In the post-2000 era, however, the NGOs' struggle to be taken into account by the state in official policy decisions has resulted in a process of institutionalization that makes it increasingly impossible for them to hold the Mexican government accountable for citizens' social welfare. In fact, the institutional expectation for "official" NGOs is that they will act in partnership with government agencies to propose and implement solutions to particular social problems emphasized in the agencies' strategic plans. However, there remains no official channel through which NGOs might engage in broader critiques of the neoliberal model in order to confront the root causes of the problems they seek to address since "official" NGOs are expressly prohibited from attempting to influence the legislative process.

The issue is not just whether, from the perspective of target populations, NGOs function as Trojan horses of neoliberal values or cultivators of democratic practice. Rather, it has to do with the nature of the model of social solidarity they come to mediate in particular historical and cultural contexts. That is, who is called into action on behalf of whom, and in what ways do they act? Although the language of democratic citizenship has now been adopted by political elites both on the Right and in the center, the earlier emphasis that popular pro-democracy movements placed on accountability and the redress of inequality has largely been removed from official political discourse in Mexico. Calderón's congratulatory speech to the winners of the 2010 Premio Nacional de Acción Voluntaria y Solidaria holds Mexican citizens personally accountable for their contributions to the "common good" but largely avoids the issue of the government's own role in producing the conditions of deprivation and vulnerability, which make these virtuous interventions necessary. The removal of the expectation of the government's obligation to honor the individual and social rights of citizens thus enables a collapsing of the categories of philanthropy and civic action within the official discourse. The contradictions produced by neoliberal reforms and the enduring structural inequalities that neoliberalism has failed to resolve are thus naturalized. As the process of retrenchment has unfolded, Mexico has witnessed the concomitant naturalization of neoliberal modes of social action, albeit refracted through the historical legacies of particular forms of organization and intervention (see Postero and Goodale, Chapter 1 in this volume). Deepening poverty and exclusion and even epidemic violence are presented as opportunities for the enactment of civic virtue rather than grounds for a refounding of the social contract. Indeed, Calderon's speech (and the creation of the Premio itself) emphasizes the moral obligation of Mexicans to ameliorate one another's social suffering as the only legitimate means of repairing a *patria* divided by wealth and bloodshed. In so doing, Calderon rhetorically transforms rights into gifts and charity into democratic activism.

PART THREE

CARE AND PUNISHMENT: BIOPOLITICS AND NEOLIBERAL VIOLENCE

CHAPTER 7

NEOLIBERAL RECKONING

Ecuador's Truth Commission and the Mythopoetics of Political Violence

Christopher Krupa

Ecuadorians have not had to deal with the guerrilla groups and drug traffickers that plague its neighbors. In fact, in the 1980s, Ecuador was considered an island of peace in a convulsed Latin America.

—Osvaldo Hurtado, *Structural Problems of Ecuadorian Democracy* (2009)

Your successful campaign against terrorism has kept Ecuador an island of peace in South America. . . . We are proud we could be of assistance against subversion.

—U.S. Department of State to Government of Ecuador, March 25, 1988

The shortest way between two points, between violence and its analysis, is the long way round, tracing the edges sideways like the crab scuttling.

—Michael Taussig, *Defacement* (1999)

INTRODUCTION: ISLANDS OF PEACE AND HISTORY

Early in 2007 the government of Ecuador announced its plans to form a "truth commission" to investigate allegations of widespread human rights abuse committed by previous administrations. The presidential decree (Ministerial Accord #305) that set the commission in motion was one of the first major acts of state undertaken by President Rafael Correa, sworn in less than four months earlier. The timing of Correa's motion was not unusual. Many of the thirty-plus truth commissions formed around the world since 1974 have followed closely on the heels of regime change. As Jonathan Tepperman notes, "Unthinkable just a short time ago, such gestures now accompany practically every transition from civil war or authoritarian rule. Announcing the creation of a truth commission has become a popular way for newly minted leaders to show their democratic bona fides and curry favor with the international community" (2002, 128). What was unusual in Ecuador's case, however, was that no such transition was taking place—unlike its predecessors, Ecuador was not emerging from civil war, authoritarian rule, or anything close to genocidal state violence. The truth the commission was after, rather, went further back. Its mandate instructed it to "realize a deep and independent investigation of human rights violations occurring *between 1984 and 1988*" (Government of Ecuador 2007, 1; emphasis added)—a twenty-five-year gap between violence and its reckoning that stretches even modest definitions of what "late," "transitional," or even "posttransitional" justice might imply today (Collins 2010; Olsen, Payne, and Reiter 2010; Shaw and Waldorf 2010).

More curious still was the very suggestion that Ecuador, of all places, had a past warranting such an investigation at all. Ecuador is commonly regarded as one of the only countries in the continent to have endured the 1980s free of state violence—the proud "island of peace in a convulsed Latin America," as ex-President Osvaldo Hurtado famously put it. This image has given Ecuador an ambiguous place in continental analyses of neoliberalism's path of emergence. As Greg Grandin writes:

> With a few important exceptions such as Costa Rica, Mexico, and Ecuador, state- and elite-orchestrated preventative and punitive terror was key to ushering in neoliberalism in Latin America. The prerequisite for the rapid economic restructuring

> that took place throughout the Americas beginning full throttle in the 1980s . . . had as much to do with the destruction of mass movements as it did with the rise of new financial elites invested in global markets. (2004, 14)

This is an eloquent summary of the story of neoliberalism's foundational violence in the Americas—a tale of origins that instrumentalizes terror as the means through which Latin America was made into a blank slate for transnational capital and its political advocates to implement their agendas without radical opposition. Ecuadorian neoliberalism, as a key exception, has long been deprived of an origin myth—an island of peace adrift in the waves of history made elsewhere. What then are we to make of the U.S.-backed "campaign against terrorism" referenced in the interstate correspondences of the period and their suggestion that elements of "subversion" had to be eliminated for such a peace to prevail? This altogether different, more violent history, buried below the official narratives of Ecuadorian exceptionalism, is what the Truth Commission was charged with unearthing. But why? And why now? What might the victims of this untold history have to contribute to twenty-first-century Ecuador?

COMMISSIONING RUPTURE

> Truth commissions . . . construct the national self with regard to the violent national past . . . and they assert a discontinuity with that same past. . . . The present order is presented as purified, decontaminated and disconnected from the old authoritarian order.
> —Richard Ashby Wilson, "Anthropological Studies of National Reconciliation Processes" (2003)

The years 1984–1988 are not an arbitrary focus for the Truth Commission's investigation. They mark the presidential term of wealthy coastal businessman León Febres Cordero, commonly credited for having led "the first right-wing neoliberal government in Ecuador" (Montúfar 2000, 9). Billed in the mid-1980s by Ronald Reagan as an "articulate champion of free enterprise" and by the International Monetary Fund as "a model debtor,"[1] it was Febres Cordero who is considered to have first oriented the national political economy toward financial-sector deregulation, export-oriented production, the elimination of price and wage controls, foreign investment, and the privatization of state services (Conaghan 1988; Hey and Klak 1999; Zuckerman 1986)—the origins of what Alain de Janvry et al. (1991, 1579) would later describe as Ecuador's "classically neoliberal program."

As is well known, Rafael Correa organized his victorious 2006 presidential campaign around the promise to "end the long and sad night of neoliberalism," a promise he repeated at his inauguration the following January with the emphasis that his election should be seen as marking "not merely an *epoch of change*, but rather a *change of epochs*" for Ecuador and Latin America as a whole (Conaghan 2008, 47; Escobar 2010, 5). Answering the question raised by Correa's promise—just how long and how sad was Ecuadorian neoliberalism, really?—was, this chapter argues, the central task facing the Truth Commission. Its job was to turn a national public secret of state violence into a proper origin myth—to document the true terrors of Ecuadorian neoliberalism at the moment of its purported transcendence.

To suggest this is to argue that the primary commodity produced by truth commissions and their "incredible machines of documentation" may be neither truth nor justice but a national-temporal orientation that might be shorthanded as *rupture* (O'Neill 2005, 331). As Nenad Dimitrijevic argues, truth commissions' "comprehension of the relationship between the past, the present, and the future rests on a poorly formulated idea of a new beginning, where the act of the regime change is perceived as a watershed between a 'then' and a 'now' " (2006, 371). This pushes Tepperman's point further: rather than simply accompanying political transitions, truth commissions have become central agents in their manufacture. The painstaking work of these commissions calls upon history and memory to bear witness to violence's pastness and, at the same time, spectacularizes the transition into a period of peace, democracy, and human rights. It is around rupture that periods qua periods are formed—the thens and nows structuring any historical imaginary. As Olivia Harris long ago cautioned anthropologists, the act of periodization should not be regarded as "an innate function of the way that human beings conceptualize and give meaning to the past" (1995, 11). It is rather a major technology of temporal subjectification, "frequently grounded in myths which posit a sharp break in the flow of events according to criteria which are themselves derived from ethical and political concerns"—concerns that, it follows, are contemporaneous to the moment of period making itself, not the historical locations they reference (Harris 1995, 21).

At the start of 2007 the political concerns of the Correa administration centered on the consolidation of a governing platform based on the rather ostentatious discourse of epochal shift and more specifically on defining the altogether amorphous promise of postneoliberal transition. Correa's flair for rhetorical hyperbole has by now become one of his trademarks, part of his characteristic style of governing. "Never have Ecuadorians seen a president so obsessed with, and so skillful at, communications and public relations," Catherine Conaghan (2008, 47) notes. Forming a Truth Commission in South America's only country thought not to need one, some twenty-five years after the violence in question, may evidence this mode of rule based on "direct, unmediated appeals to public opinion" (ibid.). But Correa's invocation of a specialist institution of transition making right at the moment he was promising Ecuadorians a major one makes its Truth Commission seem not so unusual at all. Set against the dislocated and "exceptional" world of Ecuadorian neoliberalism, what the commission offered Correa was a highly conventional story of foundational violence into which the broader experience of neoliberal Ecuador could be metonymically condensed. The opening line of the commission's final report, released to the public in July 2010, makes this point its core argument: "Ecuador was a victim, *equal to other countries in the Latin American continent*, of grave human rights violations committed by the state, which imposed terror through its projects of political, economic, and cultural domination" (Comisión de la Verdad 2010, vol. 1, 11; emphasis added).[2]

As Harris (1995) emphasizes, periodization and rupture making rest on a blurring of historic and mythic genres. This identification of a sacrificial scene that constitutes the neoliberal order and the abstraction of that order into the continental history of neoliberalism is the blueprint for a new national myth. With that, what the commission promises Correa's Ecuador is a proper neoliberal past and a solid justification for a very different sort of future. Later I discuss the manufacture of this past and the violence found to have been buried in it. First, however, I examine the more general linkages between myth and violence that make Ecuador's Truth Commission—and perhaps others—such a powerful force of historical production.

SPEAKING CORPSES: THE MYTHOPOETICS OF VIOLENCE

> Myth . . . is a language which does not want to die: it wrests from the meanings which give it its sustenance an insidious, degraded survival, it provokes in them an artificial reprieve in which it settles comfortably, it turns them into speaking corpses.
>
> —Roland Barthes, *Mythologies* (1972 [1957])

In likening myth to a speaking corpse, Barthes (1972 [1957]) has sharply pinpointed a rather unique property shared by both violence and mythic production—a capacity of each to develop generative potencies out of acts of destruction. He distinguished myth from everyday or "historical" speech by the former's imposition of new meanings on the latter's already-signified communicative chains. More specifically, this means that the fully composed sign in linguistic relation 1 becomes the signifier in linguistic relation 2 (which he called its "form"), creating space for a new signified (or meaning, which he called a "concept") to be imposed on it, forming an entirely new sign (which he called the "signification"). Myth "bears on objects already prepared," Barthes argued (ibid., 154); it appropriates them, distorts them, and deforms them; it performs "a robbery by colonization" (132) to the extent that "through the concept, it is a whole new history which is implanted in the myth" (119). Barthes's point in examining myth in this way was to understand how certain political projects naturalize their claims upon reality—how certain powerful "concepts" or meanings imparted on dimensions of a given reality come to appear as indisputable organic traits of those dimensions themselves. To Barthes myth making centers on the "passing from history to nature": "it abolishes the complexity of human acts, it gives them the simplicity of essences" and makes "things appear to mean something by themselves" (143).

In a similar vein, Begoña Aretxaga argues that violence tends to create two products: the corpse or victim and a "surreal, uncanny, and chilling" realm of meaning, affect, and fantasy produced around it (2000, 46). Aretxaga calls this second product violence's "surplus." In her analyses of state terrorism in the Basque country, she shows how this fantastical realm of meaning developed veracity through its creation out of the indisputable materiality of the victim's body. Such is how, she argues, something so fantastical and amorphous as the state comes to achieve a veneer of objective presence through violence, a retroactive attribution of agency to an object constituted in its suchness only by its effects (Aretxaga 2000). Elaine Scarry (1985) drew a similar argument from her analysis of torture, calling this realism function of violence "analogical substantiation"—a signification slippage that allows the incontestable materiality of the body in pain to lend facticity to all sorts of truth claims, starting with the solidification of the agent or regime of violence itself. It is this quality of violence, she argued, that "permits one person's pain to be translated into another person's voice, that allows real pain to be converted into a regime's fiction of power" (ibid., 18). Allen Feldman (1991) referred to this as the "legitimizing potential of the politically encoded corpse" (253), a conversion of the body of the dead into a material "surface" on which "historical maps are made manifest," debated, and exchanged (233). To extend Aretxaga's argument in this regard, one of the greatest potentialities of violence might lie in the incapacity for its surplus to ever fully be consumed, once and for all. It is violence's signifiers, more than its victims, that circulate, continually positing "history as a cultural object susceptible to alteration," always open to new mythical renderings (ibid.).

The power of a truth commission rests on its ability to invest corpses with speech and to make what they say matter. It means wrestling with the semiotic properties invested in victims' bodies at their point of production, the truth-making surplus of violence itself (linguistic relation 1), and, through appropriation, imparting a "whole new history," a second-order signification, in them (linguistic relation 2). In what follows I trace the mythosemiotic work of Ecuador's Truth Commission and examine its conversion of historical artifacts into mythic devices for the postneoliberal age.

THE APPARATUS OF HISTORICAL PRODUCTION: HOW ECUADOR'S TRUTH COMMISSION WORKED

> Whoever seeks power must first control the apparatuses for the production and mimesis of history as material spectacle.
> —Allen Feldman, *Formations of Violence* (1991)

Ecuador's Truth Commission was publicly inaugurated in a massive ceremony in Quito's Plaza Grande on January 8, 2008. By the end of the month, state funding had been channeled to the commission, along with more than

300,000 declassified documents from the Council of National Security, the Ministry of National Defense, the National Police headquarters, and the U.S. Department of State (provisioned under Correa's parallel Law of Transparency). The commission secured political backing (enforced by the Ministry of Justice and Human Rights) to enter military buildings and private dwellings to inspect suspected sites of torture and detention, collect archives, and record testimonials. On September 10 and 11, 2008, the commission hosted an international conference on its work, drawing participation from experts who had worked with truth commissions in Argentina, Chile, Paraguay, South Africa, Peru, and Guatemala and advisory support from the California-based Center for Justice and Accountability and the United States Institute of Peace. In April and May 2009, convocations were published in national newspapers and on web pages requesting that nearly 300 named individuals present themselves to the commission to be interviewed about their involvement in human rights violations committed during the Febres Cordero years. By the end of its investigations in December 2009, 650 testimonies had been collected, 600 rights violations documented, 127 scenes of violation identified, and 456 victims named. Although these figures refer to violations that occurred between 1984 and 1988 "and other periods" stretching up through 2008, as the Ministerial Accord states,[3] these "other" twenty years seem to serve mostly as a comparative foil. The commission's final report showed that 311 of these victims, or 68 percent, suffered their abuse in the first four years.[4]

The commission's research followed a very specific and somewhat unique process. Research into any case began only with a voluntarily offered testimony by someone claiming victim status (victimhood here is associative, including family and friends of those directly affected), allowing the investigative process to present itself as an apolitical and disinterested attempt to simply verify an accusing body's claims. Each testimony was then assessed by a team of lawyers and psychologists, who broke it down and reorganized it into five different data streams (one each on the victim, the legal aspects, the perpetrators, and so on). These data streams then entered what the commission called the "validation phase," which sought to verify that the reported actions indeed occurred and did so in the manner presented. Research teams checked the dates, places, and names for accuracy and scoured the archives for corroborating evidence. Interviews with named perpetrators, summoned publicly, were launched within this phase. It was by adding this level of fact checking to the testimony that the commission's executive secretary, Cristhian Bahamonde, felt the Ecuadorian team was "pioneering a new approach" to how truth commissions might work. This was "not to doubt the victim," he stressed to me—"but it has been a while." As Bahamonde put it, "The new thing here is that it is not just the victim speaking but also the mediating research body."[5]

If this validation was intended to both overcome doubt in these potentially time-altered testimonies and to strengthen their truth-value, it also effected a transformation in the status of the victim's memory, ascribing to it not the bedrock location of absolute truth (regardless of any inaccuracies), as some anthropologists of human rights have advocated (see Sanford 2005), but rendering it both potentially flawed (though redeemable) and one source of archival data among others. Of the two versions of the violations—the victim's and the commission's—only the latter would survive the process and be officialized in the final report. This archival validation set the standards for a particular violation's inclusion in the national history of state violence.

A second transformation of victims' testimonies followed, guided by the commission's rather novel methodological goal to not reproduce a compendium of testimonials of individual rights violations but rather to reconstruct the actual *events* in which reported violations occurred. This they did by combining multiple testimonies of victims and perpetrators as well as supporting documents into what the commission refers to as a "case," a unit defined by its temporal occurrence, which often includes multiple individually counted violations (e.g., torture, detention, sexual abuse) committed upon a number of victims (some "cases" include as many as ninety victims). This overarching case-based organization of the material represents a further movement of the victim through the validation process from its singularity to multiplicity, a second level of abstraction from individual affliction into a one-of-many exemplar, whose archival significance is indexed primarily by its performative moment—its place in the event history of a chain of violent scenes. The organization of the commission's final report reflects this goal, which reads as a chronological narration of 108 cases, grouped into two volumes (1984–1988, 1989–2008), with each numbered case introduced by a sidebar that details its place and date of occurrence, the name(s) of the victim(s) and those "presumed responsible" (each linked to an index that lists all known information about them and often a photo), and the violations committed at the event.

* rubric of violations inclusion

What needs to be stressed in this outline of the commission's method is its production of a progressive series of abstractions from the particular to the general, a movement of attention from victim to event, from event to period, and from period eventually into an analytical profile of neoliberal excess, with violence highlighted as central to the foundations of neoliberalism in Ecuador. The following sections examine this profile in greater detail, showing how the commission expanded it into a thesis that envelops its entire report, making it as much an analytical document as an archival one. The truth it has produced, we shall see, is more rhetorical than testimonial, written more in what I have been calling, from Barthes, a mythic genre than a historical one. Like most truth commissions, Ecuador's had no juridical power to act on its findings and bring those deemed responsible to trial. As Tepperman notes, the "lack of trials is an essential aspect of the commissions' identity. . . . Unlike courts, they do not seek punishment or retribution" (2002, 130). However, like others, Ecuador's commission, headed by a lawyer, did seek to prepare the grounds for possible trials in the future.[6] It sought to show not only that rampant state violence did occur in the mid-1980s but also, as the commission's team repeatedly stressed to me, that it occurred in a fully *systematic*, *designed*, and *political* manner[7]—the grounds for charging Febres Cordero and his associates with having committed *crímenes de lesa humanidad*, crimes against humanity, to which an entire 500-page volume of the final report is dedicated to arguing in detail. Significantly, this volume, volume 2, appears before those (volumes 3 and 4) tracing the chronology of actual human rights violations. The latter appear, in the end, as the former's appendix—the evidence one might wish to consult if not entirely convinced by the overarching argument.

It is in the shadows of international law and juridical purification that the commission's more national mythic production is set. This is not surprising, given its role in essentially mediating a dialogue between two states, twenty-five years apart, about the ways that violence might be foundational to generating the social and political order each proposed. Myth, law, violence—what triad more completely maps out the fertile terrain of state investment in its own legitimacy? What better devices could a state draw on for writing its origin story and for discrediting those of its competitors? Starting with this question of origins and the struggles to narrate them effectively, the following sections turn our attention specifically to the 1984–1988 period, the main years of concern for Ecuador's Truth Commission. Looking first outside the commission's purview, the rest of this chapter moves increasingly toward unpacking the ways it builds an argument about how we should understand the violence of the period today.

ORIGIN STORIES: FEBRES CORDERO, ALFARO VIVE CARAJO, AND THE PATH TO NATIONAL RECONSTRUCTION

In his first presidential address of 1984, Febres Cordero added to clear and expected statements of his economic plan to "open the doors to foreign capital" the more unexpected declaration of his administration's "commitment to fighting all forms of terrorism" and its zeal "to eliminate the great scourge of our time." What makes this such an interesting statement is that nothing of any magnitude existed in the Ecuador of 1984 to justify antiterrorism as a founding principle of the new regime. A small guerrilla group known as Alfaro Vive Carajo (Alfaro Lives, Damn It, or AVC), the target of Febres Cordero's remarks, had formed in February 1983, but its actions throughout the following year had been entirely symbolic. Taking its name from the leader of Ecuador's 1895 Liberal revolution, the AVC was then known only for having stolen General Eloy Alfaro's swords from a museum in Guayaquil and his bust from a museum in Quito, for a press conference in September 1983, which announced its existence, and for plastering major cities in Ecuador with graffiti announcing "1983: Year of the People. Alfaro Lives, Damn It!" On the first of these actions, which most memorably brought the AVC to public awareness, founding member Edgar Frías notes in his memoirs the sense of historicist praxis it left on the guerrillas:

> The recovery of the swords of Alfaro and Montero, more than just a political-military action that showed the incipient structure of the AVC, had a spiritual, romantic, and magical connotation. It was like an encounter with the past, as we might have said to *don* Eloy: we are here to continue your struggle . . . you haven't died . . . you live. Damn it. It was like writing ourselves directly into the Civil Registry of History. It was our baptism. (1999, 21)[8]

It was Alfaro's claim to be leading an anti-imperialist uprising uniting all popular sectors against the conservative theocracy that then ruled Ecuador, as well as his proto-guerrilla style of organizing the revolutionary taking of Quito, that AVC leaders drew on in forging what they framed as the "historical objectives" of late twentieth-century Alfarismo—a mission that they saw as at once antioligarchic and nationalist but "neither Socialist nor Social Democratic" in ideology (see the 1985 platform reproduced in Frías 1999, 30). As AVC leader Arturo Jarrín put it in a 1985 interview, Alfaro's struggle "continues today because the objectives of Alfarismo, which are democracy, social justice, economic independence, national sovereignty, and pan-American patrimony, continue to be a felt necessity of the Ecuadorian people" (cited in Frías 1999, 108). The electoral victory of Febres Cordero crystallized the urgency of channeling this historic mission into a "direct confrontation with the oligarchy," giving rise to the AVC's organizing slogan of "democracy in arms" (ibid.).

Febres Cordero, in contrast, baptized his governing platform under the sign of radical discontinuity with the past. Although his predecessor, Osvaldo Hurtado (who assumed power when President Jaime Roldós died in a mysterious plane crash),[9] is often credited with "putting Ecuador on the road to neoliberalism" by launching an economic austerity plan that the next administration would only deepen,[10] Febres Cordero exaggerated their political differences to the extent of branding Hurtado a communist sympathizer whose social-reform programs had enabled the rise of the AVC (Hey and Klak 1999, 70; see also Conaghan 1988, 133; North 2004, 198; Salamea 1988, 29): "next to Osvaldo Hurtado," Febres Cordero famously said, "Mao Tse Tung is a child."[11]

Febres Cordero's effort to distance himself from the Hurtado administration was strategic. It not only placed the entire blame for the mounting fiscal crisis and socioeconomic instability on that administration and a misplaced notion of its leftist agenda but also allowed Febres Cordero to position his government and its aggressively right-wing, market-oriented political and economic platform as the only viable solution to national unrest. What Ecuador needed at a time like this, the president maintained, was a completely new kind of state leading a project of total national reconstruction—not incidentally the name of the right-wing coalition party (National Reconstruction Front, FRN), under which Febres Cordero assumed the presidency.

However, the claim that *national* reconstruction would start with not only a refoundation of the *state* but also one ostentatious in its control of ("legitimate") violence against a "terrorist" threat drew on its own historic reference, one that in fact should be credited with constructing Ecuadorian nationalism around its "island of peace" characterization. As Ecuadorian sociologist Erika Silva Charvet (2005) persuasively argues, Ecuador's identity as a "peaceful nation" was born in the 1940s, when official pleas for international sympathy framed its border wars with Peru as an imperial crusade against a "small" and "peaceful" country governed by a state too weak to be the agent of such aggression or to mount a proper defense against it. Revisionist histories written at the time equated the "Peruvian expansionism" of the 1940s with the "Cuzco expansionism" of the Incas, postulating a precolonial territorial and sociological integrity to the Ecuadorian nation before its political formation, ever threatened by violence from the outside. This newfound identity, based on Ecuador's "incapacity to dominate geography," Silva Charvet claims, "presented us with a reality—always mythically elaborated— . . . [showing] us to be more like the vanquished than the conquerors" (99): a crucial step toward what would become Ecuador's official cultural unification programs in the 1970s (Krupa 2011). At issue in this "mythical reality," Silva Charvet (2005) argues, was the translation evoked between violence effected upon both the national body and the cultural body, in which memory of Peru's 1941 invasion "implied for the large majority of Ecuadorians the mutilation of part of themselves, . . . expressed in the autoperception of being *tullidos, baldados, incompletes* [cripples, incompletes]" (100). What the violence showed was the need for a "unity of the population around the state and the existence of a political class with a better-developed sense of national consciousness—finally!" (126), Silva Charvet jests, "A modern bourgeois state!" (47).

Undergirding Ecuador's exceptionalist myth, in other words, is a certain idea of the state as itself "incomplete" for its incapacity to use force to defend its territory, shamed by its inability to dominate violence, and thereby requiring a sort of refounding through the consolidation of a new class project led by a unified, politically attentive bourgeoisie. This discourse linking territorial integrity, Peruvian expansionism, and militarist confrontation will emerge again in official explanations of the development of guerrilla activity in 1980s Ecuador (discussed later). However, twenty-five years after Febres Cordero's rise to power, Ecuador's Truth Commission would read his refoundational script as evidence of his intent to commit violence against his political opponents, a deliberate exaggeration of the state of domestic crisis and outright fabrication of a condition of internal war to justify and legitimize the strong military response to follow. The evidence suggests, its report maintains, "that the government of Febres Cordero was already predisposed, from the start of its formation, to govern on the basis of an institutionalization of violence [and in a way that tried to make] it appear legitimate in the eyes of society" (CV, vol. 2, 273). "We can confirm," it goes on to say, "that there existed a planned and concerted policy, systematic and generalized, which produced, as analyzed in this Report of the Truth Commission, violations of human rights from the very core of the government of Febres Cordero" (ibid., 284).

The notion that a new sort of state would be assembled around this notion of "crisis" was actually built into the bureaucratic structure of the Febres Cordero administration. Early in his term he formed a high-level working group called the Cabinet of Crisis, composed of top officials in the armed forces and national police, who coordinated an antiterrorist offensive under the aegis of designing, the Truth Commission suggests, "actions promising to show the [government] as savior, making frequent recourse to the phrase 'national reconstruction'" (CV, vol. 2, 276). This group's formation, the commission adds, shows that by "1985, only a few months after its possession [of the presidency], the government of Febres Cordero had already structured its antiterrorist policy, inspired by the model of President Reagan" (ibid., 270). And yet, this violence is said to have had a deeper political and economic logic: "What the antiterrorist policy was referring to [was a plan] to wipe out the formation of all sources that put in danger the implementation of neoliberal policies directed by Febres Cordero, giving them a dimension of internal war" (ibid., 272). It "had as its end the establishment of its model of the nation, a political-economic model easily identifiable: neoliberalism" (ibid., 265). And again:

> The necessity of implementing in Ecuador neoliberal politics, by applying economic and social measures that would pull the country out of crisis, required declarative

allocutions describing a situation in which stronger and more impactful values prevailed—such as terrorism—which tried to identify society's common enemy and whose response to it would [encourage society to] unite around the government and its politics. (CV, vol. 2, 270)

This framing of the violence as instrumental to the foundation of Ecuadorian neoliberalism summarizes what I am calling the Truth Commission's central thesis and governing myth. Supporting it is a series of secondary arguments about the broader frames of meaning in which the violence of the period was carried out and legitimated by the state. Three of these frames—excess, sacrifice, and externality—come together in the commission's overall attempt to show that violence depended on a faulty yet instrumental image of a country deep in crisis, for which the figure of the victim, embellished with conflicting meanings, emerged as the most condensed symbol of neoliberal murder.

FRAMING ATROCITY: EXCESS SURPLUS AND THE SACRIFICIAL ECONOMY OF NEOLIBERAL MURDER

> The subversion has to be killed like turkeys the night before the feast.[12]
>
> —Ecuadorian Secretary of Public Administration Joffre Torbay Dassun, 1985

In 1985, the same year that Febres Cordero publicly signed Ecuador to the International Convention against Torture and Other Cruel, Inhuman, or Degrading Treatment or Punishment, his secretary of public administration, Joffre Torbay Dassun, candidly outlined a more sacrificial agenda for how the regime was imagining its relationship with human rights (in Zuckerman 1986, 485; see also Pozo 2007, 350). The latter would prove a better summary of the year ahead. Quito's Ecumenical Commission on Human Rights documented 59 cases of torture in 1985, 43 of which occurred in the second half of the year (Americas Watch Committee 1988). In the same year, presidential orders to block a strike called by the United Workers' Front to protest a 60 percent increase in gas and transit prices resulted in at least five deaths (Zuckerman

1986, 487). A parallel strike on the coast left two students dead from police gunshots. "Esta es la hora de la patria contra la antipatria" ("this is the time of the homeland against the antihomeland"), Febres Cordero remarked during the height of the violence in September, brutally vindicating the sacrificial economy of state violence right at the moment when the nation it claimed to be consolidating was coming most undone (*El Comercio* 1985, cited in Pozo 2007, 282).

Through all of this, Alfaro Vive Carajo maintained just enough presence to serve as a focal point for military and police violence. Although ex-militant Juan Fernando Terán calls 1985 "the year registering perhaps the most complete and audacious operatives of the Alfarista political-military trajectory" (2006a, 13), the year in retrospect seems a tragic summary of the false starts, media spectacles, crushing defeats, and fateful blunders that plagued the guerrilla movement throughout its short existence. At least two clandestine national conferences were held in 1985, resulting in sophisticated organizational advances but also in capture of many trying to attend; an arms cache stolen (with help from Colombia's M-19) from a police unit in Quito was recovered when a cow fell into the hole in a park where it was hidden; in August, businessman Nahim Isaías Barquet was kidnapped for ransom by the AVC and the M-19, resulting in the torture and execution of AVC members and civilians; a month later, a botched rescue attempt by the state left Isaías Barquet and his kidnappers dead; other failed kidnapping attempts left AVC members hospitalized and in police custody; various radio stations were occupied, and two journalists were captured to spread the AVC's message, denounce the torture of its members, and call for a mass uprising against Febres Cordero; the Mexican Embassy was briefly occupied by the AVC to denounce Ecuador's rupturing of diplomatic ties with Nicaragua; and so on. Despite beginning the next year with the hope that *it* "would be the year in which the 'myth about the impossibility of implanting a rebel force in the country' would be destroyed," things turned even worse for the AVC in 1986, when discoordinated and poorly supported actions resulted in many deaths, including that of its leader, Arturo Jarrín (ibid., 19). Terán's summary of the movement's trajectory speaks clearly of its power and even existence, being mostly a fantastical creation of the state:

> Alfaro Vive Carajo would never have become more than another clandestine and ephemeral organization were it not for the words and actions of León Febres Cordero. . . . Not even in its best moments was the AVC anything more than an assemblage of two or three hundred militants with permanent operative capacity. However, even in its worst moments, thanks to the arrogance and imprudence of León Febres Cordero, the AVC appeared to be everywhere and much bigger than it actually was. . . . In his speeches and excessive actions, including those before becoming president of the republic, León Febres Cordero amplified this illusion. (Terán 2006b, 67–68)

Foreign witnesses to the period confirm this assessment. In 1986 Sam Zuckerman wrote that the state's "crackdown against a tiny, politically isolated armed underground has made illegal arrest, kidnapping and torture commonplace" (484). Two years later the Americas Watch Committee and the Andean Committee of Jurists noted that the government of Febres Cordero "has exploited the insurgency to justify repression against non-violent popular organizations and movements that oppose its conservative policies" (Americas Watch Committee 1988, 18; see also North, Kit, and Koep 2003, 106–107). Ecuador's Truth Commission would later expand these observations into an argument about how the violence of the period was meant to work, noting that people

> were seized in the streets for the sole reason of having long hair, for walking in a certain way, for being dressed in a manner considered suspect, for "erroneous" looks, or for participating in social movements. The exercise of state violence created an atmosphere of fear and terror within the scene of an internal war, a scene necessary to establish a hard-line government. (CV, vol. 2, 284)

The commission's statistical reconstruction of victim's testimonies and archival materials in fact shows only 19 percent of the 295 victims of the period to have had anything to do with the AVC or revolutionary activity at all (CV, vol. 2, 288).[13]

Such statistical reckonings with atrocity have long been valuable tools in efforts to deconstruct violence's truth claims. Well before truth commissions were invented, Ida Wells-Barnett used a similar method in the United States to prove that fewer than a third of all victims of lynching were even accused of rape, the dominant justification for its continuation among Southern whites at the end of the nineteenth century (Wells-Barnett 2002 [1895], 71). This evidence led her to a profound reframing of the modal category of "victim," showing how its official production under the identity of "black rapist" belied a more accurate identity as an emblem of black political and economic emancipation, over which white Southern society was attempting, through violence, to regain control. Similar to what Terán suggests about the AVC, the fantastical elaboration of a "rape mythos" in the American South enabled violent responses that confirmed the reality of an illusion of its own making (Wiegman 1993).

In the Truth Commission's reframing of the violence of 1984–1988, the category of "victim" was overdetermined by an excess, an exaggerated body count relative to the guerrilla threat that was meant both to retroactively confirm the reality of that threat and to eliminate the broader, nonarmed opposition to the conservative neoliberal project being implemented. Similar to William Robinson's pithy summary that "If the economic component [of neoliberal democracy] is to make the world available to capital, the political component is to make it safe for capital" (2006, 98), the commission argues that generalized fear among popular sectors was to be a midway product on the road to unrestricted capitalist restructuring of state and economy: "The necessity of implanting the neoliberal economic model . . . determines who its enemies are: whichever sectors oppose the development of capital and, consequently, those who would [be said to] oppose democracy" (CV, vol. 2, 270). Febres Cordero's homogenization of all of the victims and targets of state violence under the banners of "terrorist" and "subversive," common discursive strategies of the period, are discussed in the Truth Commission's report as efforts to criminalize all political opposition to the regime, "actions of a psychological nature [intended] to accentuate social polarities and differences, reprimanding [those involved in] street protests . . . and at the same time define the actions of oppositional or subversive groups in a way that its constituents were shown to be 'barbarous,' 'violent,' and 'delinquent'" (ibid., 272–273).[14]

What this analysis opens up is an understanding of the ways that violence always seems to arrive accompanied by a story, particularly about the victims, one that explains their death or harm in relation to their own actions or identities (Krupa 2009). This is precisely the point that Aretxaga (2000) and Scarry (1985) have astutely identified as the starting point for attempts to grapple with violence's generative powers—its "dual production," in Aretxaga's terms, of a victim out of the raw material of the body and a fantastical world of meaning out of its immediate process of transformation. Both authors went further still, noting how these stories of violence's victims were simultaneously stories of its protagonists, agentive performances constituting the latter by hard evidence of their worldly effects. It was this inauguration of an open-ended process of dialectical semiosis, I have argued, that made state violence so workable for truth commissions, so malleable to mythic resignification, so submissive to new political ends, including those rooted in appeals to historic transition, temporal rupture, and epochal shift. The incredible work of Ecuador's Truth Commission shows its clear understanding of this struggle over victim signification. What we are asked to trace, as readers of its report, is a resignification of the period's victims—made, by their death, into communist subversives, they are remade, by their unearthing, into evidence of and witnesses to neoliberal excess.

It is the synthetic exactitude with which the notion of "sacrifice" summarizes the generative imagery that enveloped Febres Cordero's relation to violence, his practice of it as an investment into the coproduction of neoliberal victim and state, that inspires the Truth Commission to read Secretary Torbay's unfortunate remark (quoted earlier) as among the most revelatory of the regime's logic. "In the period of Febres Cordero," the report states, "what was prevalent was the idea of the sacrifice of the other, akin to the sacrifice of turkeys, [that] the life of the persecuted was only utilitarian, only served to consolidate a politics based on neoliberalism" (CV, vol. 2, 309). Its critical rewriting of Torbay's remarks—"individuals will be killed who put in danger the stability of a system . . . [and], thanks to their elimination, the country will enjoy greater peace"—exposes the regime's efforts to nationally disperse responsibility for the violence and, under the claim that "the sacrifice is necessary because it is demanded by society to realize its own proper peace," to "compromise Ecuadorian society in a crime of state, as if it had given its approval from the start" (ibid., 308). Speaking of a different sort of sacrifice, Febres Cordero exemplified this position in a 1990 letter to the editor of *El Universo* newspaper, in which he claimed that "It is true, accepted, and recognized by everyone that the decision adopted by my government and carried out by the valiant expressions of sacrifice by the armed forces . . . freed the country and Ecuadorian society in general of worse and incomparably bad deeds" (cited in CV, vol. 2, 311). This sacrifice was feted to its own private feast in 1986, when Ronald Reagan threw a dinner in honor of Febres Cordero, calling him a "national leader who is clearly devoted to the political and economic freedom of his people" and commending him for his work in combating hemispheric "subversion" (Ronald Reagan Presidential Library 1986).[15] Evidence that the sacrifice was worthwhile was provided in media spectacles displaying huge caches of arms supposedly recovered from AVC storehouses, gruesome photos of dead "subversives," and live broadcasts of military takeovers of AVC bases (see CV, vol. 2, 287–291; Dávalos 2007)—what Febres Cordero called the "real, positive, tangible, and beneficial" results of his antiterrorist offensive (cited in CV, vol. 2, 310).

Plain to for all to see was that national reconstruction was a project that had to be built on the body of the sacrificial victim. In "la hora de la patria contra la antipatria," one of the key registers of sacrificeability was foreign connections, particularly those indexing historic threats to national sovereignty. Throughout Latin America, since at least the end of World War II, the label of "communist" has routinely carried the mark of the extranational, antipolitical, and unpatriotic. But in the 1980s this mark carried a particular significance in Ecuador. Its fateful loss of territory to Peru in the 1940s left that country as the master symbol of the external threat to national security and of the fragile condition of Ecuadorian sovereignty. This experience, we noted earlier, is routinely identified to this day as the origin of Ecuador's "exceptional" status as South America's "island of peace," more a mark of shame than of pride, the identity assumed by a defeated people and of a state unable to defend itself against external aggressors (Silva Charvet 2005). Less than four years before Febres Cordero took office, President Roldós's unsuccessful attempt to regain the lost lands in the Guerra de Paquisha dramatically confirmed that identity's relevance to the present and reinstated Peru's status as the quintessential symbol of foreign threat.

A newly declassified government document, written in October 1985 and titled "The Concept of Strategic National Security," shows how the Febres Cordero regime built what it termed a "hypothesis" of the "external conflict" in direct relation to this history. The document's authors (signed by León Febres Cordero and the general secretary of the Council of National Security, Edgar Vásconez Troya) posit that "PERU, having broken the status quo, would invade Ecuadorian territory, opposing the maintenance of . . . Territorial Integrity and National Sovereignty," has "proven the violence and speed of its actions in conquering vital objectives, with the aim of imposing political-territorial conditions that threaten the survival of the State" (Presidencia de la Republica 1985, 3). The Truth Commission reads this formative document of Febres Cordero's security discourse as suggesting two things: first, that the completely unsubstantiated claim that Peru remains an active threat to Ecuadorian sovereignty "shows the intention of the government to deepen that situation of crisis and insecurity necessary to implement a regime in a permanent state of war" (CV, vol. 2, 272)—this is revealed as being first an official *hypothesis* of a war not yet evident, part of the fantasy that Febres Cordero was developing around the notion of national crisis needing armed resolution; and, second, that oppositional groups such as the AVC "received instructions, support, and even financing from outside, in particular from Peruvian institutions: and with this," the report adds, Febres Cordero "wanted to make it appear as if the insurgent groups supported the Peruvian thesis, against the Ecuadorian *patria*" (274). Although entirely false,[16] this discursive overlapping of the AVC and Peru at once aimed to legitimate the violence directed at the opposition (as both revenge and national defense), impel the lacking "unity of the population around the state," which Silva Charvet identified as one of the central enduring effects of the 1940s' war, and, in a broader sense, finally show the state to have mastered the violence that left its sovereignty an open wound and its state shamefully incomplete ever since.

From Febres Cordero's efforts to define a mode of historicist praxis capable of overturning this entrenched nationalist myth, to the figuration of his opponent's bodies as sacrificeable to that cause, to the Truth Commission's work to rewrite those efforts as the markings of a period demanding closure, the study of the inextinguishable surplus of violated bodies seems to confirm Appadurai' s depiction of myth, paraphrasing Edmund Leach, as "a language of argument, not a chorus of harmony," that "kind of past whose essential purpose is to *debate* other pasts" (1981, 202). When it comes to reckoning with nationalist histories of violence, we are perhaps prone to finding that it is myths all the way down.

CONCLUSIONS: NEOLIBERAL RECKONING

> "Everyone" may know something very well without its becoming a fact, without its creating a new consciousness which would entail people assuming it in the . . . sense of its becoming a true identity.
> —Diane Nelson, *Reckoning* (2009)

Rafael Correa did not, strictly speaking, invent Ecuador's Truth Commission. Victims' groups had been pressing for one since the end of Febres Cordero's presidency and were twice successful in gaining state support.[17] Both attempts emerged under presidents—Abdalá Bucaram (1996–1997) and Lucio Gutiérrez (2003–2005)—who, like Correa, framed their elections as popular rejections of Ecuador's *partidocracia* (the political oligarchy of traditional ruling parties); both presidents were ousted from office by popular uprisings before completing their term, taking even token support for the commission down with them (see Krupa 2011). Perhaps the conditions were not yet ripe for transforming the island of peace's public secret into a truly historic identity.

Supporters of the commission have understood its delay to be largely an effect of Febres Cordero's continuing political influence over the country. As Eduardo Tamayo wrote in a new introduction to his 1994 book on the Febres Cordero regime:

> There has not been justice [in Ecuador] precisely because Febres Cordero abandoned the government [in 1988] but not power. From his home in El Cortijo in Guayaquil he continued governing the country at least until 2006. His party continued to control the Congress, and through the Congress he exercised great influence over the executive functioning and the Supreme Court of Justice, the Supreme Electoral Tribunal, the Constitutional Tribunal, and the organisms of State control. (2008, 3)

The Truth Commission's public figurehead, Sister Elsie Monge, explained this to me in a related fashion, emphasizing both the power of the ex-president's discourse and the comparative weight of the Ecuadorian violence vis-à-vis other countries of the region:

In general, in Ecuador, there has been a deliberate effort to say this is an island of peace and to cover up everything for this. This was the image that we were having to overcome, the island of peace. "Ecuador: Island of Peace." This island of peace thing minimized, covered up all sorts of abuse, see, and what's more is that we had two neighbors in which the repression was so great, Colombia and Perú with Sendero Luminoso, no? So, clearly, we never got to this magnitude, and so *no pasa nada* [nothing ever happens]. This was the phrase of Febres Cordero: here, *no pasa nada*, after massacring the people, *no pasa nada*. So what we are always saying is that clearly [in other countries] the magnitude [of deaths] was much greater, but the difference isn't between 100 or 1,000—one is too many, one disappearance. In other words, these aren't numbers but persons. In any case, these are the reasons I think that, here, *no pasaba nada* [nothing ever happened].[18]

Perhaps to even frame the delay as unusual or requiring explanation is to miss the point. The transition the commission was marking was not one of regimes but of periods. With that caveat, Correa's drawing on the commission at the moment he took up power was, by all accounts, highly conventional. This conventionality of Ecuador's story was what gave it its force. Indeed, it was very much part of the message that readers were to take from its work:

With the Truth Commission, created by Rafael Correa, hope has recently returned to not keep buried under a thick coat of impunity those acts which disturb and distort the democratic system and affect the victims who, in all these years, haven't been able to achieve that in this country a policy of truth, justice, and reparation be applied as they have done in other countries that lived through equal or worse situation to that of Ecuador. (Tamayo 2008, 3–4)

And "What is the fundamental feature of Febres Cordero-ism?" asks Tamayo, reflecting on the period in 2008:

Inspired by the ultra-conservative president Ronald Reagan and the British prime minister Margaret Thatcher, Febres Cordero attempted to implement the neoliberal model in the country through the politics of an authoritarian state that frequently used the resources of fear and terror to paralyze and divide all those who opposed his project. (2008, 4)

The message, it appears, is getting through.

If the 1980s onward have been broadly defined in Latin America through the experience of neoliberalism (see Schild, Chapter 8 in this volume), the period has also, in a not unrelated fashion, come to be understood as its "age of accountability" (Olsen, Payne, and Reiter 2012), a time when "Truth-telling . . . has increasingly come to be seen as . . . a positive end in itself" (Collins 2010, 21). However, with the truth of neoliberalism increasingly being found in its violence (see Zilberg, Chapter 9 in this volume), itself a producer of objects made to hold value "in themselves," a key question in the study of its institutions of accountability is how the *end* of violence meets up with the sorts of *ends* to which such powerful assertions of temporal rupture might be put (Nelson 2009). This is very much the sort of question that motivated Barthes in his efforts to identify certain modes of political engagement as *mythical*. It was the political utility of a communicative sign that ultimately, for Barthes, defined myth as a distinct genre: "we know that myth is a type of speech defined by its intention . . . much more than its literal sense," he noted (1972 [1957], 124).

Following Barthes's cue, this chapter has examined the mythopoetics of Ecuador's truth commission and asked how the raw material of a violence buried in public secrecy for twenty-five years was brought to light and made meaningful to a country said to be embarking on its postneoliberal transition. We identified the core of this new meaning complex as twofold: the accentuation of a sense of national-temporal rupture, a specialist service of truth commissions worldwide, and the metonymization of Ecuadorian neoliberalism with the violence shown to have started it. Nonetheless, the real glue in this story has been an attempt to better understand the semiotic potency of violence and the inextinguishable surplus (of meaning, fantasy, explanation) produced alongside or as part of, violence's victims. It was the malleability of this surplus that, we argued, was the basis of the truth commission's mythopraxis in Ecuador as perhaps elsewhere—its summoning up of the corpses of violence past and setting them to speech.

Yet violence, we noted, was somewhat peculiar in the scope of its capacity to speak truth. Part of its story seems to be that there is no story at all and that the entire truth of the matter is right there in the material evidence of the violated body, exactly as Dana Polan defined the spectacular as that which presents a world "without background, a world in which things exist or mean in the way they appear" (1986, 61). Violence, ever spectacular in this way, is akin to how Barthes (1972 [1957]) discussed mathematics and poetry, two languages apparently immune to interpretation, too already full and finished for mythic appropriation—an "anti-language" or a "murder of language, a kind of spatial, tangible analogue to silence" (ibid., 134) claiming to present "the transcendental quality of the thing, its natural (not human) meaning" (132), as Elaine Scarry (1985) famously also defined the politics of pain. "In passing from history to nature, myth acts economically," Barthes (1972 [1957]) notes; "it organizes a world without contradictions because it is without depth, a world wide open and wallowing in the evident, it establishes a blissful clarity: things appear to mean something by themselves" (143). But in instances where "the meaning is too full for myth to be able to invade it, myth goes around it, and carries it away bodily" (ibid., 132). Every line of a poem, once "captured by myth [will be] transformed into an empty signifier, which will serve to *signify* poetry" (ibid., 134), every mathematical formula made into a "pure signifier of mathematicity" (ibid., 132).

What we have examined in this chapter is the work of transforming each particular act of violence (this torture, that disappearance) in Ecuador between 1984 and 1988, every one of its 295 reported victims, into a pure signifier of violence itself and, with that, of neoliberal rationality. As Donald Donham rhetorically asks, "Can we imagine a current analyst in the human sciences . . . who poses a problem as one of 'violence,' while adopting a positive attitude toward it? Does not speaking of 'violence' always already contain a condemnation?" (2006, 19). By dredging up violence from the recesses of collective memory, Correa's institutionalization of the truth commission as an index of postneoliberal transition quite masterfully figures this sense of condemnation as the axis of historical subjectivity in the postneoliberal republic. More than simply a purification of violence from the state, it is this historicist compromise forged between citizen and state around condemnation and transcendence that marks the ends of violence in the work of Ecuador's truth commission.

> The pain, the fear, and suffering of the victims and families have to be known as part of the collective history of this country . . . this was a dark epoch that assassinated dreams and hope. This

government, humanist and democratic, in the name of the Ecuadorian state, apologizes to the victims. It apologizes to the victims and renews its compromise to transcend/rise above [*superar*] this bourgeois and repressive state [applause].

—Rafael Correa, speaking at the public launch of the Truth Commission's Final Report, July 6, 2010

CHAPTER 8

CARE AND PUNISHMENT IN LATIN AMERICA

The Gendered Neoliberalization of the Chilean State

Veronica Schild

WITHOUT A DOUBT, NEOLIBERALISM HAS lost political legitimacy over the past decade in Latin America, especially since the recent global financial crisis and its devastating economic impact. Resistance to neoliberalism in the region is manifold and widespread. The massive demonstrations and work stoppages in 2012 in Chile, following on the heels of the high school and university student demonstrations of 2011, are but the latest in a series of oppositions to the continuing hegemony of neoliberalism in Latin America. Yet, alternatives to the present modality of capitalist accumulation and the economic and state institutions buttressing it, although important, are also few, as are effective inroads into the transnational regulatory frame for global capitalism. Not all resistances to neoliberalism, in other words, have coalesced into possibilities for change, much less into full-fledged alternative forms of government and transformed systems of accumulation, including redefined modalities of social reproduction. Neoliberalism, aptly characterized as an "emergent *pensée*," continues to be a dominant form of governance. This form is marked on the one hand by "pious anti-poverty rhetoric" and on the other by "unstinting support for the prerogatives of foreign investors and domestic elites, together with a relentless emphasis on the need to keep politics firmly within the confines of the reigning orthodoxy" (Wood 2009, 138). Although once associated with the so-called Washington Consensus, it is entrenched today in the so-called post–Washington Consensus, or the agenda for a more comprehensive development adopted since the late 1990s under the World Bank's tutelage.[1]

This chapter focuses on Chile, a paradigmatic case of a successfully entrenched, or "deep," neoliberalism. It explores the transformation of the state in that country, or its neoliberal governmentalization, through a grounded discussion of neoliberalism as an entrenched, mature form of governance. This discussion reminds us that actually existing neoliberalisms are inevitably composite or hybrid structures. They are the outcome of ongoing political contestation, embedded in specific economic and sociocultural contexts, and, in this sense, they are best understood as ongoing processes, not as an end state.[2] Thus understood, neoliberalisms in their multiple, regional expressions are also never far from the global reach of international financial institutions like the World Bank and the International Monetary Fund (IMF).

What the transformations in Chile reveal is an active involvement of the neoliberal state—in its present, "enabling" form—in the configuration of a fully fledged hegemonic project and social reorganization characterized by a commitment to the "aggressive re-regulation, disciplining and containment" of targeted populations (Peck and Tickell 2002, 389). This chapter addresses specifically the centralized dimensions of power and renewed coordinating capacities of a state and links them to a cultural revolution associated with a longer process of neoliberal state formation (Corrigan and Sayer 1985). For analytical purposes I distinguish two dimensions of the emerging neoliberalized, or enabling, state: an "ameliorative" or caring dimension and a punitive dimension. Moreover, a basic premise of this chapter is that the neoliberalized state is gendered both in its Janus-faced configurations and its effects.

In addressing the challenges posed for mobilization and contestation of an entrenched or mature neoliberalism and in particular of a neoliberalized state like the Chilean, the discussion focuses on the configuration of an ameliorative form, intent on improving the population through forms of reregulation and disciplining of a "caring" kind. This caring side is bolstered by a coercive or punitive side, what sociologist Loïc Wacquant (2008) terms the "penal state." The punitive dimension of Chile's enabling state gathered momentum under the third Concertación (Reconciliation) government of socialist Ricardo Lagos (2000–2006), and its strengthening was continued by Michelle Bachelet, at the helm of the fourth and last center-left coalition government (2006–2010). The criminalization of protests and the indiscriminate use of repression and the legal system against a society that is increasingly mobilized have left no doubt about the renewed momentum of aggressive forms of disciplining under Sebastian Piñera's center-right government.

The chapter's main focus is on the "caring" state, or the configuration of forms of social regulation that are behind the formidable efforts at social integration and social engineering afoot for the past two decades in the name of meeting the unmet social and political expectations of those many Chileans who are excluded from the market and its promises. It relies on extensive research on the transformation of feminism and the women's movement in Chile, with a particular focus on the processes of institutionalization of a dominant liberal feminist agenda, and on the convergence of this agenda with the neoliberal project since 1990.[3] The chapter suggests that the neoliberalization of the state under way as an ameliorative and caring form has powerful implications for the reorganization of social life, not to mention for the increasing microregulation of individuals. Women's efforts, including an expanding and rich transnational feminist expertise, have played a fundamental role in the reconfiguration of this ameliorative neoliberal state. In the following pages I offer a grounded analysis of the neoliberalization of the Chilean state and argue that what we are witnessing is, in fact, a feminization of the social state in two senses: first, in terms of the extensive resources found in the efforts of different categories of women—from clients to experts and to a vast army of female personnel (*profesionales* and *técnicas* in Chilean terms) working in the public, volunteer, and private sectors; and second, in terms of the legacy of practices and expertise and broader feminist knowledge. These efforts and knowledge underlie the new terms of social regulation of women, who are the explicit and implicit targets of social-assistance policy, and of men, whose often pathologized, when not marginalized, masculinities, to borrow Kate Bedford's terms, are also the targets of aggressive and punitive forms of regulation and control (Bedford 2007; see also Wacquant 2007). To illustrate this discussion, the chapter turns to Chile Solidario (Chile in Solidarity) and its principal component, Programa Puente, the most recent and internationally acclaimed piece of Chilean social-policy innovation. Like its counterparts in Mexico (Oportunidades) and Brazil (Bolsa Familia), Chile Solidario aims to eradicate hard poverty, or "indigence," to use the current neologism, through a system of conditional cash transfers designed to enhance the capacities of families to escape poverty through their own efforts.

Before turning to the complex and contradictory contemporary processes responsible for the configuration of the neoliberalized state as an ameliorative and caring form in Chile, I review the broader historical processes that have led to the retrenchment of neoliberalism in Latin America. This next section distinguishes two moments of neoliberalism, which, it suggests, are captured by reference to the Washington Consensus and the post–Washington Consensus. It also outlines the value of insights offered by the governmentality approach to neoliberalism as a political project first proposed by Michel Foucault, in particular for exploring the enabling state as a governmentalized neoliberal state.

NEOLIBERALISM: FROM ECONOMIC AND INSTITUTIONAL "MODERNIZATIONS" TO A MODE OF GOVERNANCE

In 1997 the Inter-American Development Bank, in its assessment of a decade of neoliberal reforms in Latin America, pondered the question, all pain and no gain? The reference was to the unimpressive overall levels of economic growth in the region coupled with a failure of the market to effectively address poverty and inequality. By the mid-1990s the whole region had undergone drastic structural reforms, including trade and financial liberalization, deregulation, and privatization, associated with the policy recommendations of the Washington Consensus. Throughout the 1980s and 1990s countries in the region had been subjected to deep and drastic reforms aimed at increasing their global competitiveness through labor-market flexibilization measures, that is, by dismantling labor's social, economic, and political gains, however incipient in many cases.[4] Economic growth during the 1990s was weak, however, and by 1997 the so-called tequila financial crisis of 1994–1995 had affected Mexico. Soon other major financial crises plagued the region, first in Brazil (1999), then in Ecuador (1999–2000); these were followed by a meltdown in Argentina (2001–2002). Financial crises also affected Uruguay (2002) and the Dominican Republic (2003). According to figures from the Economic Commission for Latin America and the Caribbean (ECLAC), the poverty rate for the region declined from 48.3 percent in 1990 to 44 percent in 2002, but it still remained higher than the 1980 rate of 40.5 percent (see Fraile 2009). In addition to this lackluster progress in poverty reduction in the region, income inequality grew in the 1990s.[5] By the end of the 1990s and the early 2000s, millions of Latin Americans had joined the ranks of the unemployed or faced precarious working conditions, thanks to the replacement of formal contracts with a panoply of so-called atypical contracts, which often translated into either no contract at all or limited, renewable contracts without benefits. Moreover, they did so with limited social protection and faced the prospects of poverty in their old age as their ability to accumulate enough to draw a pension evaporated.

In 1998 Latin American leaders met in Chile to discuss the need to move beyond so-called first-generation neoliberal reforms and to focus on social and institutional change. They endorsed the "Santiago Consensus," a clear signal of their commitment to move beyond the so-called Washington Consensus. The Santiago Consensus was a commitment to growth that preserved the neoliberal macroeconomic essentials but combined them with presumably sensible, or judicious, forms of social spending, both to guarantee political stability and to rob fuel from critical alternatives emerging in the region.

Neoliberal structural reforms opened up the region to the influence of financial agencies and multilateral interests supporting their interests. As Tony Wood reminds us:

> Whether in the shape of the IMF, rating agencies, hedge funds or multilateral corporations, a host of outside actors entirely immune from democratic accountability have a decisively increased say over the fate of hundreds of millions, with the power to hold recalcitrant governments to ransom or blackmail them onto the path of macroeconomic orthodoxy. (Wood 2009, 146)

The World Bank, in particular, focuses on "improving" public-sector institutions and the performance of public policies. Its own agenda of institutional reforms and innovations can be summarized as the "governance agenda," which focuses on improving state capacity. The governance agenda has been characterized as follows:

> One of its important dimensions is the recognition that politics matter for development. It suggests that sustaining development requires reforming not only the policies but also the institutional framework in which policies are formulated. It has become apparent that effective democratic institutions are urgently needed to complement macroeconomic changes, provide safety nets, and assuage the adverse social consequences of structural adjustment programs. (Santiso 2001, 14–15)

What this has meant, concretely, is that the bank's lending priorities have increasingly turned to regulation and reform of nationally based judiciaries and legal bodies, parliamentary oversight bodies and ombudspersons, the civil service, not to mention its continued support of decentralization efforts that reach all levels of government.[6]

New lending has encouraged institutional reforms aimed at good governance and promoted partnerships with society (including profit and nonprofit sectors), or the so-called public-private partnerships in the delivery of social goods, ostensibly to maximize benefits to society. The relations and practices in social spending between local, national, and international sectors came to be regulated by the principle of conditionality.[7] A 2007 survey of two decades of institutional reforms in Latin American countries by the International Development Bank reveals that the region has indeed experienced considerable institutional reform in practice and characterizes this as "a silent revolution in which many dimensions of the state have been gradually transformed" (Fraile 2009, 217–218; Lora 2007, 5). Clearly, the era of the post–Washington Consensus is characterized by more, not less, influence and is resulting in the very reconfiguration of the state. This does not mean, however, that we are witnessing the demise of sovereign Latin American states. The territorial permeability—or the transnational and hence limited, or "fragmented," "graduated" sovereignty (Ong 2006)—has been a fact of postcolonial state formation from the start. The territorially sovereign Latin American state is a myth that was debunked some time ago. The permeability and transnational links of national peripheral states have been recognized either explicitly or implicitly in the work of the *dependistas* and Immanuel Wallerstein. What has changed is how we think about them. That the point needs to be stated anew as an important insight into the nature of postcolonial states is an indication of the enduring capacity for the so-called methodological nationalism of mainstream social science and development expertise to frame the discursive terrain of critical scholarship.

Against a narrow, conventional reading, then, neoliberalism, has never been simply about getting the economic order right, but it has, above all, been a political project for helping societies adapt to an unencumbered economy.[8] Economist Gabriel Palma calls the discourse of neoliberalism of "prudent-macroeconomics-cum-smaller-states" mainly a camouflage for a sophisticated exercise in the restoration of class power, or "capital attempting to regain its power and control through a more refined form of legitimisation and a more advanced technology of power" (Palma 2008, 18). The more recent reforms associated with the post–Washington Consensus define the retrenching of neoliberalism as a political form or as a form of governance committed to market-led growth and guided by principles of sound fiscal management, efficiency, and accountability. The dominant vision of the good society in this elaboration of neoliberal economics, then, tacitly relies on social intervention for its actualization. A strictly political economy account, however, is at best incomplete in helping us grasp what Palma aptly calls "the novel reconfigurations of political and institutional power encapsulated by the neo-liberal revolution" (Palma 2009, 840). This is precisely what Michel Foucault's analysis of modern forms of power and government made us aware of in his insightful lectures on neoliberalism, when he insisted on the political intention of the reworking of liberal economic ideas on both sides of the Atlantic after World War II (Foucault 1991a; Lemke 2001).

Following Michel Foucault's ideas about neoliberalism as a mode of governance that encompasses but is not limited to the state, we could describe the transformations of the past two decades as an emergent neoliberal political rationality with far-reaching implications for the reorganization of social life and the state, particularly for the production of subjects and new forms of citizenship (Brown 2003, 1; Lemke 2001, 2007). In this sense, while foregrounding the market, neo-liberal rationality, as Wendy Brown states, "is not only or even primarily focused on the economy; rather it involves extending and disseminating market values to all institutions and social action, even as the market itself remains a distinct player" (Brown 2003, 3).

Modern states, we could argue, following Foucault, whether directly or indirectly, have always been involved in the formation of subjects who conduct themselves in ways that are appropriate to dominant social projects. Neoliberalized states are no exception. In this sense, neoliberalism is a political project—a veritable revolution in government intent on reorganizing society, which is informed by a political rationality based on the norms and values of the market. The notion of "political rationality," or rationality of government, helps us to understand political power as a dominant discursive field that offers not only a particular political grammar and vocabulary within which "problems" are defined but also the ethical principles and explanatory logic that are proper to it (Rose 1999b, 28).

What Bourdieu once called the "left hand of the state" refers to those activities that aim to regulate subordinate classes and populations by protecting and expanding life chances (Wacquant 2009). The successes or failures of programs of policy reform are typically assessed and evaluated as if the efforts expended on their configuration and implementation left no traces beyond those they claimed to have left. And yet, these are always cultural-political processes in a material sense inasmuch as they involve individuals acting in specific organizational settings, articulating and expressing specific understandings through the traditions and practices of the culture in which they live. Furthermore, they are always gendered in their configuration, their intent, and their effects. Typically, the so-called social-policy field relies explicitly and implicitly on women's private and public efforts in the area of care and on naturalized conceptions of such work.

Feminist critics of Latin American neoliberalism have characterized the so-called retrenchment of the social dimension of the state of the 1980s and early 1990s as a "remasculinization" of the state.[9] This was, in their view, the corollary of the reduction in public spending and privatizations in health, education, and welfare, which resulted in thousands of public-sector job losses. David Harvey reminds us eloquently that at present we still live in a kind of society in which "the reproduction of daily life depends upon the production of commodities through a system of circulation of capital that has profit-seeking as its direct and socially accepted goal" (Harvey 2001, 312; Smith 2004, 226). However, the production system itself hinges critically on the care activities that enable societies to subsist, thrive, and reproduce themselves by delivering new workers to the market. The production of commodities, in other words, depends on the reproduction of life, and in the history of capitalism this has been women's responsibility par excellence. The actual work of caring for the young, the old, and the sick, which is essential for reproducing societies, did not disappear with neoliberal restructuring but was reprivatized. That is, it was absorbed by women alongside their productive activities, removed from the ledgers, and rendered invisible. Indeed, as feminists have shown convincingly, the globalization of capitalism and the subjection of institutions and practices of the social field to the rationality of the market have been achieved on the backs of the majority of women. Latin America is no exception.[10]

Attention to the more recent changes in neoliberal governance suggests that we need to reconsider the characterization of neoliberal states as "remasculinized" states *tout court*. On the contrary, this chapter suggests that in cases of the retrenching of neoliberalism, in which states acquire renewed prominence and visibility in the ethical and coercive regulation of societies in the guise of enabling states, what we are witnessing is in fact a refeminization of the social dimension of the state. This chapter argues that in this reconfiguration of the neoliberal state, gender has acquired renewed prominence and that this is in large measure the outcome of feminist struggles and of legacies of practices of women's solidarity. Moreover, this development is not merely an outcome of the diffusion of a North American feminism but rather results from an articulation of transnational feminist discourses with local ones embedded in an older tradition of solidarity with the poor as empowerment inherited from social Catholicism.[11] Furthermore, this articulation needs to be thought of as embodied and grounded in myriad practices of women in their capacity as agents—whether as clients, experts, or practitioners—involved in strategies of empowerment. Today these distinctively Latin American feminist strategies of empowerment are critical resources for projects of intensified social regulation of poor people.

For analytical purposes, in thinking about the transformations of the minimalist, also known as "subsidiary" states, into enabling states, we can distinguish between two stages of neoliberalism by attending to the ongoing processes of gendered neoliberalization of the state. An initial stage is characterized by the overt and excessive use of coercive power, including the coercion of the market, to impose drastic privatizations and economic and institutional reforms intent on opening up national economies to international competition. A second stage is associated with the expansion of social spending and with the rise of an interventionist, “enabling” state. This second stage has as its central preoccupation the ethical regulation of populations.

Social policy has been a crucial mechanism for the goals of the enabling state, namely, turning societies into entrepreneurial societies through the “self-responsibilization” of individuals—as entrepreneurial selves—who can function in the new economy. This has been an explicitly gendered project, and feminist discourses of empowerment and the specific practices of women’s movements have played a pivotal role. Socially interventionist neoliberal states are, in other words, not less neoliberalized but more, and they continue to be underpinned by coercive power. Both the criminalization of dissent and the punitive management of poverty through policing, the justice system, and prisons make this amply clear. Because of the degree of social penetration of the ethos of the market, these enabling states constitute “deeper” or more “mature” instances of neoliberalism. I use neoliberalization in this second sense to make reference to the remaking of the governmentalized state that takes the form of a caring state.

CHILE’S NEOLIBERALIZED STATE AS THE “ENABLING” STATE

The 1973 military coup headed by Augusto Pinochet oversaw the dismantling of the labor and welfare regimes associated with Chile’s developmentalist model (1924–1973) and the implementation through ruthless means of an early version of the market-based strategy of development later known as the Washington Consensus. The overtly coercive neoliberal strategy of the “Chicago boys” led to stunning results in Chile’s labor regime that are nothing short of revolutionary. Intervention in the countryside included the rounding up and killing of peasants suspected of having supported the agrarian reform, or, in the case of those who were spared, their expulsion from the land. Nearly 40 percent of expropriated lands were handed over to those deemed loyal to the regime, whereas only about one-third of expropriated lands were returned to former owners. The result was the exodus of the majority of resident peasants from the land. Those who remained in the countryside became waged rural workers, while many more migrated to towns and cities to increase the ranks of the urban poor. The peasantry as a group no longer exists in Chile (Riesco 2009, 285).

The political and economic coercion of the 1970s and 1980s also had drastic and transforming effects on urban labor. Throughout the twentieth century, Chile's labor movement was a major social and political actor, and its power culminated in its active participation in Salvador Allende's short-lived Popular Unity government. In the aftermath of the 1973 coup, the movement was brutally repressed, rolled back, and undermined by a series of emergency measures (the "state of siege" measures of the 1970s), which were subsequently entrenched in the 1979 Plan Laboral (Labor Plan). Throughout the 1980s, the ruthless and sudden mass-privatization program and the dismantling of public services, in particular of social services, led to the loss of 50 percent of public-sector jobs, according to ECLAC figures. Moreover, an estimated one in three workers became unemployed during the severe economic crisis of 1981–1985. The effects of these sudden and dramatic changes on the majority of working-class and middle-class Chileans were devastating. A population bereft of any kind of social recourse felt them even more acutely. The programs introduced in the early 1980s, such as the emergency work programs Programa de Empleo Minimo and Programa Jefes de Hogar, and social programs to palliate hunger among children, were means-tested and doled out only to those deemed to be living in extreme poverty.

Since 1990 labor has failed to recover the social and political power it once had, and labor relations have not changed. In fact, official figures indicate that the overall wage policies of the four Concertación governments have, with some exceptions, remained conservative.[12] Chile's success as the region's most globalized capitalist economy—boasting, for example, the largest number of free-trade agreements in the world—is an achievement of the Concertación, and it has been built on the backs of workers whose ranks today include unprecedented numbers of women. The ECLAC figures on women's employment rates, based on Chile's national census, carried out by the Instituto Nacional de Estadísticas, continue to show that Chilean women have among the lowest levels of employment in the region. However, statistics from the compulsory private pension schemes tell a very different story.

These figures show that "70 percent of Chilean women of working age are actively engaged in wage employment, as against 84 percent in the case of men" (Riesco 2009, 295). Working conditions for the overwhelming majority of Chileans are precarious; large numbers work in temporary jobs, typically without contracts or with only limited contracts—the so-called atypical contracts. The precarization of labor, or its flexibilization, has been made possible by the labor code, which remains largely untouched. Workers are very limited in their ability to negotiate favorable contracts, are forced to engage in complicated and narrowly defined bargaining processes, and have also been restricted in their capacity to create industry-sector networks. In fact, the only significant change to the labor code during the Concertación was an amendment introduced in 2007 that prevented large companies from subcontracting significant proportions of their work to temporary employment agencies.[13]

By 1989, on the eve of the end of the dictatorship, Chileans were a poorer, dispossessed, and vulnerable lot. Faced with a poverty level of approximately 40 percent, addressing the so-called *deuda social* (social debt) became paramount for the incoming center-left coalition, the Concertación government. After twenty years, when the coalition of Socialists and Christian Democrats ceded power to the center right in 2010, some positive changes had been achieved, especially in public-sector wages, the minimum wage, and access to public health. However, the pensions and education systems continued to be private and exclusionary, the health-care system had been partially privatized, working conditions for the majority remained precarious, and workers were still poorly paid.[14] It should come as no surprise, then, that increasingly vocal labor demonstrations demand improved working conditions, with contracts, decent pensions, and guaranteed shifts and call for general strikes with cross-sector alliances.[15]

CHILE'S POST–WASHINGTON CONSENSUS: CONTINUITIES AND CHANGE UNDER THE CONCERTACIÓN

The commitments to fiscal discipline and market-led economic growth based on low wages and primary exports were the sine qua non of Chile's transition to democratic rule in 1990. Moreover, the principles guiding Chile's neoliberal modernization project during the 1970s and 1980s have become entrenched as a new political rationality. The changes in the state-society relation premised on the powerful discourse of liberal individual rights (not to mention the so-called politics of consensus, within which these rights are to be exercised), all of which have been justified and entrenched as the new "modern" form of politics, have changed the terrain for social mobilization, above all for forming alliances for meaningful change.

The return to liberal democratic politics in 1990, then, not only ushered in strategies for repaying Chile's "social debt," as the first Concertación framed the poverty problem, but also posed the question of coercive power anew. Today Chile is one of the most unequal countries in the world, where the wealthiest have incomes that are thirty times greater than those of the poor.[16] Organization and contestation are very much part of political life; however, the possibilities for forming and sustaining broader alliances to challenge the status quo are constrained by a neoliberalized state that has increasingly acquired a Janus face, with both caring and punitive dimensions. The actions of a presumably responsive, caring state—one that extends health care, pensions, and educational opportunities to the poorest sectors of the population—are buttressed by an unflinching reliance on coercion and the brutal use of force if need be. State violence, in other words, has not become a thing of the past in Chile but has taken newer, explicit forms, as is illustrated by the systematic deployment of militarized police units in poor social and urban spaces, by the remarkably high levels of incarceration for males, by the construction of prisons, and by the criminalization of dissent and social mobilization. The banner of citizen safety, *seguridad ciudadana*, is waved by television networks with their daily diet of crime and murder perpetrated by those living in poor urban areas.

Two trends characterize the present moment of institutional transformation and action and frame the context for action and resistance in Chile's entrenched neoliberalized context. First, increased forms of social intervention through public-private partnerships promoted by World Bank discourse and practice, which follow the principles of fiscally responsible or targeted social spending first introduced during the Pinochet period. Second, increased forms of punitive intervention, also in the form of public-private partnerships, through the mobilization of the penal system to address the issue of "citizen safety." These trends are deeply marked by gender, and they are not unique to Chile. Moral education of those deemed worthy of it, as well as punishment, including incarceration if need be, of those who are considered dangerous, are the two institutional interventions that aim to govern populations in contexts of immiseration and stark inequalities.

Under the socialist government of Michelle Bachelet (2006–2010), the gendered neoliberalization of the state continued apace. Containing the effects of the informalization of the economy, underemployment and the constant threat of immiseration were framed in terms of the rights of citizens to personal security. Although new prisons were built—ten new ones through private contractors announced by the Lagos government and two new ones announced by Bachelet's government in November of 2007—official figures show that the delinquency rates have actually dropped in the past four years, and studies are unable to establish a correlation between drug use and crime.[17] The country today has the highest rate of male incarceration of all Latin American countries, including Brazil; of a total prison population of 43,723, only 6.7 percent of those incarcerated are women. The prison population rate per 100,000 inhabitants is 262. By comparison, the Brazilian rate is 219, while the rates for the other two countries of the Southern Cone, Argentina and Uruguay, are 163 and 193, respectively.[18]

Much as Elana Zilberg describes in Chapter 9 of this volume, strategies of containment and militarization of poor areas, borrowed from the United States, have also become widespread. For example, the Safe Neighborhoods Program, enacted in 2001 by the Lagos government and placed under the Ministry of the Interior, which was further expanded during the Bachelet government, uses crime and drugs as the justification for combining the use of police and social intervention in so-called marginal or conflicted neighborhoods. The Piñera government has folded the Safe Neighborhoods Program into the more comprehensive crime prevention and security program, Chile Seguro, National Strategy for Public Safety in Chile, 2010–2014. La Victoria, a *población* on the southern periphery of Santiago that is internationally known for its history of political organization and resistance during the military regime and more recently for its innovative forms of resistance and organization against neoliberalism, is one of those neighborhoods where "the state intervenes by dispatching the national police to keep residents under surveillance" (Zibechi 2007b). This is, to borrow Zibechi's apt characterization, a "battle-hardened neighbourhood," one where few families did not have a relative killed, imprisoned, or "disappeared" during Pinochet's rule. It is also a place with an estimated official unemployment rate of 30 percent (in 2003) and the lowest reported per-capita income in the poorest municipality on Santiago's southern periphery (Finn 2006, 229–230). Community members in La Victoria talk about the ways in which a politics of zero tolerance, "fueled by fear campaigns regarding citizens' safety, has been borrowed and instituted in Santiago, expanding the spaces of exclusion and the power of surveillance throughout the city" (ibid., 232). The objectives of the Safe Neighborhoods Program is "to combat crime and street peddling in downtown Santiago," as the authorities themselves admit.[19] The program involves social organizations and neighborhood councils in each target area in security and crime prevention activities. In the words of one community member, "We are watched by the police 24 hours a day. Any activity that occurs is supposed to be reported to the police" (Zibechi 2007b).

Moreover, this militarized response to crime meted out in the name of citizens' right to safety has been accompanied by the criminalization of political mobilization. Under Ricardo Lagos's watch, the antiterrorist law first used by the military government to repress political dissent was rehabilitated and has been used ever since to repress, brutally if necessary, the actions of indigenous groups and to protect the interests of landowners and the timber industry. During the Bachelet government, the use of this law was further extended.

The enhanced law-and-order plan, the Plan de Seguridad Ciudadana, which was unveiled in 2011 by the incoming Piñera government, builds on the achievements of the Concertación and proposes an expansion of the police force. It also recommends the creation of an alliance between the different branches of Chile's security forces to enhance policing capacities in low-income areas considered to be vulnerable to crime. Under the guise of an alliance with citizens, the plan promises to further enhance police capacities for surveillance and repression in poor and working-class neighborhoods. The expansion of the punitive dimensions of the ameliorative state is also evident in the government's harsh response to recent protests and mobilizations. Since the student uprisings of 2011, the category "delinquent" has been expanded to apply to Chilean citizens involved in constitutionally sanctioned dissent, while the use of police repression and the courts to criminalize social mobilizations has become indiscriminate.

The return to elected democracy in 1990 saw the rise of a politics of consensus, focused explicitly on liberal notions of individual rights and obligations. For more than twenty years, Chileans have been encouraged through legislation and other institutional means to take responsibility for their own lives by procuring their own individualized means for a successful life and to actively exercise choice in a whole range of areas from employment, pensions, and health to the education of their children. If the implementation of some of the economic and institutional reforms during the dictatorship (1973–1989), which began this reregulation of Chilean society, relied primarily on economic coercion and violence, since 1990 the process of reregulation has been buttressed by a powerful discourse of active, responsible citizenship. The Concertación is responsible for the construction and consolidation of an ameliorative, neoliberalized state form—the enabling state—which the incoming center-right government of Piñera has vowed to extend. This ameliorative state form has entrenched a distinctive mode of governance.

The "caring" arm of the state displays its own forms of violence that are subtle and cloaked in a benign concern with the improvement of the poor. Starting in 1990, the reconfiguration of Chile into an enabling state relied on an extensive legacy of nonprofit, transnationalized, antipoverty initiatives, many of which had been under the protection of the Catholic Church. The church's Vicaría de la Solidaridad played a fundamental role in this alternative social sector by supporting a panoply of poverty-alleviation programs from soup kitchens and production workshops to skills-training workshops and also delivering relief packages of food and clothes. Women, in their capacity as clients, volunteers, and professionals working in near-volunteer conditions, were the dominant force behind these activities. This rich legacy, including study centers and nongovernmental organizations (NGOs), as well as social Catholic and Left-imbued expert knowledge and practices of solidarity, proved to be an invaluable resource for the retrenchment of neoliberalism as a mode of governance. Indeed, the articulation of the distinct political rationality of the ameliorative state was made possible following the 1989 elections by the turn en masse of the Chilean political and intellectual

Left, including some sectors of the women's movement and feminists, to a brand of pragmatic politics concerned with advancing a progressive agenda through pragmatic politics that successfully oversaw the intensification of a rapacious, dispossesive capitalism, as we have seen.[20] In this context, the 1990s witnessed in Chile a convergence between modes of institutionalizing a pragmatic, liberal feminist agenda for gender equality and so-called innovative forms of regulation and self-regulation in the social field, which are central to the political agenda of neoliberal governance. In Gramscian terms, the twenty years of the Concertación were a period of the retrenchment of capitalist class power and control, as well as the transformation of neoliberalism into a reigning hegemony with the capacity to shape social life and subjects, all in the name of democracy.

The center-right government led by Piñera promises to further retrench the Janus-faced neoliberalized state. In the aftermath of the 2008 global financial crisis, poverty levels have increased once again, from 13.7 percent in 2006 to 15.1 percent, as revealed by the latest Caracterización Socioeconómica Nacional figures (2009), and the government has vowed to eliminate indigence by 2014 and poverty by 2018. In 2011 Piñera's government inaugurated the Ministerio de Desarrollo Social (Ministry of Social Development) and charged it with improving the tools for measuring poverty and the oversight and further development and implementation of social programs like Chile Solidario and Programa Puente to combat indigence. Piñera's electoral platform promised that the new ministry would be housed in the presidential palace, La Moneda, and that it would be under his direct supervision.

PUBLIC AND PRIVATE CARE OF OTHERS: THE FEMINIZATION OF THE ENABLING STATE

Women are at the center of social-policy innovations that have been critical for the reconfiguration of the enabling state in Chile. These policies bear strong traces of the practices and feminist popular-education contents of the solidarity work of the women's movement during the 1980s, mentioned earlier. George Steinmetz, writing in a different context, has pointed out that gender is "always already there" in the configuration of the social dimension of the state, although at some points it may become "a central and explicit object of social regulation" (1993, 52). Throughout the twentieth century, modern state formation, in its social dimension, relied in Chile and elsewhere on the efforts of feminists, activists, and professionals. This process of social formation has also invoked fairly consistent, heteronormative assumptions about social reproduction and the need to solve the contradictions generated by capitalism. These are echoed in transnational regulatory agencies that play an influential role in offering direction and resources for the implementation of solutions at the national level.

Heteronormative families have been the explicit object of social regulation over the years. It would be incorrect, however, to reduce the focus on the family of present-day antipoverty programs and indeed of the panoply of programs and subsidies that are part of the social network of public and private assistance only or even primarily to the conservative, Catholic underpinnings of state action in Chile. The transnational trend is linked with the state's own need for heteronormativity. Care of and concern for the population includes projection into the future, which is premised on the production of new generations. To this end, states need to regulate not only sexuality but also norms of femininity and masculinity (Bedford 2007). The present preoccupation with "families" views women as agents in the reconfiguration of the family unit, and its assumption of women as informed, responsible, and achieving operates in conjunction with age-old implicit assumptions about irresponsible masculinity, especially as embodied among poor people.

The vast field of antipoverty policymaking and delivery, both in the public and private areas of social action, and of social governance more generally—for example, in health care and education, including most recently early childhood education and care—relies on novel assumptions about women's subjectivity, which have been naturalized as the new universal truth. For instance, in the context of the innovative care-related policy changes associated with so-called conditional cash transfer programs like Chile Solidario and the Programa Puente, explored in more detail later, the linchpin for the success of the programs is no longer the figure of woman-for-others, inspired by Catholic conservatism, but the woman as a "subject of rights." Although the focus of this program is the nuclear family, especially children, women are the real targets for conditional social assistance. This emerging femininity, which defines women as capable agents of change, is premised not on women's ostensibly distinctive and superior moral qualities—as was the case in the past—but on the recognition of their individual rational capacities. Women as empowered individual subjects of rights, capable of autonomous action, including the exercise of choice as producers and consumers (even as clients of social assistance programs) is the innovative assumption of these new social programs. This is a singular victory of feminism, albeit a contradictory one.

The terms of a liberal variant of feminism, one that focuses on advancing the equal rights of women and pivots on a notion of woman as a subject of rights, has provided the resources for the moral education of poor women. Women are to be empowered as autonomous, sovereign subjects—in effect, they embody the unencumbered subjectivity of the neoliberal vision of market society—who aspire to take their rightful place in the world of work. This appeal to women as entrepreneurial subjects, in a strict and narrow sense, has taken for granted social reproduction and care as women's natural, and by extension invisible, responsibility. Indeed, in the project of emancipating women by bringing them to the market, the family has until recently been seen as the site of a natural division of labor. The burden of multiple expectations and demands associated with active engagement in the job market, along with the responsibility for care work and the expectation of self-care as "modern" women or, in the case of those who are very poor and are expected to prepare themselves to exercise their autonomy, as market subjects, has fallen squarely on women's shoulders.

Implicit in the expectations of this "modern" Chilean woman is a new model of masculinity, whose actualization lies in the hands of women. This ideal of responsible masculinity is countered, though not explicitly, by that old specter, the irresponsible, neglectful, and even violent male, especially those unmarried or unemployed. The irresponsible poor male is the target of the punitive state, and as the revised Plan de Seguridad Ciudadana of 2011 makes clear, the definition of citizen safety has been gendered and expanded by the inclusion of policies and programs whose objective is to combat violence against women.[21] Clearly, this new femininity is employed today for the regulation of women's lives, and through them, social regulation is exercised down to the molecular level of the family unit. In this sense, we can argue that this powerful legacy of feminism has been mainstreamed into the repertoire for the regulation and control of Chile's population.

The women's extra burdens are a subject of long-standing criticism by feminists who evaluate gender-sensitive programs. Moreover, feminist critics have long shown that the impact on women of their taken-for-granted and invisibilized, seemingly infinite capacity to absorb the emotional and physical demands and tensions of care work is particularly dramatic for women from poor economic sectors.[22] As far as social programs targeted at the poorest sectors of society are concerned, they may encourage and entice their female clients by appealing to this new femininity, but in the end women's freedom is trumped by the age-old implicit assumption that makes them primarily responsible for the well-being of their families.

INSTITUTIONALIZATION OF FEMINIST LEGACIES

The convergence of the legacies of Chile's contemporary feminism and women's activism with the neoliberal project is linked to the institutionalization of feminism in the 1990s.[23] This institutionalization refers to the vast network of professionals, activists, and experts housed in the government bureaucracy, private and public agencies, and specialized university programs, as well as to the production of gender-sensitive knowledge that circulates through it. This is, furthermore, a transnationalized network. In 1990 the first Concertación government, under Christian Democrat Patricio Aylwin, created the Servicio Nacional de la Mujer (SERNAM), the National Women's Bureau, to meet its commitment to UN-based agreements on gender equity. This agency proved to be critical for the subsequent articulation of this gender expertise with direct and indirect input in social-policy innovation. Pivotal in the articulation of feminist- and gender-sensitive work have been the drafting and implementation of official equal-opportunity plans, which focus on responding to the main challenges Chilean women face in their struggle for equality with men.[24] The commitment to eliminate all forms of economic, social, political, and cultural inequalities between women and men has led to some important legislative changes.[25] More important, for our purposes they have helped shape a discourse that has contributed to "regendering" the organizational style and terms of work through which an array of innovative services is made available to clients of social assistance.

In addition, the solidarity practices developed in women's activist work in support of organized women's efforts in poor areas constitute another important legacy of feminism and the women's movement. Throughout the 1980s, NGOs used feminist popular-education contents and techniques, the so-called feminist curriculum, to offer training to women in a range of self-improvement (*desarrollo personal*) and empowerment workshops. In the 1990s these feminist popular-education techniques and contents were adopted as a method to reach potential clients of social assistance and came to be identified with more generic forms of "social intervention." Thus, practices and discourses perfected first by feminist experts and activists in NGOs and then implemented by a veritable army of dedicated, typically working-class, women active on the ground in Chile's poor neighborhoods, have been successfully incorporated into innovative forms of social regulation.

Michelle Bachelet's government represents the culmination of what scholars refer to as feminist policymaking. Her "gentler," pro-equity agenda included programs for women, pensions, employment, and educational reform.[26] Bachelet argued that inequalities "begin at the moment one is born and determine the nature of one's life and death, and a pro-equity agenda would contribute to the country's growth and development" (Borzutzky 2010, 91). Her government responded to the well-documented question of women's double burden by addressing the unresolved issue of child-care provision in the context of the Concertación's long-term commitments to fuel economic growth and global competitiveness, while also reducing poverty. The program Chile Crece Contigo (Chile Grows with You) was introduced in October 2006 as a partial answer to the problem of childcare. The program guarantees access to nursery schools and kindergartens for children up to the age of three on a means-tested basis, that is, for the two poorest quintiles of the population. It also makes preschool coverage for four- and five-year-olds universal (MIDEPLAN 2007). The initial impetus for this child-care program came from the Lagos administration, which called on SERNAM in 2004 to come up with proposals to facilitate women's participation in the labor force.[27] Piñera's center-right government recognizes Chile Crece Contigo as an important achievement and remains committed to its further development.

Since 2000, the coordination of the vast array of public and private forms, tactics, and techniques of social regulation has come to rest in the state with the creation of the Red de Protección Social, or Social Protection Network. This system includes the panoply of innovative social-assistance programs developed by the agency Solidarity and Social Investment Fund, or

FOSIS, as well as those offered by a range of public and private agencies working with women, children, schoolchildren, and the unemployed. Among these, the Fundación PRODEMU stands out for its evolution from a strictly clientelistic organization to a valued partner in the implementation of gender-sensitive social programs.

The foundation PRODEMU (Programa de Promoción y Desarrollo de la Mujer, or Program for Women's Promotion and Education) is a quasi-governmental organization that taps into the pool of women clients living in poverty. It was set up in 1990 to capture a poor female clientele that had been courted successfully for generations by an intricate network of volunteer-led, Catholic-inspired *centros de madres*, or mothers' centers. Control of these organizations had been legally transferred by the outgoing dictatorship in 1989 at its eleventh hour to the military, and after some wrangling with the opposition, the incoming Concertación managed to obtain legislative approval to set up PRODEMU. This organization offers a litmus test of the extent to which the discourses and practices of feminist solidarity have become part of the work of making poor women over into empowered subjects of rights. Since their creation in 1964 by the Christian Democratic government of Eduardo Frei Montalva as part of its massive plan for social integration of marginal urban and rural social sectors, mothers' centers have proved to be an immensely valuable political tool. The president's wife was always the head of the umbrella agency, a position Lucia Hiriart de Pinochet used very effectively during the 1980s to mobilize right-wing middle- and upper-class volunteers and to deliver ready-made political clienteles in exchange for much-needed social assistance.[28]

Since the mid-1990s the organization has become an established ally of SERNAM and is now a recognized and reliable partner in the delivery of social programs developed by agencies like FOSIS (Schild 2007). In its present form, PRODEMU defines itself as an *escuela de la mujer* (women's school) with the mission of preparing poor women by offering skills training and empowerment workshops, or *formación*, to them. Their goal is to teach women to help themselves by learning to see themselves as "principal and responsible protagonists" in "a process of development and growth." Under Michelle Bachelet's government, PRODEMU renewed its commitment to help poor urban and rural women through a line of work that emphasized education and skills for "employability." This means helping specific categories of women (e.g., rural women, microentrepreneurs) not only identify themselves as "subjects of rights" through training in personal development but also prepare for the market and presumably unfold their entrepreneurial talents, pursue their individual "life projects," and exercise their rights as active citizens. The commitment to educating women for a new femininity through the implementation of modules on *desarrollo personal* (personal development) or *formación* has been a fundamental component of PRODEMU's educational efforts with women since the mid-1990s. Despite the focus of the present discourse on the family, the reworking of an important legacy of solidarity practices of the women's movement as a taken-for-granted technique for making women over into empowered, active citizens is preserved. In fact, PRODEMU has renewed its commitment to help prepare women as subjects of rights by adding "of responsibilities" (PRODEMU 2011). Clearly, these forms of intervention of the caring, ameliorative state lead one to think that no one seems to leave the poor alone anymore, to paraphrase Bryan Roberts, writing in a different context, and that poor people have today a woman's face (Roberts 2004).

What these innovations also suggest is that the neoliberalized state, in its ameliorative form, relies heavily on the public extension of women's practices and emotional investments in care. Thousands of women are now employed in the implementation and delivery of the panoply of social programs that compose the Social Protection Network. Chile Crece Contigo alone, for example, accounted for an estimated 16,000 workers in 2006 and 2007 in two of the public agencies (JUNJI and Integra) in charge of the well-being of children, which, together with private and municipal-level partners, are in charge of managing the program (Staab and Gerhard 2010, 16). Furthermore, for the past twenty years, public- and private-sector partners in the provision of social programs have engaged in a process of professionalization, including expecting increasingly stringent professional or technical accreditation from the predominantly female personnel they hire. What remains unchanged, however, are the poor working conditions for such positions. Employment in both the private and public sectors of social-program delivery seems to be offered on a fixed-term basis, with short, renewable contracts, and there are very few permanent positions. Women employed as educators, social workers, nurses, or technical personnel (e.g., counselors, monitors, or *promotores* working directly with clients) typically work under precarious conditions and are poorly paid. Implicit in these work arrangements is a persistent understanding that care work, whether private or public, is women's work. Moreover, judging from the pattern of female employment and remuneration that characterizes public care work, it is clear that, although it is a central component of the neoliberalization of the state, it continues to be taken for granted. Furthermore, although the myriad activities through which the ameliorative state is reconfigured have represented opportunities for social and career advancement for middle- and lower-middle-class professionals and activists, much of this work continues to be typically "female work" and is thus—with few exceptions—work that is undervalued and underpaid.

PROGRAMA PUENTE OR THE ENTRENCHED FEMINIZATION OF THE STATE

With the latest generation of policy innovation, represented by Chile in Solidarity and its key component, Programa Puente, the myriad contributions of feminist expertise and the women's movement's pedagogic legacy have been mainstreamed. In his speech to the nation on May 21, 2003, President Ricardo Lagos outlined the gains made by the program Sistema de Protección Social Chile Solidario, created in 2002, which aimed at integrating those deemed by the national census to live in extreme poverty. The goal of the program, he stated, is to teach indigent individuals "to stand up and make their rights count." Overcoming indigence, Lagos told the nation, "requires the will of those suffering from it."

The program targeted the estimated 225,073 families—identified by the two-page survey, or "Ficha CAS II," implemented by municipal governments—to be living in indigence and promised to deliver assistance tailored to their specific needs through a direct and personalized approach with each family. Chile Solidario and Programa Puente were further expanded by Bachelet's government. They are considered a valuable legacy of the Concertación, although with some ostensibly serious flaws in implementation, including the targeting methods used to identify potential clients, which the present, center-right government of Piñera, vows to correct.[29]

The goal of the program is to reach those living in extreme poverty through a combination of psychosocial support and an offer of preferential access to social assistance programs and services in health care, education, infant nutrition, scholarships, subsidies, pensions, and other public and private services, grouped together as a *red social* (social network) of social assistance and coordinated nationally, regionally, and locally until recently by the Ministry of Planning, or MIDEPLAN. A critical component for participants is access to a monetary voucher as a condition of meeting the program's requirements.

The execution of Programa Puente is a joint responsibility of the agency FOSIS and the municipal governments. Both hire personnel (under the precarious terms already discussed), and in some cases the total income of the person hired is made up of a combination of part-time work paid by the agency and the local government. Municipal governments play a central oversight role in the implementation of Chile Solidario. The program has three components: first, personalized and intensive psychosocial support and the delivery of a *bono de protección familiar* (family protection voucher); second, *subsidios monetarios garantizados* (guaranteed monetary subsidies), as families progress through the first phase; and, third, preferential access to programs of social advancement, employment, and social security. The Programa Puente is the initial, critical component through which those who successfully complete it gain access to this innovative system of social protection. The integration of indigent families targeted for assistance depends on Programa Puente. *Apoyo familiar*—family support—is the name given to the program personnel who act as intermediaries between the beneficiaries and the network of public and private services. These counselors are typically women with degrees in social work or a related field from accredited institutions, and they often work under economically precarious and physically dangerous conditions.

In Programa Puente, one *apoyo familiar* counselor is assigned per family to work with its members for twenty-four months and to help them understand the seven dimensions identified as necessary for attaining what the program calls the "minimum conditions of quality of life," which are seen as requirements to move from indigence to poverty. These areas are, in broad terms, the procurement of legal identification documents, health care, education, and family dynamics—with a focus on preventing family violence, housing, employment, and income generation. Although the Programa Puente aims to work with families, the real targets of its socioeducational and intermediation efforts are women. Indeed, MIDEPLAN's own evaluations conclude that "the experience of the System of Social Protection Chile Solidario shows a high degree of feminine presence and participation" (MIDEPLAN 2007). The counselor relies on popular education techniques and uses a cheerful board game to discuss the areas outlined in the program. Although all family members are invited to take part, typically women are the ones who take the lead and remain committed to the goals. They have a strong incentive to do so because they are the ones who receive the cash vouchers, or *bonos*, on behalf of the family. Vouchers are released to clients as they cover the various modules of the program and complete the tasks outlined, for example, attending a clinic to obtain a free gynecological examination or ensuring that the children are up for school at 7 a.m., and so on. Meeting these goals and, more important, offering proof of commitment by signing a contract with the counselor to that effect are the conditions for receiving the cash vouchers. The counselors' work is also regulated by the exercise of contracts with their clients because these documents must be submitted electronically on a regular basis directly to the ministry in charge.

According to an official document prepared by MIDEPLAN for a seminar on social protection and gender, the

> positive impacts in the psychosocial realm for women who have been through psychosocial support reveal an improvement in their self-esteem, self-valorization, and their ability to propose life projects, among the most important. It is understood that in many cases the personal projects of the beneficiaries are definitely aimed toward the improvement and wishes of the family, but they function as concrete opportunities for advancing in the consolidation of autonomy for the women. (MIDEPLAN 2008, 2)

The document suggests that women in popular sectors have historically been the ones to occupy the local community space and translates this into a reference to popular women's "primordial role in the overcoming of their condition of poverty." With regard to this role of women in the local space, the document concludes that the experience of Chile Solidario shows that "a prior condition for participating in institutional and community-based networks is women's self-recognition (*auto-reconocimiento*) and self-perception (*auto-percepción*) as subjects of rights."[30] What this evaluation reveals is that what was once the prerogative of feminist education, namely consciousness-raising efforts through popular education to help build a women's movement, has come to be seen as a natural and legitimate task of the gender-sensitive state.

The experience of those on the ground, however, suggests a more complex process, one that has contradictory outcomes. Families do not necessarily graduate from the program, and the money may not be controlled by the woman in the household or may not be invested in the sensible, rational form envisioned during the discussions on family budgeting, which are part of the family-dynamics dimension. Moreover, for those who graduate from the program, escape from indigence is not necessarily permanent, as the fluctuating figures on poverty and indigence suggest. A 2010 study of six poor districts in Santiago shows that numerous Chileans, including many who do not qualify for social-assistance programs, are in fact permanently teetering on the edge of the economic abyss. An estimated one-third of Chile's population—not the 15.1 percent officially classified as poor—live in conditions of economic vulnerability. For them, any major (perhaps catastrophic) event—from the loss of employment to increases in food prices or in basic services, an illness, an accident, the birth of a child, or access by one of the children to higher education—can cause them to lose their foothold and fall below the poverty line.[31] To use the Programa Puente's own metaphor, the bridge from indigence seems to be crossed regularly, but in both directions, by large numbers of Chileans whose economic status is precarious indeed. Moreover, for those who are invited to cross the bridge from indigence to poverty, the inevitable cessation of the cash voucher upon "graduation" from the program very often means retracing their steps back across the bridge.

Whether the program meets its self-defined expectations, especially in the current economic crisis, which has resulted in unstable employment and rising food prices, is the topic of renewed scholarly and political debate in Chile and beyond.[32] It is not, however, the focus of this discussion. Instead, my aim has been to highlight the style of work used in Programa Puente and the language used to analyze its benefits for women in order to draw attention to the continuities of this innovative device of social regulation with a long legacy of feminist work with women. Programa Puente is, in effect, a pedagogic initiative intent on making indigent women over as subjects of rights. The term *apoyo familiar* is used interchangeably in official documents and reports with *monitores* or *promotores*, terms that reveal the strong continuity with other forms of educational intervention with poor people and are the hallmark of social programs of the Concertación and that reach further into the past as part of the repertoire of feminist popular education and Freirian critical pedagogy. The figure of the monitor and, later, promoter (in effect, a popular educator) was central in Freire's pedagogy and then a key element of the work of women's NGOs with poor people. For the past twenty years, this figure of the popular educator who helps poor people empower themselves has been a critical component of innovative social programs. Then and now, this has predominantly been a female figure working with women living in poverty.

According to MIDEPLAN, "the strengthening of the closest and most informal social links to favor cooperative practices of different types is an objective of the system (Chile Solidario), whose foundation is based on a proposal about personal, family, neighborhood, and community self-direction (*autogestión*), which privileges organization and associativity (*asociatividad*)." During the dictatorship the goal of women's organizing in popular sectors was to enable women's empowerment and foster their social and political participation. Today this task seems to have been taken over by the state, and the question is empowerment for what? The pedagogic effort under way does not promote autonomous organization and solidarity ties but rather "social capital" among extremely poor clients by teaching them to see themselves as empowered people who are capable of exercising their individual freedom in the various realms in which they live. Empowerment for participation as a preoccupation of the ameliorative state, then, seems to have become a form of regulation that aims to set parameters for women's activism.

CONCLUSIONS

Antonio Gramsci claimed that without being embedded in a state or organized into some system of power, revolutions are not genuine. This is a comment that haunts me these days as I ponder how we get "from here to there" or what is necessary for social movements to help usher in a postneoliberal order rather than become ensnared in the present as resources for reforming neoliberalism. As a Chilean of a generation that invested itself in the dream of a revolution achieved through the democratic means of Salvador Allende's Popular Unity government, I am predisposed to accept what Gramsci referred to as pessimism of the intellect, which necessarily accompanies but is distinguishable from, an optimism of the will. The new challenges to narrow conceptions of citizenship and belonging, the clamoring for decentralized, participatory forms of politics, and the newly crafted, promoted, and embodied subjectivities of women's and urban popular movements—to name two of the new social movements that emerged in Latin America during the dark days of military rule—have all made important contributions to democratizing liberal democracy. They have also, however, contributed powerful resources to the local reconfiguration of the neoliberal governmental states in the region. This is visible in Brazil, where the hopes of the many who counted on President Lula's leftist government seem to have been dashed as the Brazilian gendered, neoliberalized state acts both to care for those worth caring for (e.g., through the widely popular and widespread Plan Zero Hunger and other initiatives of the caring state) and to punish and warehouse those deemed to be superfluous (e.g., through the militarization of *favelas* and the incarceration of ever-increasing numbers of people).[33]

In this chapter I have explored the ongoing institutional transformations in Chile and their link to the struggles of feminists and the women's movement. Rather than signaling the end of neoliberalism, they, I have suggested, correspond to a second moment in the neoliberalization of the state: its transformation into an "enabling" state with both punitive and caring dimensions. The enabling state is a socially interventionist state intent on adapting Chilean society to the present economic order through projects of self-responsibilitzation of society, accomplished in turn through the caring or punitive reregulation of individuals. What a historically sensitive, grounded examination reveals is that women, with their ascribed capacities for care, are explicit handmaids of this ambitious project. Through their expert and professional knowledge and actions, as well as their presence in private-public partnerships, where they deploy their capacities as practitioners and clients, women are actively involved in bringing about the self-responsibilization of society and individuals. Thus, gender has "always already been there" in the configuration of the Chilean ameliorative state as an implicit or explicit object of social regulation.

In charting a course beyond neoliberalism, I believe that it will be important to first recognize that, in cases of mature neoliberalism, like the Chilean case discussed here, the feminist movement's fundamental emancipatory promise is tightly imbricated with its entrenchment in a particular political form. Feminists have argued that the dismantling of social dimension of states as part of Latin American neoliberal restructuring in the 1980s is best described as a "remasculinization" of the state. This is a bleak snapshot of a moment in what has turned out to be a much more ambiguous process of neoliberalization that is characterized by an infusion of feminist ideas and practices into the institutions of the state. Indeed, Chile's example suggests that our present struggle to get "from here to there," to move beyond neoliberalism, may have to begin with a careful, self-critical questioning of the Janus-faced state and of its caring and punitive resources and effects.

CHAPTER 9

"YES, WE DID!" "¡SÍ SE PUDO!"

Regime Change and the Transnational Politics of Hope Between the United States and El Salvador

Elana Zilberg

El Salvador is a place where three crucial issues in U.S.–Latin America relations converge with unusual clarity—immigration, free trade, and security.
—Kevin Casas-Zamora, "President Obama in El Salvador" (2011)

WHEN THIS VOLUME WAS PROPOSED, I argued strongly that the framework of an emergent postneoliberal imaginary, put forth as it was by its Bolivianist coeditors, was frankly unimaginable in the context of El Salvador. In my view, the close economic and security relationships between the United States and El Salvador were not up for grabs. As I have argued elsewhere, if anything, during the eight years of the Bush administration, ARENA (Allianza Republicana Nationalista, or the National Republican Alliance), El Salvador's ruling right-wing party, had successfully resumed its cozy Cold War relations with the United States precisely through its staunch stand against the Pink Tide elsewhere in Latin America and its eager endorsement of the Dominican Republic and Central American Free Trade Agreement (DR-CAFTA) on the one hand and its support of Bush's "war on terror" and its close collaboration with U.S. regional strategy for heightened and integrated security on the other. The latter involved, among other things, establishing a Transnational Anti-Gang (TAG) unit, which involved direct collaboration between U.S. and Salvadoran law-enforcement agencies. The U.S. Southern Command had renewed its military presence in Central America, and El Salvador was once again a central client within the U.S. "protection racket" (Huggins 1998; Stanley 1996) and its "global military gift economy" (Klima 2002), Moreover, the country was utterly dependent on the flow of immigrant remittances from the United States and thus was obliged to court favor for its large diaspora living in legal limbo in the United States. Both the ARENA party and the Bush administration had repeatedly held the Salvadoran electorate ransom with the threat of the loss of remittances and the massive deportation of Salvadorans if the leftist opposition party were to take the Salvadoran presidency (Zilberg 2011).

My dark prognosis for the prospects for a postneoliberal era in El Salvador was to be challenged the following year when the FMLN (Frente Farabundo Martí para la Liberación Nacional, or the Farabundo Martí Front for National Liberation) presidential candidate, Mauricio Funes, was successfully elected to office and with the glowing approval of the Obama administration. Had the Pink Tide finally swept ashore in El Salvador, that otherwise recalcitrant isthmus of Latin America's postauthoritarian Right? Would Obama's election lift the weight of U.S. imperialism sufficiently to relax the patronage politics that had stifled Salvadoran sovereignty for so long? How might these transnational politics of hope, captured in the twin elections of Obama and Funes, reconfigure the hegemony of neoliberal policies on the one hand and hard-line regional and global security agendas on the other? Would these "transformational" presidencies usher in, as Funes promised, "a preferential option for the poor" and, as Obama promised, "a new chapter in U.S.–Latin American relations"?

As Casas-Zamora noted in his commentary on Obama's March 2011 trip to El Salvador, "El Salvador is a place where three crucial issues in U.S.–Latin America relations converge with unusual clarity—immigration, free trade, and security" (2011). To what extent, then, have the transnational politics of hope ushered in by the twin elections of Funes and Obama reconfigured this triumvirate of issues at the crux of Salvadoran sovereignty? In this chapter I consider the first two years of the Funes administration from the vantage point of this volume's concern with the possibilities for alternative political, economic, moral, and cultural models of neoliberalism. I do so through an examination of what I have elsewhere termed "neoliberal securityscapes" and more specifically through the lens of the making of the so-called transnational gang crisis (Zilberg 2011, 1–6).[1] In keeping with this volume's attention to Latin America, my focus here is El Salvador. However, I contend that an analysis of the realpolitik in El Salvador necessarily includes a discussion of ongoing entanglements between the El Salvador and the United States and of the continuing salience of "the interstate regime" between the United States and Latin American countries (Menjívar and Rodríguez 2005). First, I discuss how neoliberalism as an economic model, a political philosophy, and a mode of personal conduct unfolded in both the United States and El Salvador through a transnational framework. Next, I discuss the relationship between neoliberal and security discourses and practices. Finally, I consider how the Funes and the Obama administrations have or have not reconfigured the web of relations and the field of forces that undergird these neoliberal securityscapes and link El Salvador and the United States in complicity.

NEOLIBERALISM IN A TRANSNATIONAL CONTEXT

In El Salvador, well before the implementation of DR-CAFTA in 2006, privatization had affected all aspects of life including health care, education, banking, and public utilities. William Robinson makes the somewhat ironic and tragic argument that the FMLN unwittingly provided the United States a pretext for massive intervention—not only through military but, in fact, largely economic aid and training. The latter involved cultivating a new elite, or what Robinson terms a "neoliberal polyarchy," that would challenge the old agricultural oligarchy as well as the more progressive "import-substitution" economic model and govern instead through a "market democracy" (2003, 87–101). Although the peace accords did contain a limited land-reform agreement, by the close of the war the Salvadoran government had removed all subsidies on agricultural products, leaving the beneficiaries of land reform without technical and financial assistance. El Salvador shifted from being a net exporter to a net importer of basic foodstuffs, such as beans and rice (Zilberg and Lungo 1999). The cost of the "basic [food] basket," the term of art in Salvadoran economic analyses, continued to rise each year.

By war's end, labor was El Salvador's primary export, and immigrant remittances exceeded coffee as the number-one source of foreign revenue (Funkhouser 1995; Lungo 1997; Orozco 2000; Pedersen 2002). The shocks to the Salvadoran economy over the next fifteen years would be cushioned only by the massive influx of remittances from Salvadorans working abroad. This flow of capital from immigrants proved to be an important safety net for Salvadorans affected by the postwar neoliberal structural adjustment. It also anticipated the formal dollarization of the Salvadoran economy in 2001. The much-valorized figure of *el hermano lejano* (the faraway brother), a hardworking, responsible individual who migrates abroad in order to support the individual's family in El Salvador, became a perfect sign for the neoliberal subject—at least in El Salvador. The recipients of those remittances were increasingly interrelated as consumers rather than laborers, foreshadowing the proliferation of huge shopping malls and branded identities (Rivas 2007; Zilberg 2011).

Needless to say, international migration did not abate with the end of the war; in fact, poverty and crime rates actually increased.[2] Informal and criminal economies actively exploited new zones of ambiguity opened up by deregulation (Comaroff and Comaroff 2006). [3] In this new entrepreneurial and import-oriented society, these sectors of the economy became the only available alternatives to international migration for an increasing number of Salvadorans. Like immigrant remittances, extortion became a fundamental means of survival within El Salvador's neoliberal economy. In this sense, migrants, gangs, and criminals were mimetic of the normative ideological figures of the neoliberal era, the entrepreneur and the consumer (Zilberg 2011).

Salvadoran migration to the United States brings the transnational and simultaneous effects of neoliberalism into view. Although it is often noted that neoliberalism appeared as discourse, practice, and subject of academic analysis earlier in Latin America than in the United States, I maintain that, in the Salvadoran case, the "spatial and temporal" separation between developments in Latin America and the United States does not hold. In the 1980s Salvadoran refugees fled the effects of Reagan's "new cold war" in Central America, only to find themselves in American cities already eviscerated by the deindustrialization of the 1970s and undergoing the effects of aggressive union busting and outsourcing alongside the flow of cheap, unprotected labor for the new service economy. Most Salvadorans settled in the Los Angeles area, where the California homeowners' tax revolt of 1978, Proposition 13, and the downsizing of the defense industry a decade later had taken a particularly hard toll. In the 1990s the neoconservative "Reagan revolution" of the 1980s was extended through the Clintonian embrace and consolidation of a neoliberal agenda. The Clinton era represented a dramatic inversion of the binary opposition between conservatives and liberals that had characterized official U.S. politics on domestic issues since the Great Depression. Republicans had successfully disorganized and inverted Democratic discourse precisely over the issues of state intervention, privatization, and deregulation.

The passage of the North American Free Trade Agreement (NAFTA) in 1994 further accelerated all of the aforementioned processes. During the same period, the institutional apparatus of the capitalist welfare state was entering its last moments before the full onset of neoliberalism in 1996 with the passage of welfare reform legislation.[4] The state, which had produced a social-service industry upon which the underclass fed, was to be redesigned along entrepreneurial lines. The welfare-dependent culture of poverty in the inner city was to be transformed into a culture of enterprise, family, and self-help. Both the government and the individual were to be disciplined according to the logic of the market. Welfare reform also found its way into the 1996 Illegal Immigration and Immigrant Responsibility Act, which also targeted immigrant access to social services and welfare, regardless of legal status or age.

NEOLIBERAL SECURITY

The liberal conception of individual responsibility, which was radically revived under neoliberalism, would also underpin the moral framework of an increasingly punitive criminal-justice system. Criminals refused to accept responsibility for their actions. This growing severity and scope of law enforcement, accompanied by an increasingly punitive criminal-justice system, seems to contradict the neoliberal logic to minimize state intervention. Indeed, Foucault's anticipation that American neoliberalism would be accompanied by a more tolerant penal justice system has not been borne out.[5] Rather, zero-tolerance strategies, "just deserts," and "truth in sentencing" appear to be part and parcel of the neoliberal logics of individual responsibility and deregulation. The latter involved the removal of any number of state protections: standards for probable cause, access to legal representation, and judicial review. At the same time, new categories of crime and of felonies were added to the rolls of criminal and mandatory sentence enhancements, which bumped misdemeanors up to felonies. Under neoliberalism, the state continued to govern, but it did so through crime (Simon 2007). The result was the mass incarceration of African American and Latino men.

Like the Personal Responsibility and Work Opportunity Act of 1996, the Illegal Immigration Reform and Immigrant Responsibility Act (IIRAIRA), passed the same year, was equally beholden to this notion of the "responsibilization" of the individual. Under the IIRAIRA, offenses that were neither "aggravated" nor "felonies" under criminal law now constitute "aggravated felonies" within immigration law. These included nonviolent "crimes of moral turpitude," such as driving while under the influence of alcohol, simple battery, shoplifting, and selling small amounts of drugs (Coutin 2007, 21). This expanded definition of aggravated felonies was applied retroactively and set into motion "expedited removal" proceedings, through which immigration officials could remove unauthorized entrants without a court hearing as long as these individuals did not express a credible fear of persecution.

Even though only a minority of those deported had criminal records (most were still deported for illegal entry or overstay of their visas, both civil offenses) and an even smaller number were active or alleged gangs members, the criminal alien and the criminal deportee as hardened criminals and active gang members became ubiquitous and highly feared "new criminal types" (Siegel 1998) in the United States after the Cold War and post–civil war El Salvador, respectively. Indeed, in El Salvador, *el marero* (the gangster) came to represent the negative counterweight to the entrepreneurial *el hermano lejano* (Zilberg 2011).

In the United States, market fundamentalism required, it seemed, the spread of tactics of policing and discipline, which sought to ensure the continuous production of marginalized bodies in the form of cheap labor and criminals. Labor migration served the interests of the marketplace, and incarceration furnished the means with which the nation-state could secure the basis of its sovereignty and legitimate its monopoly on coercion. However, it seems that nationalism was not as successful as capitalism in this regard.

Despite the apparent contradictions between the political economy of free trade and the postdisciplinary regime of zero-tolerance policing, both seem to produce the spaces of circulation and interconnection associated with globalization, whether through sanctioned or transgressive mobility.

Whereas in the 1990s, the U.S. criminal-justice system was becoming more and more draconian, postwar El Salvador was marked by a proliferation of newly guaranteed rights under the law. The 1992 peace accords ushered in an era dominated by reforms in human and civil rights, all of which culminated in the new 1998 penal code. A new civilian police force replaced the old security apparatuses of the authoritarian state. Indeed, the rights embedded in postwar social or political liberalism seemed to be out of step with the emerging neoliberal order and its emphasis on responsibilities over rights.[6] However, as soon as the 1998 penal code was signed into law, ARENA, other right-wing parties, and even elements within the FMLN called for the reform of the reforms—arguing that the high levels of postwar crime and violence were the result of the liberal excesses of democratization. The increasing Americanization of Salvadoran culture through migration and deportation was also regularly cited as the source of increasing crime rates. Remittances were said to have made Salvadorans lazy and vulnerable to all sorts of vices (Zilberg and Lungo 1999).

Postwar violence led to extreme disillusionment. Suspicion and fear were the prevailing structures of feeling in postwar El Salvador (Cortez 2001; Kokotovic 2006; Moodie 2010; Nelson 2009; Zilberg 2007a). The great majority of Salvadorans no longer expected that the state could provide for either their economic or their physical security. Many championed vigilante-style or what Daniel Goldstein terms in the Bolivian case "flexible" or "self-help" justice through private security patrols and vigilante lynchings (2004). As early as 1998, a public-opinion poll indicated that 46 percent of the Salvadoran population believed that people had the right to take justice into their own hands and wanted to see the military step in where the new civilian police force was failing (Instituto Universitario de Opinión Pública 1998). Private security flourished under these conditions. Although the new Policía National Civil (National Civil Police, PNC) struggled just to furnish and equip its local and regional offices, private security firms (fewer than 10 in 1992) increased to more than 80 in 1995 and 265 in 2001. The number of private security agents more than tripled, from 6,000 in 1996 to 18,943 in 2001, far outnumbering officers in the National Civil Police. These businesses benefited directly from the state's failure to contain the violence. Violence could be co-opted within a market logic despite the more common perception that investment requires stable and docile markets.

By 2003 the human rights agenda ushered in by the 1992 peace accords had been eclipsed by the rise of, and indeed return of, the security state in the form of citizen or public security discourses. The ARENA government (much like Honduras and Guatemala) launched El Plan Mano Dura, and legislation, El Ley Antimara. During the next two years, more than 30,000 youth and young adults accused of being gang members were arrested. Not only did Mano Dura represent a major blow to the postwar human rights agenda in El Salvador, but it also signaled the successful transnationalization of U.S.-style zero-tolerance gang-abatement strategies. Moreover, it brought the Salvadoran military back into policing functions by establishing joint police and army patrols. Soldiers were back on the streets of San Salvador for the first time since the end of the civil war (Zilberg 2007b).

REMILITARIZATION

If the peace accords had succeeded in delinking the military and the police, *manodurista* policies enabled their reconnection and harkened back to an earlier moment in Salvadoran history, when the police were a division of the Salvadoran Armed Forces. Indeed, the plan's introduction of joint patrols of police officers and soldiers threatened to bring the military back into politics and to strengthen the hand of *los señores de la guerra* (the warlords), whose power had diminished considerably since the signing of the peace accords in 1992.[7] Plan (Súper) Mano Dura was distorting the role of the military in contemporary El Salvador. As one Salvadoran constitutional lawyer said to me:

> The military now say, "Look, now we have deployments . . . [so] we need a larger budget. We need the United States to send new transport vehicles, we need new arms, we need more aid, more uniforms because we're in a military campaign against the gangs or the thieves. . . . It distorts not only the role of the police, who need a guard to protect them so that they can protect me, but also the role of the military. The military regains their profile.

> We have a minister of defense who opines over the death penalty, who offers his opinion about public security . . . the environment. . . . The military leaders that we had, *los señores de la guerra*, as we called them in the conflict in the eighties, feel once again [that they have a political voice].
>
> The UMO, these anti-riot units that were formed by France, lately have started to be trained [using] the helicopters of the air force . . . in simulating rescues. . . . But who's going to guarantee me that this anti-riot unit will not use the air transport training to repress a protest rally? *I have the right to worry because of the history of my country.* (Zilberg 2011, 202; emphasis added)

The United States, of course, had played a central role in that history. And there was considerable concern that its newly opened International Law Enforcement Academy for Latin America (ILEA) in San Salvador might repeat that history. The self-proclaimed mission of the program was to combat international crimes, such as drug trafficking, organized crime, and terrorism, by providing high-quality training to members of law-enforcement agencies throughout the world.[8] Most Salvadoran human rights organizations opposed the agreement, saying that the ILEA was the new School of the Americas (SOA).[9] The Human Rights Institute of the University of Central America (IDHUCA), however, somewhat counterintuitively, argued that the ILEA was the last hope for realizing the peace accord's goal of a *civilian* police force truly independent of the military. It was, after all, the ineffectiveness of the PNC that had been leveraged to launch joint patrols with the military.[10] The fear of U.S. participation was, of course, not unfounded. Many of the worst violators of human rights in El Salvador had attended the School of the Americas. They were trained by the FBI and stationed at Fort Benning and Fort Bryant in North Carolina for training in the infantry or military intelligence. This historical alliance between the Salvadoran and U.S. military was renewed when ARENA eagerly threw its lot in with the Bush's "coalition of the willing." Tellingly, the Iraq war drew directly on the United States' Latin American policy up through the Cold War. El Salvador, which provided a school for the United States to execute imperial violence through proxies, is an iconic case of how Latin America has long served as a "workshop of empire" (Grandin 2006). It was no coincidence then that the "Salvador option"—the use of local paramilitary forces, otherwise known as death squads—was proposed by then Vice President Dick Cheney as a successful model on which to base counterinsurgency operations in Iraq after direct intervention by U.S. troops had failed (ibid.; Lomas 2006). In this sense, the newness of the "war on terror" was largely an invention (Masco 2005).

Furthermore, the remilitarization of Salvadoran society was also accompanied by an increase of the U.S. military's presence in the region. Prior to 9/11, the U.S. Southern Command had already begun to shift its focus to the "securitization" of nontraditional security threats, which had previously fallen under the domains of social policy or policing. However, these disparate threats—immigration and gangs, as well as criminal activities such as human trafficking, document forging, money laundering, and drug production—lacked a unifying logic. The September 11 attacks on New York and Washington, D.C., by al-Qaeda and the ensuing "war on terror" provided not only that logic but also the rationale the U.S. military establishment needed to justify increased military aid to the region (Loxton 2007).

At much the same moment, U.S. Attorney General Alberto Gonzales and Salvadoran president Elias Antonio Saca announced a new collaborative effort to combat La Mara Salvatrucha and the Eighteenth Street gangs through the use of a Transnational Anti-Gang unit. The TAG would be made up of the U.S. Federal Bureau of Investigation, the U.S. Department of State, and El Salvador's National Civil Police, with an "embedded" prosecutor from the Salvadoran attorney general's office. It would also facilitate the efficient implementation of CAFÉ (the Central American Fingerprinting Exploitation initiative). The day after this announcement, the chiefs of police of El Salvador, Guatemala, Honduras, and Belize met in Los Angeles to draft a proposal for the Third Annual International Gang Conference in San Salvador. The same year, the federal Interagency Taskforce on Gangs (which comprised governmental officials from five agencies, including the departments of Homeland Security, Defense, State, and Justice, together with the U.S. Agency for International Development), launched its U.S. Strategy to Combat Criminal Gangs from Mexico and Central America. These transnational security agreements derive their logic and form from the premise that such gangs operate as sophisticated transnational criminal organizations that have elaborate communication systems and networks that span Central America, Mexico, and the United States (if not beyond).

The implied interconnections between gangs, immigrants, and terrorists were further bolstered by military strategists who argued that the division between gangs as a law-enforcement concern and terrorists as a military concern could no longer be maintained where "distinctions between war and crime are becoming increasingly blurred" (Manwaring 2005). This "gang crime–terrorism continuum" (Wilson and Sullivan 2007) was popularized by pundit Newt Gingrich in his documentary titled "American Gangs: Ties to Terror?" (2005). Gingrich argued that these possible links between immigration, gangs, and terrorism clearly support, first, bringing law enforcement and immigration agencies together and, second, bringing national security and law enforcement into one unified effort—"for, if not, our very civilization maybe at risk." It comes as no surprise, perhaps, that Fox News and Gingrich would be a conduit for popularizing links between gangs and terrorists and feeding our imaginations with alarmist reportage. However, this "gang-crime-terrorism continuum" and the justification of the United States as a security state also became a legitimate topic of debate among military strategists. In a special to the website titled *Defense and the National Interest*,[11] Wilson and Sullivan advocate applying "third generation street gangs (3G2), netwar, and fourth generation warfare (4GW) to investigate typologies and relationships of third generation street groups and terrorist groups" (2007, 1). They, too, argue that the division between gangs as a law-enforcement concern and terrorists as a military concern can no longer be maintained where "distinctions between war and crime are becoming increasingly blurred" (ibid., 3). Their publication follows on previous works that argue that gangs, as a mutated form of "urban insurgency," pose a serious challenge to state sovereignty. As such, gangs were both political and criminal in nature and thus required police and military forces to provide collective security and stability (Manwaring 2005).

The Bush era's geopolitics of disaster provided new opportunities for the ruling right-wing party, ARENA, to pass its own antiterrorist law. The 2006 law was directed not only against gangs but also against leftists protesting the privatization of water and street vendors demonstrating against restrictions on their access to public space. Once again, the Salvadoran government had successfully deployed the gang crime–terrorism continuum to repackage its internal enemies in terms of the United States' governing security paradigm.

Take, for instance, this speech delivered by El Salvador's then minister of foreign affairs, Marisol Argueta, on September 18, 2008, before the conservative American Enterprise Institute in Washington, DC. Argueta appealed to the United States to concern itself with the possibility of a victory by the leftist opposition party in the upcoming elections. Quoting Ronald Reagan, the new Cold War president, Argueta said, "The security of the United States is at stake in El Salvador." Latin America, she asserted, was threatened by a wave of neosocialist groups that take power through democratic elections and populist appeals. "If power goes to the wrong hands, El Salvador may well be the next populist failure in the hemisphere" (Argueta, cited in Tim 2008).

There was nothing particularly new in Argueta's Washington speech. It was the foreign-policy counterpart to ARENA's regular warnings to the Salvadoran people during each electoral campaign since the FMLN was legalized as a political party in 1992 with the signing of the Salvadoran peace accords. ARENA had consistently held the power of the United States in the region over the heads of Salvadoran voters. In the 2005 presidential election, ARENA argued that if Shafik Handal, the FMLN candidate that year, was elected, the United States would discontinue temporary protected status for Salvadorans living abroad and so end the flow of family remittances, on which the country was enormously dependent.

The Bush administration supported ARENA's discourse. It objected to Handal's leftist ties as the former the head of the Salvadoran communist party and his strident criticism of neoliberalism as a continuation of U.S. imperialism, not to mention his close relations with Venezuelan president Hugo Chávez and Bolivian president Evo Morales. In violation of Salvadoran sovereignty, the U.S. ambassador openly warned Salvadorans in newspaper headlines that the election of Handal would have a serious and negative impact on U.S.-Salvadoran relations. Poised between the danger of gangs to the north and antineoliberal and socialist victories to the south in Venezuela and Bolivia, El Salvador had once again became strategically placed within U.S. interests (Zilberg 2011).

POSTNEOLIBERAL EMERGENCE?

The year 2009 proved to be an auspicious year for the Salvadoran Left and for U.S.-Salvadoran relations. ARENA's tried and true threat of a communist takeover failed to convince either side—either the Salvadoran electorate or the U.S. government. With consistent and concerted pressure from the Salvadoran diaspora and their allies in the United States (many of whom were Latin Americanists in U.S. universities), the United States promised to honor the results of the election regardless of its outcome (Perla 2010). When on June 1, 2009, Mauricio Funes was inaugurated as the first FMLN president in El Salvador, Secretary of State Hillary Clinton, dressed in red, radiated the approval of the Obama administration from the audience. Also present was Cuba's Vice President Lazo, the first official Cuban visitor to El Salvador since 1962. Lazo received a standing ovation to the roar of "Cu-ba, Cu-ba, Cu-ba!" hours before the Funes administration "correct[ed] a historic error" by renewing diplomatic relations between the two countries (Garret 2009). Not only had the Funes election ended twenty years of uninterrupted rule by ARENA, but Funes was also the first remotely leftist president since the founding of the modern Salvadoran state. His election was, in his words, "the night of the greatest hope in El Salvador." Invoking slain Archbishop Romero as his "teacher and the spiritual guide of the nation," Funes promised that his government would have "a preferential option for the poor, for those who need a robust government to get ahead and to be able to compete in this world of disequilibrium under fair conditions. . . . The Salvadoran people are watching," he declared, and "Archbishop Romero will be the final judge." In both countries, the magic of casino capitalism and its emperors had lost some of the allure, if not actual power, that they had enjoyed and fed off during the past two to three decades. However, like Obama, Funes faced a daunting financial crisis, which was further exacerbated by the corruption of the previous regime and the loss of remittance income from Salvadoran immigrants in the United States. Salvadorans were out of work at home *and* abroad.

In what ways might the transnational politics of hope, condensed in the dialectical image of the "Obama-Funes inauguration," reconfigure the web of relations and field of forces undergirding the neoliberal securityscapes mapped in the foregoing sections of this chapter? Would these developments signal the beginning of the end of neoliberalism or at least the most vulgar and predatory expressions of its logic? Where would questions of human rights, immigration, and security policy—national, regional, and global—fall in this moment of potential, of seeming emergence? Would these "transformational" politics usher in a "new chapter in the story of the Americas" and signal the end of U.S. unilateralism in Latin America—a welcome break from the revival of the Cold War–inspired policies of the Bush administration (Hursthouse and Ayso 2010)?

For his part, Obama failed the first test of his new policy toward Latin America. On June 27, 2009, the president of Honduras, Manuel Zelaya, was ousted by the Honduran military when troops arrested him in his pajamas and sent him into exile in Costa Rica. President Funes put his troops on alert at the Salvadoran-Honduran border. Zelaya's removal was largely attributed to his support of the Venezuelan- and Cuban-initiated alternative international trade organization, the Bolivarian Alliance for the Peoples of our Americas (ALBA). Initially, President Obama joined the rest of the world in condemning Zelaya's ousting as both an illegal coup[12] and a disturbing throwback to a pattern characteristic of earlier authoritarian regimes in Latin America. But the United States' position would waver in the coming months, and Zelaya would not be reinstated. The United States would, instead, endorse the results of an election that the majority of Hondurans boycotted and that lacked, according to the UN secretary general, the Organization of American States, and the Carter Center, conditions for free and fair elections (Pine 2010). Under the new Honduran president, Porfirio Lobo, Honduras withdrew from ALBA. At nearly the same time, Funes announced that he would not support El Salvador's joining ALBA despite the FMLN's strong approval of the alliance.

The close economic relationship between the United States and El Salvador was clearly not up for grabs, and the FMLN could come to power only by accepting some form of U.S. domination and moderating its agenda. The Funes-FMLN ticket was from the outset a marriage of convenience (Garrett 2010). Funes had come to victory promising a new politics of the Left and with the support of a surprising coalition of forces. Both the right wing and private sectors could be counted among the "friends of Mauricio Funes."[13] A long-time television journalist committed to a free and critical press, Funes had no direct ties to the leftist party or to the revolutionary war and ran on a distinctly centrist and reformist platform. Although his vice-presidential candidate, Salvador Sánchez Cerén, continued to represent the FMLN's more orthodox leftist core, Funes had taken care to publicly align himself with then Brazilian president Lula and with the "good left" (Pine 2010). Indeed the "bad left," namely presidents Hugo Chávez and Evo Morales, were both noticeably absent at Funes's inauguration.

During his first year in office, Funes designated 43 percent of his administration's budget for social projects and established a new office of social inclusion, headed up by his Brazilian wife, Vanda Pignato (a well-known promoter of gender equality).[14] The president also focused on implementing social policies to mitigate the effects of the recession on poor people in El Salvador. Among these were the provision of free lunches, school supplies, uniforms, and shoes to public-school students; free medical services; and the Plan de Agricultura Familiar, or Family Farming Plan, to assist small farmers with credit, insurance, technical help, and the procurement of seeds and fertilizer (*Americas Quarterly* 2011). In this sense, the Funes administration, not unlike the Chilean case discussed by Veronica Schild in Chapter 8 of this volume, has expanded state support in health care, pensions, and education for "responsible citizens" and for women in particular. However, as in Chile, this "caring" and "ameliorative" state is still firmly entrenched in a neoliberal political rationality. Funes has maintained respect for corporate privatization, refused to open investigations against the previous government for corruption, and generally has not challenged the underlying premises of neoliberalism.[15] Funes remained committed to maintaining his country's "friendship" with the United States, as well as his loyalty to both CAFTA and dollarization even at the expense of alienating his party. His steadfastness paid off with millions of dollars in loans and other assistance to Funes's antipoverty program. He also secured an additional $790 million in a "stand-by agreement" from the International Monetary Fund to help alleviate the economic crisis (Pine 2010). Obama granted Funes's request for a fifteen-month extension to the Temporary Protected Status program, which allowed 240,000 Salvadoran beneficiaries to continue working legally in the United States (Garrett 2010).

Most surprising, however, is Funes's failure to support social justice and human rights reforms. When Funes assumed office, he stated that his government would take "the human being as the beginning and the end" of its political program, assume a policy of "zero tolerance" toward all forms of human rights violations, strengthen the national system for the protection of human rights, and establish new relations with international human rights organizations by promoting the development of human rights through national legislation. Both national and international human rights groups, however, have found his human rights record lacking on a number of fronts (Instituto de Derechos Humanos de la UCA 2011).

Although he apologized to the nation on behalf of the state for the 1980 assassination of Archbishop Oscar Romero and instituted an annual national holiday to commemorate Romero, he does not support retracting the 1993 amnesty law, which absolved perpetrators of war crimes. In fact, Funes endorsed legislation sponsored by ARENA that would tie the Supreme Court's hands in reexamining the amnesty law, CAFTA, and dollarization. Although ARENA has since backed away from the controversial Decree 743, Funes's collaboration in not only signing but also participating in the formulation of the law has severely damaged his credibility and led to massive protests. Relationships between Funes and the FMLN, already strained, have only been damaged further, leading some to conclude that Funes and the FMLN are indeed "separate entities" (Hayden 2009). The FMLN is purportedly seeking to bring a "truly red president" into office in 2014 (Brockwehl and Pitarque 2010).

Again as in the Chilean case, the contemporary Salvadoran state can be characterized as a "Janus face . . . with both caring and punitive dimensions." The "enabling state" operates within and is buttressed by a coercive state apparatus (Schild, Chapter 8 in this volume). On this front, the Funes administration has dashed hopes that it would adopt an entirely new approach to security in general and youth gangs in particular. The FMLN had opposed the *manodurista* policies of the preceding two ARENA governments and favored combating crime by attacking its root causes, such as social exclusion and poverty. Although the new National Civil Police strategy has purportedly designated 50 percent of its budget for prevention (Garrett 2010), Funes has not only continued ARENA's hard-line approach but has also called for the continued and expanded role of the Salvadoran military in civil policing matters. Under ARENA's zero-tolerance plans, the military had been limited to patrols with the police. Funes has since enabled the military to set up checkpoints, perform searches, pursue suspects, and make arrests.

As a result, the army requested an addition $10 million to support these deployments, which were increased from 1,300 to 3,800 troops (Wolf 2010). Moreover, upon taking office, Funes reappointed the previous ARENA minister of defense, Col. David Mungía Payés, who was in charge of these military police. Although Mungía Payés has not himself been accused of human rights violations, he is a 1973 graduate of the School of the Americas and also the former chief of intelligence and commanding officer of the Batallón Belloso, one of the deadliest, rightist military squadrons during the civil war. Most recently, Funes replaced Manuel Melgar, an FMLN loyalist, with Munguía Payés as minister of justice and public security.[16] He subsequently replaced the civilian head of the PNC with "retiring" general Francisco Ramón Salinas Rivera. Salinas has, not surprisingly, brought his loyal staff from the military to serve under him at the PNC—further blurring the lines between military and police culture. A third military officer has been placed as second in command in the state intelligence unit.

Cleary, the military's political profile has not weakened under the new FMLN administration despite the party's historic distrust of the military and its direct role in sidelining the military in the peace accords. Given the 2009 military coup in Honduras, many are concerned that strengthening the Salvadoran military's hand in internal policing could leave future governments vulnerable to military overthrow (Brockwehl and Pitarque 2010). At the very least, human rights organizations are worried that human rights violations will increase with the military's increased contact with the Salvadoran population (Ayala 2011).

The military is also the centerpiece of Obama's El Salvador agenda, revealing, as Nick DeGenova argues, that Obama is deeply conjoined with his predecessor. Rather than "the presumed return to normal," the Obama presidency signifies the normalization of the state of emergency, the entrenchment of the Homeland Security State, and persistent demands on the security apparatuses of states throughout the work in the U.S. global policing project (DeGenova 2010). Obama's Central American Citizen Security Partnership offers $200 million in technical assistance to military-security forces, which he says will "confront the narco-traffickers and gangs that have caused so much violence" (ibid.). Observers believe the initiative is once again militarizing daily life under cover of drug wars. "What makes Obama different is the Obama doctrine," says Héctor Perla, assistant professor of Latin American and Latino studies at the University of California, Santa Cruz, who was in El Salvador during Obama's visit there in March 2011:

> The Obama doctrine uses the rhetoric of respect for human rights, the rhetoric of peace, poverty alleviation and social justice on the one hand, while promoting militarization with the other hand. . . . In El Salvador, the U.S. is talking about policies of growth and security, promoting "citizen security" . . . but when you look close, you see an expansion of many of the same policies of the Bush administration, only now you will have Plan Centroamerica to connect and integrate Plan Mexico to the north and Plan Colombia to the south. (Perla, cited in Lovato 2011)

A member of the Concertación Feminista Prudencia Ayala (the Prudencia Ayala Feminist Consensus), thirty-five-year-old Roxana Marroquín commented as follows: "Obama's visit to the tomb of Monseñor Romero is super complicated because of what the U.S. has traditionally signified for us: a state that financed the Salvadoran military to block a revolutionary process." Marroquín lost more than a dozen family members, including her father, during the war. "The visit to Monseñor's tomb is not an act of reparation. It's an act of protocol and leaves me even more indignant, especially when he comes here with more money for guns for the military. How are we to trust that this *anti-narcoticos* plan will do anything but increase violence?" she asks (cited in Lovato 2011). The "war on terror" has been eclipsed once again by the "war on drugs." Now in its fourth futile decade, under Obama, that war has been successfully extended into Central America. Either way, it is the United States that sets the framework for the governing paradigm within which antipoverty programs and immigration policy are absorbed.

On the immigration front, the Obama administration has also overseen the continuation and intensification of enforcement policies begun under the Bush administration. This trend, variously referred to as the "securitization of migration" (Tirman 2004) or the "crimmigration crisis" (Stumpf 2006) entails the increasing interpenetration of criminal, immigration, and antiterrorist law, as well as the militarization of the U.S.-Mexican border. Obama has consistently said that he would devote resources to identifying and removing aliens with criminal records rather than targeting immigrants in workplace sweeps. Yet immigrant-rights advocates argue that the majority of immigrants captured through the much-touted Secure Communities program did not have criminal records (Griesbach 2011). Moreover, although Obama opposed SB 1070, the Arizona state law that empowered police to stop and question people about their immigration status, he responded by sending an additional 1,200 National Guard troops to the border and boasting that there were "more boots on the ground near the Southwest border than at any time in our history" (Obama 2010).

Meanwhile, the DREAM (Development, Relief, and Education for Alien Minors) Act is the only component of immigration reform to have gained any traction—although it has still not been voted into federal law. The DREAM Act would permit certain undocumented immigrant students who have grown up in the United States to apply for temporary legal status and to eventually obtain permanent legal status and become eligible for U.S. citizenship if they go to college or serve in the U.S. military. The act would also eliminate a federal provision that penalizes states that provide in-state tuition without regard to immigration status. Advocates argue that, if enacted, the DREAM Act would have a life-changing impact on the students who qualify, dramatically increasing their average future earnings—and consequently the amount of taxes they would pay—while significantly reducing criminal-justice and social-services costs to taxpayers. The act was first introduced in 2001 but floundered until the military option was added to its original focus on education in 2007, when it was attached to the 2008 Department of Defense Authorization bill (S2919). The DREAM Act's military-service component echoes the U.S. military's intense focus on recruitment in Latino schools and neighborhoods, and many Latino activists argue that it is a de facto military draft for Latino youth. These efforts to target first- and "one-and-a-half"-generation Americans of Latin American origin gained considerable momentum after September 11, 2001, as part of the U.S. military's crisis in meeting its recruitment quotas.

Indeed, public attention was initially drawn to this phenomenon when it was discovered that the first marine to die in Iraq was a Guatemalan immigrant. The death of the "immigrant soldier," U.S. Marine Lance Corporal

José Antonio Gutiérrez, has since served as an important political text for proponents and opponents of military recruitment in Latino communities. Corporal Gutierrez grew up as an orphan on the streets of Guatemala City. In 1988, at the age of fourteen, Gutiérrez came to the United States as an undocumented immigrant and subsequently legalized his status as a minor in the foster-care system. He later joined the U.S. Marines and was deployed during Operation Bagdad. In a much-publicized ceremony, Gutiérrez was awarded posthumous citizenship, and his Guatemalan-based sister and her family were granted green cards. Once again, immigrants have been called upon to fill jobs that Americans are not filling—the patriotic duty to defend the homeland. In exchange, they have been offered a fast track to legalization and/or naturalization, and in some cases immigrants facing criminal charges have been given the option of joining the military as an alternative to incarceration followed by deportation (National Gang Intelligence Center 2007). Scholars and journalists have remarked on the macabre ironies that the immigrant—whether documented or undocumented, alive or dead—presents with regard to questions of citizenship and belonging, particularly in a rabidly anti-immigrant climate (Amaya 2006; Lovato 2005; Mariscal 2005; Pérez 2008; Plascencia 2009).

Following the United States' lead once again, Funes's most recent proposal for crime prevention also involves military service. As such, it echoes the disciplinary logic of the DREAM Act and the Junior Reserve Officer Training Corps (JROTC) programs in junior high and high schools in the United States. Funes has called for military training and service for several thousand at-risk youth between the ages of sixteen and eighteen. These young people would receive six months of training in military discipline and physical fitness, but without weapons. They would be trained to work in civil protection and risk-prevention efforts during emergencies. They would then receive six months of vocational and skills training, as well as instruction in mountain climbing and other sports and first aid. The entire process would take a year, and during that time they would receive $250 a month and would stay in "citizen training centers" specifically set up for the purpose and run by the army. The goals of the program are to promote "social integration," to harness "the productive potential of youth," and to keep youth "out of the reach of criminal groups" (Ayala 2011).

CONCLUSION: A RETURN OF THE DISCIPLINARY STATE?

In the immediate aftermath of regime change in the United States and El Salvador, the neoliberal securityscapes linking the two countries have only been strengthened. Both countries remain in a "permanent state of exception," and neoliberal logics still dominate despite and indeed through the discourses of financial crisis, disaster, and their affective insecurities. With few exceptions, neoliberalism, like U.S. hegemony, remains firmly entrenched in El Salvador. What is more, as with the United States, this economic framework has become increasingly undergirded by the remilitarization of civilian life.

One new dimension of U.S. imperialism, notes Catherine Besteman, is an unprecedented emphasis on military solutions for civil, economic, and humanitarian concerns and as a means of controlling the ungoverned (cited in Goldstein 2010, 200–201). In this sense the rise or return of the security state in the Salvadoran and U.S. cases differs sharply from the Bolivian case, captured so compellingly in Goldstein's work. Drawing on Gramsci's characterization of the liberal state as a "night watchman," Goldstein argues that the security state is "the necessary counterpoint to neoliberalism's 'privatization' of civil society, its attempt to devolve onto civil institutions, local communities, and individuals the tasks of governance" (ibid., 491). Quoting Gramsci, he depicts the neoliberal state as one that "progressively reduce[s] its own authoritarian and forcible interventions" (ibid.). Goldstein argues that "even as the state warns of imminent security threats, the state seeks to reduce its own role in security provision through expanding individual 'responsibilization'" (ibid., 492). In stark contrast, neoliberal security in the Salvadoran and U.S. cases and their shared regional-security agendas are characterized by greater state intervention on two levels. The first by the criminalization of more and more domains of everyday life and the growing intersection between criminal, immigration, and antiterrorist law, and the second by a return to and an extension of the military into criminal and civilian matters. Thus, both criminalization and militarization are dominant features of the neoliberal securityscapes in which the United States and El Salvador remain enmeshed.

Of course, militarization is by no means a new feature in any of these cases. As Goldstein rightly notes, under the National Security Doctrine, the military was charged with defending "democracy" in Latin America from the 1960s through the 1980s (Goldstein 2010). However, some postauthoritarian market democracies have turned to the military once again, albeit now in their efforts to "govern through crime" (Simon 2007). I concur with Besteman, who insists that "the contexts in which citizens take responsibility for their own protection are not defined by an absence of power but rather by a particular structure of power" and that U.S. imperialism is "a critical dimension of this structure" (cited in Goldstein 2010, 201).

Where neoliberal security has failed to "responsibilize" recalcitrant sectors of the population, be they Latino immigrants or children of those immigrants in the United States or "native" and deported immigrant youth in El Salvador, the disciplinary apparatus of the state has returned via military service. In the United States, this is still through "voluntary" service—although given the limited opportunities available particularly to the DREAM Act generation, military service is a "choiceless choice." In El Salvador, where the military is also perhaps the only expanding labor sector (outside private security and call centers), the proposed mandatory enlistment of youths from a particular sector of society represents potentially an even sharper return to rehabilitation through disciplinary institutions of the state.

That said, military service as a technique for crime prevention with at-risk Salvadoran and Latino youth must be understood within the broader context of "military neoliberalism" (RETORT 2005) and the "co-constitution of US military policy and neoliberal economic ideology" (Ettinger 2011, 1). Since the Reagan and Thatcher era, the privatization and marketization of the state's monopoly on the use of coercive force through government contracts with private military and security firms has radically altered the balance of public- and private-sector functions in wartime. This trend of rolling back the U.S. defense bureaucracy was accelerated in during the George W. Bush administrations (ibid., 6). Both Triple Canopy and Blackwater, under contract with the Pentagon, have actively recruited experienced Salvadoran soldiers from the civil war and poorly paid Salvadoran police officers (Harman 2005) and young soldiers to work as private security in Iraq. Moreover, private security contractors (retired members of the U.S. military special operations and the Drug Enforcement Administration in particular) are important actors in the United States' war on drugs in Latin America. The disciplinary functions of the contemporary military, therefore, operate within and pale in comparison to the larger logics of the free market and privatization.

It seems fair, albeit regrettable, to say then that neither the Funes nor the Obama presidencies has been successful in ushering in a new chapter in U.S.-Salvadoran relations. For the time being, their continued commitments to the combined logics of neoliberalism and militarism make it difficult to discern possibilities for alternative models that might begin to unravel the neoliberal securityscapes in which the two countries remained enmeshed.

POSTSCRIPT: INSURGENT IMAGINARIES AND POSTNEOLIBERALISM IN LATIN AMERICA

Miguel Ángel Contreras Natera

Translated by Nancy Postero

THE EMANCIPATORY IDEAL OF A UNIFIED society, one that is reconciled with itself and allows people to become their own masters, constitutes a central illusion of the colonial-modern logos in Latin America. This totalizing myth of indivisibility, of homogenization, of a society transparent to itself was of a piece with the absolutist logic of the various modernizing projects in the region. Thus, the modernizing projects involved a cruel process of conquest, destruction, and cultural colonization. Society, as a plural space characterized by heterogeneity and a polyphony of voices, has been silenced and "foreclosed" (*forcluida*)[1] by the legal dimensions of politics in the colonial-modern logos. Thus, a comprehensive overview of Latin American colonial modernity reveals a modernity marked by successive failures and tragedies: of colonization and exclusion, of fracture and fragmentation, of breaches and conflict between Latin American cultures and peoples (see Dussel 2003, 368).

Today a complex polyphony of the social, cultural, and popular movements is pushing society toward randomness. Rancière argues that "the political"—which he defines as the dimension of antagonism and conflict that exists in social relations—depends upon a radical questioning of the colonial-modern logics of "policing" on the continent. "Policing," in Rancière's view, points to the establishment of regimes of law and meaning that define acceptable ways of doing, ways of being, and ways of saying, making one activity visible and another not; one word understood as a part of the discourse and another understood as noise. The political is the sphere of rupture with those configurations of law and meaning that define, as Rancière would put it, those who have roles or "parts" in society and those who do not. It is those who by definition do not have a place in that configuration who carry out the ruptures, taking the "part" of those who supposedly do not have a part. This rupture is manifested as a series of acts that rerepresent the space in which those parts, their parts, and the absence of parts were defined. Thus, the logic of "the political" acts on the logic of policing, displacing, contesting, and straining the forms of representation established by policing (Contreras Natera 2004, 112–113; Rancière 1996, 44–45).

The denial of the temporal and spatial alterity intrinsic to the social sphere in Latin America is inscribed in the origin of the law, which constitutes the colonial-modern logic of politics. In the words of Eduardo Grünner "it is not that violence is a transgression of a pre-existing Law, nor that the Law comes to make amends for an unexpected violence: violence is the foundational condition of the Law, and of course it persists beyond that foundation" (1997, 32). Conceiving of power as the institutionalized representation of the law constituting the unity of society in Latin America conceals the original symbolic violence that generated this way of representing power and society. Moreover, the democratic liberal format that supplemented the colonial-modern logos assumes a society essentially determined by the economy. As a result, the naturalization of the liberal pathos directs one to question every possible constriction of individual freedom, the principle of private property, or free competition. It is worth remembering that these naturalized principles of the liberal democratic format link ethics and economy, objectifying a system of depoliticized concepts that covers up a political intentionality and, above all, foreclosing analysis of the unthinkable legacy of colonial-modern logos in the region.

In Latin America, the destabilization of the colonial-modern logos has implied the emergence of the political through the irruption of social, cultural, and popular movements and in a renovation of both politics and policing expressed in the growing debates about the necessity of convening national constituent assemblies in a large majority of the countries in the region. The visibility of policing as legal violence, inscribed and naturalized by social and political laws, has been one of the thematic axes of social, cultural, and popular movements. As these destabilizing efforts reveal the character of the colonial-modern logos, they have an important effect: policing is invalidated as a naturalized universal once the idea of one transcendent natural order has been dislocated.

By covering up the violence instituted as the law and erasing the historical constraints of its constitution, the colonial-modern logos naturalized the universal enunciation of the law of the world. Strictly speaking, it hypostatized the principle of legality of the demo-liberal format, ascribing material existence to it. The irruption of the political expresses an innovation in social relations that unleashes the creative forces of constituent power. The constituent power of the peoples in Latin America must be understood as intimately related to the profound epochal break that has made possible processes of subjective de-identification:

> Constituent power is the capacity to return to the real, to organize a dynamic structure, to build a shaping form that, through commitments, balances of power, regulations and diverse equilibria, nonetheless always recovers the rationality of the principles, that is, the material adjustment of the political to the social and to its indefinite movement. (Negri 1994, 46)

Thus, the central purpose of a renewed critical theory is to direct our gaze toward the potentials of the rebellion, transformation, and rupture carried out by antisystemic movements and to boost their obstructed capacities in order to establish the conditions of possibility for democratic, socialist, and plural processes of individual and collective self-determination. In the words of Gilles Deleuze, it is to build "rhizomatic" alternatives that take into account the production of a resistant, counterhegemonic, emancipatory, and radicalized subjectivity (see Deleuze and Guattari 1997, 6). In fact, the political spring in Latin America is a powerful and silent "molecular" transformation that takes shape in the discourses, gestures, and attitudes of the emergent forms of radicalized subjectification.[2] It is prefigured in the destabilization of five hundred years of history of the colonial-modern logos and its regimes of exclusion, *forclusión* (foreclosure), and segmentation. In this sense, the questioning at the time of the five-hundred-year anniversary in 1992 permitted the assertion of a counterhistory that made visible previously foreclosed memories, ways of life, forms of knowledge, and languages. Current struggles for land and autonomy are based on these vindications. But, above all, the demands for human justice can be realized only through just treatment of the Other. Consequently, what is essential is the theoretical and practical production of critical and radicalized imaginaries of resistance that construct a different human reality and recover the political as a deliberate means of creating the future.

THE IRRUPTION OF THE POLITICAL

In recent decades, the scattered and fragmented emergence of a political spring has begun changing the scope and content of social, political, and popular struggles in Latin America. This political spring is taking place on the "inscribed surface" (Foucault 1991b, 83) of the Washington Consensus and is beginning to fracture both the political and economic agreements that supported the multilateral and national institutions and policies of structural adjustment. These insurgent cycles of collective action and popular protests have succeeded in destabilizing a group of meanings sedimented in common sense by decades of neoliberal policies and centuries of colonial practices. The rupture with the regimes of law and meaning, that is, with policing, has altered the loci of enunciation of "the political" in the region by breaking up the symbolic distribution of the corpus of colonial modernity.

The political in social and popular movements does not emerge as an organizational proposal but as the opening of a dispute over the forms of symbolic ordering within policing. They are, then, two incommensurable logics that come into conflict as the contentious irruption breaks down the boundaries established by the regimes of visibility and meaning of the colonial-modern logos. In any case, the conflict between these logics presumes that they have nothing in common but interruptions, fractures, and exclusions. Thus, the intense social and popular mobilizations and the election of leftist democratic governments are shaping a profound transformation in both the normative horizons of Latin American societies and the theories that served as interpretative keys in the region. One could say that the current distancing from traditional readings of Latin American societies is in and of itself a symptom of the profound fractures they are experiencing.

Today's complex social-historical processes are characterized by renewed hopes and creative possibilities for the future. Above all, they represent a pluralizing tendency, as social and popular struggles overflow their bounds. These insurgent imaginaries subvert the hierarchical meanings of the fields of production of Euro-Western knowledge. They raise a defense of nature to counter the neoliberal modernizing destruction and liberate the potentialities of a critical and radicalized subjectivity. In a field of force intersected by contesting social, political, and cultural powers, these insurgent imaginaries are contributing to the questioning of colonial-modern hierarchies. This implies cultural resignification processes that destabilize hegemonic political subjectification in Latin America.[3]

Thus, in the evocative words of Enrique Dussel, the twenty-first century demands enormous creativity in the definition of transformative horizons in the societies of the region. Even the horizon of socialism (if it still has a profound and evocative meaning) must be developed as a cultural revolution, as Bolivian president Evo Morales indicates. Therefore, the construction of a new social and political theory cannot simply answer to the suppositions of the capitalist and colonial modernity of the last five hundred years. It cannot begin from liberal-bourgeois axioms, but neither can it begin from those of real socialism. This is where the fundamental challenges will be found for the resistance, counterhegemonic, and emancipation processes of social and popular movements and, above all, of the peoples of the region (Dussel 2006, 7).

In light of the consequences of neoliberal globalization, we are seeing social and cultural explosions, citizen mobilizations, and forms of resistance that are transforming the social makeup of Latin American societies. Their actions are activating a new field of cultural, environmental, and collective rights and calling for a new juridical regime that responds to the forms of property, life, and appropriation of the means of production, that these emerging socialization processes are promoting. The resistance, counterhegemony, and emancipation of indigenous people through claims for dignity, culture, and territory; peasant mobilizations against transgenic agriculture; popular struggles for the recognition of social rights; and the plurality of social movements all agitate for fundamental ruptures with the symbolic organization of colonial modernity.

That said, we must recognize that the disruptive, antagonistic, and conflictive actions of social and popular movements in the region were built in part on the "inscribed surface" of the neoliberal decline.[4] Since the late 1980s and the early 1990s, the resistance movements against neoliberal hegemony have been expanding throughout Latin America and even the world. In fact, the emergence of critical molecular powers against the neoliberal program can be dated back to the popular uprisings in Venezuela, Ecuador, and Argentina in the late 1980s and the early 1990s. The Zapatista insurrection in the Lacandona jungle on January 1, 1994, will become one of the fundamental events of reactivation of critical molecular powers. The plurality of congresses, documents, and mobilizations produced by the Zapatista insurrection had a molar impact on a family of movements around the world, reactivating a strategic debate about regional integration processes—starting from a reaffirmation that the goals of national economies should be to produce autonomous and harmonious economic development. The relevance of this movement in the criticism of the capitalist system is fundamental, given that, in the 1970s, Cold War conflicts were staged in the Third World, prefiguring the Third World as a space of resistance, counterhegemony, and emancipation of neoliberal hegemony. In the 1990s, this spatiality of resistance began to be intertwined with a vast global nebula of alter-globalization movements.

These mobilizations began to construct emergent forms of critical subjectification through discourses, gestures, and attitudes. This growing network has a definitively pluralist character: it brings together indigenous people, peasant and urban movements, feminist and ecological movements, labor unions, and others. The plurality of their demonstrations and the horizontality of their relations have helped create international solidarities. Global resistance meant the insurgence of a critical imaginary, which would build another horizon of the future as a condition of its possibility. The massive strikes in France in the winter of 1995–1996 helped prepare a new field of political confrontation with neoliberal globalization, which culminated in the blockade of the 1999 World Trade Organization (WTO) meeting in Seattle, in the G8 demonstrations in Genoa, and in the collapse of the WTO program as a consequence of the pressure by critics of capitalism at the Cancún meetings in 2003.

In Latin America, from 2002 onward one observes an exponential growth in the number of conflicts compared to previous years. This increase appears to be connected to a worsening of the crisis and, above all, to the attempts by the governments in the region to deepen the structural-adjustment plans and privatization policies. The crisis of the neoliberal model at a more systemic level has been accompanied by an attempt to impose projects centered in security, linked to disciplinary neoliberalism, with an emphasis on the creation of good investment climates for foreign investment and the rule of law. Finally, disciplinary neoliberalism shapes the social schema by criminalizing and prosecuting protests, as well as through the exponential growth of state and parastatal repression. In any case, social and popular responses to this policy have increased in recent years.

The collapse of the neoliberal model and the street actions of the *piqueteros* in Argentina; the struggles against privatization in Paraguay and Peru; the conflicts in El Salvador against the privatization of the Social Security Institute; the "water war" in Cochabamba, Bolivia; the multiple protests in Honduras against the water-privatization law; the protracted conflicts over health care in Chile and Nicaragua; the popular mobilizations in April and December 2002 supporting President Chávez and the experience of citizen participation in water delivery in Venezuela; the profound social and cultural conflict as a consequence of the actions of the People's Assembly in Oaxaca and the Zapatista movement in Chiapas, Mexico; the mobilizations supporting presidential candidate López Obrador in Mexico; the struggles of the landless movement for "social property" and against the transgenic agricultural model in Brazil; the intense indigenous mobilizations in Bolivia and Ecuador; the clear rejection of the Free Trade Pact in Colombia and Costa Rica; the diplomatic and social attempts to consolidate the ALBA (Bolivarian Alliance for the Peoples of Our Americas); the debates about the National Constituent Assembly in Ecuador, Bolivia, and Venezuela; the Andean political principle based on indigenous notions of the *pachamama*, or Mother Earth, of "command by obeying"; and others are all signals of the emergence of a set of profound transformations in the subjectivities of the peoples of the region.

But, besides this, the turn of the popular feeling in the region to the Left—with the electoral triumph of Nestor Kirchner, Lula da Silva, Evo Morales, Rafael Correa, Daniel Ortega, and Hugo Chávez Frias; the political polarization in Peru and Mexico; and the attention drawn to the Cuban problem all awaken horizons to the future laden with counterhegemonic possibilities. In a strict sense, social and popular mobilizations and the election of democratic leftist governments break up the regimes of visibility of the colonial-modern logos. These "disagreements" have implied a quest for ways to symbolically organize politics to encourage democracy, communitarianism, and solidarity. The contestation itself unleashes a process of subjectification that reconfigures the field of experimentation. This presumes the presentation of new collective challenges, the empowerment and construction of common objectives, and the revalorization of solidarity and collective action.

To understand the irruption of conflicts in Latin America, one has to locate them in the context of neoliberal hegemony, where neoliberalism is the dominant discursive form in the historical capitalist system. In any case, to place oneself in this tectonic fracture of change and transformation means to take as a reference point the concomitant and dramatic effects of neoliberal discourse. Neoliberalism can be described as a hegemonic strategy for economic globalization, given that (1) the main institutions of international economy (the Organization for Economic Co-Operation and Development, the International Monetary Fund [IMF], and the World Bank) support and promote it; (2) it occupies a fundamental political, cultural, and economic place in the United States (still the undeniable leader) and other Anglo-Saxon countries (mainly Great Britain, New Zealand, and Canada); (3) neoliberal adjustment policies have been consolidated as a prescription in almost all advanced capitalist countries; and (4) it has been configured as the pragmatic solution for restructuring postsocialist economies as they seek to become incorporated in the global economy (Jessop 2003, 216).

In the 1990s the global turn toward neoliberal practices consolidated a set of rules of negotiation, economic policies, and basic orientations that converged in the institutional forces around the so-called Washington Consensus:

The creation of new institutional practices, such as the ones established by the IMF and the WTO, provided convenient vehicles through which financial and market

> powers could be exercised. The model needed the collaboration of the principal capitalist powers and the Group of Seven (G7), leading Europe and Japan to align with the United States to shape the global financial and commercial system in ways that effectively obliged all nations to submit to it. Proscribed nations, defined as those that would not adapt to these global rules, could then be faced with sanctions or coercive or even military force if necessary. (Harvey 2008, 10)

However, it is important to remember that neoliberal hegemony has been discontinuous, asymmetric, and partial.

NEOLIBERAL GLOBALIZATION: FOUNDATION AND CRISIS

Neoliberalism has transformed itself into a political program and the dominant teleo-eschatological utopia of economic globalization processes, both because of its dissemination through structural adjustment policies and the forcefulness of the diverse interventions that characterized the neoliberal offense. The naturalization of neoliberal practices was extended as institutional reform, as discursive adjustment, and as a form of epochal common sense with omnipresent effects on social imaginaries. In that sense, its "possessive individualist" conception has turned into an epochal common sense with wide cultural and political repercussions in the daily life of the societies within the historical capitalist system (Macpherson 1970, 16).

Neoliberal globalization is based on the free flow of merchandise and capital and in the absence of state interventions in these flows. This implies a reconfiguration of the role of the state in the global economy to facilitate merchandise and capital flows and promote neoliberal competition. With that, neoliberal globalization has contributed to the formation of transnational legal regimes centered in Western economic concepts of contract and intellectual property. Multilateral institutions such as the IMF, the World Bank, and the WTO have significantly contributed to consolidating this transnational legal regime through their economic-policy recommendations over the last decade. Global markets for finance and advanced services operate through this transnational legal regime centered not in the state but in the market. Neoliberals like Hayek (1985, 1991) start from the notion of a spontaneous, self-regulated natural order whose functioning does not depend on sovereign decisions, administrative controls, or collective deliberations. Reality is considered as a materiality that preexists its social and historical forms, that is to say, something identified as real and natural, so that social reality would be structured by laws of causality analogous to the laws of natural sciences. In that sense, what is represented as the natural order of the market is removed from history to naturalize and deify liberal-capitalist society.

This idea of possessive human nature with fixed and invariable features (competitiveness, selfishness, and individuality) determines the conduct, interests, and desires of the individual in the neoliberal version. As a guiding idea, this implied forms of subjectivity with extremely broad repercussions in the imaginaries of globalized societies. As this idea becomes socially and culturally naturalized, it produces what we can call "spiritual neoliberalization."[5] Thus, from the neoliberal perspective, since the individual is symbolically and cognitively disconnected from the whole, it makes no sense for individuals to locate themselves in relation to the entirety of society. All of this points to major social dysfunctions, profoundly pathological ways of functioning, and processes of "derealization" of the other and the social.[6] A whole set of features defines this individual: allegiance to oneself, forms of enclosure, relationships marked by extreme narcissism, avoidance strategies, and inconsistencies.

Thus, in order to legitimize a new meritocratic elitism by means of conspicuous consumption, a pattern of seduction was configured, based on a culture centered on money, power, and ambition. Spiritual neoliberalization implied the formation, in the realm of consumption, of a mythical and demobilized way of living for the professional and intellectual middle class, marked by high salaries, ideological and political conservatism, and a renewed promotional, internationalist, and individualist culture. The design, fashion, diet, decoration, jewelry, and perfumes would contribute to reinforcing the image, knowledge, and beauty of individual success for the highly remunerated professional and intellectual middle class in open contrast to the insecurity, ignorance, poverty, and ugliness of the mass of "foreclosed" (*forcluidos*) others.

In a strict sense, the factual horizon of neoliberal hegemony is characterized by the exacerbation of systemic unresolved contradictions. In the 1980s, as the transformation of the productive model and the dominant regulation of post–World War II capitalism was deepened, the system of conventions that cognitively and ideologically marked the Fordist-Keynesian model was substantially changed. We witnessed a profound movement from a society based on security and labor guarantees to a society of instability, risk, and uncertainty, based fundamentally on full mercantile availability and the substitution of property rights for social rights. In a strict sense, we see the subordination of any right of citizenship to property rights. In summary, production has become flexible. It has had to adapt to fundamentally stochastic, chaotic, and turbulent markets that are subordinated to the imperatives of competition, technological innovation, and financial globalization.

The new landscapes of flexible production are characterized by deindustrialization, the return to primary production, hypertechnologization, and productive dislocation with its consequent effects on the workplace: precariousness, flexibilization, disaffiliation, and the pauperization of labor. The main social issue, according to Robert Castel (1997), is the generalization of phenomena like flexibilization, impoverishment, and clandestine immigration, as well as the perpetuation of profoundly racist regional regimes or any other phenomenon that expresses marginality and segregation, which indicate the consolidation of subclasses and situations of new poverty. These are becoming structural due to the post-Fordist model of maximum mobility and flexibility in the use of the natural and economic resources and especially of the characteristics of the labor force, according to the region. Statistical indicators cannot capture the phenomena of precariousness, the growing feeling of insecurity, or the multiple ways the social bond is weakening. The danger lies in the loss of the symbolic density of democracy, which is a result of the loss of salaried positions: a growing number of people find themselves obliged to live in the uncertain culture of the informal market.

Thus, work, as a principle of social integration, has been brutally questioned as unstable and flexible, and balkanized jobs are imposed. Work flexibility eliminates the guarantees necessary for life. Having a job and impoverishment become compatible. An increase in employment rates does not solve the problems of unemployment. Indeed, exclusion becomes compatible with unstable and flexibilized jobs. Thus, the same forms of subproletarization, physiological misery, vagrancy, and banditry that had accompanied the emergence of industrial capitalism at the end of the eighteenth century are reappearing. The worst forms of domination, servitude, and exploitation have been restored, forcing everyone to fight against everyone else to obtain that already lost job.

The crisis of the salary society also means disaffiliation from labor unions as allocating organizations. The mechanisms of collective inscription and regulation have broken up as a simultaneous consequence of the neoliberal offensive and the crisis of the social rule of law. This means that the supports of "social property," in the words of Robert Castel (1997), have not completely disappeared as a result of the commotion of the profound crisis of the state; however, its links have unraveled, and now leave entire categories of individuals without protection, who then become individuals through deprivation. This leads to a double challenge: on the one hand, unprotected individuals live that situation as individuals, at least through the suffering of finding themselves in that condition. On the other hand, they are less individual because of the possibilities they have to develop personal strategies or to find room for action by themselves and for themselves.

Therefore, as Chapter 5 by Cerutti and Grimson on Buenos Aires demonstrates, the central social question is the deepening problem of workers without jobs, who occupy the place of supernumeraries (excess workers) in the societies of the historical capitalist system, the "ordinary useless" of the world, using the expression of Jacques Donzelot (1979). Supernumeraries are characterized by flexibilization, impoverishment, instability, and vulnerability. We are, in Ulrick Beck's view (2000), witnessing the irruption of instability, discontinuity, and informality in the salaried sector, as well as the extension of the Third World now embedded in the industrialized societies:

> The result is a new type of social fascism as a social and civilizing regime. This regime, paradoxically, coexists with democratic societies, hence their novelty. This fascism can operate in various ways: through spatial exclusion; territories disputed by armed actors; the fascism of insecurity; and of course the deadly financial fascism, which sometimes dictates the marginalization of entire regions and countries that do not comply with the conditions called for by capital, according to the IMF and its faithful advisors. (Escobar 2005, 29)

To be sure, the destructive course of neoliberal globalization raises urgent questions, challenges, and dilemmas with regard to possible radical social-historical alternatives to this state of affairs. The time scale for such actions can be measured in decades, but not in centuries. Therefore, only a radical alternative to the established way of controlling the social metabolic reproduction can offer ways out of the structural crisis of capital. The basic premise is that capitalism should be profoundly transformed, surpassed as a mode of production and as a form of social organization to free the utopian and emancipatory contents of the plurality of social and popular movements in their social, political, and cultural struggles against the neoliberal capitalist order. In order to do this, it is necessary to probe deeply into the spaces and opportunities that create the political agency of social and popular movements and recover the undetermined content of politics and the political.

THE POLITICAL SPRING

To the extent that coloniality is the other face of modernity in the region, the modernization of the neoliberal project implies the exacerbation and deepening of new and renewed forms of colonization. Multilateral institutions (e.g., IMF, World Bank) and the foreign policy of the United States and the European Union are fundamental points of reference in thinking about global coloniality and its concomitant effects (Mignolo 2005a, 23). The Washington Consensus was built on the modern colonial assumption that Latin America was a homogeneous block with similar economies and problems that needed economic and political answers of a global character, and it was on that understanding that the policy instruments designed to resolve problems of economic instability in Latin America were established. Consequently, in the course of the last two decades, the economies in the region went through a process of deep changes as structural adjustment programs were imposed.

However, the processes of the capitalist restructuring in the region, induced by the model of "financialization" of the economy—which simultaneously includes processes of deindustrialization, return to primary economic production, flexibilization and the precariousness of employment, privatization, and the subsequent dismantling of the state public sector—have displaced and intensified the axes of political and economic unrest in the region. In a way, the deepening and intensification of social conflict expresses the dual crisis of neoliberal hegemony: a recessionary economic crisis that extends to a regional and an international level alongside a crisis of legitimacy (although this appeared to be overcome, even though in an unstable way, during the first half of the 1990s). The intense effects of social, political, and structural conflict are inscribed in the field of forces that resulted from the structural transformations forged in the imposition of neoliberalism in our countries.

In the second half of the 1990s, Latin America was marked by the consolidation, emergence, and extension of social and popular movements, whose organizational characteristics and forms of struggle, inscriptions of identity, theories of collective action, and understandings of power, politics, and the state all distinguish them from earlier movements in the region (Algranati, Seoane, and Taddei 2004, 143–144). The conflictive, disruptive, and antagonistic effects of social and popular movements are located in the liminal edges of the crisis of neoliberal hegemony. The fundamental reason for this is clear: the exploitation and increase in productivity in Latin America is also a process of exploitation and accelerated and progressive destruction of genetic biodiversity and cultural diversity. Nature, transformed into a resource or commodity, must be exploited. This colonial-modern paradigm of construction and production of relationships of subordination and inferiority continues to have devastating effects in Latin America.

Thus, in the words of Boaventura de Sousa Santos:

> It is not a coincidence that at the end of the millennium, a big part of the planet's biodiversity is located in the territories of indigenous peoples. . . . Today, just like what happened at the dawn of the world capitalist system, pharmaceutical, biotechnology and genetic engineering transnational companies try to transform indigenous people into genetic resources, into instruments of access, no longer to gold and silver, but through their traditional knowledge, to the flora and fauna in the form of biodiversity. (Santos 2005, 149)

To be sure, the specific forms of exploiting natural and cultural resources imposed by the West have had a destructive and reifying effect on the networks of life of the region.

In the last few years, social and popular movements have managed to significantly reconfigure the public agendas of Latin American nation-states and provide new meanings to the Western liberal democratic format, naturalized as the form that corresponds best to the realities of the region. The emergence of the indigenous movements in Mexico, Chile, Bolivia, Peru, Ecuador, and others; the demand for and defense of social rights (health care, education, shelter), threatened as a consequence of the mercantilization and neoliberal privatization processes in Argentina, Brazil, Mexico, and Venezuela, to mention only the most representative countries; the struggles for the defense of basic human rights in the countries of the Southern Cone in the context of authoritarian regimes; and, above all, the head-on rejection of the Free Trade Area of the Americas have all mobilized large multitudes demanding profound changes in the region.

The numerous initiatives, which include the defense of social rights under threat; the appearance of new ethical-political principles of the popular movements; the visibility of the "cultural politics"—in Arturo Escobar's sense—in the indigenous, feminist, and ecological movements; and the appearance of peasant movements contesting the diffusion of the transgenic agricultural model are all manifestations of collective expressions countering the offensive of the modernizing neoliberal project (see Alvarez, Dagnino, and Escobar 1998). But also, as a consequence of the actions of social and popular movements, the differences between and interrelation of cultures and peoples in the region have multiplied, creating new spaces of experiences and redefining the horizons of meaning.

The emergence of these plural forces has taken on a political life not separated from social and political dynamics. Based on social and cultural demands, the collective action of these movements has led the region to a level of turbulence and violence not seen for many years. The political assemblages[7] of social and popular movements (changes in political agendas, transformations in the repertoires of protests, and the new modalities of mobilization) unfold horizons of meaning and alternative concepts of development, citizenship, and democracy rights, which destabilize profound cultural meanings and set up a cultural reconfiguration. Fundamentally, this reconfiguration by the social and popular movements promotes alternative political cultures centered in cooperation and solidarity and potentially contributes to extending and deepening the meaning of rights and democracy in Latin America.

In any case, the processes of cultural resignification that drive social and popular movements in Latin America are bearers of new meanings of both the political and policing in the region, implicitly or explicitly. They build new symbolic definitions of social power and political legitimacy in contemporary circumstances. The principles that have governed what constitutes the political and policing in the societies of the region were deeply configured and determined by the processes of colonization and, above all, by the reception by the elites of the region to the Western liberal democratic format. Thus, social and popular movements find themselves in the modality of transgression, as what Rancière (1996) would call "speaking beings" endowed with words (voice) that do not merely express noise, suffering, and fury but also have other meanings, cultures, and knowledge.

This is about a cultural plurality that cannot be contained in the colonial-modern logos but rather shows up there as an absence and, at the same time, as an indispensable space for all interlocution. The colonial-modern logos had deprived the people of voice and condemned it to silence or animal-like noise simply by expulsion from the meaning-making realm of politics. As Rancière suggests, the people, as the subjects of democracy and, consequently, generative of the political, are not merely community members in a given territory. It is the supplementary part in relation to any counting of parts of the population that makes it possible to identify "the part of those who have no part" with the whole of the community (Rancière 1999, 9).[8]

The coloniality of power, understood as the global hegemonic model of power installed since the conquest, has imposed principles of the political and policing according to the needs of capital and for the benefit of European white people. Thus, time and space were marked according to a logic imposed from the outside, the effects of which still persist in the postindependence period. In that sense, the struggles to recuperate an autochthonous narrative of time and space have become an essential part of the debate about the political and politics carried out by diverse social and popular movements in the current moment. Although the aim of the Western liberal democratic format is to reduce the political to policing, the practices, thoughts, and *cosmovisiones* (worldviews) of social and popular movements try to free the political moment of its subordination to the societal frameworks naturalized by the liberal democratic format (Laclau 2005, 305).

From this perspective, social and popular movements with emanations in distinct national spaces offer a plethora of possibilities to the incipient processes of resistance, counterhegemony, and emancipation in the region. The makeup of the social and popular movements has denaturalized colonized identities, opening spaces to promulgate new possibilities of identity existence. This is particularly relevant if we consider that the exclusion of alterity (such as blacks, indigenous peoples, mestizos, workers, women, homosexuals, poor people, marginalized people) has been central to the symbolic and material violence limiting identity construction in Western liberal society.

The search for new theories and languages has become one of the fundamental challenges in the last few years. To the extent that this quest is understood as a symptom of global transformations, the interactions between critical intellectual productions and social and popular movements around excluded cultures and wisdoms would by right become a decisive heterogeneous, antagonistic, conflictive, and open "force field," as Walter Benjamin (1968 [1940]) defined it. This assumes the identification of conflictive fields between neoliberal globalization and counterhegemonic globalization. Conflictive social fields are also battlefields between rival forms of knowledge, where analytical priority is given to struggles that resist hegemonic globalization and propose alternatives to it. To define the conditions whereby social and popular movements can engage in new processes of political creation—something previously dominated by major political institutions and major political parties—is, I believe, the central task of a critical social and political theory in the region.

Therefore, it is necessary to develop a critical theoretical perspective that contributes to the renovation of social and political theory and reinvents forms of social and political emancipation that are pluralistic, radical, democratic, and socialist. This critical theoretical project presupposes the overcoming of Euro-Western assumptions and concepts in two complementary ways. On the one hand, it presumes that by laying bare the assumptions and concepts of colonial modernity, it would reveal the coloniality of power and knowledge in its entirety. The idea of the coloniality of power and knowledge is the most important contribution of social scientists of the region to the critical social and political theory in the last decade. On the other hand, it would imply—in the sense that I have been presenting here—extending the principles and criteria of social, political, and cultural inclusion through new synergies between the principle of equality and the principle of recognition of differences. At present, the demands of cultural recognition (through memories, knowledge, identities, and cultural citizenships) are intertwined with the demands of economic redistribution (through wages, fair jobs, and full social citizenship).

Through the intensity of social and popular struggles, insurgent imaginaries are emerging and creating an incipient norm based on decolonization, democracy, solidarity, and dialogue. In summary, critical and decolonizing intellectual production is oriented to revealing the hidden logic, as Karl Marx would say, of the colonial-modern logos, together with the social and popular movements. The idea of a critical theory implies that theoretical-conceptual inquiries are not formulated in a passive and neutral way, simply recording inexorable social historical processes, but rather as a normative evaluation of interventions that are both theoretical-epistemological and practical-political. Thus, a critical theory that transcends Europe's narrative history of itself and focuses its search on cultures and wisdoms foreclosed by the colonial-modern logos will become a critical theory that is inscribed in the deconstructive turn of the colonial-modern logos. In Dussel's terms, these new historical subjects should practically and daily articulate a "critical ethics" on which to base their decisions. In this sense, as we know from Karl Marx's famous formula, knowledge must be oriented toward change and social transformation.

Hence, the importance of dislocating the foundations of the colonial-modern logos, empowering forms of radicalized subjectivity, and, above all, inventing new modes of articulation that surpass the state/party/union form. Without a doubt, the reactivation of this critical power will make it possible to confront the complex challenges that confront us. In particular, it is this plurality of sources of thought, the revalorization of traditional cultures, and the social and political forces that will make it possible to dislocate the colonial-modern logos. To do so, it is critical to combine the action of social and popular movements in favor of forms of direct democracy in a diversity of realms with radical and urgent changes in the state. The strategy must consist in intensifying the contradictions and conflicts in the mechanisms of power. For that, social and popular struggles must maintain a critical distance from the state.

In the strengthening of processes opened by the action of social and popular movements and the elections of democratic leftist governments, we have the creative spaces necessary to promote and provide democratic, radical, and socialist meaning in the construction of that "other world" that is possible. As Laclau and Mouffe (1985) suggest, before even beginning to threaten an order, there must exist the possibility of negating it. Without that utopia, there is no possibility at all of building a radical, democratic, and socialist imaginary. Thus, the presence of this new imaginary, the symbolic meanings of which completely negate the previous social order, is absolutely essential for the constitution and strengthening of all critical and deconstructive thinking. Following Walter Benjamin (1968), we have survived for too long in this state of emergency.

NOTES

CHAPTER THREE

1. http://www.menpet.gob.ve/repositorio/imagenes/file/Documentos/varios/InformedeGestion2011dePDVSA.pdf, accessed November 27, 2012.

2. For examples of theories of neoliberal governmentality, see Ferguson and Gupta (2002), Rose (1999a), and Yan (2003).

3. These latter two companies had established cultural programs in Venezuela many years before Bigott did so.

4. In 2007 FUNDEF's name was changed to Encuentros de Diversidad Cultural (Meetings of Cultural Diversity).

CHAPTER FOUR

The research on which this chapter is based is part of a larger study that I have been working on since 2005 with my friend and colleague Dr. Diego Jaramillo, emeritus professor of political philosophy at the University of Cauca in Popayán. We have had many fruitful discussions about the topics discussed here, and although sometimes we agree and sometimes we disagree, I take fully responsibility for the opinions expressed here. Over the years the research has been supported by a grant from the Fulbright Commission, as well as by travel grants from the Elliott School of International Affairs, part of George Washington University. This support is gratefully acknowledged.

1. Diego Jaramillo, interview by David Gow, Popayán, June 24, 2005.

2. A notable exception to this generalization appears in a special issue of the *Latin American Research Review* (45, 2010), titled "Living in Actually Existing Democracies."

3. For Bolivia, see Postero (2007) and Van Cott (2008); for Brazil, see Avritzer (2005, 2009), and Tendler (1997); for Ecuador, see Bebbington (2006), Paley (2009), and Van

Cott (2008); for Mexico, see Campbell (2003) and Grindle (2007); and, finally, Cameron (2010) for Bolivia, Ecuador, and Peru.

4. In their article, Bebbington et al. (2006, 305) deal with the concept and practice of public spaces of social gathering (*espacios públicos de concertación local*), another way of thinking about and analyzing alternative government.

5. Cited in Sanford (2004, 257).

6. CIA (2009). In 2008 the Comisión Económica para América Latina y el Caribe (CEPAL) classified 25.1 percent of the population as indigent and highly vulnerable to indigence (income up to 0.6 times the poverty line), while 30.3 percent was classified as poor and highly vulnerable to poverty, a total of 54.4 percent of the population. Economic Commission for Latin America and the Caribbean (ECLAC) (2009); United Nations Development Program (2011, 135–213).

7. Luis Carlos Galán of the Liberal Party; Bernardo Jaramillo Ossio of the Patriotic Union, the political party established after the 1985 peace accords signed by Las Fuerzas Armadas Revolucionarias de Colombia (FARC); and Carlos Pizarro Leongómez of the Alianza Democrática M-19, the political party established by the Movimiento 19 de abril (M-19) shortly after it demobilized in 1990.

8. The ANC worked in five commissions, and delegates were free to choose which one they wished to join. Muelas was vice president of the second commission, responsible for territorial organization, municipalities, and indigenous territories. Peña was a member of the fourth commission, which addressed the administration of justice (Dugas 1993b, 60). And Francisco Rojas Birry, the third indigenous delegate, was vice president of the first commission, which dealt with principles, rights, responsibilities, guarantees, and fundamental liberties.

9. Departmental governors were directly elected for the first time in 1992, following earlier changes in 1988 that led to the direct election of mayors and council members.

10. In 2009 interviews conducted with those who had been members of the departmental assembly during Tunubalá's administration, including those who had ostensibly supported his policies, indicated that many in Cauca would have voted for *anyone* rather than support the Liberal Party, so profound was their disgust.

11. Miguel Fernández, one of the leaders of the strike, interview by David Gow, Popayán, August 6, 2006.

12. Guerrilla groups would also do this but only for a limited time—until they were forcibly displaced by the army.

13. Wilson Bonilla, interview by David Gow, Popayán, May 16, 2007.

14. Floro Tunubalá, interview by David Gow, Clarete, June 6, 2005.

15. Asamblea Departamental del Cauca (ADC), Actas Originales, primer período, tomo 1, 2001, vol. 50, acta #1, January 2, 9–18.

16. Her name was proposed by the president of the Central Unitaria de Trabajadores de Colombia, who belonged to the union of bank employees.

17. Floro Tunubalá, interview by David Gow, Popayán, May 28, 2007.

18. This tends to become a self-fulfilling prophecy: the governor expects little of the assembly, and the assembly expects little of the governor. Tunubalá and other members of his cabinet admitted that they had not attached much importance to trying to work with the assembly.

19. ADC, vol. 50, acta #1, 15.

20. Gobernación de Cauca (2003a).

21. *El País* (2003b).
22. Gobernación del Cauca (2003b).
23. *El País* (2001).
24. *El Liberal* (2001).
25. *El Espectador* (2001).
26. *El Mundo* (2001).
27. *El Tiempo* (2003); *El Liberal* (2003).
28. *El País* (2003a).
29. *El País* (2003b).
30. *Voz* (2003).
31. Acta de Consejo de Gobierno, Gobernación del Departamento del Cauca, October 14, 2003, 1.
32. Memorias, Asamblea Comunitaria, Municipio de San Sebastian, June 2003. Cited in "Una aproximación a los Derechos Humanos y el Derecho Internacional Humanitario en el Cauca," 2001–2003, Gobernacion del Cauca, Popayán, 2003, 101.
33. Acta de Consejo de Gobierno, Gobernación del Departamento del Cauca, October 14, 2003, 2.
34. Floro Tunubalá, interview by David Gow, Clarete, June 16, 2005.
35. Ministerio de Hacienda y Crédito Público (n.d., 3).
36. Gobernación del Cauca (2002, 13).
37. Ministerio de Hacienda y Crédito Público (2002, 79).
38. Gobernación del Cauca (2003a, 4–5).
39. *El Informativo* (2001).
40. Ministerio de Hacienda y Crédito Público (2005, 180).
41. The budget for the health sector came directly from the Ministry of Health.
42. Ministerio de Hacienda y Crédito Público (2004, 159–160).
43. Cámara de Comercio del Cauca (2008, 125).
44. Henry Caballero, interview by David Gow, Popayán, June 29, 2005.
45. Floro Tunubalá, interview by David Gow, Clarete, June 16, 2005.
46. Milton Guzmán, interview by David Gow, Cali, May 26, 2007.
47. In the final document produced at the workshop and read by Henry Caballero, who was to become secretary of government in the new administration, mention is made of the violence occurring in Cauca that very day, including the assassination of four local leaders by the paramilitary and the death of an indigenous leader at the hands of the FARC (La María 2000, 47).

CHAPTER FIVE

This chapter draws in part on our previous research published in "Buenos Aires, neoliberalismo y después . . . ," in A. Portes, B. Roberts, and A. Grimson, *Ciudades Latinoamericanas* (Buenos Aires: Prometeo, 2005). We are grateful for the comments of Alejandro Portes, Bryan Roberts, and the project members in various countries. We also thank Elizabeth Jelin for her suggestions.

1. By 1939, the Buenos Aires metropolitan area already accounted for 60 percent of the industrial production in Argentina (Meichtry 1993).
2. In order to control inflationary expectations, the government put its money supply under a dollar-standard regime. The Convertibility Law adopted a fixed exchange rate between the peso and the U.S. dollar and severely restricted the issuance of money by the

Central Bank of the Argentine Republic, turning this institution into a currency-exchange board. The coexistence of this type of exchange with a positive, although declining, inflation rate produced a significant overvaluation of the peso over the years. This overvaluation very negatively affected the competitive opportunities for local industry.

3. The Law of Economic Emergency and the Law of State Reform.

4. Foreign trade grew from US$12.164 billion in 1987 to US$37.283 billion in 1994.

5. The growing rates for the gross domestic product were of 9.9 percent, 8.9 percent, 5.2 percent and 7.2 percent between 1991 and 1994 respectively. (Ministry of Economics and Public Services. Secretary of Economic Programming. Economic Report, 1998).

6. To understand the reasons for this widespread consensus on convertibility and extreme neoliberalism in Argentina, it is necessary to comprehend the cultural consequences of the hyperinflation of 1989 in Argentine society (see Grimson 2003a).

7. "Piquete" here refers to a roadblock (cf. English "picket line"). Thus, piqueteros are organizations of the unemployed that set up roadblocks to prevent vehicles from passing. The term initially had stigmatizing connotations in some media, but the organizations themselves have given it a positive meaning, linked to strength and resistence, and usually chant encouraging phrases like "¡Piqueteros carajo!" during their demonstrations.

8. The *cacerolazo* is a popular protest where people create noise by banging pots, pans, and other utensils.

9. This section is based on ethnographic research in 2002 and 2003 by Alejandro Grimson. Pablo Lapegna, Nahuel Levaggi, Gabriela Polischer, Paula Varela, and Rodolfo Week also participated in the field work in popular neighborhoods in Buenos Aires.

10. The first, Villa 7 of Soldati, is a shantytown, founded in the 1960s, now home to many migrants from Bolivia and Paraguay. A neighborhood association, or *junta*, formally represents the town with the municipal authorities and acts as an intermediary to obtain and distribute building materials and to give out food boxes provided by the municipal administration to each family. In the villa, there are numerous grassroots organizations (e.g., fourteen community kitchens, three organizations of unemployed workers, a housing cooperative). The second neighborhood, La Fe, is located in the southern part of Buenos Aires, in Monte Chongolo, in the Lanús zone. A traditional working-class suburban neighborhood, La Fe was occupied without authorization in the 1980s but with a collective plan that respects the urban grid design and lot size. The deindustrialization of the late 1970s and early 1980s struck hard there, leaving cemeteries of abandoned factories. This neighborhood was long run by Peronist Party politics until the late 1990s, when a new organization of unemployed workers became prominent. A third neighborhood, Billinghurst, located in the northwest suburbs, is an industrial and labor center that has been in crisis in recent years. In this area, the more skilled and educated population occupied and struggled to reopen a key source of labor: a metal factory called Forja. In an area without either strong territory-based traditions or major neighborhood organizations, demand for labor is channeled through unions. Therefore, of the four neighborhoods and processes that we have analyzed, Forja is the only one whose protagonists are exclusively men. Finally, the western case study, the neighborhood of El Tambo, is an urbanized settlement in La Matanza, one of most populated parts of the metropolitan area, with high levels of extreme poverty. El Tambo has a long-standing organization to push for land and housing rights and was the origin of the national Federación de Tierra y Vivienda (Federation of Land and Housing, or FTV). It is also the focal point of two

major organizations of unemployed workers, the FTV and the Corriente Clasista y Combativa (the Classist and Combative Current, or CCC).

11. In 2003 the beneficiary was given approximately 150 pesos (about US$50).

12. A much-quoted and eloquent example is that of MTD of La Matanza, which, after having played an important role in the first mobilizations in the late 1990s, decided not to accept plans and was eventually reduced to only a few members.

CHAPTER SIX

The ethnographic fieldwork on which this chapter is based was carried out in the Tulancingo Valley of Hidalgo and Mexico City between 2002 and 2007. It was generously funded by the John L. Simpson Memorial Research Fellowship in International and Comparative Studies and the Chancellor's Opportunity Predoctoral Fellowship from the University of California, Berkeley, as well as the Pacific Fund of the University of the Pacific.

1. Personal communication, April 2004.

2. Name withheld, interview by Analiese Richard, Tulancingo, September 20, 2002.

3. Name withheld, interview by Analiese Richard, Tulancingo, May 2003.

CHAPTER SEVEN

1. Febres Cordero's close relations with Washington helped make Ecuador one of the first recipients of Baker Plan loans in 1985. By 1987 the national debt had reached $9.6 billion, just shy of Ecuador's total GDP of $10.6 billion the same year.

2. Further references to this text are indicated as CV, followed by the volume number.

3. Article 1 of the accord creates the commission to investigate human rights abuses "between 1984 and 1988 and other periods." Article 2a lists its first objective to conduct an investigation into "human-rights violations occurring between 1984 and 1988 and other special cases."

4. This figure includes 34 extrajudicial executions, 212 illegal privations of freedom, 262 acts of torture, 52 of which involved sexual violence, and 18 attempts to kill.

5. Cristhian Bahamonde, interview by Christopher Krupa, November 5, 2009.

6. Efforts are currently under way by the state to prosecute perpetrators named in the commission's report. On July 19, 2010, the commission handed over its archives to the Public Prosecutor's office (*Fiscalía General del Estado*). The following day, state Resolution 049-2010-FGE formally created a subsection of the *Fiscalía* charged with investigating, in a formal legal manner, the human rights violations identified in the report and assembling the evidence needed to bring those responsible to trial. The commission currently operates as an advisory team, along with new provincial agents, to this governmental entity (called the Investigative Unit of the Truth Commission).

7. Certainly, state violence continued after Febres Cordero, Bahamonde explained to me, but it was of a different character, framed not in the language of politics per se but rather as "combating delinquency" or reflecting "abuses of power or force" at different levels of the police or military. Correa himself has sought to emphasize the distinction between these periods but has placed the line of demarcation between periods somewhat differently. In his remarks at the ceremonial launch of the commission's final report on July 6, 2010, Correa noted that although the report names violations of human rights occurring under his administration, those that took place in 2007 and 2008, he claims,

were already investigated and those responsible brought to trial. "This marks, yet again, the difference between the abuse of power in the decade [*sic*] of the eighties and nineties and all that, with the new history in which dignity and truth are not luxuries but rather the essence of this reality, of the reality of our administration (*gestión*)." Bahamonde, interview by Christopher Krupa, November 5, 2009.

8. Despite the phrase "Alfaro Lives," it is the unusual circumstances of his death that both forecast the violence to come in the AVC's confrontation with Febres Cordero and warns of an ambiguous relationship between Ecuador's "popular sectors" and an emancipatory political project claiming to act in its name. In 1912 Alfaro was captured by his conservative rivals on the charge of plotting a coup and briefly held in a Quito jail, where he was killed and dismembered by an urban "mestizo mob" who reportedly drank his blood, dragged his body parts through the city, and set them on fire in El Ejido park (Halperin Donghi 1993, 196; Ayala Mora 2002, 189; Krupa 2011).

9. Conflicting reports produced by national and international research teams led many to believe, to this day, that Roldós was murdered (on the reports, see Hurtado 1990, 118–119). The list of suspects is long and includes U.S. oil companies (whose interests were supposedly threatened by his nationalist hydrocarbon laws); the CIA (Roldós refused to attend Reagan's inauguration in protest of the U.S.'s Central America policy, had good relations with the Sandinistas, and formed a Charter of Conduct among a number of Andean countries to limit the capacity for U.S. intervention); the Peruvian military (with whom he was engaged in a round of highly tense border disputes, called the Guerra de Paquisha); the Ecuadorian business elites, including Febres Cordero (whose economic interests were supposedly undermined by his private-sector reforms); and even a vengeful evangelical God (angered for his barring of the Summer Institute of Linguistics from Ecuador). See, for instance, the remarks of former president Abdalá Bucaram (1990, 30): "What killed Roldós was his anti-imperialist politics, his antiarmament policies. What killed Roldós was the politics of the patriarchs of the constituent assembly (Febres Cordero, Otto Aresemena, Raúl Clemente)." Bucaram later suggests the plane was shot down by the Peruvian military: "It was in the middle of a warlike conflict . . . we can't deny as well the fact that Peru had a direct line to the CIA." John Perkins, in his *Confessions of an Economic Hit Man* (2004), cites the case of Roldós as a key example of the sort of hits the CIA, in collusion with U.S. oil or other business sectors, would make on political figures who threatened their interests (for a critique of Perkins's analysis of the Roldós affair, see Niall Ferguson (2008, 309–310), who claims that Ecuador was too insignificant to warrant such an action).

10. As AVC leader Arturo Jarrín (in Frías 1999, 108) himself noted in his 1985 interview, "the regime of Osvaldo Hurtado, without being a regime clearly defined as oligarchic, was a regime that was unquestionably at the service of the oligarchy."

11. As Febres Cordero remarked in his 1989 trial over the misuse of state funds (specifically the hiring of Israeli Ran Gazit to design an antiterrorism program; see Zambrano Pasquel 1990): when coming to power in August 1984, "among the diverse and very grave difficulties of social and economic order that we found the country immersed in, we also found disturbing elements fomenting due to the indolence and suspected tolerance that allowed terrorist groups trained in the exterior to organize and realize a mounting scale of illicit and illegal actions" (in CV, vol. 2, 266). "In other words," say the authors of the Truth Commission report (ibid., 268), "the person guilty for this situation, according to Febres Cordero, was Hurtado, insinuating that it was his government, soft and irrespon-

sible, that had compromised with sectors of the Left, which took up arms to destroy the institutionality of the state."

12. "A la subversión hay que matarla como a los pavos, a la víspera."

13. "The Ecuadorian insurgency did not have terrorist motives, did not have the character of generalizing a threat, nor did it realize indiscriminate actions against the civil population. In contrast to the government of the times, its actions did not generate terror in society" (CV, vol. 2, 297).

14. "The acts of social and political opposition in Ecuador were considered, in Febres Cordero's discourse as: wicked, criminal acts, actions disconnected from the political fabric, and acts of resistance against the neoliberal politics. The government identified the opposition solely in its penal dimension, not in its dimension of political struggle" (CV, vol. 2, 289).

15. To this Febres Cordero replied: "You and I, Mr. President, have in us something like a cowboy spirit, and with that spirit we are trying to improve the lot of our countrymen. Our peoples and all mankind, Mr. President, are going through a period of strains and unprecedented problems. You, as I in my own country, are responsible for taking the reins of the state with the conviction that in so doing we are effectively serving our peoples" (Ronald Reagan Presidential Library 1986).

16. The AVC did have quite well-known links with Colombia's M-19 and viewed Nicaragua's Sandinistas as models. Several of its founding members also received combat training in Libya. None of these countries carried the symbolic and historic weight, however, that Peru did as the emblem of antinational aggression. Foreignness itself, as a mark of the antinational, of course, was relative. Febres Cordero received extensive support from the United States and paid $150,000 in state funds to an Israeli operative for counterterrorist military training.

17. These groups include the Committee of Family Members of Political Prisoners, the Committee of Families against Impunity, and the Ecuadorian No Impunity Committee.

18. Sister Elsie Monge, interview by Christopher Krupa, May 26, 2010.

CHAPTER EIGHT

This chapter originated in a presentation at the Wenner-Gren Conference on Revolution and New Social Imaginaries in Postneoliberal Latin America," held at the Center for Iberian and Latin American Studies, University of California, San Diego, May 2–3, 2008. I want to thank Mark Goodale and Nancy Postero, as well as two anonymous reviewers, for their suggestions on an earlier draft of the chapter. I am also grateful for Malcolm Blincow's input into this version of the chapter.

1. After serious challenges by experts within and outside the institution, the bank changed its lending focus in the late 1990s from stabilization and structural adjustment to a more comprehensive approach to development that takes up once again the issue of poverty, recognizes a role for the state, and also takes up environmental concerns. For a critical assessment of the World Bank's post–Washington Consensus agenda, see Van Waeyenberge (2006).

2. Peck and Tickell (2002, 383). See also Larner (2000).

3. This research has been funded over the years by the Canadian International Development Research Centre and the University of Western Ontario through a Faculty of Social Science VIP and Alumna Research Grant and the Agnes Cole Dark Fund. The

most recent update of transformations in the social-policy field during the government of President Michelle Bachelet (2006–2010) was completed with the assistance of Francisca Gallegos, with funding from an International Research Award of the University of Western Ontario.

4. For a summary of the mechanisms used to increase labor flexibility in six key countries, Argentina, Brazil, Bolivia, Chile, Mexico, and Uruguay, see Fraile (2009). The literature on these labor reforms, both laudatory and critical, is by now vast. For a very useful and detailed discussion of the reforms pursued in these six countries, refer to the special issue of ILO's journal, *International Labour Review* 148 (2009): 3.

5. The simple average Gini coefficient for the region increased from 0.505 to 0.514, or by nearly one point, according World Bank figures (cited in Fraile 2009). The Gini coefficient is a standard, international measure of inequality, ranging from 1 to 0, with 0 standing for complete equality.

6. The issue of improving state capacity has become paramount for the World Bank. According to Santiso (2001), between 1987 and 1998, the bank financed 169 civil-service reform programs in eighty countries. Moreover, in 1996 the bank began supporting programs to address the issue of corruption, including those aimed at strengthening institutions, addressing corruption in institutions like parliamentary oversight bodies and ombudspersons (see World Bank 2000).

7. *Conditionality* is the governance principle regulating aid relations and practice, as well as social spending within countries, including in innovative approaches to eliminating poverty.

8. Feminist scholars have also tended to follow this narrow approach to the study of neoliberalism. Although they may be sensitive to questions about the gendered effects of neoliberal economic and institutional reform, they have tended to overlook the broader question of the powerful cultural effects of neoliberalism. Much less attention has been paid to the making of neoliberal forms as cultural forms. For a detailed elaboration of this point, see Schild (2007).

9. On the remasculinization of the Latin American state, see Craske (1999).

10. For an early and comprehensive discussion, see Sparr (1994). For Latin American case studies, see Lind (2005) and Schild (2002).

11. Feminist popular education, inspired by Paulo Freire's method of popular education, acquired prominence as NGOs emerged in the region in the 1980s to play a very visible role in local development.

12. The minimum wage and public-sector wages are the exceptions. As Riesco points out, after the military coup, these were cut to less than a third of their former levels (2009, 287).

13. The practice is still allowed in some very specific cases. For a discussion of this legislation, see Riesco (2009, 295–296). For a comprehensive overview, see Frank (2004). For a discussion of the more recent changes, see Riesco (2009) and Fraile (2009).

14. The project that had been launched in 1981 to completely privatize the health system failed, although efforts to privatize it continue apace (Riesco 2009, 298; Cid 2007). Universal coverage was replaced by an expensive and discriminatory system of private insurance plans. Today more than 80 percent of the population continues to use the public health-care system. A large number of users of private plans gravitated to the public system during the crisis of the late 1990s. The Concertación government under Ricardo Lagos increased health spending and also, through its Plan Auge, revised and increased the number of illnesses covered by the public plan.

15. This is evident in the dockworkers' strike of February 15 and 16, 2012. The organizing multisectoral committee, composed of unions of blue- and white-collar workers and a number of other social organizations, called for a national civic and productive strike for later in 2012.

16. The poorest segment (or decile) receives 1.2 percent of the national income, whereas the wealthiest receives 41.2 percent. This extreme disparity is the reason Chile ranks number 10 in income inequality in the world (de Rementería 2007).

17. This is according to studies by the nongovernmental organization Paz Ciudadana and statistics from the Instituto Nacional de Estadísticas (National Institute for Statistics, INE), cited in de Rementería (2007). See also Castro (2007).

18. These figures were downloaded from "World Prison Brief South America" of the International Centre for Prison Studies, http://www.prisonstudies.org/info/worldbrief/wpb_country.php? (accessed December 10, 2012). I am grateful to Loïc Wacquant for pointing out this site to me.

19. See http://www.gob.cl/especiales/chile-seguro-plan-de-seguridad-publica-2010-2014/ (accessed December 10, 2012).

20. This turn to what Gabriel Palma characterizes as an accommodationist politics was widespread in the region, and it has prompted him to ask, "Why has the mainstream of Latin American socialism mutated from a 'dangerous' idea/movement to the capitalist elite's best friend?" (Palma 2008, 11).

21. Indeed, in a vision of what Kate Bedford (2007) refers to as pathologized, already marginalized masculinities haunt feminist-influenced policymaking both at the national level, most recently under Michelle Bachelet, and transnationally.

22. Although no time-use survey has been done in Chile, an experimental survey conducted for the greater Santiago area in 2008 shows that women continue to be responsible for most of the unpaid care work, including child care, care for the elderly and other adults, domestic work, and work for other households or for the community. See Instituto Nacional de Estadísticas (2008).

23. See Schild (2003, 2007) and Richards (2004) for a discussion of this process and its implications.

24. The first plan was introduced in the aftermath of the 1995 UN women's conference in Beijing. The revised plan (Plan de Igualdad entre Mujeres y Hombres 2000–2010), explicitly recognized modern Chilean women as active agents with "life projects" that they control and that presumably include family life, children, and paid employment. In its attempts to make institutional inroads into women's equality, SERNAM's achievements and limitations have had mixed results. See Franceschet (2003) and Baldez (2001).

25. For a discussion of achievements, setbacks, and roadblocks in feminist politics and policymaking, culminating with the so-called feminist agenda of Michelle Bachelet, see Haas (2010).

26. See Haas (2010) and Borzutsky (2010).

27. For a critical overview and assessment of the Chile Crece Contigo program, see Staab and Gerhard (2010).

28. For a study of the contradictory effects of Centros de Madres–Chile during the Pinochet regime, see Lechner and Levy (1984). See also Schild (2007).

29. This critique is in response to the increased numbers of Chileans living in poverty and indigence, which the Piñera government attributes to errors in the measurement of poverty and problems with social programs. See Skoknic (2010) for a critical review

that points to the economy, the global crisis, and the poor quality of jobs as the real culprits.

30. "Sistemas de apoyo psicosocial, mujer y familia," Notas técnicas sobre protección social y género, documento no. 5, Documento temático elaborado por MIDEPLAN como material de apoyo al Seminario Protección Social y Género, http://www.mideplan.cl, October 2008, 2 (accessed December 2012).

31. The study included interviews with personnel who were implementing the program, social assistants attached to local governments, and other functionaries involved with *desarrollo comunitario*, in addition to clients and potential clients. See Ramírez and Fouillioux (2010).

32. Programa Puente in particular became the focus of a very positive World Bank review, and it has been addressed by an extensive literature on innovative social policy in Latin America. Critics have challenged the use of means-tested programs instead of labor reform and wage mechanisms to address the question of persistent poverty and inequality. Their critique has gathered momentum as the global financial crisis affects Chile's open economy. See Ramírez and Fouillioux (2010). For a cautious assessment of the implications of conditional cash-transfer programs like Programa Puente and Chile Solidario for women, see, for example, Molyneux (2008) and Tabbush (2009).

33. Recently, for example, Brazilian army sources admitted publicly "that techniques employed in the occupation of the Morro da Providéncia favela are the ones Brazilian soldiers use in the United Nations peacekeeping mission in Haiti" (Zibechi 2007a).

CHAPTER NINE

1. I deploy the concept of the "securityscape" (Gusterson 2004; Weldes et al. 1999) to refer to the patterns of circulation that result from the effort of states to police and control the mobility of immigrants and youth. The securityscape results from the spatial patterns of policing, immigration, deportation, and reentry into the United States that connect Los Angeles and its Salvadoran immigrant community to El Salvador. Although rooted in a longer history of U.S.–Latin American security relations, the contemporary securityscape emerged during a period characterized by the consolidation of neoliberal structural-adjustment programs in both countries. As I argue in this chapter, a treatment of neoliberalism must account for the place of security policies and vice versa. In other words, there is an intimate relationship between political economy and security programs.

2. United Nations Development Program (2005). This abysmal economic situation was not simply an ongoing Third-World condition. Rather, the austerity programs and structural-adjustment policies of the 1990s had increased and deepened poverty. Although there were "social compensation funds" attached to those programs, "putatively intended to 'target' the poor," they "isolat[ed] poverty from the process of capital accumulation and economic development." In so doing, they treated poverty as an individual pathology rather than as a consequence of the socioeconomic exclusion immanent in the economic system itself (Robinson 2003, 246).

3. For a discussion of the relationship between neoliberalism and criminal economies see Comaroff and Comaroff (2006).

4. Or what was then referred to as the "devolution" of the welfare state.

5. Foucault argued that, although eighteenth-century reformers sought to "eliminate all crime through the internalization of the gaze," neoliberals "only seek a degree of compliance—i.e., an acceptable level of return on society's investment." Zero-tolerance

gang-abatement strategies and the accompanying legislation, however, depend on the creation of a limitless supply of crime by subjecting more and more actions to penalties and increasing the penalties for actions already deemed criminal. As such, the neoliberal security under investigation here diverges from Foucault's expectations that neoliberalism would entail "a balance between the curves of the supply of crime and negative demand," where a certain degree of crime is to be tolerated (Foucault 2007, 256).

6. The 1993 amnesty law, which granted impunity to perpetrators of human rights abuses committed during the civil war was, of course, an enormous exception to the hegemony of human rights discourse in post–civil war El Salvador.

7. See Robinson on regime change in El Salvador for a discussion of how the peace accords involved sacrificing the Salvadoran military and the power of the landed oligarchy, who had not adjusted to the new neoliberal agenda introduced by the United States via the new Right in El Salvador, represented then by the new ruling political party, ARENA, and U.S.-sponsored think tanks such as FUSADES (2003, 87–102).

8. The ILEA, originally established under Bill Clinton in 1995, has additional training facilities in Hungary, Botswana, and the United States. The U.S. and the Salvadoran governments signed a bilateral agreement to establish ILEA San Salvador on September 21, 2005.

9. The U.S. military academy, the SOA, was the training ground for many of the Salvadoran military officers accused of gross human rights violations during the civil war. In fact, the primary reason I had met with Burgos (personal interview, September 9, 2006) was to discuss his organization's controversial collaboration with the ILEA. The IDHUCA's role here was particularly delicate, given the Jesuit university's history not only as ardent defender of human rights during the civil war but also because of the still-unresolved murder of six Jesuits priests and their housekeeper on the UCA campus by the Salvadoran military during the final FMLN offensive in 1989.

10. The IDHUCA, along with then police chief Ávila (ARENA's 2009 presidential candidate), pointed to the need for better technical training for the police. Burgos was adamant that bad management of crime scenes, the incapacity to bring technical proof to court hearings, poor expertise in ballistics, forensic medicine, and so on generated "more impunity and more suffering."

11. The stated aim of the *Defense and the National Interest* website is to

> foster debate on the roles of the U.S. armed forces in the post–Cold War era and on the resources devoted to them. The ultimate purpose is to help create a more effective national defense against the types of threats we will likely face during the first decades of the new millennium. Contributors to this site are, with a few exceptions, active/reserve, former, or retired military. They often combine a knowledge of military theory with the practical experience that comes from trying their ideas in the field. As you browse our site, please pay particular attention to the e-mails from our deployed forces in such places as Kosovo, Bosnia, Afghanistan, Iraq and other Middle Eastern Countries. (Wilson and Sullivan 2007)

12. The U.S. embassy in Tegucigalpa sent a cable to Washington with the subject, "Open and Shut: The Case of the Honduran Coup," asserting that "there is no doubt" that the events of June 28 "constituted an illegal and unconstitutional coup." The embassy listed arguments being made by supporters of the coup to claim its legality and dismissed them thus: "None . . . has any substantive validity under the Honduran constitution."

The Honduran military clearly had no legal authority to remove President Manuel Zelaya from office or from Honduras, the embassy said, and their action—the embassy described it as an "abduction" and "kidnapping"—was clearly unconstitutional (Naiman 2010).

13. Included here were Miguel Menéndez, the wealthy owner of several Salvadoran corporations, and Carlos Cáseres, a board member of a Salvadoran coffee conglomerate (and now secretary of the treasury).

14. Pignato is behind the initiative Cuidad Mujer, a project supported by the Inter-American Development Bank and led by El Salvador's Ministry of Social Inclusion. Ciudad Mujer seeks to improve the living conditions of Salvadoran women through an integrated focus and the promotion of women's rights.

15. One exception is the Salvadoran state's stance against the mining rights of the Canadian-U.S. company Pacific Rim in the state of Cabañas. PacRim has sued the Salvadoran government for an infringement of corporate rights granted under CAFTA. Funes's continued opposition to PacRim's claims, however, is ironically a continuation of the position held by former president Saca, of the ARENA party. Saca surprised everyone by supporting Salvadoran sovereignty over free trade.

16. Some analysts argue that the United States was behind Melgar's resignation. The United States believes that Melgar, who was an FMLN commander during the civil war, was responsible for the 1985 Zona Roja attack, in which four off-duty U.S. military personnel and eight civilians were killed (Allison 2011).

POSTSCRIPT

1. Translator's note: The author uses the term *forcluida*, a Spanish translation of Lacan's French term *forclusión*. According to Evans (1996, 65), Lacan uses this term to refer to a specific defense mechanism in which "the ego rejects an incompatible idea and behaves as if the idea never occurred to the ego at all." It is thus different from repression, in that "the forclosed element is not buried in the subconscious, but expelled from the unconscious" (ibid.) Although somewhat awkward, we use the English word "foreclosed."

2. Translator's note: Here the author is distinguishing between two paradigms of analysis of behavior. Behavioral scientist William Baum explains: The "molecular view" sees

> behavior as consisting of discrete units, usually called responses. . . . The molar view of behavior offers an alternative. It sees behavior as composed of behavioral patterns (called activities) that, by their very nature, are temporally extended. Activities or patterns differ from discrete responses in that they are integrated wholes, existing not only in space but spanning time. Thus, instead of momentary responses like the lever press or the footstep, the molar view sees the activities of lever pressing and walking. Whereas the molecular view names its discrete units with ordinary nouns, the molar view usually names activities with gerunds. (Baum 2004, 349)

3. Following Rancière, I understand political subjugation as the production—through a series of actions—of an instance and a capacity of enunciation that were not identifiable in a given field of experience, whose identification, therefore, is on an equal footing with the new representation of the field of experience of the political (Rancière 1996, 52).

4. Editors' note: We note here that not all of the social movements that coalesced in the 1980s directly challenged neoliberalism to begin with or emerged from contestations with it. Some, in fact, emerged from the spaces provided by neoliberalism, which allowed the expressions of alternative cultural identities that later came to challenge both the colonial modern paradigm and neoliberalism.

5. In a conversation with Colombian anthropologist Arturo Escobar during his visit to Caracas in June 2006, the two of us posited the use of the concept of "spiritual neoliberalization." By it we refer principally to the profound porous and spiritual influence of the precepts of neoliberalism on the imaginaries of Venezuelan and global intellectuals and to the undeniable colonization of Latin American reality, which signified the intracapillary reception of its programs and substantive horizons. To quote my friend Tito Tamburini, we can say that a "spiritual mercantilization" was constituted in the imaginary of the region.

6. Translator's note: derealization is a subjective experience of unreality of the outside world, a dissasociative state brought on by various psychiatric disorders, sleep disorders, or acute drug intoxication.

7. Translator's note: the author uses the Spanish *agenciamiento* as a translation from Delueze and Guattari's French term *agencement*. "Assemblage" appears to be the accepted best translation into English, but as Phillips (2006) points out, it is not a perfect translation. He suggests "arrangement" might be better.

8. Translator's note: I am relying here on the translation of "Rancière's Ten Theses on Politics" in Bowlby and Panagia (2001).

REFERENCES

Agamben, Giorgio. 1998. *Homo Sacer: Sovereign Power and Bare Life*. Stanford, CA: Stanford University Press.

Aguilar Valenzuela, Ruben. 1997. "Apuntes para una historia de las organizaciones de la sociedad civil en Mexico." *Cuadernos de la Sociedad Civil* 1, no. 2: 9–32.

Albó, Xavier. 2000. "El sector campesino-indígena, actor social clave." *Opiniones y Analisis* 52: 75–112. La Paz: Fundación Fundemos.

Albro, Robert. 2010. *Roosters at Midnight: Indigenous Signs and Stigma in Local Bolivian Politics*. Santa Fe, NM: School for Advanced Research.

Algranati, Clara, José Seoane, and Emilio Taddei. 2004. "América Latina, neoliberalismo y conflicto social: Las configuraciones de los movimientos populares." In *Mundialización de las resistencias estado de las luchas 2004*, edited by Samir Amin and François Houtart, 125–152. Bogotá: Ruth Casa Editorial y Ediciones Desde Abajo.

Allison, Mike. 2011. "A Changing of the Guard in El Salvador: The Appointment of a Retired General as Minister of Justice Is Part of a Trend of Militarising State Institutions." *Al Jazeera*, November 29.

Alvarez, Sonia, Evelina Dagnino, and Arturo Escobar. 1998. *Cultures of Politics, Politics of Culture*. Boulder, CO: Westview.

Amaya, Edgardo. 2006. "Security Policies in El Salvador, 1992–2002." In *Public Security and Police Reform in the Americas*, edited by John Bailey and Lucía Dammert, 132–147. Pittsburgh: University of Pittsburgh Press.

Americas Quarterly (Online). 2011. "Funes Completes Two Years as Salvadoran President." June 1. Accessed December 8, 2012. http://www.americasquarterly.org/node/256.

Americas Watch Committee. 1988. *Human Rights in Ecuador*. New York: Americas Watch Committee.

Andean Information Network. 2007a. "Bolivia's Gas Nationalization: Opportunity and Challenges (1)." November 21. Accessed November 21, 2007. http://ainbolivia.org/index.php?option=com_content&task=view&id=106&Itemid=29.

———. 2007b. "Bolivia's Gas Nationalization: Opportunity and Challenges (2)." December 4. Accessed December 5, 2007. http://ain-bolivia.org/index.php?option=com_content&task=view&id=106&Itemid=2.

———. 2008. "Bolivia's Gas Nationalization: Opportunity and Challenges (3)." January 16. Accessed January 16, 2008. http://www.ain-bolivia.org/index.php?option=com_content&task=view&id=109&Itemid=29.

Appadurai, Arjun. 1981. "The Past as a Scarce Resource." *Man* 16: 201–219.

———. 2004. "The Capacity to Aspire: Culture and the Terms of Recognition." In *Culture and Public Action*, edited by Vijayendra Rao and Michael Walton, 59–84. Stanford, CA: Stanford University Press.

Arditti, Benjamin. 2008. "Arguments About the Left Turns in Latin America: A Post-Liberal Politics?" *Latin American Research Review* 43, no. 3: 59–81.

Aretxaga, Begoña. 2000. "A Fictional Reality: Paramilitary Death Squads and the Construction of Terror in Spain." In *Death Squad: The Anthropology of State Terror*, edited by Jeffrey A. Sluka, 46–69. Philadelphia: University of Pennsylvania Press.

Arze, Carlos, and Tom Kruse. 2004. "The Consequences of Neoliberal Reform." *NACLA Report on the Americas* 38, no. 3: 23–28.

Auyero, Javier. 2001a. *La política de los pobres: Las prácticas clientelistas del peronismo.* Buenos Aires: Manantial.

———. 2001b. Introduction to *Parias urbanos: Marginalidad en la ciudad a comienzos del milenio*, edited by Loïc Wacquant, 9–32. Buenos Aires: Manantial.

Avritzer, Leonardo. 2005. "Modes of Democratic Deliberation: Participatory Budgeting in Brazil." In *Democratizing Democracy: Beyond the Liberal Democratic Canon*, edited by Boaventura de Souza Santos, 377–404. London: Verso.

———. 2009. *Participatory Institutions in Democratic Brazil.* Baltimore: Johns Hopkins University Press.

Ayala, Edgardo. 2011. "Military Service Plan for At-Risk Youth Raises Controversy." San Salvador: Associated Press International (IPS), June 29.

Ayala Mora, Enrique. 2002. *Historia de la revolución liberal ecuatoriana*, 2nd ed. Quito: Corporación Editora Nacional.

Bailaba Parapaino, José. 2004. "Inducción y etnocidio chiquitanto, II." *Consignas*, July 21. Accessed November 3, 2012. http://consignas.espacioblog.com/post/2005/09/22/induccion-y-etnocidio-chiquitano-ii.

Baldez, Lisa. 2001. "Coalition Politics and the Limits of State Feminism." *Women and Politics* 22, no. 4: 1–28.

Baptista, Felix, and Oswaldo Marchionda. 1992. "¿Para qué afinques?" BA thesis, Escuela de Antropología, Universidad Central de Venezuela.

Barthes, Roland. 1972 [1957]. *Mythologies.* Translated by Annette Lavers. New York: Hill and Wang.

Baum, William. 2004. "Molar and Molecular Views of Choice." *Behavioural Processes* 66: 349–359.

Bautista S., Rafael. 2011. "¿Qué significa el Estado Plurinacional?" In *Descolonización en Bolivia: Cuatro ejes para comprender el cambio*, 169–205. La Paz: Vicepresidencia del Estado.

Bebbington, Anthony. 2006. "Los espacios públicos de concertación local y sus límites en un municipio indígena: Guamote, Ecuador." *Debate Agrario* 40/41: 381–404.

———. 2009. "The New Extraction: Rewriting Political Ecology in the Andes?" *NACLA Report on the Americas* 42, no. 5: 12–15.

Bebbington, Anthony, Gonzalo Delamaza, and Rodrigo Villar. 2006. "El desarrollo de base y los espacios públicos de concertación local en América Latina." *Debate Agrario* 40/41: 299–324.

Beck, Ulrich. 2000. *Un nuevo mundo feliz: La precariedad del trabajo en la era de la globalización.* Barcelona: Editorial Paidós.

Bedford, Kate. 2007. "The Imperative of Male Inclusion: How Institutional Context Influences World Bank Gender Policy." *International Feminist Journal of Politics* 9: 289–311.

Benjamin, Walter. 1968 [1940]. "Theses on the Philosophy of History." In *Illuminations*, edited by Hannah Arendt, translated by Harry Zohn, 253–264. New York: Harcourt Brace Jovanovich.

———. 1986 [1978]. "Critique of Violence." In *Reflections: Essays, Aphorisms, Autobiographical Writings*, edited by Peter Demetez, 277–301. New York: Harcourt Brace Jovanovich.

Berlant, Lauren. 2007. "Nearly Utopian, Nearly Normal: Post-Fordist Affect in *La Promesse* and *Rosetta*." *Public Culture* 19, no. 2: 273–301.

Bloch, Ernst. 1986. *The Principle of Hope.* Translated by Neville Plaice, Stephen Plaice, and Paul Knight. Cambridge, MA: MIT Press.

Bornstein, Erica. 2012. *Disquieting Gifts: Humanitarianism in New Delhi.* Stanford, CA: Stanford University Press.

Borzutzky, Silvia. 2010. "Socioeconomic Policies: Taming the Market in a Globalized Economy." In *The Bachelet Government: Conflict and Consensus in Post-Pinochet Chile*, edited by Silvia Borzutzky and Gregory B. Weeks, 87–116. Gainesville: University Press of Florida.

Bourdieu, Pierre. 1999. "Rethinking the State: Genesis and Structure of the Bureaucratic Field." In *State/Culture: State-Formation After the Cultural Turn*, edited by George Steinmetz, translated by Loïc Wacquant and Samar Farage, 53–75. Ithaca, NY: Cornell University Press.

———. 2003. *Las estructuras sociales de la economía.* Barcelona: Editorial Anagrama.

Bowlby, Rachel, and Davide Panagia. 2001. "Jacques Rancière: Ten Theses on Politics." *Theory and Event* 5: 31.

Brockwehl, Alexander, and Juan Pablo Pitarque. 2010. "Concessions of a Leftist Party: The FMLN's Dilemma in the Face of Funes' Centrist Policies." June 28. Washington, DC: Council on Hemispheric Affairs.

Brown, Wendy. 1998. "Democracy's Lack." *Public Culture* 10, no. 2: 425–429.

———. 2003. "Neoliberalism and the End of Liberal Democracy." *Theory and Event* 7, no. 1: 1–21.

———. 2005. *Edgework: Critical Essays on Knowledge and Politics.* Princeton, NJ: Princeton University Press.

Bucaram, Abdalá. 1990. *Las verdades de Abdalá.* Quito: Ediduende.

Burawoy, Michael, and Katherine Verdery. 1999. *Uncertain Transition: Ethnographies of Change in the Postsocialist World.* Lanham, MD: Rowman and Littlefield.

Burchell, Graham. 1996. "Liberal Government and Techniques of the Self." In *Foucault and Political Reason*, edited by Andrew Barry, Thomas Osborne, and Nikolas Rose, 19–36. Chicago: University of Chicago Press.

Bustos, Pablo. 1995. "Argentina: Un capitalismo emergente?" In *Más allá de la estabilidad: Argentina en la época de la regionalización y la globalización*, edited by Pablo Bustos and Pablo Gerchunoff, 11–38. Buenos Aires: Fundación Friedrich Ebert.

Calcaño, Isabel Cristina. n.d. "El Arte y la Ley de Mecenazgo: ¿Una muy necesaria . . . fantasía?" Accessed March 14, 2008. http://www.veneconomia.com/site/files/articulos/artEsp67_47.pdf.

Calderón, Felipe. 2010. "Palabras del presidente Calderón en el Premio Nacional de Accion Voluntaria y Solidaria." Los Pinos, December 16. Accessed February 15, 2011. www.presidencia.gob.mx.

Cámara de Comercio del Cauca. 2008. "Análisis de coyuntura económica: Cauca 2000–2007." Popayán.

Cameron, John. 2010. *Struggles for Local Democracy in the Andes*. Boulder, CO: First Forum.

Campbell, Tim. 2003. *The Quiet Revolution: Decentralization and the Rise of Political Participation in Latin American Cities*. Pittsburgh: University of Pittsburgh Press.

Canessa, Andrew. 2006. "Todos somos indígenas: Toward a New Language of National Political Identity." *Bulletin of Latin American Research* 25, no. 2: 241–263.

Carothers, Thomas. 2002. "The End of the Transition Paradigm." *Journal of Democracy* 13, no. 1: 5–21.

Carroll, Thomas F. 1992. *Intermediary NGOs: The Supporting Link in Grassroots Development*. West Hartford, CT: Kumarian.

Carvajal, Rolando. 2010. "Sumitomo confirma que tributó 358 millones en 10 anos, pero nada por el agua que utiliza." Accessed April 21, 2010. http:/boliviaenvideos.com/2010/04/sumitomo-confirma-que-tributo-358.html.

Casas-Zamora, Kevin. 2011. "President Obama in El Salvador." Washington, DC: Brookings Institution, March 16. Accessed June 27, 2011. http://www.brookings.edu/research/opinions/2011/03/16-obama-el-salvador-casaszamora.

Castel, Robert. 1997. *La metamorfosis de la cuestión social: Una crónica del asalariado*. Buenos Aires: Editorial Paidós.

Castro, Álvaro. 2007. "Más cárceles: Tapar el sol con un dedo?" *El Mostrador: Columna*, November 21. Accessed December 10, 2012. http://m.elmostrador.cl/opinion/2007/11/21/mas-carceles-%C2%BFtapar-el-sol-con-un-dedo/.

Centeno, Miguel Angel. 1994. *Democracy Within Reason: Technocratic Revolution in Mexico*. University Park: Pennsylvania State University Press.

Central Intelligence Agency (CIA). 2009. *CIA World Factbook*. New York: Skyhouse. Accessed October 23, 2012. https://www.cia.gov/library/publications/the-world-factbook/fields/2172.html.

Centro de Estudios Bonaerenses (CEB). 1995. "La industria: Un desempeño heterogeneo." *Informe Coyuntura* 5, no. 43 (April): 69–81.

Cerrutti, Marcela, and Alejandro Grimson. 2004. "Buenos Aires, neoliberalismo, y después: Cambios socioeconómicos y respuestas populares." *Cuadernos de IDES, Instituto de Desarrollo Económico y Social* 5 (October): 61–121. http://rimd.reduaz.mx/coleccion_desarrollo_migracion/ciudades_latinoamericanas/c1.pdf.

Chaudhry, Peter. 2011. "Unconditional Cash Transfers to the Very Poor in Central Viet Nam: Is It Enough to 'Just Give Them the Cash'?" In *What Works for the Poorest?* edited by David Lawson, David Hulme, Imran Matin, and Karen Moore, 169–178. Warwickshire, UK: Practical Action.

Cid, Camilo. 2007. *La política neoliberal y su impacto en la salud y las pensiones en Chile.* Santiago. Accessed November 30, 2007. http://cep.cl/Cenda/Cen_Documentos/Pub_CCid/Ensayos/Camilo_Cid_070420.doc.

Collins, Cath. 2010. *Post-Transitional Justice: Human Rights Trials in Chile and El Salvador.* University Park: Pennsylvania State University Press.

Colombia, Républica de. 1991. *Nueva Constitución Política de Colombia.* Pasto: Minilibrería Jurídica Moral.

Comaroff, Jean, and John L. Comaroff. 2000. "Millennial Capitalism: First Thoughts on a Second Coming." *Public Culture* 12, no. 2: 291–343.

———. 2006. *Law and Disorder in the Postcolony.* Chicago: University of Chicago Press.

Comisión de la Verdad. 2010. *Informe del la Comisión de la Verdad.* Quito: Ediecuatorial.

Comisión Económica para America Latina y el Caribe (CEPAL). 1997. *Panorama social para América Latina.* Santiago: CEPAL.

Conaghan, Catherine M. 1988. *Restructuring Domination: Industrialists and the State in Ecuador.* Pittsburgh: University of Pittsburgh Press.

———. 2008. "Ecuador: Correa's Plebiscitary Presidency." *Journal of Democracy* 19, no. 2: 46–60.

Consejo Regional Indígena del Cauca (CRIC). n.d. "La María, Piendamó territorio de convivencia, diálogo y negociación: Territorio y autonomía." Popayán.

Constitución Política del Estado (CPE) Bolivia. 2008. "Texto Final Compatibilizado." October. Accessed November 5, 2012. http://www.patrianueva.bo/constitucion/.

Contreras Natera, Miguel Ángel. 2004. "Ciudadanía, Estado y democracia en la era neoliberal: Dilemas y desafíos para la sociedad venezolana." In *Políticas de ciudadanía y sociedad civil en tiempos de globalización*, edited by Daniel Matos, 111–132. Caracas: UCV-FACES.

Cook, Bill, and Uma Kothari. 2001. *Participation: The New Tyranny?* London: Zed.

CORDIPLAN. 1990. "El Gran Viraje: Lineamientos Generales del VIII Plan de la Nación, Enero." Presentación al Congreso Nacional, Presidencia de la República de Venezuela, Oficina Central de Coordinación y Planificación.

Coronil, Fernando. 2000. "Magical Illusions or Revolutionary Magic? Chávez in Historical Context." *NACLA* 33, no. 6: 34–41.

Correas, Oscar. 2007. "The Criminalization of Social Protest in Mexico and Latin America." Paper presented at the annual meeting of the Law and Society Association, Berlin, Germany, July 25.

Corrigan, Phillip. 1994. "State Formation." In *Everyday Forms of State Formation: Revolution and Negotiation of Rule in Modern Mexico*, edited by Gilbert Joseph and Daniel Nugent, xviii–xix. Durham, NC: Duke University Press.

Corrigan, Phillip, and Derek Sayer. 1985. *The Great Arch: English State Formation as Cultural Revolution.* Oxford: Basil Blackwell.

Cortez, Beatriz. 2001. "Estética del cinismo: La ficción centroamericana de posguerra." *La Nación: Ancora*, March 11. Accessed November 28, 2012. http://www.nacion.com.

Coutin, Susan. 2007. *Nation of Immigrants: Shifting Boundaries of Citizenship in El Salvador and the United States.* Ithaca, NY: Cornell University Press.

Craig, David, and Doug Porter. 2006. *Development Beyond Neoliberalism? Governance, Poverty Reduction and Political Economy.* London: Routledge.

Craske, Nikki. 1999. *Women and Politics in Latin America.* Oxford: Polity.

Dagnino, Evelina. 2003. "Citizenship in Latin America: An Introduction." *Latin American Perspectives* 30, no. 2: 211–225.

Das, Veena, and Deborah Poole. 2004. "State and Its Margins." In *Anthropology in the Margins of the State*, edited by Veena Das and Deborah Poole, 1–33. Santa Fe, NM: School of American Research Press.

Dávalos, Isabel. 2007. *Alfaro Vive Carajo! Del sueño al caos*. Film (35 mm).

Deakin, Nicholas. 2001. *In Search of Civil Society*. Basingstoke, UK: Palgrave Macmillan.

DeGenova, Nick. 2010. "Antiterrorism, Race, and the New Frontier: American Exceptionalism, Imperial Multiculturalism, and the Global Security State." *Identities* 17, no. 6: 613–640.

Degregori, Carlos Iván. 1990. *El surgimiento de Sendero Luminoso: Ayacucho 1969–1979*. Lima: IEP.

de Janvry, Alain, Alison Graham, Elisabeth Sadoulet, Ramón Espinal, Walter Spurrer, Hans-Peter Nissen, and Frederico Welsch. 1991. *The Political Feasibility of Adjustment in Ecuador and Venezuela*. Paris: Organisation for Economic Co-Operation and Development.

Delamata, Gabriela. 2002. "De los 'estallidos' provinciales a la generalización de las protestas en Argentina: Perspectiva y contexto en la significación de las nuevas protestas." *Nueva Sociedad* 182 (November–December): 121–138.

de la Peña, Guillermo. 2007. "Civil Society and Popular Resistance: Mexico at the End of the Twentieth Century." In *Cycles of Conflict, Centuries of Change: Crisis, Reform, and Revolution in Mexico*, edited by Elisa Servin, Leticia Reina, and John Tutino, 305–345. Durham, NC: Duke University Press.

Deleuze, Gilles, and Felix Guattari. 1997. *A Thousand Plateaus*. Translated by Brian Massumi. Minneapolis: University of Minnesota Press.

Departamento del Cauca. 2001. "Documento del Proyecto: Plan Alterno al Plan Colombia en el Departamento del Cauca." Governor's Office, Popayán, Cauca.

Departamento de Nariño. 2001. "Memorias de la III Cumbre de Gobernadores de la Región Sur Colombiana. El Sur una Propuesta para la Vida." Pasto, Nariño.

de Rementería, Ibán. 2006. "Implosión política y explosión social." *El Mostrador: Columna*, September 27. Accessed November 30, 2007. http://www.elmostrador.cl/modulos/noticias/constructor/noticia_imp.

———. 2007. "Delincuencia y política." *El Mostrador: Columna*, October 15. Accessed November 30, 2007. http://www.elmostrador.cl/modulos/noticias/constructor/noticia_imp.

Dezalay, Yves, and Bryant Garth. 2002. *Global Prescriptions: The Production, Exportation, and Importation of a New Legal Orthodoxy*. Ann Arbor: University of Michigan Press.

Dimitrijevic, Nenad. 2006. "Justice Beyond Blame: Moral Justification of (the Idea of) a Truth Commission." *Journal of Conflict Resolution* 50, no. 3: 368–382.

Donham, Donald L. 2006. "Staring at Suffering: Violence as a Subject." In *States of Violence: Politics, Youth, and Memory in Contemporary Africa*, edited by Edna G. Bay and Donald L. Donham, 16–33. Charlottesville: University of Virginia Press.

Donzelot, Jacques. 1979. *La policía de las familias*. Valencia: Editorial Pre-Textos.

Dorfman, Adolfo. 1983. *Cincuenta años de industrialización en la Argentina (1930–1980): Desarrollo y perspectivas*. Buenos Aires: Solar.

Dugas, John. 1993a. "La Constitución Política de 1991: Un pacto político viable?" In *La Constitución de 1991: Un pacto político viable?* edited by John Dugas, 15–44. Bogotá: Universidad de los Andes.

———. 1993b. "El desarrollo de la Asamblea Nacional Constituyente." In *La Constitución de 1991: Un pacto político viable?* edited by John Dugas, 45–76. Bogotá: Universidad de los Andes.

Duménil, Gerard, and Dominique Lévy. 2004. *Capital Resurgent: Roots of the Neoliberal Revolution*. Cambridge, MA: Harvard University Press.

Dussel, Enrique. 2000. *Polarizing Mexico: The Impact of Liberalization Strategy*. Boulder, CO: Lynne Rienner.

———. 2003. "La globalización y las víctimas de la exclusión: Desde la perspectiva de la ética de la liberación." In *Culturas y poder: Interacción y asimetría entre las culturas en el contexto de la globalización*, edited by Raúl Fornet-Betancourt, 359–386. Bilbao: Editorial Desclée.

———. 2006. *20 Tesis de Política*. México City: Ediciones Siglo XXI and CREFAL.

Economic Commission for Latin America and the Caribbean (ECLAC). 2009. *Social Panorama of Latin America 2009*. Santiago: ECLAC. Accessed June 9, 2010. http://www.eclac.cl/publicaciones/xml/0/37840/PSI2009-presentacion-SE-CEPAL.pdf.

Egan, Nancy. 2007. "'Una lucha de razas, secular y honda': The Proceso Mohoza, Bolivia, 1899–1905." Master's thesis, University of California, San Diego.

El Espectador. 2001. "Caravana de muerte en Naya." April 18, 4A.

El Informativo. 2001. "El acuerdo de reestructuración de pasivos del Departamento del Cauca (I)." 105 (February 2–10): A6.

El Liberal. 2001. "Sigue la zozobra por presencia 'para.'" April 19, 6B.

———. 2003. "Asesinado alcalde de Bolívar." October 8, 6B.

El Mundo. 2001. "Fue una masacre anunciada." April 17, B4.

El País. 2001. "Masacradas seis personas en el Naya." April 14, C3.

———. 2003a. "Alcaldes en la boca del lobo." October 9, 1, 6.

———. 2003b. "En el Cauca, los alcaldes cumplen desde el exilio." October 12, A3.

Elson, Diane. 1995. "Male Bias in Macro-Economics: The Case of Structural Adjustment." In *Male Bias in the Development Process*, 2nd ed., edited by Diane Elson, 164–190. Manchester: Manchester University Press.

El Tiempo. 2003. "FARC mataron al alcalde de Bolívar." October 8, 2, 9.

Elyachar, Julia. 2002. "Empowerment Money: The World Bank, Non-Governmental Organizations, and the Value of Culture in Egypt." *Public Culture* 14, no. 3: 493–513.

Engle Merry, Sally. 1997. "Legal Pluralism and Transnational Culture: The Ka Ho'okolokolonui Kanaka Maoli tribunal, Hawai'i." In *Human Rights, Culture and Context: Anthropological Perspectives*, edited by Richard Wilson, 28–48. London: Pluto.

———. 2006. *Human Rights and Gender Violence: Translating International Law into Local Justice*. Chicago: University of Chicago Press.

ERBOL (Educación Radiofónica de Bolivia). 2010a. "Indígenas marchan contra el gobierno y demandan consulta sobre hidrocarburos." April 14. La Paz.

———. 2010b. "García Linera: No nos vamos a convertir en guardabosques del norte." April 26. La Paz.

Escobar, Arturo. 1995. *Encountering Development: The Making and Unmaking of the Third World*. Princeton, NJ: Princeton University Press.

———. 2005. *Más allá del Tercer Mundo: Globalización y diferencia*. Bogotá: ICANH y la Universidad del Cauca.

———. 2010. "Latin America at a Crossroads: Alternative Modernizations, Post-Liberalism, or Post-Development?" *Cultural Studies* 24, no. 1: 1–65.

Espinosa, Myriam Amparo. 2005. "Movimientos sociales en La María-Piendamó, territorio de convivencia, diálogo y negociación." In *Retornando la mirada: Una investigación colaborativa interétnica sobre el Cauca a la entrada al milenio*, edited by Joanne Rappaport, 129–151. Popayán: Editorial Universidad del Cauca.

Ettinger, Aaron. 2011. "Neoliberalism and the Rise of the Private Military Industry." *International Journal* 66, no. 3: 731–752.

Evans, Dylan. 1996. *Dictionary of Lacanian Psychoanalysis*. London: Routledge.

Fabricant, Nicole, and Nancy Postero. Forthcoming. "Contested Bodies, Contested States, Performance, Emotions, and New Forms of Regional Governance in Santa Cruz, Bolivia." *Journal of Latin American and Caribbean Anthropology*.

Farthing, Linda. 2009. "Bolivia's Development Dilemma: Development Confronts the Legacy of Extraction." *NACLA Report on the Americas* 42, no. 5: 25–29.

Feldman, Allen. 1991. *Formations of Violence: The Narrative of the Body and Political Terror in Northern Ireland*. Chicago: University of Chicago Press.

Ferguson, James. 2006. *Global Shadows: Africa in the Neoliberal World Order*. Durham, NC: Duke University Press.

Ferguson, James, and Akhil Gupta. 2002. "Spatializing States: Toward an Ethnography of Neoliberal Governmentality." *American Ethnologist* 29, no. 4: 981–1002.

Ferguson, Niall. 2008. *The Ascent of Money: A Financial History of the World*. New York: Penguin.

Finn, Janet. 2006. "La Victoria Comprometida: Reflections on Neoliberalism from a Santiago Población." *Research in Economic Anthropology* 24: 207–239.

Fischer, William. 1997. "Doing Good? The Politics and Anti-Politics of NGO Practices." *Annual Review of Anthropology* 26: 439–464.

Forment, Carlos A. 2003. *Democracy in Latin America 1760–1900*. Vol. 1, *Civic Selfhood and Public Life in Mexico and Peru*. Chicago: University of Chicago Press.

Foucault, Michel. 1991a. [1978]. "Governmentality." In *The Foucault Effect*, edited by Graham Burchell, Colin Gordon, and Peter Miller, 87–104. Chicago: University of Chicago Press.

———. 1991b. "Nietzsche, Genealogy, History." In *The Foucault Reader*, edited by Paul Rabinow, 76–100. London: Penguin.

———. 1997. *Ethics: Subjectivity and Truth*, edited by Paul Rabinow. New York: New Press.

———. 2007. *The Birth of Biopolitics: Lectures at the Collège de France, 1978–1979*, edited by Michel Snellart. New York: Palgrave Macmillan.

Fox, Jonathan. 1994. "The Difficult Transition from Clientelism to Citizenship: Lessons from Mexico." *World Politics* 46, no. 2: 151–184.

Fox, Jonathan, and Luis Hernández. 1992. "Mexico's Difficult Democracy: Grassroots Movements, NGOs and Local Government." *Alternatives* 17, no. 2: 165–208.

Fraile, Lydia. 2009. "Lessons from Latin America's Neo-liberal Experiment: An Overview of Labour and Social Policies Since the 1980s." *International Labour Review*, 148, no. 3: 215–233.

Franceschet, Susan. 2003. "States and Women's Movements: The Impact of Chile's Servicio Nacional de la Mujer on Women's Activism." *Latin American Research Review* 38, no. 1: 9–40.

Frank, Volker. 2004. "Politics Without Policy: The Failure of Social Concertación in Democratic Chile, 1990–2000." In *Victims of the Chilean Miracle: Workers and Neo-*

liberalism in the Pinochet Era, 1973–2002, edited by Peter Winn, 71–124. Durham, NC: Duke University Press.
Fraser, Nancy. 1997. "Rethinking the Public Sphere: A Contribution to the Critique of Actually Existing Democracy." In *Justice Interruptus: Critical Reflections on the "Post-socialist" Condition*, edited by Nancy Fraser, 69–98. New York: Routledge.
Frías, Edgar. 1999. *A.V.C. por dentro*. Author's independent publication.
Fundación para el Debido Proceso Legal (FDPL). 2010. *Criminalización de los defensores de derechos humanos y de la protesta social en México*. Mexico City: FDPL.
Funkhouser, E. 1995. "Remittances from International Migration: A Comparison of El Salvador and Nicaragua." *Review of Economics and Statistics* 7, no. 1: 137–146.
Garcés, Fernando. 2011. "The Domestication of Indigenous Autonomies in Bolivia: From the Pact of Unity to the New Constitution." In *Remapping Bolivia: Resources, Territory, and Indigeneity in a Plurinational State*, edited by Nicole Fabricant and Bret Gustafson, 46–67. Santa Fe, NM: School for Advanced Research Press.
García Linera, Álvaro. 2011. "Las tensiones creativas de la revolución: La quinta fase del proceso de cambio." Vicepresidencia del Estado Presidencia de la Asamblea Legislataiva Plurinacional.
García Villegas, Mauricio. 1993. *La eficacia simbólica de derecho: Examen de situaciones colombianas*. Bogotá: Ediciones Uniandes.
Garrett, Linda. 2009. "The Funes Inauguration." Washington, DC: Center for Democracy in the Americas.
———. 2010. "El Salvador: Expectations for Change and the Challenges of Governance, the First Year of President Mauricio Funes." Washington, DC: Center for Democracy in the Americas.
Gingrich, Newt. 2005. "American Gangs: Ties to Terror?" *Fox News*, July 3.
Gobernación del Cauca. 2002. "Informe de gestión enero–diciembre 2001." Popayán.
———. 2003a. "Informe de Gestión. Administración en minga por el Cauca. 2001–2003." Popayán.
———. 2003b. "Una aproximación a los Derechos Humanos y el Derecho Internacional Humanitario en el Cauca," Secretaria de Gobierno, Derechos Humanos, Convivencia y Participación Social. Popayán.
Goldstein, Daniel. 2004. *The Spectacular City: Violence and Performance in Urban Bolivia*. Durham, NC: Duke University Press.
———. 2010. "Towards a Critical Anthropology of Security." *Current Anthropology* 51, no. 4: 487–517.
González Bombal, Inés. 1989. *Los vecinazos: Las protestas barriales en el Gran Buenos Aires, 1982–83*. Buenos Aires: IDES.
González González, Fernán E., and Silvia Otero Bahamón. 2010. "La presencia diferenciada del estado: Un desafío a los conceptos de gobernabilidad y gobernanza." In *Gobernanza y conflicto en Colombia: Interacción entre gobernantes y gobernados en un contexto violento*, edited by Claire Launay-Gama and Fernán E. González González, 28–36. Bogotá: Cinep-Irg.
Goodale, Mark. 2009. *Dilemmas of Modernity: Bolivian Encounters with Law and Liberalism*. Stanford, CA: Stanford University Press.
———. n.d. "The Violence of Ambiguity: Constitutional Revolution and the Problem of Radical Social Change in Bolivia." Unpublished manuscript.
Gordon, Sara. 1998. "Entre la filantropía y el Mercado: La Fundación Mexicana para el Desarrollo Rural." In *Organizaciones Civiles y Políticas Públicas en Mexico y*

Centroamerica, edited by Jose Luis Mendez, 293–320. Mexico City: Académia Mexicana de Investigación en Políticas Públicas.

Gorz, André. 2003. *Miserias del presente, riqueza de lo posible*. Barcelona: Editorial Paidós.

Government of Ecuador. 2007. Ministerial Accord no. 305.

Gramsci, Antonio. 1971. *Selections from the Prison Notebooks*. New York: International Publishers.

Grandin, Greg. 2006. *The Last Colonial Massacre: Latin America in the Cold War*. Chicago: University of Chicago Press.

Green, Linda. 2011. "The Nobodies: Neoliberalism, Violence, and Migration." *Medical Anthropology* 30, no. 4: 366–385.

Griesbach, Kathleen. 2011. "Policing Bodies at the Border and the Borders Within: Immigration Enforcement and Detention in San Diego County and North Carolina." Master's thesis, University of California, San Diego.

Grillo, Ralph D. 1997. "Discourses of Development: The View from Anthropology." In *Discourses of Development: Anthropological Perspectives*, edited by Ralph D. Grillo and R. L. Stirrat, 1–33. New York: Berg.

Grimson, Alejandro. 2003a. "La nación después del deconstructivismo." *Sociedad* 20–21: 147–162. Buenos Aires.

———. 2003b. "La vida organizacional en zonas populares de Buenos Aires." Center for Migration and Development, Working Paper Series, Princeton University, March 15. http://cmd.princeton.edu/papers/wp0315e.pdf.

———, ed. 2007. *Cultura y neoliberalismo*. Buenos Aires: CLACSO.

Grimson, Alejandro, and Gabriel Kessler. 2005. *On Argentina and the Southern Cone: Neoliberalism and National Imaginations*. New York: Routledge.

Grindle, Merilee S. 2007. *Going Local: Decentralization, Democratization, and the Promise of Good Governance*. Princeton, NJ: Princeton University Press.

Grünner, Eduardo. 1997. *Las formas de la espada: Miserias de la teoría política de la violencia*. Buenos Aires: Ediciones Colihue.

Gudynas, Eduardo. 2010. "The New Extractivism of the 21st Century: Ten Urgent Theses About Extractivism in Relation to Current South American Progressivism." *Americas Program Report*, January 21. Washington, DC: Center for International Policy.

Gudynas, Eduardo, Rubén Guevara, and Frederico Roque. 2008. "Heterodoxos: Tensiones y posibilidades de las políticas sociales en los gobiernos progresistas de América del Sur." Montevideo: CLAES y OXFAM. Accessed August 29, 2011. http://www.democraciasur.com.

Guigale, Marcelo M., Olivier Lafourcade, and Connie Luff. 2003. *Colombia: The Economic Foundations of Peace*. Washington, DC: World Bank.

Guss, David. 1993. "The Selling of San Juan: The Performance of History in an Afro-Venezuelan Community." *American Ethnologist* 20, no. 3: 451–473.

———. 2000. *The Festive State: Race, Ethnicity, and Nationalism as Cultural Performance*. Berkeley: University of California Press.

Gusterson, Hugh. 2004. *People of the Bomb: Portraits of America's Nuclear Complex*. Minneapolis: University of Minnesota Press.

Gutiérrez, Irma Eugenia. 1990. *Hidalgo: Sociedad, Economía, Política y Cultura*. Mexico City: Universidad Nacional Autónoma de México.

Haas, Liesl. 2010. *Feminist Policymaking in Chile*. University Park: Pennsylvania State University Press.

Haddick, Robert. 2011. "This Week at War: Outsourcing the Drug War." *Foreign Policy*, August 12. Accessed November 1, 2011. http://www.foreignpolicy.com.

Hale, Charles A. 1989. *The Transformation of Liberalism in Nineteenth-Century Mexico*. Princeton, NJ: Princeton University Press.

Hale, Charles R. 1994. *Resistance and Contradiction: Miskitu Indians and the Nicaraguan State, 1894–1987*. Stanford, CA: Stanford University Press.

Hall, Stuart. 1996. "The West and the Rest: Discourse and Power." In *Modernity: An Introduction to Modern Societies*, edited by Stuart Hall, David Held, Don Hubert, and Kenneth Thompson, 185–228. London: Blackwell.

Halperin Donghi, Tulio. 1993. *The Contemporary History of Latin America*, edited and translated by John Charles Chasteen. Durham, NC: Duke University Press.

Hardt, Michael, and Antonio Negri. 2001. *Empire*. Cambridge, MA: Harvard University Press.

Harman, Danna. 2005. "Firms Tap Latin Americans for Iraq." *USA Today*, March 3. Accessed March 15, 2008. http://www.usatoday.com/news/world/iraq/2005-03-03-latinamerica-iraq_x.htm?csp=34.

Harris, Olivia. 1995. "The Coming of the White People: Reflections on the Mythologisation of History in Latin America." *Bulletin of Latin American Research* 14, no. 1: 9–24.

Harvey, David. 2001. *Spaces of Capital: Towards a Critical Geography*. New York: Routledge.

———. 2005. *A Brief History of Neoliberalism*. Oxford: Oxford University Press.

———. 2007. "El neoliberalismo como destrucción creativa." Translated by Germán Leyens. August 2. Accessed September 24, 2008. http://www.rebelion.org/noticia.php?id=65709.

Hayden, Tom. 2009. "El Salvador Rising." *Nation*, June 29, 431–459.

Hayek, Friedrich. 1985. *Derecho, legislación y libertad: Una nueva formulación de los principios liberales de la justicia y de la economía política*. Madrid: Unión Editorial.

———. 1991. *Los fundamentos de la libertad*. Madrid: Unión Editorial.

Heller, Agnes. 1990. *General Ethics*. Oxford: Blackwell.

Herrera Rivera, Luz Angela. 2003. *Región, desarrollo y acción colectiva: Movimiento de integración del Macizo Colombiano*. Bogotá: CINEP.

Hershberg, Eric, and Fred Rosen, eds. 2006. *Latin America After Neoliberalism: Turning the Tide in the 21st Century?* New York: New Tide/NACLA.

Hetherington, Kevin. 1998. *Expressions of Identity: Space, Performance, Politics*. Thousand Oaks, CA: Sage Publications.

Hey, Jeanne A. K., and Thomas Klak. 1999. "From Protectionism Towards Neoliberalism: Ecuador Across Four Administrations (1981–1996)." *Studies in Comparative International Development* 34: 66–97.

Hintze, Susana. 2003. *Balance y perspectivas de las políticas públicas en Argentina*. Universidad Autónoma Metropolitana, Primer Seminario Internacional "Balance y perspectivas de las políticas y la gestión pública Latinoamericana," México.

Hirschman, Albert O. 1984. *Getting Ahead Collectively: Grassroots Experiences in Late America*. New York: Pergamon.

Howard, April. 2009. "Salt of the Earth: Bolivia Extracts Its Lithium, Environment Be Damned." *In These Times*, May 6. Accessed November 3, 2012. http://www.inthesetimes.com/article/4360/salt_of_the_earth/.

Huggins, Martha. 1998. *Political Policing: The United States and Latin America*. Durham, NC: Duke University Press.
Hursthouse, Guy, and Tomás Ayso. 2010. "From ¿Cambio? The Obama Administration in Latin America: A Disappointing Year in Retrospective." Council on Hemispheric Affairs (COHA), January 26. Accessed November 3, 2012. http://www.coha.org/cambio-the-obama-administration/.
Hurtado, Osvaldo. 1990. *Política democrática: Los últimos veinte y cinco años*. Quito: Corporación Editora Nacional.
———. 2009. *Structural Problems of Ecuadorian Democracy*. Quito: Cordes.
Instituto de Derechos Humanos de la UCA (IDHUCA). 2011. "Derechos Humanos 2010." Accessed October 10, 2011. http://www.uca.edu.sv/publica/idhuca/documentos/final-balance2010.pdf.
Instituto Nacional de Estadísticas (INE). 2008. "Encuesta experimental sobre uso del tiempo en el Gran Santiago." May 30. Santiago: INE.
Instituto Universitario de Opinión Pública (IUDOP). 1998. "Delincuencia y Opinion Pública." *ECA-Estudios Centroamericano* 599: 785–802.
Inter-American Development Bank (IADB). 2008. "Bolivia: The Bank's Strategy with Bolivia, 2008–2010." Accessed April 25, 2011. http://www.gavega.com/uploads/1/0/8/8/1088147/idb_-__country_strategy_with_bolivia.pdf.
International Center for Not-for-Profit Law (ICNL). 2011. *NGO Law Monitor—Mexico*. Accessed May 5, 2011. http://www.icnl.org.
James, Cyril Lionel Robert. 1989. *The Black Jacobins: Toussaint L'Ouverture and the San Domingo Revolution*. New York: Vintage.
Jaramillo Salgado, Diego. 2001. "Un gobierno alternativo en una región olvidada de Colombia: Entrevista al taita Floro Alberto Tunubalá, gobernador de departamento del Cauca." *Journal of Iberian and Latin American Studies* 7, no. 2: 151–166.
———. 2005. "Procesos de resistencia de los movimientos sociales en el Cauca y la experiencia de un gobierno alternativo." *Revista Utopía* 21: 19–40. Popayán, Cauca.
Jelin, Elizabeth. 2003. "Citizenship and Alterity: Tensions and Dilemmas." *Latin American Perspectives* 30, no. 2: 309–325.
Jessop, Bob. 2003. "Reflexiones sobre la (i)lógica de la globalización." In *Cansancio del Leviatán: Problemas en la mundialización*, edited by Juan Carlos Monederos and Juan Carlos, 205–230. Madrid: Editorial Trotta.
Kaup, Brent. 2010. "A Neoliberal Nationalization? The Constraints on Natural-Gas-Led Development in Bolivia." *Latin American Perspectives* 37, no. 3: 123–138.
Kessler, Gabriel. 1996. "Algunas implicancias de la experiencia de desocupación para el individuo y su familia." In *Empleo e integración social*, edited by L. Beccaria and N. López, 111–160. México: Fondo de Cultura Económica.
Klein, Herbert S. 1992. *Bolivia, the Evolution of a Multi-Ethnic Society*, 2nd ed. New York: Oxford University Press.
Klima, Alan. 2002. *The Funeral Casino: Meditation, Massacre, and Exchange with the Dead in Thailand*. Princeton, NJ: Princeton University Press.
Knight, Alan. 1990. "Racism, Revolution, and Indigenismo: Mexico, 1910–1940." In *The Idea of Race in Latin America, 1870–1940*, edited by Richard Graham, 71–113. Austin: University of Texas Press.
Kohl, Ben. 2010. "A Work in Progress." *Latin American Perspectives* 37, no. 3: 107–122.

Kohl, Ben, and Linda Farthing. 2006. *Impasse in Bolivia: Neoliberal Hegemony and Social Resistance.* London: Zed.

———. 2009. "'Less than Fully Satisfactory Development Outcomes': International Financial Institutions and Social Unrest in Bolivia." *Latin American Perspectives* 36, no. 3: 59–78.

Kokotovic, Misha. 2006. "Neoliberal Noir: Contemporary Central American Crime Fiction as Social Criticism." *Clues: A Journal of Detection* 24, no. 3: 15–29.

Krupa, Christopher. 2009. "Histories in Red: Ways of Seeing Lynching in Ecuador." *American Ethnologist* 36, no. 1: 20–39.

———. 2011. "Mestizo Mainstream: Reaffirmations of Natural Citizenship in Ecuador." In *Subalternity and Difference: Investigations from the North and the South,* edited by Gyanendra Pandey, 149–166. New York: Routledge.

Laclau, Ernesto. 2005. *La razón populista.* Buenos Aires: Fondo de Cultura Económica.

Laclau, Ernesto, and Chantal Mouffe. 1985. *Hegemony and Socialist Strategy: Towards a Radical Democratic Politics.* London: Verso.

La María. 2000. "Memorias: Encuentro de organizaciones sociales—construcción de alternativas al Plan Colombia." La María Piendamó, Cauca, Colombia.

Larner, Wendy. 2000. "Neoliberalism: Policy, Ideology, Governmentality." *Studies in Political Economy* 63 (Autumn): 5–25.

Larson, Brooke. 2004. *Trials of Nation Making: Liberalism, Race, and Ethnicity in the Andes, 1810–1910.* Cambridge: Cambridge University Press.

Laserna Rojas, Roberto, Carlos Miranda Pacheco, and Mario Napoleón Torrico. 2009. "Control estatal de recursos naturales y rentismo." In *Poder y Cambio en Bolivia, 2003–2007,* edited by Roberto Laserna and Rubén Vargas, 9–60. La Paz: Fundación PIEB.

Laurie, Nina, Robert Andolina, and Sarah Radcliffe. 2002. "The Excluded 'Indigenous'? The Implications of Multi-Ethnic Policies for Water Reform in Bolivia." In *Multiculturalism in Latin America: Indigenous Rights, Diversity, and Democracy,* edited by Rachel Sieder, 252–276. New York: Palgrave Macmillan.

Lazar, Sian. 2008. *El Alto, Rebel City: Self and Citizenship in Andean Bolivia.* Durham, NC: Duke University Press.

Lechner, Norbert, and Susana Levy. 1984. "Notas sobre la vida cotidiana III: El disciplinamiento de la mujer." Material de Discusión, 57. Santiago: FLACSO.

Lemke, Thomas. 2001. "'The Birth of Bio-Politics': Michel Foucault's Lecture at the Collège de France on Neo-Liberal Governmentality." *Economy and Society* 30, no. 2: 190–207.

———. 2007. "An Indigestible Meal? Foucault, Governmentality, and State Theory." *Distinktion: Scandinavian Journal of Social Theory* 15: 43–64.

Leve, Lauren, and Lamia Karim. 2001. "Privatizing the State: Ethnography of Development, Transnational Capital, and NGOs." *Political and Legal Anthropology Review (PoLAR)* 24, no. 1: 53–58.

Li, Tania Murray. 2007. *The Will to Improve.* Durham, NC: Duke University Press.

Lind, Amy. 2005. *Gender Paradoxes: Women's Movements, State Restructuring, and Global Development in Ecuador.* University Park: Pennsylvania State University Press.

Lomas, Laura. 2006. "The War Cut Out My Tongue: Domestic Violence, Foreign Wars, and Translation in Demetria Martínez." *American Literature* 78, no. 2 (2006): 357–387.

Lomnitz, Claudio. 2001. *Deep Mexico, Silent Mexico: An Anthropology of Nationalism.* Minneapolis: University of Minnesota Press.

Lomnitz, Larissa. 1998 [1975]. *Cómo sobreviven los marginados.* Mexico City: Siglo XXI.

Lora, Eduardo, ed. 2007. "The State of State Reform in Latin America." Washington, DC: International Development Bank.

Lovato, Roberto. 2005. "The War for Latinos." *Nation*, October 3. Accessed June 23, 2011. http://www.thenation.com/article/war-latinos.

———. 2011. "Dispatch from El Salvador: Obama's Drug War Feels Eerily Familiar." *Huffington Post*, March 31.

Loxton, James. 2007. "Imperialism or Neglect: The Militarization of US Aid to Latin America Since 9/11." *Security and Citizenship Program Bulletin*, no. 1 (January): 1–7.

Lungo, Mario. 1997. *Migración internacional y desarrollo.* San Salvador: Fundación Nacional para el Desarrollo.

Macdonald, Laura, and Arne Ruckert. 2009. "Post-Neoliberalism in the Americas: An Introduction." In *Post-Neoliberalism in the Americas*, edited by L. Macdonald and A. Ruckert, 1–19. New York: Palgrave Macmillan.

Macpherson, C. B. 1970. *La teoría política del individualismo posesivo.* Madrid: Editorial Fontanella.

Madrid, Raúl L. 2008. "The Rise of Ethnopopulism in Latin America." *World Politics* 60: 475–508.

Magazine, Roger. 2003. "An Innovative Combination of Neoliberalism and State Corporatism: The Case of a Locally Based NGO in Mexico City." *ANNALS of the American Academy of Political and Social Science* 590: 243–256.

Mallon, Richard, and Juan V. Sourrouille. 1975. *Economic Policymaking in a Conflict Society: The Argentine Case.* Cambridge, MA: Harvard University Press.

Mamani Ramírez, Pablo. 2004. *El rugir de las multitudes.* La Paz: Yachaywasi Editores.

———. 2006. "Territorio y estructuras de acción colectiva: microgobiernos barriales." *Ephemera* 6, no. 3: 276–286.

Manwaring, Max G. 2005. "Street Gangs: The New Urban Insurgency." *Strategic Studies Institute*, March. Accessed March 5, 2011. http://www.carlisle.army.mil/.

Mariscal, Jorge. 2005. "Homeland Security, Militarism, and the Future of Latinos and Latinas in the United States." In "Homeland Securities," special issue, *Radical History Review* 93 (Fall): 39–52.

Masco, Joseph. 2005. "Active Measures; or, How a KGB Spymaster Made Good in Post-9/11 America." In "Homeland Securities," special issue, *Radical History Review* 93 (Fall): 1–12.

Mehta, Uday Singh. 1997. "Liberal Strategies of Exclusion." In *Tensions of Empire: Colonial Cultures in a Bourgeois World*, edited by Frederick Cooper, 59–86. Berkeley: University of California Press.

———. 1999. *Liberalism and Empire: A Study in Nineteenth-Century Liberal Thought.* Chicago, University of Chicago Press.

Meichtry, Nora. 1993. "Urban High Primacy as a Social Construction: The Case of Argentina." PhD diss., University of Texas at Austin.

Menjívar, Cecilia, and Néstor Rodríquez. 2005. *When States Kill: Latin America, the U.S., and Technologies of Terror.* Austin: University of Texas Press.

Meridian International Research. 2008. "The Trouble with Lithium 2: Under the Microscope." William Tahil, research director.

MIDEPLAN. 2007. "Chile Crece Contigo: Sistema de Protección Integral a la Infancia." Dossier Informativo para Encargados Comunicacionales de Ministerios, Servicios, Gobiernos Regionales y Municipalidades. Accessed December 7, 2007. http://www.crececontigo.cl/download.php?c=upfiles/materiales&a=4753efa82a60e_Dossier_informativo_CHCC.pdf.

———. 2008. "Notas Técnicas sobre Protección Social y Género: Sistemas de Apoyo Psicosocial, Mujer y Familia." Documento no. 5. Accessed December 10, 2012. http://siis.ministeriodedesarrollosocial.gob.cl/seminario_genero2010/doc/2008/Not_tecnica%205_sistemas%20de%20Apoyo.pdf.

Mignolo, Walter. 2005a. *Historias locales/Diseños globales: Colonialidad, conocimientos subalternos y pensamiento transfronterizo.* Madrid: Ediciones Akal.

———. 2005b. *The Idea of Latin America.* Blackwell Manifestos Series. Oxford: Blackwell.

Ministerio de Hacienda y Crédito Público. 2002. "Informe sobre la viabilidad fiscal de los departamentos. Vigencia 2001." Bogotá: Dirección General de Apoyo Fiscal.

———. 2004. "Informe sobre la viabilidad fiscal de los departamentos. Vigencia 2003." Bogotá: Dirección General de Apoyo Fiscal.

———. 2005. "Informe sobre la viabilidad fiscal de los departamentos. Vigencia 2004." Bogotá: Dirección General de Apoyo Fiscal.

Miraftab, Faranak. 1997. "Coqueteando con el enemigo: Desafíos de las ONG para el desarrollo y el empoderamiento." *Cuadernos de la Sociedad Civil* 1, no. 2: 33–57.

Molyneux, Maxine. 2008. "The 'Neoliberal Turn' and the New Social Policy in Latin America: How Neoliberal, How New?" *Development and Change* 39, no. 5: 775–797.

Montúfar, César. 2000. *La reconstrucción neoliberal: Febres Cordero o la estatización del neoliberalismo en el Ecuador, 1984–1988.* Quito: Abya-Yala.

Moodie, Ellen. 2006. "Microbus Crashes and Coca-Cola Cash." *American Ethnologist* 33, no. 1: 63–80.

———. 2010. *El Salvador in the Aftermath of Peace: Crime, Uncertainty, and the Transition to Democracy.* Philadelphia: University of Pennsylvania Press.

Moore, Donald S. 2000. "The Crucible of Cultural Politics: Reworking 'Development' in Zimbabwe's Eastern Highlands." *American Ethnologist* 26, no. 3: 654–689.

Morales, Evo. 2003. "Bolivia, el poder del pueblo." October 25. Accessed February 11, 2004. http://www.jornada.unam.mx/2003/10/25/019a1pol.php?origen=index.html&fly=1.

———. 2006. "Palabras del Presidente de la República." January 22. Accessed January 24, 2006. http://espanol.groups.yahoo.com/group/ukhamawa.

Mosse, David. 2005. "Global Governance and the Ethnography of International Aid." In *The Aid Effect: Giving and Governing in International Development,* edited by David Mosse and David Lewis, 1–36. Ann Arbor, MI: Pluto.

Naiman, Robert. 2010. "WikiLeaks Honduras: State Department Busted on Support of Coup." *Huffington Post,* November 29. Accessed July 3, 2011. http://www.huffingtonpost.com/robert-naiman/wikileaks-honduras-state_b_789282.html.

Nash, June. 1979. *We Eat the Mines and the Mines Eat Us: Dependency and Exploitation in Bolivian Tin Mines.* New York: Columbia University Press.

———. 1992. "Interpreting Social Movements: Bolivian Resistance to Economic Conditions Imposed by the International Monetary Fund." *American Ethnologist* 19, no. 2: 275–293.

Natal, A., P. Greaves Lainé, and Sergio García. 2002. *Recursos privados para fines públicos: Las instituciones donantes mexicanas*. Mexico City: Centro Mexicano para la Filantropía (CEMEFI).

National Gang Intelligence Center. 2007. "Gang-Related Activity in the US Armed Forces Increasing." January 12. Accessed November 11, 2009. http://militarytimes.com/static/projects/pages/ngic_gangs.pdf.

Navarro Wolf, Antonio. 2001. "La desmovilización del M-19 diez años después." Paper presented at the conference "Haciendo paz: Reflexiones y perspectivas del proceso de paz en Colombia," Cartagena, Colombia, March.

Negri, Toni. 1994. *El poder constituyente*. Madrid: Editorial Prodhufi Libertarias.

Nelson, Diane. 2009. *Reckoning: The Ends of War in Guatemala*. Durham, NC: Duke University Press.

North, Liisa, Wade A. Kit, and Rob Koep. 2003. "Rural Land Conflicts and Human Rights Violations in Ecuador." CERLAC Working Paper Series. Centre for Research on Latin America and the Caribbean, York University.

North, Liisa L. 2004. "State Building, State Dismantling, and Financial Crisis in Ecuador." In *Politics in the Andes: Identity, Conflict, Reform*, edited by Jo-Marie Burt and P. Mauceri, 187–206. Pittsburgh: University of Pittsburgh Press.

Obama, Barack. 2010. "Remarks by the President on Comprehensive Immigration Reform," delivered at the American School of International Service, Washington, DC, July 1. Accessed July 1, 2010. http://www.whitehouse.gov/the-press-office/remarks-president-comprehensive-immigration-reform.

Olivera, Oscar. 2004. *¡Cochabamba! Water War in Bolivia*. With Tom Lewis. Boston: South End Press.

Olsen, Tricia D., Leigh A. Payne, and Andrew G. Reiter. 2010. *Transitional Justice in Balance: Comparing Processes, Weighing Effects*. Washington, DC: United States Institute of Peace.

———. 2012. "Amnesty in an Age of Accountability: Brazil in Comparative Context." In *Real Social Science: Applied Phronesis*, edited by Bent Flyvbjerg, Todd Landman, and Sanford Schram, 204–227. New York: Cambridge University Press.

Olvera Rivera, Alberto. 1999. *La sociedad civil: De la teoría a la realidad*. Mexico City: El Colegio de México.

O'Neill, Kevin Lewis. 2005. "Writing Guatemala's Genocide: Christianity and Truth and Reconciliation Commissions." *Journal for Genocide Research* 7, no. 3: 331–349.

Ong, Aihwa. 2006. *Neoliberalism as Exception: Mutations in Citizenship and Sovereignty*. Durham, NC: Duke University Press.

Orozco, Manuel. 2000. "Remittances and Markets: New Players and Practices." Working paper, June. Washington, DC: Inter-American Dialogue. http://ww.w.thedialogue.org/PublicationFiles/Orozco%20marketplace.pdf.

Ortner, Sherry. 1973. "On Key Symbols." *American Ethnologist* 75, no. 5: 1338–1346.

Oxhorn, Philip, and Graciela Ducatenzeiler. 1998. *What Kind of Democracy? What Kind of Market? Latin America in the Age of Neoliberalism*. University Park: Pennsylvania State University Press.

Paley, Julia. 2001. *Marketing Democracy: Power and Social Movements in Post-Dictatorship Chile*. Berkeley: University of California Press.

———. 2009. "Participatory Democracy, Transparency, and Good Governance in Ecuador: Why Have Social Organizations at All?" In *New Perspectives on Democracy*, edited by Julia Paley, 147–166. Santa Fe, NM: Advanced Research Press.

Palma, José Gabriel. 2008. "Why Did the Latin American Critical Tradition in the Social Sciences Become Practically Extinct? From Structural Adjustment to Ideological Adjustment." Revised and enlarged version of a paper published in *The Handbook of International Political Economy*, edited by Mark Blyth, pp. 243–265. New York: Routledge. Accessed December 10, 2012. http://www.networkideas.org/featart/mar2009/Latin_America.pdf.

———. 2009. "The Revenge of the Market on Rentiers: Why Neo-liberal Reports of the End of History Turned Out to be Premature." *Cambridge Journal of Economics* 33: 829–869.

Panizza, Francisco. 2009. *Contemporary Latin America: Development and Democracy Beyond the Washington Consensus*. London: Zed.

Parker, Dick. 2005. "Chávez and the Search for an Alternative to Neoliberalism." *Latin American Perspectives* 141, no. 2: 39–50.

Patzi Paco, Felix.1999. *Insurgencia y sumisión: Movimientos indígeno-campesinos (1983–1998)*. La Paz: Muela del Diablo Editores.

———. 2002 "Movimiento Aymara: Una Utopia Razonada." In *Las Piedras en el Camino*, edited by María Luján Veneros, 39–66. La Paz: Ministerio de Desarrollo Sostenible y Planificación.

———. 2005. "Rebellión indígena contra la colonialidad y la transnacionalización de la economía: Trunfos y vicisitudes del movimiento indígena desde 2000 a 2003." In *Ya es otro tiempo el presente*, edited by Forrest Hylton, Felix Patzi, Sergio Serulnikov, and Sinclair Thomson. 196–276. La Paz: Muela del Diablo Editores.

Peck, Jamie, and Adam Tickell. 2002. "Neoliberalizing Space." *Antipode* 34, no. 3: 380–404.

Pedersen, David. 2002. "The Storm We Call Dollars: Determining Value and Belief in El Salvador and the United States." *Cultural Anthropology* 17, no. 3 (August): 431–459.

———. 2012. *American Value: Migrants, Money, and Meaning in El Salvador and the United States*. Chicago: University of Chicago Press.

Peña Chepe, Alfonso. 1991. "Proyecto de reforma constitutional presentado por el delgado del Movimiento Indígena Quintín Lame." *Gazeta Constitutional*, no. 26 (April 26), 16–23. Bogotá.

Peñaranda, Ricardo. 1999. "De rebeldes a ciudadanos: El caso del Movimiento Armado Quintín Lame." In *De las armas a la política*, edited by Ricardo Peñaranda and Javier Guerrero, 75–131. Bogotá: Tercer Mundo.

Pérez, Gina. 2008. "Discipline and Citizenship: Latino/a Youth in Chicago JROTC Programs." In *New Landscapes of Inequality: Neoliberalism and the Erosion of Democracy in America*, edited by Jane L. Collins, Micaela di Leonardo, and Brett Williams, 113–130. Santa Fe, NM: School of American Research.

Perkins, John. 2004. *Confessions of an Economic Hit Man*. New York: Plume.

Perla, Héctor. 2010. "Monseñor Romero's Resurrection: Transnational Salvadoran Organizing." *NACLA* (November/December): 25–32.

Perreault, Thomas. 2008. "Natural Gas, Indigenous Mobilization, and the Bolivian State." Identities, Conflict, and Cohesions Program Paper no. 12, United Nations Research Institute for Social Development.

Perreault, Thomas, and Patricia Martin. 2005. "Geographies of Neoliberalism in Latin America." *Environment and Planning A* 37, no. 2: 191– 201.

Petras, James. 2007. "Latin America: Four Competing Blocs of Power." James Petras website. Accessed November 3, 2012. http://petras.lahaine.org/?p=1700.

Petras, James, and Henry Veltmeyer. 2005. *Social Movements and State Power: Argentina, Brazil, Bolivia, Ecuador*. London: Pluto.
Phillips, John. 2006. "*Agencement:* On the Translation of *Agencement* by *Assemblage*." Accessed October 11, 2011. http://courses.nus.edu.sg/course/elljwp/deleuzeandguattari.html.
Pine, Adrienne. 2010. "Honduras' Porfirio 'Pepe' Lobo: Another Disaster for Central American Democracy Waiting in the Wing." Washington, DC: Council on Hemispheric Affairs (COHA).
Plan Nacional de Desarrollo (PND). 2006. Government of Bolivia, Ministerio de Planificación. June. Accessed August 10, 2009. http://www.ine.gob.bo/pdf/PND/00.pdf.
Plascencia, Luis. 2009. "Citizenship Through Veteranship: Latino Migrants Defend the US 'Homeland.'" *Anthropology News* (May): 8–9.
Polan, Dana B. 1986. "'Above All Else to Make You See': Cinema and the Ideology of Spectacle." In *Postmodernism and Politics*, edited by Jonathan Arc, 55–69. Minneapolis: University of Minnesota Press.
Portes, Alejandro, and John Walton. 1976. "The Politics of Urban Poverty." In *Urban Latin America: The Political Condition from Above and Below*, edited by Alejandro Portes and John Walton. Austin: University of Texas Press.
Postero, Nancy. 2007. *Now We Are Citizens: Indigenous Politics in Postmulticultural Bolivia*. Stanford, CA: Stanford University Press.
———. 2010. "The Struggle to Create a Radical Democracy in Bolivia." Special issue, *Latin American Research Review* 45: 59–78.
———. 2013. "Protecting Mother Earth in Bolivia: Discourse and Deeds in the Morales Administration." In *Environment and the Law in Amazonia: A Plurilateral Encounter*, edited by James M. Cooper and Christine Hunefeldt, 78–90. Sussex, UK: Sussex Academic Press.
———. Forthcoming. "'El pueblo boliviano, de composición plural': A Look at Plurinationalism in Bolivia." In *Power to the People?* edited by Carlos de la Torre. Lexington: University Press of Kentucky.
Pozo Montesdeoca, Carlos. 2007. *León Febres Cordero: Érase una vez en el poder*. Quito: Don Bosco.
Prada, Raúl, and Katu Arkonada. 2011. "En defensa del proceso de cambio y del Pacto de Unidad." Accessed February 5, 2011. http://nomadaboliviano.blogspot.com/2011/01/en-defensa-del-proceso-de-cambio-y-del.html.
Presidencia de la Republica (Ecuador). 1985. "Concepto Estratégico de Seguridad Nacional." Consejo de Seguridad Nacional. Declassified document, Archives of the Comisión de la Verdad, Quito.
PRODEMU. 2011. "Crecen las Chilenas, Crece Nuestro País. Memoria 2011." Accessed December 10, 2012. http://190.151.104.246/new/wp-content/uploads/2012/12/memoria2011.pdf.
Programa de las Naciones Unidos para el Desarrollo (PNUD). 2003. "El conflicto, callejón con salida." Informe Nacional de Desarrollo Humano, Bogotá.
———. 2011. "Colombia rural: Razones para la esperanza." Informe Nacional de Desarrollo Humano, Bogotá.
Proyecto de Ley Orgánica de la Cultura (Venezuela). 2000. December 4.
Putnam, Robert D. 2000. *Bowling Alone: The Collapse and Revival of American Community*. New York: Simon and Schuster.

Quiroga, Carlos Alberto. 2011. "Bolivia's Morales Scraps Fuel Hike After Protest." *Reuters*, January 1. Accessed January 5, 2011. http://af.reuters.com/article/worldNews/idAFTRE70009620110101?sp=true.

Ramírez, Pedro, and Matías Fouillioux. 2010. "Los pobres que la encuesta Casen se niega a contar." *CIPER*, August 9. Accessed February 2, 2012. http://ciperchile.cl/2010/08/09/los-pobres-que-la-encuesta-casen-se-niega.

Rancière, Jacques. 1999. *Disagreement, Politics and Philosophy.* Minneapolis: University of Minnesota Press.

Rappaport, Joanne. 2005. *Intercultural Utopias: Public Intellectuals, Cultural Experimentation, and Ethnic Pluralism in Colombia.* Durham, NC: Duke University Press.

Regalsky, Pablo. 2010. "Political Processes and the Reconfiguration of the State." *Latin American Perspectives* 173, no. 3: 35–50.

RETORT (Iain Boel, T. J. Clark, Joseph Matthews, and Michael Watts). 2005. *Afflicted Powers: Spectacle and Capital in a New Age of War.* New York: Verso.

Richard, Analiese. 2009. "Mediating Dilemmas: Local NGOs and Rural Development in Neoliberal Mexico." *PoLAR: Political and Legal Anthropology Review* 32, no. 2: 166–194.

Richards, Patricia. 2004. *Pobladoras, Indígenas, and the State: Conflicts over Women's Rights in Chile.* New Brunswick, NJ: Rutgers University Press.

Riesco, Manuel. 2009. "Change in the Chilean Social Model." *International Labour Review* 148, no. 3: 283–300.

Rivas, Cecilia. 2007. "Imaginaries of Transnationalism: Media and Cultures of Consumption in El Salvador." PhD diss., University of California, San Diego.

Rivera Cusicanqui, Silvia. 1987. *Oppressed but Not Defeated: Peasant Struggles Among the Aymara and Qhechwa in Bolivia, 1900–1980* (English translation). Geneva: United Nations Research Institute for Social Development.

Rivera Flores, Alfredo. 2004. *La Sosa nostra: Porrismo y gobierno coludidos en Hidalgo.* Mexico City: Miguel Porrua.

Roberts, Bryan R. 2004. "From Marginality to Social Exclusion: From *Laissez Faire* to Pervasive Engagement." *Latin American Research Review* 39, no. 1: 195–197.

Robinson, William. 2003. *Transnational Conflicts: Central America, Social Change, and Globalization.* London: Verso.

———. 2006. "Promoting Polyarchy in Latin America: The Oxymoron of 'Market Democracy.'" In *Latin America After Neoliberalism*, edited by Eric Hershberg and Fred Rosen, 96–119. New York: New Press/NACLA.

Romero, Simon. 2009. "In Bolivia, Untapped Bounty Meets Nationalism." *New York Times*, February 3.

Ronald Reagan Presidential Library. 1986. "Toasts at the State Dinner for President León Febres Cordero Ribadeneyra of Ecuador, January 14, 1986." Accessed February 10, 2011. http://www.reagan.utexas.edu/archives/speeches/1986/11486e.htm.

Rose, Nikolas. 1996. "Governing 'Advanced' Liberal Democracies." In *Foucault and Political Reason*, edited by Andrew Barry, Thomas Osborne, and Nikolas Rose, 37–64. Chicago: University of Chicago Press.

———. 1999a. *Governing the Soul: Shaping of the Private Self.* London: Free Association Books.

———. 1999b. *Powers of Freedom.* New York: Cambridge University Press.

Rudnyckyj, Daromir. 2009. "Spiritual Economies: Islam and Neoliberalism in Contemporary Indonesia." *Cultural Anthropology* 24, no. 1: 104–141.

Ruíz, Carlos Ariel, Nathalia Urbano, Myriam Amparo Espinosa, Eduardo Gómez, Alessandro Torres y Carolina García. 2003. *El Cauca: Alternativas de paz y gobernabilidad*. Bogota: PNUD, ARD, and USAID.

Ruíz Marrero, Carmelo. 2011. "The New Latin American 'Progresismo' and the Extractivism of the 21st Century." *Americas Program*, February 17. Accessed April 25, 2011. http://www.cipamericas.org/archives/4025.

Rus, Jan, and Miguel Tinker Salas. 2006. "Mexico 2006–2012: High Stakes, Daunting Challenges." *Latin American Perspectives* 33, no. 2: 5–15.

Salamea, Marco. 1988. *El régimen febrescorderista*. Cuenca: Universidad de Cuenca.

Salas, Yolanda. 2003. "En nombre del pueblo: Nación, patrimonio, identidad y cigarro." In *Políticas de identidades y diferencias sociales en tiempos de globalización*, edited by Daniel Mato, 147–172. Caracas: FACES-UCV.

Salazar, Milagros. 2010. "Latin America Faces an Environmental Emergency: Milagros Salazar Interviews Uruguayan Ecologist Eduardo Gudynas." July 8. Accessed April 22, 2011. http://www.ipsnews.net/2010/07/qa-latin-america-faces-an-environmental-emergency.

Saldaña-Portillo, María Josefina. 2003. *The Revolutionary Imagination in the Americas and the Age of Development*. Durham, NC: Duke University Press.

Sanford, Victoria. 2004. "Contesting Displacement in Colombia: Citizenship and State Sovereignty at the Margins." In *Anthropology in the Margins of the State*, edited by Veena Das and Deborah Poole, 253–277. Santa Fe, NM: School of American Research Press.

———. 2005. *Buried Secrets: Truth and Human Rights in Guatemala*. New York: Palgrave Macmillan.

Santiso, Carlos. 2001. "Good Governance and Aid Effectiveness: The World Bank and Conditionality." *The Georgetown Public Policy Review* 7, no. 1 (Fall): 1–22.

Santos, Boaventura de Sousa. 2005. *El milenio huérfano: Ensayos para una nueva cultura política*. Madrid: Editorial Trotta.

Scarry, Elaine. 1985. *The Body in Pain: The Making and Unmaking of the World*. New York: Oxford University Press.

Schild, Veronica. 2000. "Neo-Liberalism's New Gendered Market Citizens: The 'Civilizing' Dimension of Social Programmes in Chile." *Citizenship Studies* 4, no. 3: 275–305.

———. 2002. "Engendering the New Social Citizenship in Chile: NGOs and Social Provisioning under Neo-Liberalism." In *Gender Justice, Development and Rights: Substantiating Rights in a Disabling Environment*, edited by S. Razavi and M. Molyneux, 170–204. Oxford: Oxford University Press.

———. 2003. "Die Freiheit der Frauen und gesellschaftlicher Fortschritt: Feministinen, der Staat und die Armen bei der Schaffung neoliberaler Gouvernementalität." *Peripherie: Zeitschrift für Politik und Ökonomie in der Dritten Welt* 93, no. 23 (December): 481–506.

———. 2007. "Empowering 'Consumer-Citizens' or Governing Poor Female Subjects? The Institutionalization of 'Self-Development' in the Chilean Social Policy Field." *Journal of Consumer Studies* 7, no. 2: 179–203.

———. Forthcoming. "Localizing Transnational Feminist Interventions: Gendered Social Politics and Neo-liberal Revolutions in Government." In *Beyond the Merely Possible: Transnational Women's Movements Today/Mehr als nur das Machbare: Aktuelle Ansätze transnationaler Frauenbewegungspolitik*, edited by Uta Ruppert, Beatrix Schwartzer, and Andrea Jung. Berlin: Nomos Verlag.

Schryer, F. 1990. *Ethnicity and Class Conflict in Rural Mexico.* Princeton, NJ: Princeton University Press.

Schuster, Federico, and Sebastián Pereyra. 2001. "La protesta social en la Argentina democrática: Balance y perspectivas de una forma de acción política." In *La protesta social en la Argentina: Transformaciones económicas y crisis social en el interior del país,* edited by N. Giarraca, 42–63. Buenos Aires: Alianz.

Scott, James. 1998. *Seeing Like a State: How Certain Schemes to Improve the Human Condition Have Failed.* New Haven, CT: Yale University Press.

Semán, Pablo. 2000. "Retrato de un lector de Paulo Coelho." In *Cultura y Neoliberalismo,* edited by Alejandro Grimson, 70–90. Buenos Aires: CLACSO.

Serulnikov, Sergio. 2003. *Subverting Colonial Authority: Challenges to Spanish Rule in Eighteenth-Century Southern Andes.* Durham, NC: Duke University Press.

Shaw, Rosalind, and Lars Waldorf. 2010. "Introduction: Localizing Transitional Justice." In *Localizing Transitional Justice: Interventions and Priorities after Mass Violence,* edited by Rosalind Shaw and Lars Waldorf, 3–26. Stanford, CA: Stanford University Press.

Shefner, Jon. 2007. "Rethinking Civil Society in the Age of NAFTA: The Case of Mexico." *ANNALS of the American Academy of Political and Social Science* 610: 182–200.

Shultz, Jim. 2009. "The Cochabamba Water War and Its Aftermath." In *Dignity and Defiance: Stories from Bolivia's Challenge to Globalization,* edited by Jim Shultz and Melissa Crane Draper, 7–42. Berkeley: University of California Press.

Siegel, James. 1998. *A New Criminal Type in Jakarta: Counter Revolution Today.* Durham, NC: Duke University Press.

Silva Charvet, Erika. 2005. *Identidad Nacional y Poder,* 2nd ed. Quito: Abya-Yala.

Simon, Jonathan. 2007. *Governing Through Crime: How the War on Crime Transformed American Democracy and Created a Culture of Fear.* Studies in Crime and Public Policy. Oxford: Oxford University Press.

Skoknic, Francisca. 2010. "CASEN: Errores y aciertos para no seguir contando pobres." *CIPER,* August 12. Accessed February 24, 2012. http://ciperchile.cl/2010/08/12casen-errores-y-aciertos-para-no-seguir-contando-pobres/.

Smith, Gavin. 2004. "Hegemony." In *A Companion to the Anthropology of Politics,* edited by David Nugent and Joan Vincent, 216–230. Oxford: Blackwell.

Sparr, Pamela, ed. 1994. *Mortgaging Women's Lives: Feminist Critiques of Structural Adjustment.* London: Zed.

Speed, Shannon. 2008. *Rights in Rebellion: Indigenous Struggle and Human Rights in Chiapas.* Stanford, CA: Stanford University Press.

Staab, Silke, and Roberto Gerhard. 2010. "Childcare Service Expansion in Chile and Mexico: For Women or Children or Both?" United Nations Research Institute for Social Development (UNRISD), Gender and Development Program Paper no. 10, May. Accessed December 10, 2012. http://biblioteca.hegoa.ehu.es/system/ebooks/18280/original/childcare_service_expansion_in_Chile_and_mexico.pdf?1298889768.

Stanley, William. 1996. "Protectors or Perpetrators? The Institutional Crisis of the Salvadoran Civil Police." Washington, DC: Washington Office on Latin America and Hemisphere Initiatives.

Steinmetz, George. 1993. *Regulating the Social: The Welfare State and Local Politics in Imperial Germany.* Princeton, NJ: Princeton University Press.

Stern, Steve. 1993. *Peru's Indian Peoples and the Challenge of Spanish Conquest,* 2nd ed. Madison: University of Wisconsin Press.

———. 1998. *Shining and Other Paths: War and Society in Peru, 1980–1995*. Durham, NC: Duke University Press.

Stewart, Kathleen. 2007. *Ordinary Affects*. Durham, NC: Duke University Press.

St. John, Ronald Bruce. 2006. "Evo Morales No Che Guevara." *Foreign Policy in Focus*. Accessed August 6, 2009. http://www.globalpolitician.com/print.asp?id=1538.

Stoll, David. 1993. *Between Two Armies in the Ixil Towns of Guatemala*. New York: Colombia University Press.

Stumpf, Juliet P. 2006. "The Crimmigration Crisis: Immigrants, Crimes, and Sovereign Power." *American University Law Review* 56: 367.

Sunstein, Cass R. 2003. "The Law of Group Polarization." In *Debating Deliberative Democracy*, edited by James S. Fishkin and Peter Laslett, 80–101. Malden, MA: Blackwell.

Svampa, Maristella S., and Sebastián Pereyra. 2003. *Entre la ruta y el barrio: La experiencia de las organizaciones piqueteras*. Buenos Aires: Biblos.

Tabbush, Constanza. 2009. "Gender, Citizenship and New Approaches to Poverty Relief: Conditional Cash-Transfer Programs in Argentina." In *The Gendered Impact of Liberalization: Towards "Embedded Liberalism"?* edited by Shahra Razavi, 290–326. New York: Routledge/UNRISD.

Tamayo, Eduardo G. 2008 [1994]. *Resistencias al autoritarianismo: Gobierno de León Febres Cordero (1984–1988)*, 2nd ed. Accessed April 20, 2010. http://www.alainet.org/publica/resistencias/.

Tapia, Luis. 2011. "Consideraciones sobre el estado plurinacional." In *Descolonización en Bolivia: Cuatro ejes para comprender el cambio*, 135–168. La Paz: Vicepresidencia del Estado.

Tate, Winifred. 2007. *Counting the Dead: The Culture and Politics of Human Rights Activism in Colombia*. Berkeley: University of California Press.

Taussig, Michael. 1999. *Defacement: Public Secrecy and the Labor of the Negative*. Stanford, CA: Stanford University Press.

Tendler, Judith. 1997. *Good Government in the Tropics*. Baltimore: Johns Hopkins University Press.

Tepperman, Jonathan D. 2002. "Truth and Consequences." *Foreign Affairs* (March/April): 128–145.

Terán, Juan Fernando. 2006a. *¡AVC Alfaro Vive Carajo! Democracia en Armas* (First Regional Edition). Rosario, Argentina: Ediciones Estrategia—investigación militante.

———. 2006b. "¡Alfaro vive carajo! y la lucha por el olvido." *Ecuador Debate* 67 (April): 61–76.

Thomson, Sinclair. 2002. *We Alone Shall Rule: Native Andean Politics in the Age of Insurgency*. Madison: University of Wisconsin Press.

Thorp, Rosemary. 1994. "The Latin American Economies, 1939–1950." In *The Cambridge History of Latin America*, edited by Leslie Bethell, vol. 6, part 1, 117–158. Cambridge: Cambridge University Press.

Tilly, Charles. 1985. "War Making and State Making as Organized Crime." In *Bringing the State Back*, edited by Peter Evans, Dietrich Reuschemeyer, and Theda Skocpol, 169–191. Cambridge: Cambridge University Press.

Tim. 2008. "Election Meddling." *Tim's Blog*. Accessed December 14, 2008. http://luterano.blogspot.com/2008/10/election-meddling.html.

Tirman, John. 2004. "Introduction: The Movement of People and the Security of States." In *The Maze of Fear*, edited by John Tirman, 1–16. New York: New Press.

Tunubalá, Taita Floro Alberto. 2000. "El Pueblo Marca Nuestro Rumbo." Acceptance speech. October 29. Popayán.

United Nations Development Program (UNDP). 2005. *Informe sobre Desarrollo Human El Salvador 2005: Una Mirada al nuevo nosotros. El impacto de las migraciones.* New York: United Nations.

———. 2011. *Human Development Report 2011.* Washington, DC: UNDP.

UPI. 2010. "Bolivia Invests More in Raising Energy." *UPI News Service,* December 28.

Valdespino Castillo, R. 1992. *Hidalgo a través de sus gobernantes.* Queretaro: Talleres de Grafica Empresarial.

Valdivia, Gabriela. 2010. "Agrarian Capitalism and Struggle over Hegemony in the Bolivian Lowlands." *Latin American Perspectives* 173, no. 4: 67–87.

Van Cott, Donna Lee. 2000. *The Friendly Liquidation of the Past: The Politics of Diversity in Latin America.* Pittsburgh: University of Pittsburgh Press.

———. 2008. *Radical Democracy in the Andes.* New York: Cambridge University Press.

Van Waeyenberge, Elise. 2006. "From Washington to Post–Washington Consensus: Illusions of Development." In *The New Development Economics: After the Washington Consensus,* edited by K. S. Jomo and Ben Fine, 21–45. New York: Zed.

Vargas González, P. E. 1998. *Hidalgo: Las dificultades de la transición política.* Guadalajara, Jalisco: Universidad de Guadalajara/Universidad Autónoma del Estado de Hidalgo.

Véliz, Claudio. 1980. *The Centralist Tradition of Latin America.* Princeton, NJ: Princeton University Press.

Vera, Leonardo V. 2001. "¡El Balance es Neoliberal!" July 23. Accessed March 3, 2008. http://www.analitica.com/va/economia/opinion/1338346.asp.

Verduzco, Gustavo, Regina List, and Lester Salamon. 2002. *Perfil del sector no lucrativo en México.* Mexico City: Centro Mexicano Para la Filantropía (CEMEFI)/Johns Hopkins University Institute for Policy Studies, Center for Civil Society Studies.

Voz. 2003. "Intensos bombardeos contra civiles." September 17, 14.

Wacquant, Loïc. 2007. "The Rise of the 'Precariat' in the Neoliberal City." Lecture at the Institut für Sozialforschung, Johann Wolfgang Goethe-Universität, November 23.

———. 2009. *Punishing the Poor: The New Government of Social Insecurity.* Durham, NC: Duke University Press.

Wallace, Tina. 2003. "NGO Dilemmas: Trojan Horses for Global Neoliberalism?" In *The Socialist Register 2004: The New Imperial Challenge,* edited by Leo Panitch and Colin Leys, 202–219. New York: Monthly Review Press.

Wall Street Journal. 2011. "Update: Petrobras Plans to Explore Three New Fields in Bolivia." January 19. Acessed April 30, 2011. http://online.wsj.com/article/BT-CO-20110119-714567.html.

Webber, Jeffrey R. 2006. "Will Evo Morales Change Bolivia?" *International Viewpoint Online Magazine,* January 2006. Accessed April 24, 2009. http://www.internationalviewpoint.org/spip.php?article958.

———. 2011. *From Rebellion to Reform in Bolivia: Class Struggle, Indigenous Liberation, and the Politics of Evo Morales.* Chicago: Haymarket.

Weinberg, Bill. 2010. "Bolivia's New Water Wars: Climate Change and Indigenous Struggle." *NACLA Report on the Americas* 43, no. 5: 19–24.

Weisbrot, Mark. 2006. "Latin America: The End of an Era." *International Journal of Health Services* 36, no. 4: 4–5.

Weisbrot, Mark, Rebecca Ray, and Jake Johnston. 2009. "The Economy During the Morales Administration." Washington, DC: Center for Economic and Policy Research Issue Brief. December. Accessed January 27, 2011. http://www.cepr.net/documents/publications/bolivia-2009-12.pdf.

Weisbrot, Mark, and Luis Sandoval. 2007. "Bolivia's Economy: An Update." Washington, DC: Center for Economic and Policy Research Issue Brief. August. Accessed September 16, 2008. http://www.cepr.net/index.php/publications/reports/bolivia-s-economy-an-update.

———. 2008. "The Distribution of Bolivia's Most Important Natural Resources and the Autonomy Conflicts."Center for Economic and Policy Research Issue Brief. July. Accessed September 16, 2008. http://www.cepr.net/index.php/publicationsreports/the-distribution-of-bolivia-s-most-important-natural-resources-and-the-autonomy-conflicts.

Weldes, Jutta, Mark Laffey, Hugh Gusterson, and Raymond Duvall, eds. 1999. *Cultures of Insecurity: States, Communicsts, and the Production of Danger.* Minneapolis: University of Minnesota Press.

Wells-Barnett, Ida B. 2002 [1895]. *On Lynchings.* New York: Humanity Books.

Whitehead, Lawrence, and George Gray-Molina. 2003. "Political Capabilities over the Long Run." In *Changing Paths: International Development and the New Politics of Inclusion*, edited by Peter P. Houtzager and Mick Moore, 32–57. Ann Arbor: University of Michigan Press.

Wiegman, Robyn. 1993. "The Anatomy of Lynching." *Journal of the History of Sexuality* 3, no. 3: 445–467.

Wilson, Gary I., and John P. Sullivan. 2007. "On Gangs, Crime, and Terrorism." *Defense and the National Interest*, Draco Group, November 28. Accessed March 5, 2011. http://www.dracosecurityconsultants.com.

Wilson, Patrick. 2008. "Neoliberalism, Indigeneity and Social Engineering in Ecuador's Amazon." *Critique of Anthropology* 28, no. 2: 127–144.

Wilson, Richard Ashby. 2001. *The Politics of Truth and Reconciliation in South Africa: Legitimizing the Post-Apartheid State.* Cambridge: Cambridge University Press.

———. 2003. "Anthropological Studies of National Reconciliation Processes." *Anthropological Theory* 3, no. 3: 367–387.

Wisotski, Ruben. 2006. *El pueblo es la cultura: Conversación con Farruco Sesto, ministro de la cultura.* Caracas: Fundación Editorial el Perro y la Rana.

Wolf, Sonja. 2010. "Public Security Challenges for El Salvador's First Leftist Government," *NACLA*, July 7. Accessed December 25, 2010. https://nacla.org/node/6650.

Wood, Elisabeth Jean. 2003. *Insurgent Collective Action and Civil War in El Salvador.* Cambridge: Cambridge University Press.

Wood, Tony. 2009. "Latin America Tamed?" *New Left Review* 58 (July/August): 135–148.

World Bank. 2000. "Reforming Public Institutions and Strengthening Governance: A World Bank Strategy." World Bank Public Sector Group, PREM Network, November.

Wright, Lawrence. 2010. "Lithium Dreams: Can Bolivia Become the Saudi Arabia of the Electric Car Era?" *New Yorker*, March 22, 48.

Yan, Hairong. 2003. "Neoliberal Governmentality and Neohumanism: Organizing Suzhi/Value Flow Through Labor Recruitment Networks." *Cultural Anthropology* 18, no. 4: 493–523.

Yúdice, George. 2003. *The Expediency of Culture: Uses of Culture in the Global Era*. Durham, NC: Duke University Press.

Zambrano Pasquel, Alfonso. 1990. *Ran Gazit: La sombra tras el poder*. Guayaquil: EDINO.

Zibechi, Raúl. 2007a. "The Militarization of the World's Urban Peripheries." *Americas Program*, February 9. Accessed November 5, 2012. http://www.cipamericas.org/archives/835.

———. 2007b. "La Victoria, Chile: Half a Century Building Another World." November 13. Accessed April 28, 2008. http://www.forumdesalternatives.org/EN/print.php?type=A&item_id=4516.

———. 2010. *Dispersing Power: Social Movements as Anti-State Forces*. Translated by Ramor Ryan. Oakland: AK Press.

Zilberg, Elana. 2007a. "Gangster in Guerilla Face: The Political Folklore of *Doble Cara* in Post–Civil War El Salvador." *Anthropological Theory* 7, no. 1 (March): 37–57.

———. 2007b. "Refugee Gang Youth: Zero-Tolerance and the Security State in Contemporary US-Salvadoran Relations." In *Youth, Law, and Globalization*, edited by Sudhir Venkatesh and Ronald Kassimir, 61–89. Stanford, CA: Stanford University Press.

———. 2011. *Space of Detention: The Making of a Transnational Gang Crisis Between Los Angeles and San Salvador*. Durham, NC: Duke University Press.

Zilberg, Elana, and Mario Úcles Lungo. 1999. "'¿Se han vuelto haraganes?': Jóvenes, migración y identidades laborales." In *Tranformando El Salvador: Migración internacional, sociedad y cultura*, edited by Mario Lungo and Susan Kandel, 39–93. San Salvador: Fundación Nacional para el Desarrollo.

Zuckerman, Sam. 1986. "Reagan's Man in the Andes." *Nation* 242 (April): 484–487.

Zuñiga, Zorany. 2010. "Incidencia de las AUC en los procesos organizativos de movilización social y política del CIMA (1999–2006)." Tésis de pregrado en Ciencia Política, Universidad del Cauca, Popayán.

INDEX